Game Programming

The L Line,™
The Express Line to Learning

Game Programming

The L Line,™
The Express Line to Learning

Andy Harris

BICENTENNIAL
1807
WILEY
2007
BICENTENNIAL

Wiley Publishing, Inc.

Game Programming: The L Line,™ The Express Line to Learning

Published by
Wiley Publishing, Inc.
111 River Street
Hoboken, NJ 07030-5774
www.wiley.com

For general information on our other products and services, please contact our Customer Care Department within the U.S. at 800-762-2974, outside the U.S. at 317-572-3993, or fax 317-572-4002.

For technical support, please visit www.wiley.com/techsupport.

Wiley also publishes its books in a variety of electronic formats. Some content that appears in print may not be available in electronic books.

Library of Congress Control Number: 2006936755

ISBN: 978-0-470-06822-9

Manufactured in the United States of America

10 9 8 7 6 5 4 3 2 1

1D/RR/QR/QX/IN

About the Author

Andy Harris began learning about computing in the 1970s by playing around with the primitive computers available at that time. Before he could afford computer access, he invented computer games using a pocket calculator.

He began his teaching career as a high-school special education teacher. During that time, he kept his interest in computing, and taught himself enough to earn part-time consulting and database work. He began teaching computing at the university level part-time in the late 1980s.

Since 1995 he has been a full-time lecturer in the Computer Science Department of Indiana University / Purdue University - Indianapolis, where he manages the streaming media laboratory and teaches classes in several programming languages. His primary interests are game development, Python, Flash, PHP, Java, Microsoft languages, Perl, JavaScript/AJAX, Web-enabled data applications, virtual reality, and programming on portable devices. He has written books on many of these technologies.

Publisher's Acknowledgments

Acquisitions, Editorial, and Media Development

Project Editor
Mark Enochs

Acquisitions Editor
Katie Feltman

Copy Editor
Barry Childs-Helton

Technical Editors
Aahz and Stef Maruch

Editorial Manager
Leah Cameron

Media Development Specialists
Angela Denny, Kate Jenkins,
Steven Kudirka, Kit Malone

Media Development Coordinator
Laura Atkinson

Media Project Supervisor
Laura Moss

Media Development Manager
Laura VanWinkle

Editorial Assistant
Amanda Foxworth

Sr. Editorial Assistant
Cherie Case

Composition Services

Project Coordinator
Kristie Rees

Layout and Graphics
Heather Ryan, Erin Zeltner

Proofreaders
Arielle Mennelle, Brian H. Walls

Indexer
Kevin Broccoli

Anniversary Logo Design
Richard Pacifico

Publishing and Editorial for General User Technology

Richard Swadley, *Vice President and Executive Group Publisher*

Andy Cummings, *Vice President and Publisher*

Mary Bednarek, *Executive Acquisitions Director*

Mary C. Corder, *Editorial Director*

Composition Services

Gerry Fahey, *Vice President of Production Services*

Debbie Stailey, *Director of Composition Services*

Author's Acknowledgments

The first acknowledgment goes to my Lord and Savior.

My deepest earthly appreciation always goes to my best friend and partner, my wife Heather. I may be the one typing away, but you always work at least as hard as I do on these things.

Thanks to Katie Feltman, for making this project happen. You have the incredible knack of knowing when to push and knowing when to listen. It's a pleasure to dream about a new kind of book with you, and see it happen in front of us.

A special thanks to Mark Enochs. I can't imagine what it's like to work with authors, but you do it with grace and humor. I really appreciate your help and support through this process.

Thank you to Aahz and Stef Maruch for your technical editing insights. You have made me a better programmer.

Thanks to Jessica Petrie and Mark Hufe, for reading early manuscripts and providing your insights.

Thanks also to Ron Stephens of Python 411 for your great podcast interview.

Thank you so much to all the fine people at Wiley who do so much to make a book really happen.

Thanks to Guido Van Rossum, the author of Python. It's people like you, who are willing to give away tools of inestimable value, that make me think the technology age isn't entirely about greed.

A huge thanks to Pete Shimmers, the author of pygame, for releasing the excellent pygame library that is central to this work. Thanks also for your review of an early manuscript, and for pointing out errors in my thinking.

Thanks to the many open-source developers who freely give resources to the community. Particular thanks go to Stani Michiels, author of Stani's Python Editor, Jakob Fischer (PizzaDude) for use of several of his excellent fonts, Ari Feldman for Ari's spritelib, Reiner Prokien for Reiner's tilesets, NullSoft for the NSIS installation system, and Hector Mauricio Rodriguez Segura for the excellent HM NIS editor, Spencer Kimball, Peter Mattis and company for the GIMP, and the Audacity team for their excellent audio tool. Open-source game programming is possible because all of you have given freely to others. We are all in your debt.

Dedication

I dedicate this book to Heather, to Elizabeth, Matthew, Jacob, and Benjamin. You are my joy, and I love you all.

Contents at a Glance

Contents

Preface

From the Publisher

Welcome to *Game Programming: The L Line, The Express Line to Learning*. This book belongs to a new tutorial series from Wiley Publishing created for independent learners, students, and teachers alike. Whether you are learning (or teaching) in a classroom setting, or gaining new programming skills while you build games for fun, this book is for you. As rigorous and replete as any college course or seminar, *Game Programming: The L Line* offers instruction for developing a programmer's skill set, specifically, the skill set needed by a game programmer.

Like all titles in *The L Line, The Express Line to Learning* series, this book's design reflects the concept of learning as a journey — a trip on a subway system — with navigational tools and real-world stops along the way. The destination, of course, is mastery of the key applications and core competencies of game programming.

From the Author

Let's face it: Games are fun. Games are what brought me into computer programming so long ago, and they're a big part of why I'm still in it. There's something irresistible about immersing yourself in an imaginary world. Books and movies are a great way to experience a form of "alternate reality," but an interactive computer game is something more. You don't simply watch a game. You *participate*.

If you think games are fun to play, you should try *creating* them. There's nothing more fun than building your own gaming environment, and when you actually make something that's exciting for others to play, you'll feel a rare sense of accomplishment. If playing games is more immersive than watching movies, writing games is even more immersive than playing them. After all, the players are really playing with a universe constructed by you. In a sense they're playing with you.

Can Anyone Learn to Program?

Way back at the beginning of the computer revolution, everybody knew that programming was an arcane art best practiced by highly educated recluses. At one point, there was widespread belief that everyone should learn programming as a part of a modern literacy program. The complexity of today's technology tends to make people think once again that computer programming is difficult to learn, and not appropriate for everyone.

Nonsense.

There's no better time to learn programming than now. Python (and a number of other programming languages) have evolved over many years to be sensible, complete languages that are much easier to learn than the more obscure languages that previous generations had to endure. The open-source movement has ensured a rich set of resources — including programming languages, but also extending to audio and graphics tools, game art, and many other very useful tools for the aspiring game programmer.

How Do You Get Started in Game Programming?

When you decide you want to learn about game programming and start looking around for guidance, you'll often get all kinds of well-meaning advice. I see this kind of advice all the time on game-development forums. The line goes like this:

- **Take all the math you can.** Game programming requires algebra, trigonometry, linear algebra, and calculus.

- **Learn C++.** All serious game programming is done in C++. You're wasting your time using anything else.

- **Programming is optional.** You can learn to design games without needing to program.

- **Learn "ordinary" programming first.** Learn to program first, and then learn to program games.

While there is some truth to each of these assertions, it may not be the *entire* truth. Here's my take on each:

Take all the math you can

As you'll see, there is a little math involved in game programming, but math is never the *problem*. Instead, game programmers only concern themselves with mathematical principles when they provide the *solution* to some problem that is otherwise difficult to solve. As you progress as a game programmer, you might find that your opinion of math changes: It moves from being a topic to avoid at all costs to a useful tool you can bring to bear when you need it. I use some high-school-level trig and algebra here, but I don't expect you to be a math ace.

Learn C++

The ideas of game programming are not tied to one particular language. There are universal concepts that apply to any game development environment. Tools matter, but not nearly as much as the underlying ideas. There's nothing wrong with starting out with an easier and friendlier tool. Besides, *not* all serious game development is done in C++. However, if you learn the concepts in this book, you'll be able to apply them to any language you want.

Programming is optional

Although there are successful game designers who do not program, they are not very common. It makes absolutely no difference how good your idea is if you cannot implement it. That's like a recipe that's never been cooked. At the very least you need to know some of the basics.

Learn "ordinary" programming first

If you want to learn how to program games, you can learn programming *as* you learn game development. Why not do what you love from the very beginning? With the right materials and the right coaching, you'll write games throughout this book. (Granted, they'll be pretty simple at first, but everyone has to start somewhere.)

What Is This Book About?

It's about game programming. I use Python in this book, because Python is free, powerful, and relatively easy. My real focus is not Python itself, but *how to program games using Python.* That's an important distinction. My primary interest is that you learn to write games. Python has some great features that don't directly relate to game programming — but I won't spend a huge amount of time on those features.

Step Into the Real World

Python has some really great features that make it unique among programming languages. Although Python is worth studying for this reason alone, I chose to stress a style of programming that avoids Python idiosyncrasies in favor of more generic techniques that translate well to other languages. If you're already a *Pythonista* (a Python enthusiast), you might be disappointed that I don't emphasize such ideas as iterators and dict structures. I love those features of Python, and I encourage you to use them appropriately — but that's not the main focus of this book. Sometimes I had to make tough decisions to minimize use of a great feature in order to make the code more universal.

What Will You Learn?

When you're finished with this book, you should be able to write a game. That's the goal. Of course, you'll learn some other things along the way:

- **Programming.** You'll get a gentle but thorough introduction to the essential components of programming in any language.

- **Python.** You will learn about the Python language and its most important features. You'll learn how to write and test programs, and how Python implements many of the main ideas of programming.

- **Graphics.** You'll get the basics of any 2D graphics system. This includes how objects are drawn to the screen, how collisions are checked, and what an animation loop is all about.

- **Object-Oriented Programming.** This particular type of programming lends itself very well to game development. You'll learn how to use existing objects, and create your own objects.

- **Math.** There are a few mathematical techniques that are critical tools to the game developer. You'll get acquainted with them, and you don't need a math background to get started. I show you the essential concepts when you need them.

- **Physics.** You can't model the world if you don't know how it works. I illustrate the most essential concepts of physics and how they relate to the practice of game development. For example, to create a realistic spaceship flying through the void of space, I'll show you what you need to know about gravity — but only what you need to know. This isn't NASA boot camp.

What's in the Book?

This book is divided into four major sections.

- **Programming Fundamentals.** The first section introduces you to programming and the Python language in particular. Chapters 1 to 3 describe the essential building blocks of any programming language. You learn how to get Python running in Chapter 1. Chapter 2 shows you how to work with data. Chapter 3 is about how to build basic control structures to make your programs branch and repeat behavior.

Getting Graphical. If the first section helps you become a programmer, the middle section turns you into a graphics programmer. Chapters 4 to 6 describe how pygame can be used to turn Python into a graphical engine. You learn how to incorporate pygame, build a graphics window, and work with the essential graphical elements — all in Chapter 4. Chapter 5 shows you how to use pygame's drawing features to create a simple-but-powerful drawing program. Chapter 6 introduces you to the incredibly powerful notion of sprites.

Getting Game. This last section transitions you from being a graphics programmer to a game programmer. Chapters 7 to 10 take you through the basic game development process and beyond. You build your first complete game in Chapter 7. You learn how to build more complex sprites in Chapter 8. For the sake of providing compelling game action, Chapter 9 gives you a refresher in basic physics, explaining various ways to make objects move realistically on your screen. Chapter 10 describes a game-development engine — and shows you how to create your own.

Appendixes. This book was so much fun I didn't want to stop writing it. I added a few appendixes to help you. Appendix A has the answers to the Practice Exams provided throughout the book. Appendix B contains complete documentation for the gameEngine library highlighted in Chapter 10. Appendix C explains how you can package up your modules and games into executable programs, and how to use free tools to set up professional installation packages. Finally, Appendix D covers creating graphics and sound for your games. Appendix B–D can be found on the book's Web site at www.wiley.com/go/thelline.

Additionally, each chapter begins with the "Stations Along the Way," which outlines at a glance the topics to be covered in the chapter. This element is followed by "Enter the Station" which is a list of study questions, a pretest designed to get you thinking about each chapter's content up front (and to help you study).

At the end of each chapter are the following:

Street Jargon. This glossary lists all the important terms introduced in the chapter.

Tokens. This handy table outlines the main commands used in each chapter, and lists arguments/parameters as well as descriptions and examples.

Practice Exam. Your last stop before exiting a chapter is the Practice Exam, which will test you on the concepts you learn in each chapter. All answers can be found in Appendix A.

Step Into the Real World

These sidebars discuss problems or issues you might run into out in the real world — or additional considerations for you to mull over as you create your own game code.

Icons Used in the Book

There are several handy icons you'll find along the way:

Information Kiosk

These icons point out tips on efficient programming or additional explanations of concepts discussed in each chapter.

Transfer

These icons refer you to other places in the book for more information on a particular subject.

Watch Your Step

These icons point out potential pitfalls you might encounter as you begin programming — and advise caution when necessary.

Using the Web Site

I truly hope you enjoy reading this book. But if that's all you do, you'll miss out on the real joy of this enterprise. Everything I describe in this book, from the Python language through the graphics and sound tools and programming editor, is available for free on the companion Web site for this book (www.wiley.com/go/thelline). You won't learn this stuff just by reading about it. You really have to get in there and do it yourself. I can't emphasize enough how important it is that you write your own code. You'll have some mistakes (I sure did), but it's okay. Please look at the actual code in your editor program. Play with things. Kick the tires. Add your own features. That's how learning really happens.

For Instructors and Students

Game Programming: The L Line has a rich set of supplemental resources for students and instructors. **Instructors** can find a test bank, PowerPoint presentations with course and book outlines, and instructor's manual and samples syllabi online. Please contact Wiley for access to these resources.

Students and independent learners: Resources such as chapter outlines and sample test questions can be found at www.wiley.com/go/thelline.

Stay in Touch!

Game programming is fun because it's an extended conversation between the programmer and the user. Writing books is a lot of fun for the same reason. I can't wait to hear from you. Let me know if you're having trouble, or even if you're having fun. Send me some of your games! Check out the Web site for new goodies such as tutorials on topics that didn't make it into the book, or podcasts about new topics. Write to me at aharris@cs.iupui.edu.

Writing Your First Program

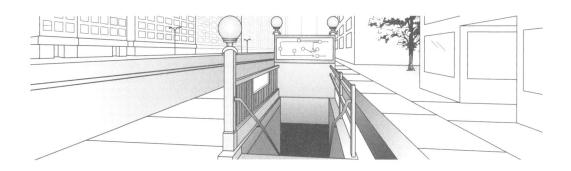

 # Enter the Station

Questions

1. Why is game programming useful?

2. How can game programming prepare you for more "serious" programming study?

3. Why is Python a good language for beginning programmers?

4. What is an interpreted language?

5. What are the advantages and disadvantages of an interpreted language?

6. How do you write the most basic Python program?

7. What is a variable?

8. How do you do basic input and output?

9. How do you name a variable appropriately?

10. How do you modify a string?

11. How do you incorporate variables into output?

You Can Learn a Lot by Writing Games

Welcome to *Game Programming: The L Line*. Over the course of this book, you will learn how to write computer games. You'll learn all the major skills of a game programmer, including how to plan programs, write code, fix mistakes, and manage complicated data.

If you have never written any kind of computer program before, gaming is a great way to start. Learning programming doesn't have to be boring. You'll have a lot of fun because you're going to be building the most interesting kind of program. Game programming provides all the same challenges as other kinds of programming, but games are also visual and interactive. Many programmers were drawn to computers because of games. Learning to program games is even more fun than playing them because you can totally create your own world. Don't worry, though. Even though this book concentrates on games, the skills you learn will translate very well to the more traditional kinds of programming. At the end of this book, you'll be a game programmer, but you'll also be a programmer.

If you've done some programming but you want to learn how to write games, you'll also like this book. A lot of books out there can teach you the mechanics of how to get images on a screen or plot out storyboards, but very few really teach you how to think like a game programmer — and that's my goal. When you imagine a game, I want you to know how to sketch out the relevant ideas, know what kinds of programming constructs you'll need, and have the ability to put your thoughts on the screen in working code. Those are the skills you'll learn in this book. You'll learn some Python, pygame, SDL, and maybe even get a refresher in some basic math and physics.

This book is really about only one thing — writing games. You'll start writing your first game in this chapter, and you'll keep writing games throughout the book. You'll learn how to make text-based games, racing games, arcade games, and even games that involve somewhat sophisticated physics and motion models. There might be some math and theory stuff interspersed, but don't expect a dry textbook. I will tell you about math or physics when it's the solution to a problem, but never for the sake of talking about theory.

Why Use Python?

This book is more about game programming in general than any specific language. When you know how to program games, you can adapt the skills learned here to other languages without too much trouble. In this book, I teach game development by using a language called Python, as well as a specific extension of Python called *pygame*. You have a number of good reasons to use these tools:

- **Python is freely available.** The Python programming language was invented by Guido van Rossum in the early 1990s. He has generously given away the language to anyone who wants it. You don't have to buy Python at all. (Technically, in fact, you *can't* buy it.) A full version of Python is available for download from this book's companion Web site (`www.wiley.com/go/thelline`). When you look at the prices for other programming environments with similar game-development capabilities (Adobe/Macromedia Flash and Microsoft VB.NET come to mind), free looks pretty good. If you add some of the powerful free editing tools and libraries that come with Python, it's even better. Cost is no barrier to programming in Python.

- **Python is platform-independent.** Python works great on a wide variety of computer environments. In this book, I'm assuming you're using Windows, but Python works well on all the primary operating systems in current use, including Mac OS, UNIX, and Linux. The pygame library used for the graphics and games is based on another standard called *SDL* (Simple DirectMedia Layer), which also works on a wide variety of computers. You can rest assured that your games will run on many types of computers.

 ## Transfer

Chapter 4 describes the relationship between pygame and SDL.

- **Python is easy to learn.** One of the original design goals for Python was to make it relatively easy for newcomers to learn. This goal has been largely realized. Python has a reasonably clean syntax (that is, rules of grammar and punctuation) that is not nearly as difficult to learn as many other languages. Writing programming code is still an exacting discipline, but Python does a lot of things automatically for you and makes writing code more straightforward than a lot of other programming languages. For example, many popular programming languages use at least one special character (a semicolon or a brace) at the end of every single line of code. Python uses a different approach, which makes the code easier for beginners to read and write.

- **Python is powerful.** Just because the language is relatively easy, that doesn't mean it's a slouch. Straight Python can do some pretty impressive things. When you attach it to the pygame library (as you will do for most of this book), Python can make some very impressive games. For comparison purposes, most games written in Flash run at 12 to 20 frames per second. Python games typically run at 30 to 50 frames per second. Although Python itself isn't an exceptionally fast language — compared to compiled languages, such as C — the technique you learn here relies on the very fast SDL library to do most of the heavy lifting. Python also incorporates all the tools needed for many sophisticated techniques, including sprites, data structures, and collision detection.

Transfer

You learn about sprites starting in Chapter 6. You learn about how data is organized beginning in Chapter 2. Collision detection is covered in Chapter 6.

Python is extensible. A lot of great add-on packages are available, and they can extend Python's basic capabilities. In the first section of this book, you will get your hands dirty with the basic version of the Python language. To get to the graphical stuff, you rely on one of Python's best features; the language was designed so people can easily add their own extensions to it, and many people have added wonderful new tools and libraries. The pygame library in particular is a wonderful way to add powerful graphics capabilities to Python. I point out this library and several others as they come up. Of course, I provide all the libraries on the Web site, too, so you can install them for yourself.

The Python concepts transfer well to other languages. Although most commercial games are not written in Python, a good number are — or they use Python as an extension language. Even if you don't end up writing Python games for a living, the basic ideas you learn in this book transfer very well to many other game-development environments.

Installing and Starting Python

Python is pretty easy to install, as programming languages go. In this book, I use version 2.4.2 and 2.5. You can find the Windows Python installer on the companion Web site for this book, or you can go to Python's main page at www.python.org and download the latest version for your operating system.

Information Kiosk

Python is a vibrant, changing language. During the time this book was developed, two more minor releases of Python occurred. I've tested the code with 2.4.4, and everything works fine. Any later version of Python should also be fine. Please be sure you're using at least 2.4 or later to ensure all the code in this book works properly.

Installing Python

Install Python to your hard drive by using the standard installation method. The entire language installation weighs in at only 9MB (which is pretty small, considering what it does). After you install it, several new elements appear on the Programs menu, as shown in Figure 1-1.

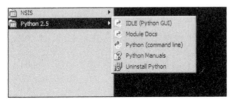

Figure 1-1: The standard version of Python comes with several interesting programs.

The programs that come with Python are pretty handy in their own right. The documentation server (Module Docs) and online help (Python Manuals) both offer a lot of help. Feel free to look at them, but don't get too overwhelmed. There's a lot of information in the documentation that you don't need at first. I show you how to use various documentation features as you need them.

Starting the engine

You can start Python in a couple ways. The simplest is to use the command-line tool, which displays a screen that looks like Figure 1-2. From the Start menu, find the Python group, and choose Python (Command Line).

Figure 1-2: It isn't pretty, but it's a good place to start.

If you run the standard Python program from the Windows Start menu, you automatically find yourself at the command-line console for Python. In the Macintosh and Linux environments, the process is slightly different:

1. **Find the command-line console for your operating system.**

In most versions of Linux you can right-click the desktop and open a terminal window from the resulting menu.

On the Mac, open the Terminal program in Applications/Utilities.

2. **Type** python **and press Enter.**

You'll know you're in the Python environment when you see a screen that looks something like what you see in Figure 1-2. (Each version of Python is slightly different, but they're all similar.)

All versions of Python include this very basic environment, called the *interactive mode.* Although it's nothing to look at, the Python console is surprisingly powerful. Python is an example of an *interpreted* language, which means the programming language is running as you type instructions into it. You can actually type in commands, and Python will respond interactively. For example, type **print "hi, there!"** and see what happens. You should get a screen like the one in Figure 1-3.

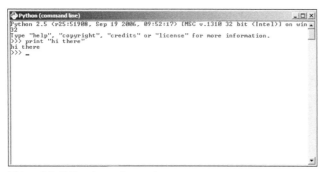

Figure 1-3: Python is greeting you!

Python is even useful in this very basic mode. Try it out by doing some simple math problems:

1. **Type some sort of arithmetic (4 + 3, for example) after the >>> symbol.**

2. **Press Enter and look at the results.**

3. **To venture into "higher math," use the asterisk (*) for multiplication and the forward slash (/) for division.**

4. **Finish by trying more complex math, including parentheses.**

Figure 1-4 shows the answer for (8 * 4 / 3) + 2. You aren't even halfway through the first chapter, and you've already got something useful!

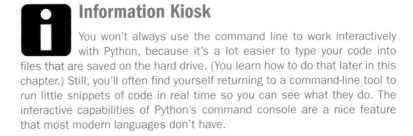

Figure 1-4: Python is a handy calculator.

Information Kiosk

You won't always use the command line to work interactively with Python, because it's a lot easier to type your code into files that are saved on the hard drive. (You learn how to do that later in this chapter.) Still, you'll often find yourself returning to a command-line tool to run little snippets of code in real time so you can see what they do. The interactive capabilities of Python's command console are a nice feature that most modern languages don't have.

Storing information in variables

Python allows you to store information and retrieve it later. To see how this works, do the following:

1. Type the following code on the command line (the >>> symbol will already be there):

```
>>> answer = 5 + 3
```

2. Retrieve the answer by typing in this code:

```
>>> print answer
```

Step Into the Real World

Who's Running What Out There?   I'm assuming that most readers use Microsoft Windows as the primary operating system for their computers, but you can write (and run) Python on most other popular operating systems. If you're using a Mac OS X or Linux machine, there's a good chance you already have Python installed. You can find out by going to a command-line console and typing **python**. If you see a message about Python, you're in luck. If you use the Mac OS, check out MacPython at www.python.org/download/mac.

When you enter the first line (`answer = 5 + 3`), nothing seems to happen, as shown in Figure 1-5.

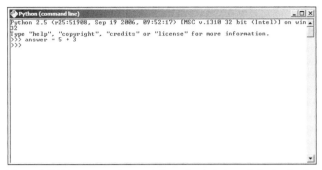

Figure 1-5: This command stores information but doesn't display it yet.

Python still calculated the math problem 5 + 3, but rather than having it print out the result, you told it to store the answer in a special element called `answer`. Python automatically created a place in the computer's memory, named it `answer`, and put this value into that place.

After Python prints the answer (`print answer`), you can see from Figure 1-6 that something interesting has happened.

Figure 1-6: Now Python prints the results.

You might be surprised that Python prints the number 8 rather than the word `answer`. Quote signs are the secret. If you tell Python to print something inside quotes (such as `"Hello, there!"`), it will print that literal value. If you don't use quotes, Python looks for a place in memory with that name, and prints the resulting value.

These named memory spaces are called *variables*. The ability to store and retrieve information from the computer's memory is one of the key elements in computer programming.

Information Kiosk

When you see a line like `answer = 3 + 5`, train yourself to read it like this: "answer *gets* three plus five." In Python (and many other languages), the equals sign doesn't always mean equality. In other words, it isn't necessarily saying that answer is equal to 3 + 5. Instead, the equals sign is used to indicate *assignment*. In other words, "find the result of the calculation *3 + 5* and store that result in a variable called *answer.*"

Transfer

In Chapter 3, you'll learn how to test for equality.

Introducing IDLE

The basic Windows and Linux installations of Python come with another nice tool for writing Python programs called IDLE. IDLE is a somewhat farfetched acronym for Interactive DeveLopment Environment. (I guess if you're smart enough to make your own programming language, you can capitalize any letter you want.)

The IDLE environment is featured in Figure 1-7.

Figure 1-7: IDLE is a little easier on the eyes than the command-line console.

IDLE has some nice features that make it an attractive tool for building Python programs. It acts like an interactive text editor that understands Python syntax. To illustrate, try this out:

1. **Start IDLE as you start any program in your operating system.**

   You can run it from the Start menu in Windows, by double-clicking the IDLE icon, or by typing `idle` into your operating system's command-line console.

2. **Notice the standard prompt.**

   When Python is waiting for you to do something, it presents a standard >>> symbol. You saw this same symbol when you ran the more primitive console version of Python.

3. **Look at the menus.**

   Unlike the standard Python console, IDLE features menus with various commands on them. Don't worry if you don't know what these mean yet. Notice there is a Help menu. That will probably come in handy soon.

4. **Type in a command.**

   Try typing the following line into the IDLE console:

   ```
   print ("hi there")
   ```

   It's important that you type exactly what you see here, including the parentheses and the quotes, or Python will not respond correctly.

5. **Press Enter to tell Python to execute the command.**

   IDLE will respond much like the command line did, printing out "hi there."

6. Notice that the color changes.

You'll see something interesting when you type commands into IDLE. The word print automatically appears in red, and the text "hi there" will be colored green. This happens because IDLE recognizes print as a built-in command, and "hi there" as the thing it should print. This feature is called *syntax highlighting*. It can make things much easier on you as you write your code.

IDLE features a number of other interesting tools that I'll point out as you continue your travels.

Storing your code in a file

It's convenient to write commands in interactive mode, but you'll soon want to write programs that are more than one command long. Python allows you to write a whole slew of commands in a text file and run them all at one time. IDLE has a built-in text editor that is perfect for storing all your commands. To use it, follow these steps:

1. Open a new window.

From the File menu, choose the New Window command. Figure 1-8 shows the original IDLE window with a new window on top.

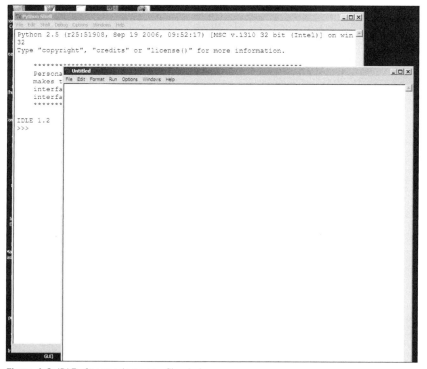

Figure 1-8: IDLE after opening a new file window.

2. **See how the new editor window is different.**

The new window looks a lot like the original, but there are some subtle differences. First, note that the new window is blank. It does not have the >>> prompt you see when you run Python in interactive mode. Also, the menu items are slightly different. This second window is a special text editor used for writing Python commands.

3. **Enter a command into the window.**

Type the following command into the new window:

```
print "Hello, World! "
```

When you press the Enter key, you might be surprised. In the standard IDLE window, everything happens interactively. As soon as you type a command, Python immediately responds, but when you use IDLE as a text editor, nothing seems to happen. The editor is letting you enter a command (or a series of commands), but the editor does not execute the commands until you tell it to. Writing commands in this way is a lot like writing a recipe. You're writing down the steps, but you aren't actually cooking (executing the commands) yet.

4. **Save your file.**

Use the Save command from the File menu to save your masterpiece as `Hello.py`.

Information Kiosk

It's important that you use the `.py` extension, because that's how your computer knows that the text file you're saving is actually a Python program and not some other text file (like a shopping list or something).

5. **Run your program.**

From the Run menu, select the Run Module command (or just press F5) to run your program. You should get a screen that looks like Figure 1-9:

Step Into the Real World

IDLE is the only editor you need to write all the programs in this book. However, you don't *have* to use it. You can actually write Python code in any text editor you wish, as long as it saves code in plain text format. (Word processors do not do this well because they write documents in specialized formats that the Python interpreter cannot need. Word processors also emphasize special formatting and layout features that are meaningless for a programming editor.) For now, stick with IDLE if you can, because you already have it, and it does plenty. As the programs get more complicated, you might want to use a more complex editor. I'll describe one such editor (called SPE) later on in Chapter 5.

Figure 1-9: Now the program is running!

When you run a program from the editor screen, Python takes all the commands from the file and executes them all at once. For these early programs, you'll see the results in the main IDLE screen. Later on, your programs will build their own output window.

Information Kiosk

If you use another text editor (one that doesn't have a "run Python" command), be sure to save the file with a .py extension. If you double-click on the file, the operating system can usually run it by associating it with the Python interpreter. However, I don't recommend you do it this way at first, because the program will disappear as soon as it finishes, and you won't be able to see it. If you cannot use IDLE (because you're working in Linux, for example), go to the command line and run your program directly from the command console by entering the following: `python Hello.py`.

Writing Your First Interactive Game

It's pretty interesting to print something to the screen, but it'd be even better if you could make a program that acts a little more like a game. Check the Cheese Shop game shown in Figure 1-10 for a silly example.

Figure 1-10: There's not much cheese at this cheese shop.

Take a look at all of the following code. Notice that it is almost English-like. Even though you may not understand everything immediately, Python code is pretty straightforward, and you'll probably be able to guess what's going on. Still, I'll explain every single part of this program after you look it over.

Here is the code for the `cheeseShop.py` program:

```
"""Cheese Shop
    cheeseShop.py
    demonstrate comments
    raw input,
    and string variables
    from Game Programming - L-line
    Andy Harris
    4/10/06
    """

#tell the user something
print "Welcome to the cheese shop!"

#get information from the user
cheeseType = raw_input("What kind of cheese would you like? ")

#we don't have that kind...
print "Sorry, We're all out of"
print cheeseType
```

The name of the Python language is a tribute to the British comedy troupe Monty Python. The `cheeseShop.py` program is inspired by one of their more famous skits. If you're going to program in this language, you may have to get some old episodes from the library. For some strange reason, computer programmers tend to love the odd humor of this group. I have to admit, I'm a big fan of them myself. You might just see another reference to them as we go on . . . The `cheeseShop.py` program welcomes the user and asks what type of cheese he would like. Regardless of the cheese requested, the program politely informs the user that no such cheese is available.

This program shows some important new ideas: documentation strings, comments, input, and output. Don't worry. None if it is all that hard to understand.

Using docstrings to document your code

Take a close look at the first few lines of the `cheeseShop.py` program. They begin and end with a triple double-quote symbol (" " "). This special combination indicates multiple lines of text. If you have several lines of text embedded inside the triple double-quotes at the beginning of the program, this text will be used as online help for the program. Each program should begin with at least the same kind of information I indicated for the `cheeseShop.py` program:

- The name of the program
- The filename where the program is stored
- The author's name
- The date the program was written or modified
- What the program does

This special documentation is called a *docstring*. Although Python ignores the information in this text block, it is very useful for human programmers. There's also an important system called `pydoc` that uses these documentation values to automatically build online help for your programs. Once programs get long and complicated, you will really appreciate your habit of good documentation. You'll be amazed at how little you understand a program you wrote after only a couple of weeks have passed. However, when you develop good documentation habits, your programs will be readily understandable because you'll leave reminders to yourself or other programmers about what the code is and does.

Building comments

The next line of code is also ignored!

```
#tell the user something
```

This command begins with a pound sign (#). Inside your code, you can add more comments by beginning a line with this symbol. In this first program, I added a comment to explain every single line of code. As you get more sophisticated, you won't need that many comments. It's still a great idea to sprinkle comments into your code when you write something clever. (Clever code means you won't understand it in a couple weeks.)

Printing output to the screen

After taking care of documentation strings and comments, we get to a line that actually does something:

```
print "Welcome to the cheese shop!"
```

You've actually used the `print` command a couple times already. This command does what it says: It prints something to the screen. The text inside the quotation marks is the stuff that Python will print out. Commands in Python (or any other programming language) are sometimes called *statements.* Some statements (such as `print`) accept some value to work with. This value is often called the *argument,* so the argument of the `print` statement above is `"Welcome to the cheese shop!"`

Watch Your Step

You must use the standard quote symbols in Python. Word processors love to put in *"smart quotes,"* which have different symbols for the beginning and end of a quote. (Look at the preceding sentence for an example of smart quotes.) Python will be confused by these characters. To avoid this headache, simply don't use a word processor to write your programming code. IDLE or another plain-text editor will produce the kind of text you need.

When Python interprets the `print` command, it will print out whatever text is inside the quote symbols. If you don't use quote signs, Python expects the name of a variable, and it will print out the value of that variable. More on that in a moment.

Getting input from the user

The next line of our `cheeseShop.py` program is really interesting:

```
cheeseType = raw_input("What kind of cheese would you like? ")
```

The `raw_input()` function allows you to get input from the user. The function requires a prompt — in this case, a question that Python asks the user: `"What kind of cheese would you like?"` The program then stops and lets the user type a value into the command console. When the user presses Enter, whatever he or she typed is transferred to the `cheeseType` variable.

Transfer

In this chapter you're learning how to use functions that come with Python, but in Chapter 3 you learn how to create and use your own functions.

Information Kiosk

If you've already programmed in other languages, you might be surprised that you don't have to create or declare a variable explicitly. When you refer to the `cheeseType` variable, Python automatically creates the variable and figures out what type it should be. Python supports a feature called Implicit Variable Declaration — which means that simply mentioning a variable creates it. The good news is it is very easy to create a variable in Python. There is some bad news: If you misspell a variable name, Python just assumes you wanted to create a *new* variable. Also, Python guesses about what type of data you intend the variable to hold — and it sometimes guesses wrong.

Creating a variable

Variables — those handy places to put things — are one of the most important parts of computer programming in any language. You will create a lot of variables as you become a programmer. It's a good idea to learn how variables should be named, because you get to name a lot of things in programming. Variable names should follow these basic rules:

- **Be descriptive.** A variable's name should indicate what the variable means. The `cheeseType` variable used in this example is well-named because it is clear that this variable is supposed to hold a type of cheese. R or p are not good variable names, because it's hard to say exactly what they mean. Generally your variable names should be long enough to clearly indicate their meaning.

Use single words. Variable names cannot contain spaces. If you want to make a variable name out of two different words (such as *cheese type*), you have two main choices: You can use the underscore character (_), as in `cheese_type`, or you can use what's called "mixed case," as in `cheeseType`. Note that only the `T` in `Type` is capitalized. Throughout this book, I use mixed case to create variable names.

Be case-sensitive. `CHEESETYPE`, `cheeseType`, and `ChEeSeTyPe` are three totally different variables as far as Python is concerned. Python is a case-sensitive language — meaning you can't get sloppy about when you use uppercase and lowercase characters in your variables or commands. It's best to stick with mixed-case to avoid problems.

Be manageable. Variable names should be long enough to be readable, but not so long that you can no longer type them. For example, `variableThatHoldsTheNameOfATypeOfCheese` is too long a variable name. You'll have trouble spelling it correctly, and it will annoy you.

Information Kiosk

The `raw_input()` function has another powerful use. If you've tried running your programs by double-clicking them from Windows, you'll find they close immediately after completion. Put the following code at the end of your program to make it wait long enough to read:

```
raw_input("press Enter to continue")
```

This command prints out the prompt, and then it waits. In this case, it doesn't bother to save the result to a variable, because you don't really care what the user typed. You're just waiting for a press on the Enter key to know the user is finished. You won't need this trick if you test your code within IDLE, but it can be handy.

Printing the results

The last two lines of code print both a text literal value and the value of the variable `cheeseType`:

```
#we don't have that kind...
print "Sorry, We're all out of"
print cheeseType
```

Figure 1-11 illustrates how this code prints the two different kinds of values.

Figure 1-11: The program prints a literal value and a variable.

When Python encounters a phrase inside quotes, it prints that phrase exactly (which is why such a value is called a *literal*). The first `print` statement is that kind of command, so Python simply prints its value.

The second `print` statement doesn't have quotes, so Python looks for a variable named `cheeseType`. If it can find such a variable, it prints the corresponding value.

Watch Your Step

When asked to print a word with no quotes, Python looks for a variable with that name and prints the value of that variable. If no such variable exists, Python will quietly create an empty variable. Be very careful with your spelling, because if you misspell a variable name, Python will complain and the program won't run.

Introducing String Variables

Many of the variables you encounter in this book contain text. These variables are called *string* variables, because the way each character's data was stored in contiguous cells reminded the early programmers of beads on a string. It's oddly poetic, and the

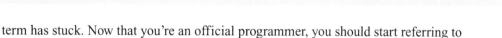

term has stuck. Now that you're an official programmer, you should start referring to text as "string data." People will be impressed with your intellectual prowess.

Building a basic string

Begin experimenting with string values by typing this command into the console.

1. **Type a string assignment into the console:**

```
playerName = "Princess Oogieboogie"
```

Python automatically creates a variable called `playerName`. Since `"Princess Oogieboogie"` is a text value, `playerName` is magically made into a string variable, and it can do all the things that strings can do in Python.

2. **Print out the value of the string:**

```
>>> print playerName
Princess OoogieBoogie
```

> ### Information Kiosk
>
> It's not really magic, of course. Python is an example of a *dynamically typed language*, which means that the programmer doesn't have to explicitly say what kind of data goes into a variable. The language guesses for you. If you know anything about computers, you know sometimes it guesses wrong. Don't worry. I'll show you how to recognize and prevent such problems as you move along.

Using string methods

Python supports a special form of programming called *object-oriented programming* (OOP). This kind of programming describes various things as *objects*. Strings are the first objects you encounter, but there are many more. You will actually build objects as the primary actors in your arcade games. (You'll get there soon, I promise.) Objects are nice, because they already know how to do things. To demonstrate, try this little exercise:

1. **Create a string variable. Type the following in interactive mode (that is, using the command line or IDLE's own interactive mode, but not the text editor — you want this code to execute immediately):**

```
>>> king = "Arthur"
```

2. **Print the uppercase version of the variable. Type this line into the console:**

```
>>> print king.upper()
ARTHUR
```

Step Into the Real World

Methods Are Things that Objects Can Do.   If you had a `monkey` object, you might expect it to have methods like `dance()`, `screech()`, and `throwBanana()`. Method names usually end in parentheses, as I have done here. The great thing about using objects is you don't have to understand how the method works. If you have a monkey, you can make it throw bananas by invoking the `monkey.throwBanana()` method. Likewise, you can get the uppercase version of a string called `king` by invoking `king.upper()`.

Python prints ARTHUR (all in uppercase). When you assigned a text value to the variable `king`, you created a string variable. String variables come with all kinds of cool capabilities, called *methods*. The `upper()` method makes a new version of the string all in uppercase. Note that `king.upper()` doesn't change the underlying value of the `king` variable. It simply returns a version of `king` formatted all in uppercase.

Transfer

For more information on IDLE and how to debug in it, turn to Chapter 2.

Examining other string capabilities

String variables have lots of other cool methods. To learn some of what a string can do, try out these steps:

1. **Ask Python for help. Go back to the Python console and type**

```
help("str")
```

2. **Read all about strings. Python responds with a huge amount of informa-tion, as shown in Figure 1-12.**

Information Kiosk

You don't have to understand all these methods now. It's good to know that they are there, and you can find them if you need them. The much more important lesson here is how the `help()` function works. You use the `help()` function with any Python object or command to find out lots of useful information about that object.

```
Python Shell                                                              _|□|x|
File  Edit  Shell  Debug  Options  Windows  Help
        S.startswith(prefix[, start[, end]]) -> bool

        Return True if S starts with the specified prefix, False otherwise.
        With optional start, test S beginning at that position.
        With optional end, stop comparing S at that position.

    strip(...)
        S.strip([chars]) -> string or unicode

        Return a copy of the string S with leading and trailing
        whitespace removed.
        If chars is given and not None, remove characters in chars instead.
        If chars is unicode, S will be converted to unicode before stripping

    swapcase(...)
        S.swapcase() -> string

        Return a copy of the string S with uppercase characters
        converted to lowercase and vice versa.

    title(...)
        S.title() -> string

        Return a titlecased version of S, i.e. words start with uppercase
        characters, all remaining cased characters have lowercase.

    translate(...)
        S.translate(table [,deletechars]) -> string

        Return a copy of the string S, where all characters occurring
        in the optional argument deletechars are removed, and the
        remaining characters have been mapped through the given
        translation table, which must be a string of length 256.

    upper(...)
        S.upper() -> string

        Return a copy of the string S converted to uppercase.

    zfill(...)
                                                             Ln: 1087 Col: 4
```

Figure 1-12: Here are some of the things string objects can do.

Building a name game with string manipulation

For an example of the power of Python strings, look at the following `nameGame` code. It uses a number of the string methods you saw when you asked Python what strings can do.

```python
""" nameGame.py
    illustrate basic string functions
    Andy Harris
    3/15/06"""

userName = raw_input("Please tell me your name: ")
print "I will shout your name: ", userName.upper()
print "Now all in lowercase: ", userName.lower()
print "How about inverting the case? ", userName.swapcase()
numChars = len(userName)
print "Your name has", numChars, "characters"
print "Now I'll pronounce your name like a cartoon character:"
userName = userName.upper()
userName = userName.replace("R", "W")
userName = userName.title()
print userName
```

The `nameGame.py` code produces the output shown in Figure 1-13.

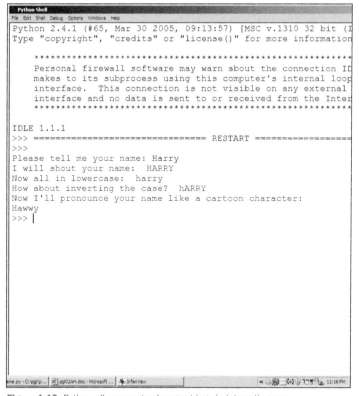

Figure 1-13: Python allows you to change strings in interesting ways.

Choosing your string methods

To build the name game, I simply looked at the various string methods and played around with them to see what I could do. Python has some fun string-manipulation commands. Table 1-1 lists the ones I used in this program.

Table 1-1   Selected String Methods

String Method	Description
stringName.upper()	Converts *stringName* into all uppercase
stringName.lower()	Converts *stringName* into all lowercase
stringName.swapcase()	Converts uppercase to lowercase, lowercase to uppercase

String Method	Description
`stringName.replace(old, new)`	Looks in the string for the value *old* and replaces it with the value *new*
`stringName.title()`	Capitalizes each word in the string
`len(string)`	Returns the length of the string

Information Kiosk

There are many more string methods available. I demonstrate more as they come up, but don't feel like you have to memorize them. You can always look up the details in the online help. The important thing is to know the kinds of methods that are available so you'll know to look them up when the time comes.

Determining the length of the name

Sometimes you might want to know the number of characters in a phrase. The `len()` function can be used for this.

```
numChars = len(userName)
print "Your name has", numChars, "characters"
```

Information Kiosk

The `len()` function is technically a method, even though it works somewhat differently from the other methods. The actual method is `__len__()`. Python allows methods defined like this to be treated as functions, so you can use `numChars = len(userName)` to retrieve the length of `userName` and store it into the variable `numChars`.

Making the cartoon version

The last few lines of the name game are a little bit interesting. See if you can figure out what I did, and why:

```
userName = userName.upper()
userName = userName.replace("R", "W")
userName = userName.title()
```

The main thing I wanted to do here was simulate cartoon speech by replacing R with W. I didn't want to worry about replacing both upper- and lowercase R values, so I did something sneaky. (Perhaps I'm a wascally wabbit.) Here's how to convert the name to a cartoon format:

1. **Make an uppercase version of userName with the userName.upper() method.**

2. **Assign the uppercase value back to `userName`.**

The `userName.upper()` construct makes a new string that is the uppercase version of `userName`, but it doesn't directly change `userName`. If I really want `userName` to change (and I do in this case), I need to assign the converted value back to `userName` using the equal-sign assignment operation. Remember, most string methods don't change the original string. If you want to modify the string, you have to assign the results of the method back to the original variable.

3. **Replace all Rs with Ws.**

The `replace()` method is a perfect tool for this. Since I converted the string to uppercase, I don't have to test for both uppercase and lowercase "r" because all "r"s are uppercase. Once again, I need to copy the value back to `userName`.

4. **Convert `userName` to title case. (Title case capitalizes the first letter of each word.)**

I converted `username` to uppercase for convenience, but now `userName` needs to go back into a more readable format. Title case capitalizes only the first letter in the word, which is how names are usually formatted.

Slicing strings

There's one more important thing to know about string variables (at least for now). You can cut them up to get new smaller strings. The Salami Slicer program (`salamiSlice.py`) illustrates how this works:

```
""" salamiSlice.py
    salami slicer
    demonstrates string slicing
    3/20/06 """

print "GUIDE:"
print "0 1 2 3 4 5 6"
print "|s|a|l|a|m|i|"
print

meat = "salami"
print "meat[2:5]", meat[2:5]
print "meat[:3]", meat[:3]
print "meat[2:]", meat[2:]
print "meat[-3:]", meat[-3:]
print "meat[1]", meat[1]
```

Figure 1-14 shows the output of the slicing program.

Figure 1-14: You can slice a string a lot of different ways.

Look carefully at the guide in Figure 1-14; it shows several positions in the string. In Python strings, character positions are best thought of as occurring *between* the characters. Slot 0 happens before the first character, 1 is between the first and second character, and so on. If you want to return a small part of a string, you can make a slice of the program, using square braces ([]) to indicate a starting point and an ending point. An example is a lot better than a lot of words, so imagine (as in the salamiSlicer.py program) you have a variable called meat that contains the value "salami". Try this experiment to re-create the effect of the salamiSlicer. py program in your console:

1. **Create a meat variable.**

Start by making meat contain the value "salami" — just type the following into the Python or IDLE console:

```
>>> meat = "salami"
```

Of course, you can make any variable you want, but to make sense of this mini-tutorial, go along with my examples first and then change them around later, just to make sure you know what's going on.

2. Get a slice of salami.

Type `meat[2:5]` into the console to see how Python slices up the string.

The program takes a slice of the value `"salami"` between slots 2 and 5. Look at the guide printed in Figure 1-14 to see that slot 2 occurs between the first "a" and the "l" in "salami." (Remember, these character slots occur *between* letters.) Slot 5 is the position between the "m" and the "i" in "salami." So the slice `meat[2:5]` returns the value `'lam'` when `meat` contains the value `'salami'`. If `meat` contained the value `'chicken'`, `meat[2:5]` would be `'ick'`.

3. Get the first three characters.

The command `meat[:3]` uses a special trick in string slicing. If you leave out the first value, Python assumes you're starting at the beginning of the text, so `meat[:3]` is the same as `meat[0:3]`. When `meat` is "salami," `meat[:3]` is `'sal'`. You can also think of `meat[:3]` as the first three letters of `meat`.

4. Get characters starting from any slot and going to the end of the word.

If you leave out the second value in the slicing operation, Python assumes you mean the end of the word. So, if you say `meat[2:]`, Python returns the values from slot 2 to the end of the word. If `meat` is "salami," `meat[2:]` means "take a slice from position 2 to the end of the word," and Python returns the value `'lami'`.

5. Get the last few characters of a word.

You can use negative values in a slice; Python will count from the *end* of the string, rather than from the beginning. This is really handy when you want the last few letters of a string. The expression `meat[-3:]` means "take a slice that begins three characters from the end of the string and goes to the last character of the string." `meat[-3:]` will return `'ami'` if `meat` is "salami." Negative slots generally count from right to left.

6. Get a specific character.

If you give only one value in the square braces, Python assumes you are talking about the letter immediately to the right of the given slot. `meat[4]` is correctly interpreted as "the character between slots 4 and 5."

Watch Your Step

Some people like to think of a single-value slice as indicating character position, but I think this is confusing to beginners. It isn't exactly correct to say that `meat[4]` means "the fourth character in the `meat` variable." If `meat` contains the value `'salami'`, then `meat[4]` is indeed "m" — but if I asked you to tell me the fourth character in the word "salami," you probably wouldn't say "m," because "m" is actually the *fifth* character in the word. The confusion stems from the fact that Python begins counting with zero. By Python's reasoning, "s" is not character 1, but character 0! It's much better to think of these character positions as the slots between letters.

Watch Your Step

You might think you could indicate the end of the string using -0, but it doesn't work.

```
meat[-0] is 's'
```

This is because mathematically, there is no such thing as negative zero. Zero is zero, regardless of the sign you put in front of it. Just use nothing to indicate the end of the string, as I do in the example.

Interpolating text

Most of your programs so far have consisted of getting information from the user, manipulating that information, and sending it back to the user. Your output often consists of a mixture of text and variables, which can be confusing. It's even worse when you mix numeric and non-numeric values together, because you can't concatenate strings with numbers. Python offers an elegant solution called *variable interpolation*. (It's another one of those fancy words for an easy idea. Try to work it into your next social conversation.) Figure 1-15 shows a silly program that calculates a user's age in decades. I ran it a few times so you can see various outputs.

Figure 1-15: I don't actually know when you'd need your age in decades . . .

Read through the code, and you'll see how handy variable interpolation can be.

```
""" interpolation.py
    demonstrates variable interpolation
    """

name = raw_input("Hi, what's your name? ")

prompt = "How old are you, %s? " % name

age = raw_input(prompt)
age = int(age)

decades = age / 10.0
print decades

print "%s is %d years old." % (name, age)
print "That is %.2f decades." % decades
```

The program uses variable interpolation several different ways:

Build a prompt using the `name` variable. The first example of variable interpolation comes in this line:

```
prompt = "How old are you, %s? " % name
```

Notice the special placeholder `%s`. This symbol means "put a string here." It allows me to continue writing the prompt without worrying about exactly what string value will go into the place held by the `%s` symbol. The next percent sign (`%`) indicates a value is coming up. Finally, `name` is the variable. When this line executes, Python builds a new string. When it sees the `%s` symbol, it looks for a string after the second `%` and places the value of that variable directly into the `prompt` string.

Information Kiosk

It isn't absolutely necessary to build the prompt in a separate string as I did here. I could have combined the string interpolation into the `raw_input` statement like this:

```
age = raw_input("How old are you, %s? " % name)
```

It's generally better to do only one job per line when you're starting out. When you get more comfortable with these ideas, you can combine them.

Interpolate two variables into one string. The next interpolation statement is a little different:

```
print "%s is %d years old." % (name, age)
```

The string inside has two symbols in it. The `%s` symbol represents a string. The `%d` indicates a decimal value (a base-10 integer) will be placed there. Since this string now expects *two* values (a string and a number), I feed it two variables. The `name` variable contains a string value and the `age` variable contains an integer.

Note that you must place the variables inside parentheses and separate them with commas if you have more than one. This type of structure is called a *tuple*. Tuples are values inside parentheses, separated by commas.

Watch Your Step

Make sure you supply enough values for your format string, or you will get an error.

Determine the formatting of floating-point values. One of the neatest things about variable interpolation is the control you have over the output. Floating-point numbers often cause problems because they can have many digits after the decimal point, but you may wish to display only a few. Look at how I solved this problem in the next line:

```
print "That is %.2f decades." % decades
```

The `decades` variable is a floating-point value.

Transfer

I divided `age` by the floating-point value `10.0` to produce a `float` response. Check Chapter 2 for more information on this process.

If you use `%f` in the format string, you are indicating that you will place a floating-point value in the output, but you don't indicate the length of that value. Usually you'll want to constrain the output to a reasonable length when you print floating-point values, because they can be difficult to read. By specifying `%.2f`, I am telling Python to print out a floating-point value with two places after the decimal point. The value is automatically rounded, using the standard algorithm.

Step Into the Real World

Many other programming languages provide some variation of variable interpolation, but they are all a little different. Python's version is really nice for a couple of reasons. First, it's pretty easy to use and understand. Also, it automatically converts values to strings and builds a nice string output. It also supports some advanced features when you use a more sophisticated data structure.

argument: The part of a statement that Python will operate on. For example, in a `print` statement, the text that will actually be printed to the screen is the argument.

comment: A comment is a specially marked element in a program that is ignored by Python. Comments are useful for explaining what you're trying to accomplish.

compiled language: In compiled languages, the code is translated completely into a machine-readable format before it runs. In general, compiled languages provide faster-running programs, but interpreted languages can be more flexible.

console: A text-based interface. You can interact with Python at the DOS or UNIX shells in a console mode. When you use IDLE, you are also presented with a special console interface. The `print` command and `raw_input()` function are used to interact with the user through the console.

docstring: A special text value that occurs at the beginning of a Python program (and in some other places that will be described in later chapters). Docstrings are used to create the automatic documentation for the program, and they are usually a multi-line string. In this book, docstring values will all begin and end with the triple quote character.

IDLE (Interactive DeveLopment Environment): A basic-but-powerful text editor and Python environment that ships with most versions of Python. Note that Eric Idle was a member of the Monty Python comedy troupe. I don't know whether there is a CLEESE or GILLIAM editor, but there should be.

interactive mode: A special way of interacting directly with the Python environment. When you use the interactive mode, you type commands directly into Python rather than storing them in a text file. Interactive mode is useful for quick code checks and accessing the online help system.

interpreted language: An interpreted language is one translated from a human-like dialect into machine-readable code in real time. Programs written in an interpreted language cannot run unless the user also has the interpreter program installed on the same system. Interpreted languages can be slow, but the programmer can interact with them in real time. The primary alternative to an interpreted language is a compiled language (such as C and C++).

method: Something an object knows how to do. For example, Python's built-in string object has a method to convert to uppercase (`string.upper()`).

object-oriented programming (OOP): A form of programming that allows the programmer to organize code in objects much like those in the real world. Most built-in Python elements (lists, variables, and so on) are objects.

pygame: A module that adds game-programming functionality to Python. The pygame library will be introduced more thoroughly beginning in Chapter 4.

Python: An interpreted programming language designed to be powerful yet easy for beginners.

SDL (Simple DirectMedia Layer): A reasonably universal graphics package. The pygame library is a special Python adaptation of the SDL graphics library.

slicing: Using the square brace ([ ]) operators to extract a subset of a string or list.

statement: A command or line of code in a programming language.

string: A variable containing text.

string interpolation: A technique for embedding variables into a string for easy formatting.

syntax: A programming language's rules of grammar and punctuation.

tuple: Values inside parentheses, separated by commas. The elements of a tuple cannot be changed.

variable: A variable is a reference to a specific place in a computer's memory meant to store information. Each variable has a name and a value.

Command	Arguments	Description	Example
print *value*	*value*: what will be printed to the screen	Prints something to the console. A value can be text in quotes or a variable name.	print "Hi there"
variable = raw_input(*prompt*)	*variable*: what receives the entered value, in this case *prompt* (a question to ask the user)	Prompts for a user response (usually text encased in quotes) and stores the response in a variable.	username = raw_input("What is your name")

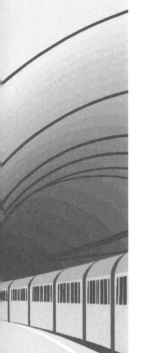

Last Stop

Practice Exam

1. Describe three ways game programming is useful for beginning programmers.

_____

_____

_____

2. Describe three reasons to use Python as a first game programming language.

_____

_____

_____

3. Which is the best description of a variable in Python?

A) A place to hold numbers but not text data.

B) A named place in memory to hold information.

C) A command without an argument.

D) Python doesn't have variables. It uses constants instead.

4. Which of the following is the best name for a variable to hold a person's shoe size?

A) `ss`

B) `thePersonsShoeSize`

C) `7 1/2 wide`

D) `shoeSize`

5. What's the best way to read the code `result = 5 + 7`?

_____

_____

_____

6. Why might you use IDLE for writing your Python programs?

_____

_____

_____

7. Why should your programs begin with a docstring?

_____

_____

_____

8. Why are comments used in Python?

_____

_____

_____

9. How does the `print` statement work?

_____

_____

_____

10. True or false (and explain why): The `print` statement prints quoted text differently than arguments without quotes.

_____

_____

_____

11. If the `raw_input()` function is used for input, why does it output something to the screen?

_____

_____

_____

12. Write a program that asks the user's name and then responds with a customized greeting. For example, if the user's name is "Elizabeth," the program says `"Hi, Elizabeth!"`

_____

_____

_____

13. What is an object method?

A) Something that happens to an object

B) A characteristic of an object

C) An attribute

D) Something an object can do

14. Name some methods of the string object.

_____

_____

_____

15. Describe the result of the following code:

```
var = "programming"
print var[3:7]
```

A) 'gram'

B) 'prog'

C) 'programming'

D) 'GRAM'

16. What is the primary purpose of string slicing?

_____

_____

_____

Working with Data

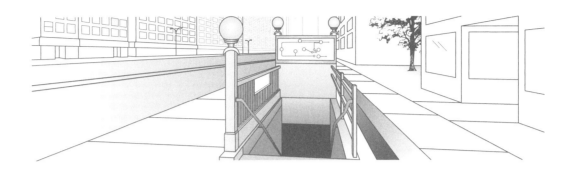

 # Enter the Station

Questions

1. How do computers store information?

2. Why do programming languages have multiple variable types?

3. How do you force a variable to be a specific type?

4. What interesting things can you do with string variables?

5. What is a list, and what can you do with it?

6. How can you step through each element in a list?

7. How can you repeat code a certain number of times?

8. How can you tell what's going on inside your programs?

9. How do you write a program when you don't know exactly what code you'll need?

A ll computer programming is about the manipulation of data. Your games will store information about where the player is, what the monsters are doing, scorekeeping, and lots of other stuff. Programmers need to understand how computers store data, and the various things you can do with that data. In this chapter you learn the basic ideas about managing data in variables and lists.

Exploring Types of Data

Computers ultimately work in the binary values of zero and one. The earliest programmers had to work directly in binary notation. It's important to understand that even modern computers still use binary notation deep inside. Fortunately, modern computer languages allow you to work with more familiar kinds of information, like text and the base-10 numbers you're already used to. Today's machines are powerful enough to do the conversion from ordinary information to binary automatically. You still have to know a little bit about this process because it has important side effects.

Each type of information comes with its own particular challenges:

 Text. Computers can't exactly store text, for example, so they use a special code to convert each letter into a number, and then convert that number to binary values.

 Integers. Likewise, binary notation doesn't have native support for negative numbers, so the computer has to have some way to convert negative numbers into binary format.

 Floating-point numbers. Numbers with decimal points introduce all kinds of other problems of their own.

Python does a good job of shielding you from this complexity when it can, but you still need to understand what's happening, because sometimes Python needs some help in determining what kind of data a particular variable contains. You learned about strings in Chapter 1. Now it's time to explore some of Python's other basic variable types.

Transfer

If you need a refresher on strings and how to work with them, take a look at Chapter 1.

Working with Numbers

Python allows you to work with numeric data as well as text. You've already seen how you can use Python to do basic calculations from the console in Chapter 1. You can combine text input with math functions to build an interactive calculator, but there are some problems that pop up. I show you the broken version first, and explain why it doesn't work. Then I show how to fix the problem.

A problem with numeric input

You might be tempted to write a simple calculator program, like the following badAdd.py program:

```
""" badAdd.py
    Tries to demonstrate adding to values input from the user
    Will not work correctly
    THIS PROGRAM HAS A DELIBERATE ERROR - see intAdd.py
    for a working version, and a complete explanation in the book
    Andy Harris
    3/20/06
    """

x = raw_input("Please tell me the first number: ")
y = raw_input("Please tell me the second number: ")

result = x + y

print x, "+", y, "=", result

print "uh-oh... Something's not right..."
```

Before reading on, look over this code carefully. The program calculates $x + y$ and stores the answer into a variable called `result`. Everything is printed out in a line like this:

```
print x, "+", y, "=", result
```

This line simply uses the comma operator to print several values in a row. It prints the value of the variable x, the plus sign, the value of y, the equals sign, and the value of `result` (which should be $x + y$).

 Information Kiosk

The comma operator adds a space, so you don't need to include your own spaces when you use it to combine text and values.

It seems completely reasonable, but it won't work right, as you can see from Figure 2-1.

Figure 2-1: I'm no math genius, but 3 + 7 is not 37.

What happened? Well, the `raw_input()` function is designed to work with the text console. It asks the user for some value, and expects the answer to be a string value. Python interprets anything from a `raw_input()` function as a string — so it stores the *string value* '3' into x, rather than the *number* 3. To the computer, the difference is very important.

Recall from Chapter 1 that you can use the plus sign (+) to add strings together, like this:

```
>>> print "py" + "thon"
python
>>> print "2" + "3"
23
```

When you use the plus sign to connect two strings, they are combined into one new string value. The second command works in the same way. Since "2" and "3" are inside quotes, Python treats them as string values — and uses the plus sign as an instruction to combine the strings, not to calculate.

Information Kiosk

Combining two text values like this is called *string concatenation*. I love it when a simple idea has such a complicated name. It makes me seem smart. Now you can tell people you've been writing "string-concatenation programs." I won't tell how easy it is . . .

Back in the `badAdd.py` program, you used the `raw_input()` function to retrieve values from the user. This function always returns a string value, so when the user thinks he's typing in numbers (say 3 and 7), the computer is actually receiving string values ('3' and '7'). Python uses the plus sign to combine these two strings (producing the string '37') rather than adding the numbers.

Information Kiosk

The plus sign works differently depending on what kind of data it is working with. If you use the plus sign with string values, it concatenates (ooh, there's that great word again!). If you use the plus sign with numeric values, it adds them. When a computer language uses the same symbol for more than one job, it's called *operator overloading*. It happens in real life — and in everyday language — all the time. Birthday presents, garage doors, and checking accounts can all be "opened," even though the act of opening a garage door is not much like opening a bank account. You might say that the `open` operator is overloaded for these kinds of objects.

Converting strings to numbers

Fortunately, Python includes a set of handy functions for converting data from one type of information to another. Take a look at the `intAdd.py` code:

```
""" intAdd.py
    Uses type conversion to create a better
    adder. This one converts all data to strings
    Andy Harris
    3/21/06 """

x = raw_input("First number: ")
y = raw_input("Second number: ")

x = int(x)
y = int(y)

result = x + y
print x, "+", y, "=", result
```

This program is very similar to the `badAdd.py` program featured earlier (except, of course, in one respect — it works correctly!).

To build the `intAdd.py` program correctly, follow these steps:

1. Get the numeric values from the user with the `raw_input()` function.

Remember, `raw_input()` returns string values, so at this point, x and y are string variables.

2. Convert x and y into integers with the `int()` function.

Take the current (string) variable x and perform the `int()` function on it, turning it into an integer. Then do the same with y.

3. Assign the integers back to the same names.

First assign the integer value of x to the variable x. This replaces the string value in x with the integer value. You're still using the same variable name, but you've changed its value from a string to an integer. Again, repeat the process with y.

4. Add up the integers.

Use exactly the same command from the previous example to add x and y:

```
result = x + y
```

This time around, because x and y are both integer values, Python knows it's supposed to add them, rather than concatenating.

5. Print the results.

Use the `print` statement to print out the values.

Information Kiosk

If you're going to combine numeric values and string values in one `print` statement, it's best to use the comma operator rather than the plus sign. Python gets confused if you try to add a number and a string, because it doesn't know whether you intend it to perform the numeric operation (addition) or the string operation (concatenation).

More surprises with numbers

There are more ways to get confused about numbers in Python. Try this code snippet in the console:

1. Ask the computer what 10/5 is by typing the following command into the console:

```
>>> print 10/5
```

2. Examine the correct result.

```
2
```

3. Now ask what 10/4 is. (Remember, the right answer is 2.5.)

```
>>> print 10/4
```

4. Marvel at how stupid the computer is.

```
2
```

It won't surprise you that 10/5 (read that "ten divided by five") is 2. But the next statement command gives a disturbing result. Apparently, 10/4 is also 2! Once again, the problem is with the way Python guesses about how data is stored in memory. You've already learned that computers store text values differently from the way they store numbers. It turns out there are many ways to store numeric data in a computer as well. Although you don't have to know all the details at this point, it's important to recognize that integers are stored differently from *real numbers* (numbers with decimal values). Computer languages often refer to real numbers as *floats* (for *floating-point numbers*) or *doubles* (a kind of floating-point number). So decimal numbers, real numbers, and floats are all the same kind of number under different names.

Both 10 and 4 are integers, so Python stores them in memory using the integer notation. When Python does math on two integer values, it (wrongly) assumes that the answer is an integer. Python won't get the correct answer (2.5) because the right answer is a floating-point value. There are a couple of ways to solve this. The following code snippet shows the easiest solution:

1. Make the 10 a floating-point number by adding a decimal point to it:

```
>>> print 10.0 / 4
```

2. If an operand is a float, then the result will be too.

```
2.5
```

3. Make the 4 a floating-point number:

```
>>> print 10 / 4.0
```

4. Once again, Python knows the result should be a float.

```
2.5
```

If you use a decimal point in a number, Python knows that number should be treated as a floating-point real number. It then assumes that the correct response is also a floating-point number. If you treat either of the original values as a float (by adding a decimal point), the problem works correctly. You can also use the `float()` function to convert a variable to a floating-point value. (Of course, there are also `str()` and `int()` functions that all convert to the appropriate type.) For example, the following function converts x to a floating-point real number, if possible. (Integer values can be readily converted to floats, but not all strings will have obvious float values.)

```
x = float(x)
```

Making a calculator

You can tie all the ideas of this section together with the Calculator program. As usual, look it over first, and I'll explain it all line by line:

```python
""" calc.py
    given any two values, calculates
    the sum, difference, product, and
    quotient of those two values
    3/20/06 """

x = raw_input("first number: ")
y = raw_input("second number: ")

x = float(x)
y = float(y)

sum = x + y
difference = x - y
product = x * y
quotient = x / y

print x, "+", y, "=", sum
print x, "-", y, "=", difference
print x, "*", y, "=", product
print x, "/", y, "=", quotient
```

The program simply combines the steps outlined earlier in this chapter:

1. Accept two variables from the user with the `raw_input()` function.

2. Convert the variables to floats with the `float()` function.

3. Perform the basic operations, storing results into variables.

4. Print out the results.

Note that the printout is a little complicated because each printout requires a combination of numeric variables and string values. I used the comma operator to combine these values into the output I wanted.

Watch Your Step

Don't use the + operator to combine text and numeric values. Python will get confused and generate an error.

This program accepts two variables, converts them to floats (so all operations will be valid), and prints out the results of the basic four arithmetic operations. The result is shown in Figure 2-2.

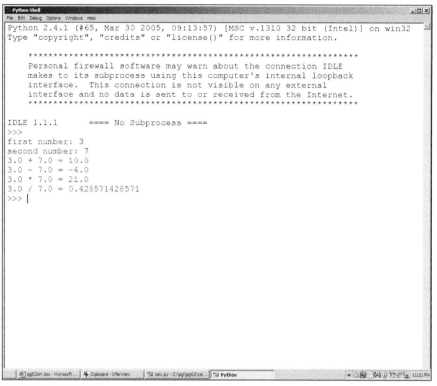

Figure 2-2: The Calculator program can do basic math.

Watch Your Step

The Calculator program works, but it isn't very robust. The user can break it quite easily by typing in the value "two" instead of 2, or by entering a 0 for the y variable (since division by 0 is undefined). You will learn how to fix these problems later. For now, just concentrate on understanding how the variable conversion and input functions work together.

Organizing Your Data with Lists

Python works well with both text and numeric data. However, games often have a *lot* of data, so we need a way of organizing large amounts of information in the computer's memory. If you're writing an adventure game, for example, you need to have some sort of inventory — which is simply a list of the useful (or not-so-useful) objects you've picked up in your travels. Python provides an incredibly handy tool for storing lots of information called the *list*. Look at the `inventory.py` program to see some of the things you can do with lists:

```
""" inventory.py
    Demonstrates lists
    4/20/06 """

inventory = [
    "toothbrush",
    "suit of armor",
    "latte espresso",
    "crochet hook",
    "bone saw",
    "towel"]

print "I packed these things for my adventure:"
print inventory
print

print "I love my", inventory[2], "and my", inventory[4]
print

print "my first few items:"
print inventory[:3]
print

print "third item:", inventory[3]
print

print "changing third item..."
inventory[3] = "doily"
print "third item is now:", inventory[3]
print

print "revised inventory:"
print inventory
print

print "adding kitchen sink"
inventory.append("kitchen sink")
print inventory
print

print "never mind... I don't need that"
inventory.remove("kitchen sink")
print inventory
print
```

The results of this program are shown in Figure 2-3.

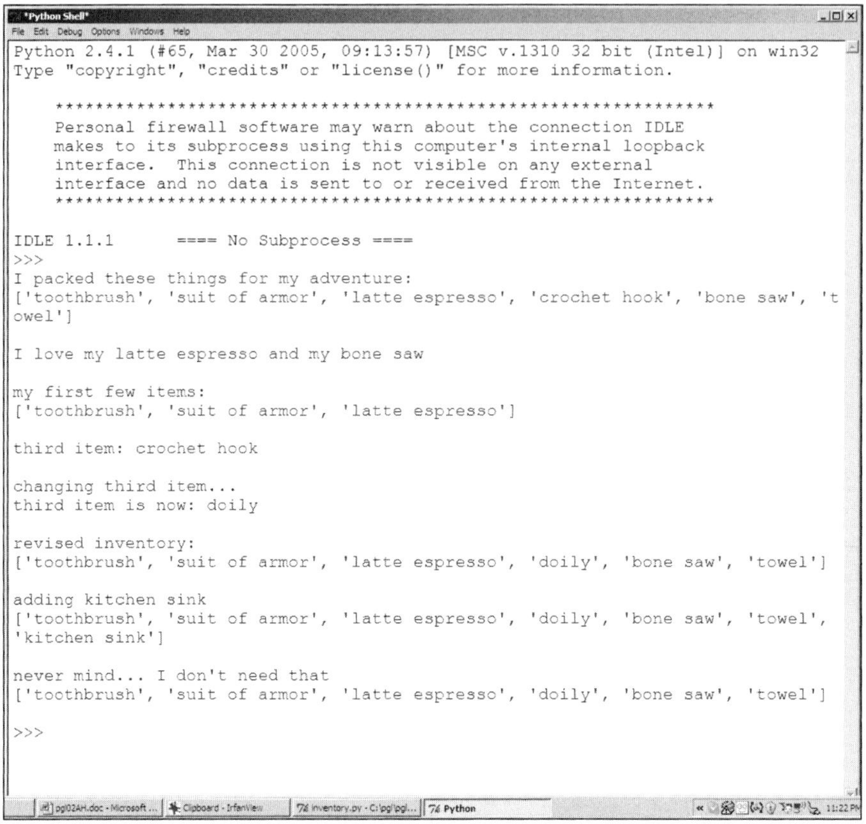

```
Python Shell
File  Edit  Debug  Options  Windows  Help
Python 2.4.1 (#65, Mar 30 2005, 09:13:57) [MSC v.1310 32 bit (Intel)] on win32
Type "copyright", "credits" or "license()" for more information.

    ***********************************************************************
    Personal firewall software may warn about the connection IDLE
    makes to its subprocess using this computer's internal loopback
    interface.  This connection is not visible on any external
    interface and no data is sent to or received from the Internet.
    ***********************************************************************

IDLE 1.1.1      ==== No Subprocess ====
>>>
I packed these things for my adventure:
['toothbrush', 'suit of armor', 'latte espresso', 'crochet hook', 'bone saw', 't
owel']

I love my latte espresso and my bone saw

my first few items:
['toothbrush', 'suit of armor', 'latte espresso']

third item: crochet hook

changing third item...
third item is now: doily

revised inventory:
['toothbrush', 'suit of armor', 'latte espresso', 'doily', 'bone saw', 'towel']

adding kitchen sink
['toothbrush', 'suit of armor', 'latte espresso', 'doily', 'bone saw', 'towel',
'kitchen sink']

never mind... I don't need that
['toothbrush', 'suit of armor', 'latte espresso', 'doily', 'bone saw', 'towel']

>>>
```

Figure 2-3: With this useful stuff, I'm sure I can slay any dragons that come by.

There are lots of interesting things going on. I'll take you through the code a step at a time so you can see what's happening. If you want, you can type the code into your console as you read along, and you'll see everything happen in real time. (That's a really great idea, by the way. Python lets you see results as you type commands in. Not all languages do that, so take advantage of it as you can.)

Creating a list

The first part of the code creates the inventory list:

```
inventory = [
    "toothbrush",
    "suit of armor",
    "latte espresso",
    "crochet hook",
    "bone saw",
    "towel"]
```

A list is a variable whose value begins and ends with square braces ([ ]). Unlike regular variables, you can assign multiple values to a list. In this example, I'm assigning a bunch of string values, but you can put any type of variable or value inside a list. Just be sure to use a comma to separate each element of the list from the other elements. I like to put the each element on its own line, but you can combine elements on the same line if you want.

Printing out the list

Once you have a list in memory, you can print it to the console like any other variable. For example, the following code

```
print inventory
print
```

prints out the value of the inventory list, like this:

```
['toothbrush', 'suit of armor', 'latte espresso',
'crochet hook', 'bone saw', 'towel']
```

The second `print` statement prints a blank line for easier-to-read output. You learn later in this chapter how to get more nicely formatted output from a list, but this is fine for now.

Slicing a list

You can slice up a list much like you can slice string variables (described in Chapter 1).

Say you want to find individual elements from the list. Take a look at this portion of the inventory code:

```
print "I love my", inventory[2], "and my", inventory[4]
```

This finds `inventory[2]` and `inventory[4]`, and inserts the values into the output. Remember, slot zero happens before the beginning of the list, so "toothbrush" is `inventory[0]`, "suit of armor" is `inventory[1]`, and so on. Even though "latte espresso" is the third element in the list from the human point of view, computers usually count beginning with zero, so "latte espresso" is actually `inventory[2]`.

You can also slice the first few elements from the list. The other slicing operators work the same way in lists as they do with strings. For example,

```
print "my first few items:"
print inventory[:3]
```

prints out the first three items — the items between position zero (actually the first position, at the beginning of the list) and position 3 (between "latte espresso" and "crochet hook"):

```
my first few items:
['toothbrush', 'suit of armor', 'latte espresso']
```

Changing a list element

You can change the values in a list. I've decided to replace my crochet hook in position three with a doily. (*Never* go into enemy territory without a doily!)

```
print "changing third item..."
inventory[3] = "doily"
print "third item is now:", inventory[3]
print "revised inventory:"
print inventory
print
```

I can write a new value to `inventory[3]` just as if it were an ordinary variable rather than part of a list. If I assign "doily" to `inventory[3]`, the crochet hook disappears, and the doily takes its place:

```
changing third item...
third item is now: doily

revised inventory:
['toothbrush', 'suit of armor', 'latte espresso', 'doily', 'bone saw', 'towel']
```

Adding and removing elements from a list

You can add on to a list after you've created it, using the `append()` method:

```
print "adding kitchen sink"
inventory.append("kitchen sink")
print inventory
```

The new inventory now contains the kitchen sink. (Of course.)

```
['toothbrush', 'suit of armor', 'latte espresso',          ↩
'doily', 'bone saw', 'towel', 'kitchen sink']
```

Information Kiosk

If you want to add an element somewhere in the middle of the list, look up the list object's `insert()` method. Be careful doing this, though, because it will change the index of all the elements that come later in the list, which might cause you problems.

You can remove any element from the list with the `remove()` method. Indicate the value of the element you want taken out of the list, and Python removes it:

```
inventory.remove("kitchen sink")
print inventory
```

Watch Your Step

There are a couple of things that can go wrong with the `remove()` method. If you try to remove an element that's not there, you will get an error. If your list has two identical elements, the `remove()` method takes out only the first one.

Looping Through Lists

Often, you'll find yourself wanting to do something to all the elements in a list. For example, if your game has a lot of superheroes in it, you need to give them appropriate introductions, as I have done in the `superhero.py` program:

```
""" superhero.py
    demonstrates using a for() structure
    to step through a list
    3/22/06 """

heroes = [
    "Buffalo Man",
    "Geek Boy",
    "Wiffle-Ball Woman"
    ]

for hero in heroes:
    print "Never fear,", hero, "is here."
```

The result of the `superhero.py` program is shown in Figure 2-4.

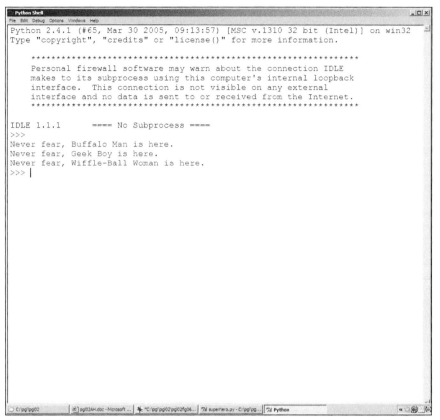

Figure 2-4: Thank goodness. All my heroes are here at last.

Step Into the Real World

Python and the Importance of Indentation If Python is your first programming language, feel free to skip this sidebar. However, programmers working on a second or third language inevitably compare languages, and that's a good thing. People moving from other languages to Python often have trouble with indentation in Python, and it makes sense to talk about it here.

If you have programmed before in some other language (C or Java, for example), a few things about Python will seem odd to you — and most of them come out in this program. By far the hardest adjustment is the importance of indentation. Most languages don't mandate any sort of indentation. For example, you could write the `superhero.py` program in JavaScript (another very popular scripting language) like this:

```
//first try - no formatting...
heroes = Array("Buffalo Man", "Geek Boy", "Wiffle-Ball Woman");
for (i = 0; i < heroes.length; i++){ hero = heroes[i];   document.write
("Never fear, " + hero + " is here! <br />");}
```

It's really okay if you can't read this particular bit of code. The point is that most programming languages don't really care where lines end, or how you indent your code. As a programmer, you're given the freedom to end lines wherever you feel like it. These languages can get away with this permissiveness by requiring very specific line-ending syntax. In most languages derived from C (a *lot* of languages these days), every line must end with a semicolon.

Even though the language gives you freedom to structure your code however you want, almost all programmers adhere by a strict set of code style standards. If you are a professional programmer or taking a programming class, your employer or teacher will never accept code written like the program above. Even if you're programming for fun, you'll benefit from buckling down on code layout. A real JavaScript version of the `superhero.py` program would look more like this:

```
heroes = Array("Buffalo Man",
               "Geek Boy",
               "Wiffle-Ball Woman");

for (i = 0; i < heroes.length; i++){
  hero = heroes[i];
  document.write("Never fear, " + hero + " is here! <br />");
} // end for loop
```

Even though this code is (probably) unfamiliar to you, the similarity between this code and the same program in Python is obvious. JavaScript doesn't use indentation to indicate that some of the code is in a loop; instead, it uses braces ({ }). Good programmers, however, get into the habit of indenting any code that happens inside a loop — just as you already do in Python.

Note that the only place Python requires any special punctuation (at least so far) is the colon (:) character at the end of the `for` line — which indicates that a block is coming up. Because of Python's understanding of indentation, no other line needs any special ending characters. Contrast that to the C-derived languages, where every single line has some sort of special ending character.

Here's what it boils down to: I don't think the Python requirement to indent your code is a problem, because you really should indent loops (and a few other structures coming up) in *whatever* language you use. Additionally, since Python uses the indentation itself as an indicator of program structure, you don't have to have a closing structure (such as the } that closes the loop in JavaScript and many other languages).

The program begins by creating a list of heroes. The next part is where things get interesting. The line

```
for hero in heroes:
```

starts a special process called a *for loop*. Loops allow your code to do things repeatedly. In this case, Python will print out a different line for every hero in the list.

`for` loops in Python are often associated with lists. Generally, you will specify a single variable (in this case `hero`) and a list (`heroes`). The line with a `for` loop has to have a colon (:) character at the end. The next line *must* be indented; indented lines identify the code that is repeated.

Look again at the printout in Figure 2-4. Notice the program printed three lines, but there is only one `print` statement in the program. Python repeated the `print` statement once for each element in the list. Here's how it works:

- **The `for` statement tells Python to create a non-list variable called `hero`.** It also tells Python there is a list called `heroes` to work with.

- **The colon at the end of the `for` line tells Python to expect a block of lines that is related somehow to the current command.** In this case, there's just one line in the group.

- **Indentation has meaning.** All the lines under this current `for` line are considered part of this line's logic, and must be indented the same amount (usually four spaces).

- **Assign the first value in the list to the non-list variable you created (`hero`, in this example).** Python takes the first element in `heroes` ("Buffalo Man") and stores it in the variable `hero`.

- **The `print` statement does its job.** In the first pass, it prints `"Never Fear, Buffalo Man is here!"`

- **The end of indentation shows the end of the loop.** Since this is the last indented line, program control *reverts* (goes back) to the `for` line.

- **Start again with the next element.** The next member of the `heroes` list is automatically placed into the `hero` variable.

- **Lather, rinse, and repeat.** The process repeats until there are no more values in the `heroes` list.

- **When the list is finished, move on.** The next (unindented) line of code occurs. Since there is no more code at the end of this program, the program ends.

Using the debugger

It's critical that you understand how Python does business, because sooner or later your code (being a human creation) will not work right and you'll have to fix it. Python comes with a wonderful resource for understanding what your code is doing: the Python *debugger*. Use the `superhero.py` program introduced in the last section to get acquainted with the debugger. You will learn how to use a very useful tool, and you'll also get important insight into how the `superhero.py` program works under the hood.

To turn on the debugger, follow these steps:

1. Go to the IDLE window and choose Debugger in the Debug menu.

A small window that looks like Figure 2-5 appears, and the console says `[DEBUG ON]`.

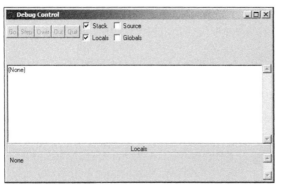

Figure 2-5: The Debug Control window when no program is running.

The new window is called the Debug Control. This little gem is a window into the actual workings of Python as it runs your program. Since you don't have a program running yet, it isn't showing much — but that will change. Note that the debugger might look a little different based on your operating system, but it will generally look like this.

Watch Your Step

If you're going to debug a program in IDLE, make sure you start IDLE first, and then load the program into the editor. If you right-click the program's name in the file manager and choose Edit in IDLE, the debugger gives you some strange and unexpected results.

2. Run the `superhero.py` program again and look at the Debug Control again.

This time it should look something like Figure 2-6.

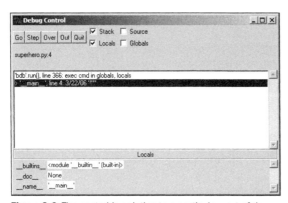

Figure 2-6: The control is pointing to a particular part of the `superhero.py` program.

When you run a program in debug mode, things work a little differently than in a normal run. During a normal run, the computer moves at the highest possible speed, doing things very quickly. If there are mistakes, they also happen so quickly that you can't see what's going wrong. (It's long been said that no human can make mistakes as quickly or efficiently as a computer.) The debugger slows everything down to a crawl so you can inspect things carefully.

3. **Take a close look at the debugger with a program running.**

The top section of the Debug Control has a series of buttons and check boxes that allow you to move through the program manually, deciding which elements you want to see. For now, leave these items alone while you inspect the other two parts of the control.

In its default setting, the Debug Control shows you two major pieces of information. The large white area is called the *stack trace*. This tells you where in the program the debugger is currently resting. When you initially run a program, it goes to the end of the first line of logic (which is in this case the end of the documentation string).

4. **Highlight the current line in the editor.**

Notice in Figure 2-6 the highlighted information stating line 4 : 3/22/06 " " ". This is the end of the first logical line of code. Click the Source check box to see that segment highlighted in the code window. Click the Step button, and the screen changes to show Figure 2-7.

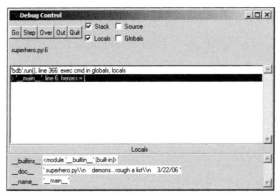

Figure 2-7: Now the debugger is looking at line 6.

5. **Go all the way through the program using the Step button; watch how the program moves through the code and prints out information only one line at a time.**

Information Kiosk

If you want to see the current line highlighted in the editor, you need to uncheck and recheck the Source check box each time. The highlight doesn't move automatically.

6. **Finish the program and restart it.**

Be sure to move all the way through the code (so the buttons are no longer selectable) and then restart the `superhero.py` program.

7. **View the local variables.**

This time, take a look at the bottom section of the window, called Locals. Keep stepping through the program until you get to line 12, which should look like Figure 2-8.

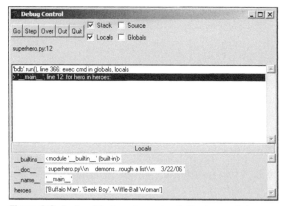

Figure 2-8: By line 12, there is a value in the heroes list.

The Locals area shows a number of strange things, but the bottom line is really interesting. It shows that you have a variable called `heroes`, and it also shows the value of that variable (the list of hero names).

8. **See what happens when the loop starts.**

Click the Step button one more time and see what happens after line 12 executes in Figure 2-9.

By the time line 13 is on deck, there are two variables. `heroes` is the list of hero names, and `hero` currently has the single value "Buffalo Man." Note that you see the stack trace (indication in the white area) of line 13 *before* it actually executes. Line 13 hasn't happened yet. It's what will happen the next time you press the Step button. (That's why the first announcement hasn't been printed to the console yet.)

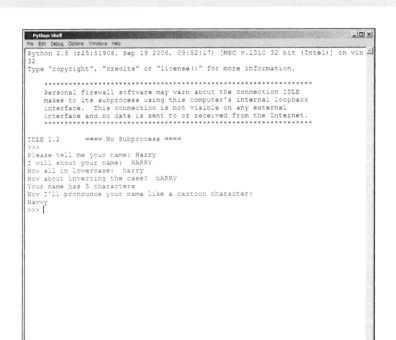

```
Python Shell                                                        _ □ X
File  Edit  Debug  Options  Windows  Help
Python 2.5 (r25:51908, Sep 19 2006, 09:52:17) [MSC v.1310 32 bit (Intel)] on win
32
Type "copyright", "credits" or "license()" for more information.

    ************************************************************
    Personal firewall software may warn about the connection IDLE
    makes to its subprocess using this computer's internal loopback
    interface.  This connection is not visible on any external
    interface and no data is sent to or received from the Internet.
    ************************************************************

IDLE 1.2      ==== No Subprocess ====
>>>
Please tell me your name: Harry
I will shout your name:  HARRY
Now all in lowercase:  harry
How about inverting the case?  hARRY
Your name has 5 characters
Now I'll pronounce your name like a cartoon character:
Hawwy
>>> |
                                                                  Ln: 20 Col: 4
```

Figure 2-9: Now you have two variables.

9. Watch the `hero` variable change.

Press the Step button a few more times and watch the value of `hero` change each time you repeat the loop.

Watch Your Step

When you're in debug mode, your program is in a limbo state between running and pausing. If you are debugging a program and you want to move on, make sure you've finished the program. You can tell this has happened when the Step button is grayed out and no longer takes input. If you want to finish the program quickly, press the Go button to finish running the program at full speed or the Quit button to stop the debugging process. If you try to run another program while Python is still debugging something else, IDLE might crash, and you have to restart it.

The process of looking through a program line-by-line and examining the value of every variable is invaluable when you try to fix programs that aren't cooperating. Python's debugger is easier and more useful than most. Be sure to take advantage of it to understand these basic programs and also to help figure out what's going wrong when your programs get more complicated.

Counting with ranges

Often you will find yourself wanting to work with each element in a list. Sometimes, though, you just want to do something a certain number of times. Python supports a special kind of list that you might find extremely handy. The `range()` function allows you to automatically build a range of values in a sequence. To see how it works, open up the console and try these things:

1. **Build a basic range of values. Type** `range(10)` **into the console and see what happens.**

   ```
   >>> range(10)
   [0, 1, 2, 3, 4, 5, 6, 7, 8, 9]
   ```

   Python creates a special list with ten elements in it. Notice that the first element is 0, and the last element is 9. If you create a range with a single value, Python creates a list with that many values going from zero to one less than the specified number.

2. **Create a range with a bottom and top value.**

   ```
   >>> range(2, 10)
   [2, 3, 4, 5, 6, 7, 8, 9]
   ```

   When you create a range with two values, the first value is the starting point of the range. The second value is the upper limit. So, when you create a range from 2 to 10, Python builds a list from 2 to 9. (Remember: Python never includes the last value.)

3. **Make a range that skips values.**

   ```
   >>> range (0, 55, 5)
   [0, 5, 10, 15, 20, 25, 30, 35, 40, 45, 50]
   ```

   If you add a third parameter to the `range()` function, Python adds that third value each time. The function `range(0, 55, 5)` creates a range of numbers from 0 to 50, counting by fives.

4. **Count backward with a negative increment.**

   ```
   >>> range (10, 0, -1)
   [10, 9, 8, 7, 6, 5, 4, 3, 2, 1]
   ```

This example begins with 10 and ends at 0, subtracting one each time. As usual, the first value is included, but the ending value (0 in this case) is not.

The `rangeDemo.py` program summarizes these various ways of working with a range.

```
""" rangeDemo.py
    demonstrates how range object
    creates automatic lists of numbers
```

```
        3/28/06 """

print "range(3)"
print range(3)
print

print "range(1, 3)"
print range(1, 3)
print

print "range(2, 5)"
print range(2, 5)
print

print "range(0, 55, 5)"
print range(0, 55, 5)
print

print "range(50, 0, -5)"
print range(50, 0, -5)
print
```

The program uses the range() function to create a bunch of special lists. The output shown in Figure 2-10 demonstrates how the range() function does its work.

Look over the results of the range demo, and you can see how ranges work:

- **If the range has one parameter,** Python creates a list with that many elements, starting with the number 0. (Remember, computers usually begin counting with zero.) The largest number will be one less than the number range, so range(3) produces a list containing the values 0, 1, and 2.

- **If the range has two parameters,** Python makes a list that starts with the first parameter, and goes to *one less* than the second parameter. The ending value is never used; it specifies only the upper limit of the range that should be produced. If you call for a range with the parameters (1, 3), the result is the values 1 and 2, but *not* 3. Likewise, range(2, 5) makes the list [2, 3, 4] but does *not* include 5.

- **If the range has three parameters,** Python uses the third parameter to indicate a step value for each new number. As an example, range(0, 55, 5) counts from 0 to 55 by fives, but repeats only the values to 50. The result is [0, 5, 10, 15, 20, 25, 30, 35, 40, 45, 50]. You can make a range count backward by using a negative number for the step value. If you do this, make sure your starting number is larger than the ending value. The function range (50, 0, -5) returns the multiples of 5 from 50 to 5, counting backward.

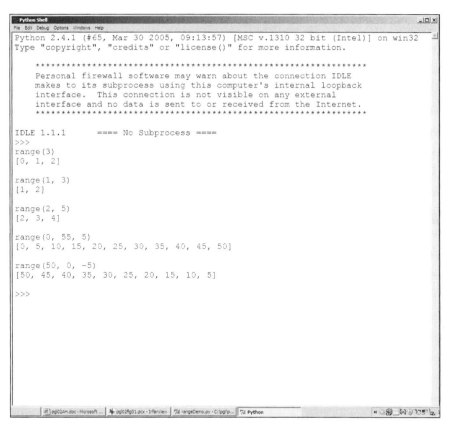

```
Python Shell                                                                    _|□|×
File  Edit  Debug  Options  Windows  Help
Python 2.4.1 (#65, Mar 30 2005, 09:13:57) [MSC v.1310 32 bit (Intel)] on win32
Type "copyright", "credits" or "license()" for more information.

    ******************************************************************
    Personal firewall software may warn about the connection IDLE
    makes to its subprocess using this computer's internal loopback
    interface.  This connection is not visible on any external
    interface and no data is sent to or received from the Internet.
    ******************************************************************

IDLE 1.1.1       ==== No Subprocess ====
>>>
range(3)
[0, 1, 2]

range(1, 3)
[1, 2]

range(2, 5)
[2, 3, 4]

range(0, 55, 5)
[0, 5, 10, 15, 20, 25, 30, 35, 40, 45, 50]

range(50, 0, -5)
[50, 45, 40, 35, 30, 25, 20, 15, 10, 5]

>>>
```
```
 pg02AH.doc - Microsoft ...   pg02fig01.pcx - IrfanView   rangeDemo.py - C:\pg\p...   Python         « ☐ 🖧 ◖·◗ 🕐 ⛶ 🔋
```

Figure 2-10: The range() function is used to make lists of numbers.

Repeating in a range

All that range stuff in the last section may sound theoretical. Why would you want to make lists of numbers? Actually, that capability turns out to be pretty useful. If you want something to happen ten times in your code, you can make a list with ten elements, and use that list in a for loop, like this:

```
>>> for i in range(10):
        print "I will not talk out in class"
```

Try entering this bit of code into the console and see what happens. The range(10) function is the easiest way there is to make a list with ten elements in it. The print line is indented after the colon that ends the for statement, so that line is repeated once for every element in the (ten-item) list. The resulting code prints out a sincere promise ten times in a row. If your transgression was greater, you can simply increase the size of the range and write out your punishment as many times as needed. (I wish I'd had Python when I was in grade school!)

Step Into the Real World

Why Does range(1, 11) Count to 10?   If you're still confused about why you must enter values 1 and 11 when you want a loop that gives values 1 to 10, you're not alone. Python's looping mechanism actually does make sense — but in order to understand what's going on, you have to look at how Python uses the `range()` function with loops. When you create a `for` loop with a range, you're basically telling Python to do these things:

● Create a special variable for the loop. This variable is sometimes called the *sentry* variable because it is used to guard access to the loop.

● Initialize the sentry to the starting value specified in the range (or 0 if no starting value is specified).

● Do the stuff inside the loop.

● Add the increment value (which defaults to the value 1 if no increment is given) to the sentry variable.

● If the sentry is still less than the maximum value, repeat the loop. If the sentry is now greater than or equal to the maximum value, end the loop immediately.

This explains why you should have a maximum value of 11 if you want your largest value to be 10 — the maximum value is never considered part of the loop.

Another strange thing: If you're coming from another language, you probably find Python's `for` loop very odd. Python doesn't really have a C-like `for` loop! The `for` loop in Python acts more like `foreach` in most languages. The very powerful `range()` function allows Python to use the same `for` where other languages have two distinctive types of loop.

You don't have to use the value of the counting variable in your loop. I didn't use it in the example just given, but you can if you want. The next example prints the results of a ten-lap race:

```
>>> for lap in range(1, 11):
        print "Now on lap:", lap
```

Notice if you want the laps to go from one to ten, you have to set the starting value to 1 (the first lap you want to represent). Set the ending value to 11, because the loop will exit when it encounters lap 11. You can use the value of the `lap` variable inside the loop.

Writing a Real Program

All this stuff may be very interesting, but the point of this book is to write some real programs. It can be hard to see how you can go from these basic ideas to an actual program. For example, suppose you wanted to print all the letters of a word in reverse order. If the user inputs the word "python," it would return "nohtyp." How could you create this program using only the skills learned up to now? Figure 2-11 illustrates the result of such a program.

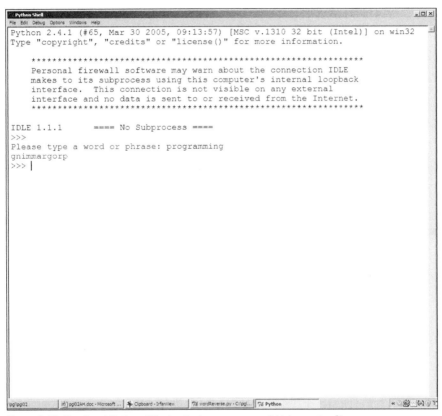

Figure 2-11: Use the skills from this chapter to reverse a word (gnimmargorp?).

Most programming really comes down to problem solving, and this problem is a great place to start. The process is not difficult, but you may need to use some discipline to work through it. Begin by asking yourself some questions:

1. **What are you trying to achieve?**

You want to print out the letters of the word in reverse order.

2. **What are you starting with?**

Every problem has a context. By the time you're worried about solving this particular problem (reversing the word), you already have a word stored in a variable.

3. **Do you already have a tool that can do this?**

So far, no. I haven't shown you anything yet that can solve this problem directly.

4. **What tools do you know that have potential?**

Quite a few, it turns out. You know how to print out any character in a word using string slicing. You know how to determine the length of a word. You know how to make a loop using a range. All these skills may come in handy.

You probably won't be able to write out your program from beginning to end. It's better to pick out basic tasks and work your way through the problem with successive approximations, always getting closer to the goal. For example, here's one way I worked through the problem (since this is actually a pretty simple problem, I'll do some preliminary testing on the console before I worry about making a full-blown program):

1. **Begin by storing a word into a variable.**

```
>>> word = "programming"
>>> print word
programming
```

Store a word into a variable and print out the variable just to be sure things are working as you want. There's no need to move on until you're sure this first step is working correctly.

2. **Use string slicing to get a feel for the problem and whether slicing has potential as a solution.**

I know I'll need to extract a letter at a time, and the only technique I know so far is string slicing. I'll try a few string slices to make sure I understand how this word is put together.

```
>>> print word[0]
p
>>> print word[10]
g
```

For this particular word, the first character is `word[0]` and the last character is `word[10]`. It has 11 characters, and their indices go from 0 to 10. It's true that other words will have different lengths, but for now simply think about how to work with this word.

3. **Make a loop that produces the correct indices.**

If you want to make a loop that can view each letter in turn, you'll need a range that can go from 0 to 10. You can build exactly such a range with the following loop:

```
>>> for i in range(11):
    print i,

0 1 2 3 4 5 6 7 8 9 10
```

This loop generates values from 0 to 10. It should be pretty easy to make a loop that prints each letter one at a time (although it's still going in the wrong direction).

4. **Modify the loop so now it prints out characters.**

Use string slicing to extract one character at a time:

```
>>> for i in range(11):
    print word[i],

p r o g r a m m i n g
```

5. Modify the range so it goes backward.

As it's currently set, the range produces values from 0 to 10. You want a range that produces values from 10 to 0. Make a new loop that produces the values you want. This is a little tricky, but think through it one step at a time. You want indices from 10 to 0. Play around with the range parameters, and you'll find that this works:

```
>>> for i in range(10, -1, -1):
    print i,

10 9 8 7 6 5 4 3 2 1 0
```

The beginning value is 10, the ending value is –1 (one less than the smallest value I want displayed), and Python should subtract 1 (by adding –1) each time. It's critical that you understand I didn't just know this. I played around with a few variations of the `range()` statement until I found a combination that does what I want.

6. Modify the program to print the characters.

Because you've done it before, it's trivial to modify this loop so it shows characters rather than indices:

```
>>> for i in range(10, -1, -1):
    print word[i],

g n i m m a r g o r p
```

7. Make a variation that will work for any word.

You should be proud of your work so far, but it has one major problem. If the value of the `word` variable is exactly 11 characters long (like the test word "programming"), everything will work great. However, you'll have problems with words of different lengths. The secret is to realize that the first parameter for the backward loop shouldn't always be 10. Think about what the value 10 really means. In this context, 10 is really the index of the last character. If the word is 11 characters long, your backward loop should start at 10. If the word is 5 characters long, the loop should start at 4, and so on. You don't have a function to find the last character's index, but you do have a function for determining the length of a string. (Hint: Remember the `len()` function from Chapter 1?)

```
>>> print len(word)
11
```

The last character's index will always be the number of characters in the word's length minus 1, or

```
>>> print len(word) - 1
10
```

8. **Make a more generic range.**

Now you can write the loop in a more generic form, so it will work for any word length:

```
>>> maxIndex = len(word) -1
>>> for i in range(maxIndex, -1, -1):
    print word[i],

g n i m m a r g o r p
```

9. **Turn these ideas into a full-fledged program.**

Now that you have played around enough to know how to build a program that can reverse a word, combine everything you've learned into a program to solve the problem. There are many right answers to this challenge, but mine is produced in the following wordReverse.py:

```
""" wordReverse.py
    demonstrates how to use loops
    for string manipulation
    3/30/06 """

inWord = raw_input("Please type a word or phrase: ")
outWord = ""

# remember, I want to count backwards to character zero,
# so negative one is the boundary

firstChar = -1

# The length of the word is how many characters are in it
# The last character is word length minus one.

maxIndex = len(inWord) - 1


# Go backwards from the last character to the first character
# counting by negative one each time through the loop

for charPos in range (maxIndex, firstChar, -1):

    # Add the current character to the output string
    outWord = outWord + inWord[charPos]

# After the loop is finished, print out the results
print outWord
```

I made a few minor modifications to this program to make it a little more user-friendly. First, I added a raw_input function to ask the user for a word or a phrase. Also, rather than simply printing out the reversed word one character at a time, I concatenated the characters into a new string called `outWord`. Finally, I printed out the resulting string value.

10. **Test your program.**

Even if you followed all my advice, it still may not work right. It might work correctly, but you don't know exactly why. Test your program by running it a few times. Use the debugger to see how exactly Python is running through the loop and creating the output variable character by character. Have fun!

In this chapter, you learned a lot about how Python works with data. You learned how to make and modify string variables, as well as how to slice strings and lists to get sub-elements. You explored Python's numeric variable types and learned how to convert variables to whatever type you wish. You built lists and picked up several functions for working with them. You used the `range()` function to build lists of numbers with interesting properties, and you were introduced to the helpful debugger. Finally, you began to investigate the process of writing programs, seeing how to go from an idea and a handful of primitive tools to something more exciting and powerful.

If data is the fuel of computer games, control structures are the engine block. In the next chapter, you'll learn about how to manage the flow of instruction through loops, functions, branching logic, and other exciting things. When your programs can make decisions, you can truly start writing games that are interesting to play.

data type: What kind of data a variable contains. Although Python automatically assigns a data type to every item of data, the programmer has to know what type a particular variable is — because each type has different methods associated with it. The most important basic data types in Python are string, integer, and float.

debugger: A special program that allows you to view your program one line at a time and watch what it's doing. IDLE has a nice debugger built in.

double: A double-precision floating-point number. Some languages distinguish between ordinary floating-point numbers (floats) and more precise numbers that can hold more information (doubles). In Python, floating-point numbers are actually doubles, so float and double refer to the same type of variable.

dynamically typed language: A programming language that assigns data types on the fly as the programmer assigns values to variables. Python is (like most scripting languages) dynamically typed.

float: A floating-point real number. This is the most common type of real number in Python.

`for` loop: A programming structure that repeats code once for each element of a list. Use with the `range()` function to make code repeat a certain number of times.

index: The number that indicates which position in a list or string contains a particular value.

`int`: The data type usually associated with integers in Python.

integer: A number without a decimal part. Python usually classifies integers as `int` (the integer data type).

list: A variable containing multiple values.

operator overloading: A mathematical operator sometimes does different things on different data types. For example, the plus sign (+) *concatenates* string data, but it *adds* integers and real numbers.

real number: A number that can include decimal values. In Python, real numbers are usually referred to as floats.

string concatenation: Combining two strings to make a larger string. This can be done with the plus sign (+).

Command	Arguments	Description	Example
`string.upper()`	None	Convert *string* to uppercase.	`print userName.upper()`
`string.lower()`	None	Convert *string* to lowercase.	`print userName.lower()`
`string.replace(a, b)`	*a:* search text *b:* replace text	Replace all instances of *a* in *string* with *b*.	`news.replace("bad", "good")`

TOKENS

Command	Arguments	Description	Example
`string.title()`	None	Capitalize the first letter of each word in `string`.	`print headline.title()`
`float(val)`	`val`: a numeric or string value to be converted	Convert `val` to a floating-point number.	`x = float(x)`
`int(val)`	`val`: a numeric or string value to be converted	Convert `val` to an integer number.	`x = int(x)`
`str(val)`	`val`: a numeric or string value to be converted	Convert `val` to a string.	`x = str(x)`
`range(start, bound, inc)`	`start`: starting value `bound`: upper limit `inc`: increment	Make a range from `start` to `bound`— using `inc`.	`print range(0, 12, 2)`
`list.append(item)`	`item`: item to add to list	Add `item` to end of list.	`inventory.append ("snakebite kit")`
`list.remove(content)`	`content`: what is to be removed (content, not index)	Remove elements containing `content` from `list`.	`inventory.remove ("nuclear waste")`
`for item in list:`	`item`: element of list `list:` list of items	Step through `list` placing each element into `item`.	`for beatle in ["John", "Paul", "George", "Ringo"]:`
`help("command")`	`command:` command, object, or module name	Get help on an object from Python console.	`help("float")`

Practice Exam

1. What kind of data goes in a string variable?

_____

2. Why should you convert numeric values you received from `raw_input()`?

_____

_____

_____

3. When does the plus sign concatenate rather than add?

_____

_____

4. Why should you be careful about dividing integer values?

_____

_____

_____

5. How do you create a list variable?

_____

_____

_____

6. How similar are string and list slicing?

_____

_____

_____

7. What's the easiest way to work with each element of a list?

A) You can't work with elements individually.

B) Use a `for` loop.

C) Copy each individual variable to a list.

D) Use a `lambda` function.

8. What two parameters does a `for` loop require in Python?

_____

_____

_____

9. Why must the line after a `for` loop be indented?

_____

_____

_____

10. Why is it good to know how to use the debugger?

_____

_____

_____

11. What are the three possible parameters of the `range()` function?

_____

_____

_____

12. Why should you organize your thoughts before you begin programming?

_____

_____

_____

13. Write a program that accepts one word of input from the user and then converts the word into Pig Latin. Take the first letter from the front of the word, move it to the end, and add "ay," so "python" becomes "ythonpay." Don't worry about whether the word begins with a vowel or a consonant (at least until next chapter!).

_____

_____

_____

14. Write a program that has a grocery list ("eggs," "cheese," and "hamburger"). Print out each element of the list in surfer-speak: "We need some eggs, dude!"

_____

_____

_____

15. Create a multiplication table that shows the products of all numbers 0 to 10. Do not pre-calculate the values. Use two `for` loops to make the code as efficient as possible.

_____

_____

_____

16. Write a program that accepts a binary number and converts it to base 10. Hint: Use `help()` to find useful features of the `int` object.

_____

_____

_____

3 Taking Control

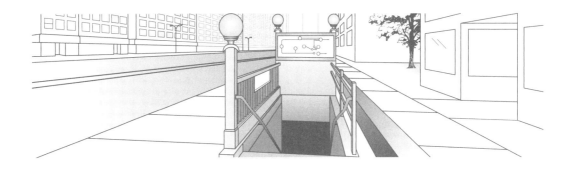

 # Enter the Station

Questions

1. How do you get a computer program to make a decision?

2. How do you compare two or more values in a computer program?

3. How do you have a program choose from a variety of options?

4. How can a program repeat until some specified condition is set?

5. How do you avoid endless loops in your code?

6. What's the best way to make a group of code structures?

7. How do you manage lots of code in a reasonable way?

8. What is encapsulation? Why is it good?

9. How do you get information into a function?

10. How do you get information out of a function?

11. How do you build a loop that has more than one exit point?

In the last chapter you learned how to work with data, the fuel of computer games. If data is the fuel of computer games, this chapter is about the engine. Control structures are the way you help your programs make decisions. You learned one control structure with the `for` loop. In this chapter, you'll learn about all the other major control structures and how to use them. By the end of this chapter, you'll know all the main concepts of programming in any language, and you'll be ready to move on to graphics!

Making Decisions with if

Computers are different than other machines primarily because they don't always act in the same way. A computer can appear to be intelligent because it seems to make decisions. Of course, computers don't *really* make decisions. The programmer creates various options and tells the computer how to respond. As an example, try the following experiment:

1. **Create a variable by opening the console and entering the following:**

   ```
   sky = "blue"
   ```

   You have created a variable called sky and set its value to `"blue"`. Nothing earth-shattering yet.

2. **Build an `if` statement.**

   Copy the following code *exactly* (including the double equals sign).

   ```
   if sky == "blue":
   ```

   After you see what this code does, I'll explain how it works.

3. **Press Enter.**

   You'll notice something new. The cursor does not appear all the way to the left of the console as it normally does. It is indented four spaces so the next text you type begins under the "k" in "sky." This is supposed to happen. You saw the same behavior when you typed a `for` loop in the previous chapter. The colon indicates that you're beginning a block of code.

    **Watch Your Step**

   If you're in IDLE, the indentation occurs automatically. If you're using a terminal, you have to indent four spaces yourself, and you'd better indent because if you don't, Python will not execute the code correctly.

4. Generate a result by entering the following `print` statement:

```
print "It's daytime!"
```

5. View the results by pressing Enter twice.

When you use a block structure (that is, a set of commands that are part of some other structure) in the console (as you're doing in this exercise) Python won't immediately display the results. Press Enter twice to see the results. The first time you press Enter indicates the end of the line. The second indicates you're done editing this block of code and Python will execute the instructions. The entire session should look like this:

```
>>> if sky == "blue":
        print "It's daytime!"


It's daytime!
```

Understanding the if statement

`If` statements are an important part of programming. They allow you to make the computer act in one way sometimes and in another way in other situations. The most important part of an `if` statement is a special structure called the *condition*. A condition is generally defined as an expression that can be evaluated as `True` or `False`. In the sky example, the condition was the text `sky == "blue"`. Conditions generally involve a comparison between a value and a variable or a comparison between two variables. If the condition is `True`, some action happens. The action does not happen if the condition is `False`. You can also set up a condition so one thing happens if the condition is `True`, and something else happens if the condition is `False`.

 Watch Your Step

Be very careful to recognize that the condition includes a double equals sign (`==`). This is different than the single equals sign (`=`) used for assignment. Python uses the double equals sign to indicate equality and the single equals sign to indicate assignment. If you swap these symbols, you will get unexpected (and usually unpleasant) results.

Building a basic if statement

`if` statements are the key to making a program appear to make decisions. Consider the following program:

```
""" Guido.py
    Illustrates if statement
    Say something nice if the user's name
    is Guido """

firstName = raw_input("What is your name? ")
print "Nice to meet you, " + firstName + "."

if firstName == "Guido":
    print "Hey, thanks for inventing Python!"
```

This program asks the user for a name. It greets everyone, but it shares a special message for anybody named Guido. (If your name is Guido and you *aren't* the guy who wrote Python, just play along, will you?) Figure 3-1 shows two runs of this program. First I answered with my own name. The second time, I pretended to be Guido.

The program runs twice in Figure 3-1, but with a different result each time. The first time through, the firstName variable contains the value 'Andy', so the condition firstName == "Guido" is False. Since the condition is False, Python skips the block and ends.

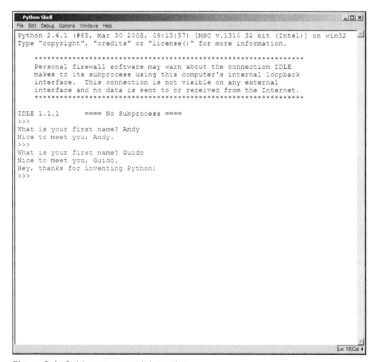

Figure 3-1: Guido gets a special greeting.

The second time I ran the program, I entered "Guido" as a first name. This time, the condition `firstName == "Guido"` is `True`, and the program executes the special greeting for Guido.

Responding to a false condition

It's good to be able to do something if a condition is `True`. Sometimes it's also helpful to have the program do something else when a condition is `False`. The `GuidoOrNot.py` program illustrates one such scenario:

```
""" GuidoOrNot.py
    Illustrates if - else structure
    Say something nice if the user's name
    is Guido and asks for Guido if user
    enters another name. """

firstName = raw_input("What is your first name? ")
print "Nice to meet you, " + firstName + "."

if firstName == "Guido":
    print "Hey, thanks for inventing Python!"
else:
    print "Have you seen Guido around?"
```

This program is much like the `Guido.py` program featured earlier, but it has an added feature in steps 4 and 5. Here's what you do step by step:

1. Ask the user for his first name just like the `Guido.py` program did.

2. Give a standard response regardless of the name the user enters.

3. If the user is Guido, thank him for writing Python.

So far, the code is just like the code in the standard `Guido.py` program.

4. Now you use the `else` clause to add some new code.

All the code indented under the condition (`firstName == "Guido"`) will be executed if that condition is `True`. If the condition is `False`, the code under the `else` clause will execute instead.

5. If the user is not Guido, use a `print` statement to ask if the user has seen Guido.

Figure 3-2 shows the `GuidoOrNot.py` program in action. As before, I ran the program twice so you can see what happens if the user types "Guido" or some other value.

Note the following characteristics of the `else` clause:

It only occurs after an **if** statement. The else clause doesn't make sense on its own. You can only use else when you're currently evaluating an if statement.

It is unindented. The else clause is unindented. That is, the term else appears directly under the if statement; it is not indented as a part of the if block. That's because it's considered an alternative to the if block. Use the Backspace key to unindent code in IDLE.

It ends with a colon. Like the if statement, the else statement begins a block. It ends with a colon (:) to indicate this fact. If you forget the colon, Python will reply with an error message.

It implies a block of code. You must put one or more lines of code after the else statement. Indent these lines just as you would indent lines under the if statement.

Use the if-else structure in situations where you want the computer to do one thing if a condition is True and something else if the condition is False.

Figure 3-2: Guido gets one greeting, and everyone else gets another.

Checking multiple conditions with elif

Sometimes you're interested in a more complex comparison. For example, you might want to see whether any other famous open-source personalities are lurking around. The `LinusOrGuido.py` shown in Figure 3-3 shows how to handle more than one condition.

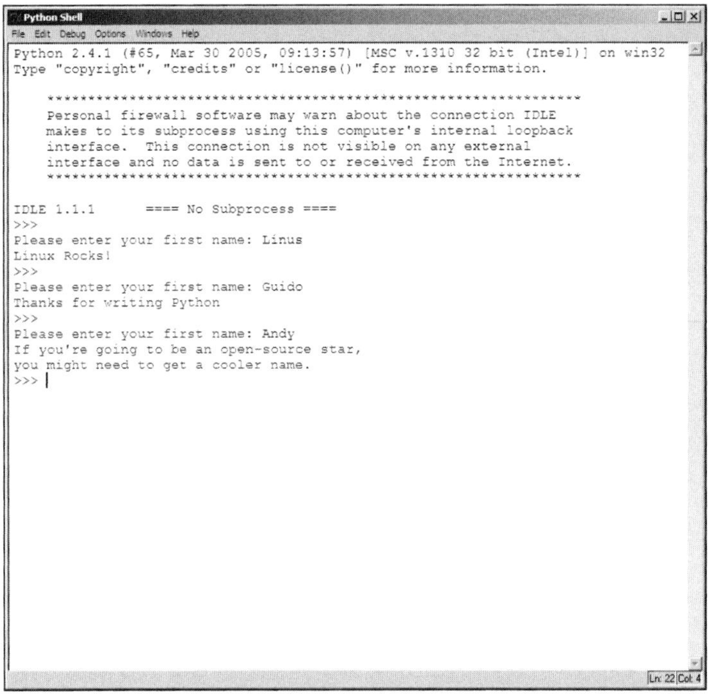

Figure 3-3: This program has different responses for Linus, Guido, and everyone else.

Look over the code listing and I'll explain exactly how it works.

```
""" LinusOrGuido.py
    Illustrates if-elif-else structure
    Checks to see if the user
    has an appropriate open-source name
    """

firstName = raw_input("Please enter your first name: ")

if firstName == "Guido":
    print "Thanks for writing Python"
elif firstName == "Linus":
    print "Linux Rocks!"
```

```
else:
    print "If you're going to be an open-source star,"
    print "you might need to get a cooler name."
```

The `LinusOrGuido.py` program adds one important element to the mix. After the `if` statement, a new statement called `elif` allows a new condition. Here's how the program works:

1. **You ask for a first name as you had it do in the other versions of the program.**

2. **Set up an `if` statement, checking for "Guido."**

Again, this is just like what you've done in previous programs.

3. **Print a greeting for Guido.**

You can write as much code as you want in the `if` block, but it must be indented.

4. **Introduce a new condition in the program.**

The `elif` clause allows you to add a new alternate condition. Python checks this new condition (`userName == "Linus"`) to see whether it is `True`. This new condition ends with a colon and starts a new block.

5. **Write code to greet Linus.**

If the second condition is `True`, I assume the program is being run by Linus Torvalds, the inventor of Linux. As usual, the code inside the block is indented.

6. **Finally, you write an `else` clause to handle all other cases.**

If neither earlier condition was `True`, the code following the final `else` clause is run instead.

Making other comparisons with if and elif

If you want to compare two string values, the equality comparison (`==`) is usually the one you want to make. Table 3-1 illustrates the other comparison operators in Python.

Step Into the Real World

Computer sports games really have a feature that works like the `raceAnnouncer.py` program. They record a series of comments from famous commentators and use conditions to determine when a situation calls for a particular comment. The next time you hear a video-game announcer explain why your quarterback got flattened, take some solace in understanding there's no real announcer broadcasting your failings; it's really just a condition at work.

Table 3-1　　　　　　　　　Comparison Operators

Symbol	What It Means	Note
==	is equal to	Works on numbers and strings.
<	is less than	Checks numbers in math. In text, checks alphabetical order.
>	is greater than	Checks numbers in math. In text, checks alphabetical order.
<=	is less than or equal to	True when the first value is less than the second or they are equal.
>=	is greater than or equal to	True when the first value is larger than the second or they are equal.
!=	is not equal to	True when the two values are not equal.

You can also compare numeric values. The `raceAnnouncer.py` program (shown in Figure 3-4) illustrates how you can use numeric comparisons and some other important features of the `if-elif` structure.

Figure 3-4: The program gives running commentary on a 10-lap race.

Step Into the Real World

This "exit the block as soon as condition's value is verified" behavior is called *shortcut evaluation*, and it is an important feature of Python. As soon as one condition is evaluated, Python knows not to worry about the others — and skips to the code following the block. This makes Python efficient because it never wastes time evaluating code that it will not run.

If you don't want the shortcut behavior, make a series of independent `if` statements rather than an `if-elif` chain.

Take a look at the `raceAnnouncer.py` code and I'll show you what it does:

```python
""" raceAnnouncer.py
    demonstrate numeric comparisons and
    elif """

for lap in range(1, 11):
    print "lap", lap
    print "    ",

    if lap == 1:
        print "starting the race"
    elif lap < 5:
        print "still in the first half"
    elif lap == 5:
        print "halfway there..."
    elif lap == 10:
        print "Finished!"
    elif lap >= 6:
        print "getting closer"
    else:
        print "something went wrong"

    print "    another great lap"

print "That was quite a race!!"
```

Transfer

Review Chapter 2 if you need a refresher on how to use the `range()` function and `for` statements.

The program acts a lot like the looping programs you saw in the last chapter, but now it says different things on different laps. Here's what you do at each step in the program:

1. **Set up a loop from 1 to 10.**

   You start a loop that uses the variable `lap`. The `lap` variables value will go from 1 to 10.

2. **Print out the lap number.**

   The program will print out all lap numbers. That way you can examine how exactly the lap number relates to the commentary.

3. **Indent the commentary by adding spaces.**

   The next `print` statement prints four spaces followed by a comma. This causes the next output (the commentary) to be indented. I did this just to make the commentary look a little better.

4. **Check to see whether it's the first lap.**

   You use an `if` statement to check for the lap number. The `lap` variable is numeric, but it can still be used inside conditions. In fact, numeric variables have a lot more options. The first check happens only if the variable lap is equal to the numeric value 1. Notice that numeric values do not have quotes. I'm not comparing `lap` to the string value `"1"`, but to the numeric value 1. Because `lap` is numeric, I can only compare it to numeric values.

   If `lap` is equal to 1, the appropriate code is activated (announcing the start of the race) and then the code jumps outside the `if` clause. None of the other conditions are activated after one of them is evaluated to `True`.

5. **Use an `elif` clause to see whether it's the first half of the race.**

   ```
   elif lap < 5:
       print "still in the first half"
   ```

   If the primary condition (`lap == 1`) was evaluated `False`, the first `elif` condition is evaluated. This one checks to see whether `lap` is less than 5. Notice that although 1 is less than 5, the "still in first half" comment did not show up in lap 1. That's because Python short-circuited all other evaluation as soon as it discovered that `lap` was equal to 1. It will only get to this particular condition if `lap` is not 1.

   Notice also that the condition only returns `True` when `lap` is *less than* 5. If `lap` is equal to 5, the condition is not `True`. (Later in the program, you'll see how to make a *"less than or equal to"* comparison.)

6. **Announce the middle point of the race.**

   The center point of the race is lap 5, so the following code announces that moment:

   ```
   elif lap == 5:
       print "halfway there..."
   ```

   This condition is very straightforward, because it's a standard comparison.

7. **Check for the end of the race.**

You might be surprised at the order of the code that looks for lap 10.

```
elif lap == 10:
    print "Finished!"
```

You can see that I'm checking for the end of the race before I place code for the final few laps. You might think the code that looks for lap 10 should be the last condition in the sequence. The important thing here is not when the code occurs, but how this short-circuiting works; I'll explain it a bit more after you look at the next clause.

8. **See whether the race is in its final laps.**

The code for checking the last laps of the race is not surprising:

```
elif lap >= 6:
    print "getting closer"
```

This code checks to see whether the lap number is greater than or equal to 6. If so, it prints an appropriate message.

 Information Kiosk

Notice the use of the >= symbol to indicate "greater than or equal to." You can also use <= to mean "less than or equal to."

The more surprising thing about this code is where it occurs in the `if-elif` code sequence. So far, I've been evaluating everything in the order it occurs — but these last two segments seem to be flip-flopped. I've done this because of the shortcut behavior described earlier. You might have expected the code to be written like this:

```
elif lap >= 6:
    print "getting closer"
elif lap == 10:
    print "Finished!"
```

I actually wrote the program like this the first time, but I got a surprise: The program never announced lap 10! See if you can figure out why before reading the upcoming explanation.

When `lap` is equal to 6, Python short-circuits the remaining `elif` clauses and repeats the loop. It doesn't bother to evaluate any other conditions, because it already found the `True` condition. This is fine when `lap` contains the values 6, 7, 8, and 9. But when `lap` contains the value 10, the shortcut behavior causes a problem. 10 is larger than 6, so Python prints the "getting closer" line and dutifully executes the `if` structure. The final `elif` clause is never evaluated!

Now look back at the order the program is really written in:

```
elif lap == 10:
    print "Finished!"
elif lap >= 6:
    print "getting closer"
```

By checking for the more specific condition first, I've got the behavior I really want. The program makes one announcement for lap 10 and another announcement for laps 6 through 9.

9. **Catch mistakes with one more `else` clause.**

It might surprise you to see an `else` clause in this code.

```
else:
    print "something went wrong"
```

After all, I've written the program so that `lap` will contain only the values 1 through 10, and I've got a condition to handle every possible value in that range. It seems wasteful to write code that should never be evaluated. Still, it's a very smart idea — because what *should* happen and what *does* happen are very different things, especially in the programming world. It's always a smart idea to put a final `else` clause in place, even if you think it will never be evaluated. At the very least, you can *know* when something bad has happened rather than having your program simply crash without explanation.

10. **Comment on the quality of the last lap.**

Consider this `print` statement:

```
print "    another great lap"
```

Although the line is very sensible, there's one problem. The code occurs immediately after the `else` clause of the `if` structure. How does Python know that this last `print` statement is not part of the `else` clause, but code that should occur *after* the `if` statement? For that matter, how does Python know that this message should occur *inside* the loop?

Indentation is the secret to code organization in Python. I indented this line at the same level as the `if` structure, so Python knows to execute that line as soon as the `if` structure finishes evaluating.

11. **Print an end-of-race message.**

No sports commentary would be complete without some breathless comments about the significance of the event just witnessed. The robot commentator obliges with one more remark:

```
print "That was quite a race!!"
```

This code begs a question similar to that of the previous line: How does Python know that this code should be executed at the end of the `for` loop, rather than each time through the loop (like the "last lap" code)?

Look back at the main code listing to see something very important about this line of code. The indentation again provides the key. I'll reproduce the code here, but this time, pay careful attention to the indentation scheme:

```
""" raceAnnouncer.py
    demonstrate numeric comparisons and
    elif """

for lap in range(1, 11):
    print "lap", lap
    print "     ",

    if lap == 1:
        print "starting the race"
    elif lap < 5:
        print "still in the first half"
    elif lap == 5:
        print "halfway there..."
    elif lap == 10:
        print "Finished!"
    elif lap >= 6:
        print "getting closer"
    else:
        print "something went wrong"

    print "     another great lap"

print "That was quite a race!!"
```

Each time I used a colon (`:`) character to indicate the beginning of a block of code, I indented the next line (or lines) of code. When I am finished with a structure, I unindent. The final `print` statement lines up with the `for` loop, so Python knows not to treat it as a part of the `for` loop, but rather as something that should be run after the loop is finished executing.

 ## Watch Your Step

In some languages, careless indentation will get you a stern look from a programming teacher — but nothing worse. In Python, sloppy indentation will cause spectacular crashes. You absolutely must be careful and consistent in your formatting or your programs will not work correctly.

Looping for a while

You've seen two of the most important control structures already. The `for` loop allows you to step through a list of items, and the `if` statement lets you use a condition to choose from two or more paths. Another important structure combines these ideas. The `while` *loop* repeats code, but it is controlled with a condition like an `if` statement.

Repeating code based on a condition

Take a look at the `minivan.py` program featured in Figure 3-5 to see this new type of loop in action.

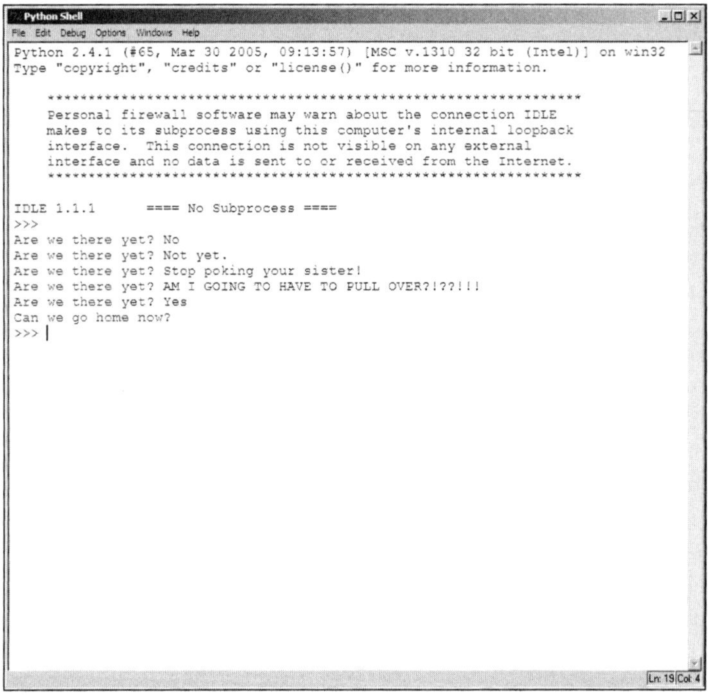

```
Python Shell
File  Edit  Debug  Options  Windows  Help
Python 2.4.1 (#65, Mar 30 2005, 09:13:57) [MSC v.1310 32 bit (Intel)] on win32
Type "copyright", "credits" or "license()" for more information.

    ************************************************************
    Personal firewall software may warn about the connection IDLE
    makes to its subprocess using this computer's internal loopback
    interface.  This connection is not visible on any external
    interface and no data is sent to or received from the Internet.
    ************************************************************

IDLE 1.1.1      ==== No Subprocess ====
>>>
Are we there yet? No
Are we there yet? Not yet.
Are we there yet? Stop poking your sister!
Are we there yet? AM I GOING TO HAVE TO PULL OVER?!??!!!
Are we there yet? Yes
Can we go home now?
>>> |
```

Figure 3-5: The user determines when this loop finishes, but never soon enough.

`While` loops are fundamentally different than `for` loops in one major way. In a `for` loop, the program steps through a list of items. You always know how many times the loop will execute, because Python loops are generally related to finite lists or similar structures with a pre-defined number of elements. A `while` loop is different. It operates based on the value of a condition. Look at the `minivan.py` code for an example:

```
""" minivan.py
    Simulates a car trip with small children
    """

tripFinished = "NO"
while tripFinished != "YES":
    tripFinished = raw_input("Are we there yet? ")
    tripFinished = tripFinished.upper()

print "Can we go home now?"
```

This code contains a loop, but the number of times the loop executes is based entirely on the user's actions. Here's how you set it up:

1. **Establish a sentry variable.**

   Just as a live sentry is a guard who controls access to a room, a *sentry variable* controls access to a loop. Most `while` loops have a sentry variable controlling all the action. In this case, I'm creating a variable called `tripFinished`. When `tripFinished` contains the value `"YES"`, my loop ends. If it contains anything else, the pain of those demands from the backseat continues.

2. **Initialize the sentry variable.**

   In Python, you create a variable by assigning it a value. The initial value of a sentry variable can be important, because it controls whether the loop occurs the very first time. More on this later, but for now, I'm setting the value of `tripFinished` to `"NO"` — like this:

   ```
   tripFinished = "NO"
   ```

3. **Set up a `while` loop.**

   The `while` loop consists of the keyword `while`, a condition, and a colon indicating the beginning of a block.

   ```
   while tripFinished != "YES":
   ```

   In this instance, the condition is the phrase `tripFinished != "YES"`. There are a couple of interesting things going on here. Notice first the `!=` operator. This symbol means "not equal to," so read this line as "while `tripFinished` is not equal to the value `'YES'`."

   `While` loops operate based on the value of a condition. If the condition is `True`, the loop keeps executing. As soon as the condition is evaluated to `False`, the loop will exit. In this particular example, the loop will keep executing as long as the `tripFinished` variable is not `"YES"`. If this variable contains any other value, the loop will keep on churning.

   The colon at the end of the statement is important because it indicates that the following indented lines are part of a block.

4. Change the sentry variable.

Inside a `while` loop, you must include some kind of code that manipulates the sentry variable. Somehow it must be possible for the `tripFinished` variable to contain the value `"YES"` or the program will simply go on forever. In this example, I'm getting a new value for `tripFinished` from the user with the `raw_input()` function.

```
tripFinished = raw_input("Are we there yet? ")
```

5. Convert input to uppercase.

You might have noticed a sneaky trick in this line:

```
tripFinished = tripFinished.upper()
```

The purpose of this code is to take any input and convert it into uppercase.

Transfer

Check back to Chapter 2 for more information on how to convert strings.

The reason I converted the input is a combination of cleverness and laziness. I want the loop to end if the user types `"yes"`, `"Yes"`, or even `"YeS"`. Python is case-sensitive, so these three values are not considered the same thing. If I want my program to ignore the case, I need to use a trick. Whatever the input is, I convert entirely to uppercase. If the user enters `"yes"` in any case (even `"yEs"`), it will be converted to `"YES"`, which triggers the condition and ends the loop.

Watch Your Step

If you use this trick to make your programs ignore case, make sure you compare the input to an all-uppercase value — or the loop will *never* end.

Avoiding endless loops

While loops are very handy and powerful, they can cause you trouble. The biggest problem is the potential for an endless loop. If your computer has ever locked up on you (that is, it seems to be frozen and refuses to accept any input at all), the chances are good you have an endless loop on your hands.

As an example, look at the following program:

```
i = 1
while i > 0:
    i = i + 1
    print i
```

This looks like a reasonable enough piece of code until you run it. Suddenly, your computer gets sluggish and responds very slowly to input. I opened the Windows XP performance viewer as I ran this code from the console. A graph of the system performance is shown in Figure 3-6.

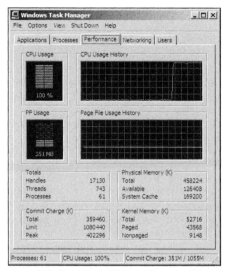

Figure 3-6: What kind of bloated irresponsible code caused that spike?

As I typed the code into the console, my machine was swimming along at 4% utilization (with seven programs open!). Notice the sudden spike to 100% utilization. That's exactly when my computer slowed down. From the performance-meter readout, you can tell that some program is hogging up every scrap of system memory. My endless loop is the culprit. That's what endless loops do. Fortunately, Python has an emergency exit. Make sure the console is the active window — and press Ctrl+C (Ctrl-D on Mac and Unix) to shut Python down.

Information Kiosk

The Ctrl+C (or Ctrl-D) command almost always works. If it doesn't, your options vary by operating system. Use Ctrl+Alt+Del on a Windows machine to get access to the Task Manager and shut down your Python program from there. Mac and Linux users can do an emergency shutdown by using the system console. Use `psef` to find the process ID of your program and use `kill` to kill the offending process.

Even professional programmers sometimes write endless loops accidentally, but obviously it's best to avoid them when you can. Look back at my code to see what went wrong:

```
i = 1
while i > 0:
    i = i + 1
    print i
```

The program looks perfectly normal, but if you run it with the debugger, you'll see the problem right away: The i variable must be larger than 0 to start the loop, so I initialized it to 1. It was indeed larger than zero, so the loop began. The i variable keeps getting larger and larger, but it's *always* larger than zero. Therefore the loop will never end.

Keep a few simple rules in mind, and you'll avoid major loop problems:

- **Initialize your sentry so the loop can start the first time.** The sentry variable should have a value that makes the condition True when the loop begins. The condition should be True during its first pass through the loop. Although this doesn't prevent endless loops, it protects you from an equally problematic situation: a loop that never starts at all.

- **Make sure the condition can become False.** As you design your condition, make sure it's possible for the sentry variable to make the condition False eventually. In my example, the value of i started larger than zero and kept getting bigger. The condition was *never* going to be triggered, so the loop never ended.

- **Be sure to change the sentry variable inside the loop.** This is the easiest mistake to make. Take a look at this classic problem:

```
i = 1
while i < 10:
    print "Hi"
```

It seems pretty stupid, but I can't tell you how many times I've made some variation of this mistake. Notice that the variable is fine and the condition makes sense. There's no code inside the loop that makes any change in the variable i. Thus i won't get any bigger — or any smaller. There's no way the condition will be triggered, so the loop will never end.

Information Kiosk

When you accidentally make an endless loop — and you will — don't panic. Use Ctrl+C (or Ctrl-D) to stop the program and review these steps to see whether you can spot the problem.

Putting Functions into Play

You know how to work with basic data in variables. You've learned that variables are more powerful when you join them together to make lists. You can also combine commands together to make a more powerful structure called a *function*. Functions are miniature programs that group together several lines of code to solve a particular problem. (You used existing functions in Chapter 1, but now you're going to make your own.) As usual, I show you a program that uses functions, and then I explain how it works.

Creating a function

If you ever went to camp as a kid, you probably remember singing the silly song "The Ants Go Marching On." If you don't remember the song, I've reproduced it in Figure 3-7. (I'll wait here if you want to go roast a marshmallow before reading on . . .)

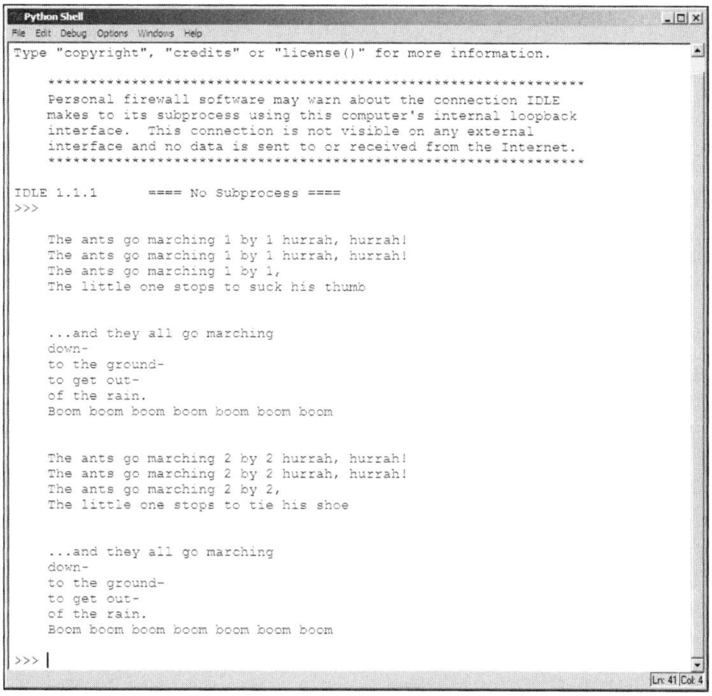

```
Python Shell
File Edit Debug Options Windows Help
Type "copyright", "credits" or "license()" for more information.

    ********************************************************
    Personal firewall software may warn about the connection IDLE
    makes to its subprocess using this computer's internal loopback
    interface.  This connection is not visible on any external
    interface and no data is sent to or received from the Internet.
    ********************************************************

IDLE 1.1.1      ==== No Subprocess ====
>>>
    The ants go marching 1 by 1 hurrah, hurrah!
    The ants go marching 1 by 1 hurrah, hurrah!
    The ants go marching 1 by 1,
    The little one stops to suck his thumb

    ...and they all go marching
    down-
    to the ground-
    to get out-
    of the rain.
    Boom boom boom boom boom boom boom

    The ants go marching 2 by 2 hurrah, hurrah!
    The ants go marching 2 by 2 hurrah, hurrah!
    The ants go marching 2 by 2,
    The little one stops to tie his shoe

    ...and they all go marching
    down-
    to the ground-
    to get out-
    of the rain.
    Boom boom boom boom boom boom boom

>>> |
                                                    Ln: 41 Col: 4
```

Figure 3-7: Python can even reproduce corny campfire songs.

Of course, there's nothing remarkable about printing a lot of text to the screen. You learned how to do that way back in Chapter 1. What's more interesting is the way this program is structured. Think back to the campfire. Sometimes the leader passes out a song sheet with the lyrics to a song on it. On that sheet, the verses are often written out, and the song is sometimes abbreviated like this:

verse 1
chorus
verse 2
chorus

Musicians sometimes call this overview a "road map," and it's a really great way to think about repetitive songs. It allows you to see the larger picture of how the song will flow together without worrying about the details of each verse and chorus. Of course, you still need to know the words to the verses, but you don't need to write the chorus more than once, because it stays the same. The song sheet separates the details of each verse and chorus from the larger flow of the song.

Functions allow you to create a road map and detail sections for your programs.

Here's the code for `ants1.py`:

```
""" ants1.py
    classic counting song
    demonstrates use of multi-line strings
    first version
    """

def chorus():
    """ prints chorus """
    print """
    ...and they all go marching
    down-
    to the ground-
    to get out-
    of the rain.
    Boom boom boom boom boom boom boom
    """

def verse1():
    """ prints first verse """
    print """
    The ants go marching 1 by 1 hurrah, hurrah!
    The ants go marching 1 by 1 hurrah, hurrah!
    The ants go marching 1 by 1,
    The little one stops to suck his thumb
    """

def verse2():
    """ prints second verse """

    print """
    The ants go marching 2 by 2 hurrah, hurrah!
```

```
The ants go marching 2 by 2 hurrah, hurrah!
The ants go marching 2 by 2,
The little one stops to tie his shoe
"""

verse1()
chorus()
verse2()
chorus()
```

This program looks a little longer than the ones you've seen so far, but it really isn't very complicated. Here's how the program works:

1. **Create a normal documentation string.**

   Remember the documentation string I've been writing at the beginning of each program. This special string usually uses the triple quote symbol. I'll be creating several docstrings in this program, and you'll finally see why they are such a good idea.

2. **Define the chorus() function.**

   A function is useful whenever you have code that might occur many times. The chorus of this song is a perfect candidate. If I define how to write that chorus one time, I won't have to keep writing it over and over again. Use the def keyword to define a new function, like this:

   ```
   def chorus():
       """ prints chorus """
   ```

   Note that the function name always ends with parentheses and a colon. A function is the beginning of an indented block. All code indented inside the function is considered a part of that function.

3. **Print a docstring for the function.**

   Python programmers usually create a short documentation string for every function as well as the main program. This can actually be any kind of string, but the triple-quote string is the most common type.

   ```
       """ prints chorus """
   ```

   The main program won't pay any attention to this text, but it's useful because it reminds you what this program does. It also alerts other programmers to how your code works.

4. **Print the chorus text.**

   The job of the chorus() function is to print out the chorus. (It's contrived, I know, but functions will get more complicated soon. Stick with me on this easy example.) I printed out the chorus as one big string. Look at it again, and you'll see something familiar:

```
print """
...and they all go marching
down-
to the ground-
to get out-
of the rain.
Boom boom boom boom boom boom boom
"""
```

This code appears inside a set of triple quotes, just like the docstrings you've been using all along. Python uses the triple quote symbol to indicate a multiple-line string. If you have a lot of text to print out, a multi-line string is pretty easy because all the carriage returns are preserved, and the code makes a lot of sense. It's true you've been using triple quotes for docstrings, but that's simply because documentation often requires more than one line.

 Watch Your Step

When you're writing a multi-line string, you're technically not writing code, so the normal indentation laws aren't strictly enforced. Still, I chose to indent all the text inside the long string for clarity's sake. It actually looks pretty good indented that way.

5. Create the `verse1()` function.

Check the indentation of the complete `ants1.py` program to see how to indicate the beginning of the next function. The `verse1()` function is very similar to `chorus()`.

```
def verse1():
    """ prints first verse """
    print """
The ants go marching 1 by 1 hurrah, hurrah!
The ants go marching 1 by 1 hurrah, hurrah!
The ants go marching 1 by 1,
The little one stops to suck his thumb
"""
```

This function has all the required elements. It begins with the keyword `def`, has the function name followed by parentheses, and a colon indicating the start of a code block.

The function begins with a short documentation string, followed by a multi-line `print` statement.

6. Second verse, same as the first.

The second verse requires a function very much like the others:

```
def verse2():
    """ prints second verse """

    print """
The ants go marching 2 by 2 hurrah, hurrah!
The ants go marching 2 by 2 hurrah, hurrah!
The ants go marching 2 by 2,
The little one stops to tie his shoe
"""
```

Although the actual text is a little different, the basic structure of this function should be very familiar to you by now.

7. **Build the road map.**

If you run the program with the debugger on, you can get all the way to this part of the code without seeing anything on the screen. Python hasn't actually done anything visible on the screen yet. Creating a function is kind of like writing a recipe. It's not really cooking, but once you have the recipe, you can use it to do useful things. The last part of the program is where all the actual work is done:

```
verse1()
chorus()
verse2()
chorus()
```

Once all the functions are defined, the program can use them to create something more complex. If you recall the song sheet analogy, this last chunk of code is just like a musician's road map. It shows the big picture of what the program will do. The details are hidden, and that's a good thing. Computer scientists call this principle *encapsulation.* Each function does a specific job. In essence, when you build a function, you are creating a new Python command. (Incidentally, that's exactly how most Python commands *are* made!) You can create complex, powerful programs by building functions that can do interesting things and then stringing these functions together to solve challenging problems.

Functions and scope

The `ants1.py` program shows how encapsulation can be used to break a large program into a series of smaller programs. The best way to handle a complicated task is to break it down into a series of smaller tasks. It's best if each of these small tasks can be self-contained, so you don't have to worry about anything but solving the immediate problem. That's exactly how programmers think about functions. A function is an independent subprogram that solves one problem well.

You can create variables inside your functions. These special variables work normally inside your functions, but as soon as your function is finished running, the value of all variables defined inside that function is gone.

Step Into the Real World

You've actually been taking advantage of docstrings all throughout this book, if you've been following my advice about the `help()` function. I love this command, because it gives you all sorts of information about the functions and commands built into Python. To review how it works, go to the console and type **help("list")** or **help("int")** to discover all the powerful features of these objects. When you incorporate docstrings into your code, you're building the documentation of your own program. After you've run the `ants1.py` program, type **help("ants1")** into the console. You'll see something like this:

```
Help on module ants1:

NAME
    ants1

FILE
    c:\pgl\pgl03\ants1.py

DESCRIPTION
    ants1.py
    classic counting song
    demonstrates use of multi-line strings
    first version

FUNCTIONS
    chorus()
        prints chorus

    verse1()
        prints first verse

    verse2()
        prints second verse
```

The `help()` function automatically turns all the docstrings in your program to a nicely formatted help file. You can even use a special module called `pyDoc` to create HTML-formatted help for online documentation of your code.

Information Kiosk

Think about the relationship between local police and state police. Local police have jurisdiction in a specific geographic area. They can operate inside that area, but not beyond certain boundaries. Another class of law-enforcement officers specializes in cases that cross local jurisdictions. It's good to have local cops, because they know the neighborhood. It's also good to have state police, because they have the capability to solve larger crimes.

Variables created inside a function (called *local variables*) are visible only inside that function. Although this may seem restrictive, this practice protects you. A large program might have hundreds — or thousands — of variables, and it's impossible to keep track of them all. If your program is broken into a bunch of functions, you only have to keep track of the variables inside your current function.

Information Kiosk

There are special variables that correspond to state troopers, too, called *global* variables. You've created global variables in all your programs so far, because you didn't know how to make functions. Once your program is subdivided into functions, it's generally better to use local variables most of the time. In the next section, "Passing Data In and Out of Functions," I'll show you how to communicate data to and from functions without having to use global variables.

An example is probably better than an explanation. Look at the code for `scope.py`:

```
""" scope.py
    illustrates scope and functions
    """

varOutside = "I was created outside the function"
print "outside the function, varOutside is: %s" % varOutside

def theFunction():
    varInside = "I was made inside the function"

    print "inside the function, varOutside is: %s" % varOutside
    print "inside the function, varInside is: %s" % varInside

theFunction()

print "back outside the function, varOutside is: %s" % varOutside
# if I uncomment the next line, the program will crash
#print "back outside the function, varInside is: %s" % varInside
```

This program creates a local and a global variable and describes how they work differently. Here's how you build the program:

1. **Create `varOutside` in the main scope of the program.**

   The `varOutside` variable is created first. It has a value indicating where it was made. Note that the code creating `varOutside` is in the main program area, not inside a function definition.

2. **Check the value of `varOutside` in the (non-function) context.**

   It won't surprise you that `varOutside` has a value and prints out correctly.

3. **Build a function.**

   For this thought experiment, I just call the function `theFunction()`.

4. Build a new variable (`varInside`) inside the function.

The `varInside` variable is created inside the function. It has a value inside the function, but will die as soon as the function finishes executing.

5. Print the values of both variables from inside the function.

Inside the function, both `varInside` and `varOutside` have a value. The `print` statements prove that both variables exist.

6. Run the function.

I've defined the function, so now I need to run it. It will work as expected, printing out the values of both variables and then gently disappearing in a poof of computing ether. When the function stops running, the `varInside` variable ceases to exist.

7. Print the variables again.

The next line of code is back at the main scope of the program. I can print out the value of `varOutside`, because it is a global variable, but I commented out the code that prints out `varInside`'s value. Figure 3-8 shows what the program looks like as written (with the `varInside` code hidden away).

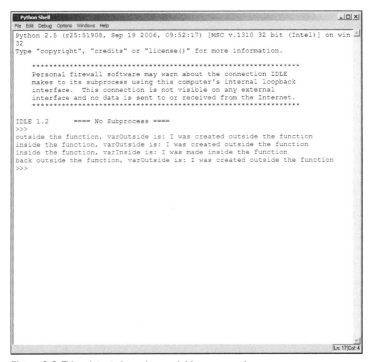

Figure 3-8: This printout shows how variable scope works.

For Figure 3-9, I uncommented the code that tries to display the value of `varInside` so you can see what happens.

Figure 3-9: If you try to reach a local variable from outside the function, the program crashes.

It seems like a bad thing that the program has crashed, but it really isn't. This tells me that Python is enforcing the rules of local variables, (that is, `varInside` has no meaning when the program is no longer inside a function) so I can declare variables all I want inside my functions and I don't have to worry about them interfering with each other and causing unintended consequences.

Passing Data In and Out of Functions

You know that functions block off a piece of code so you can work on things without having to worry about the wider picture. But this begs an obvious question: What if you *want* to send some information to a function? For that matter, what if you want a function to return some value back to the larger program? These are very valid points. To illustrate, I made another version of the ants program called `ants2.py`. (Just as you were finally getting that song out of your head!) The output of `ants2.py` is just like `ants1.py`, so I won't reprint it here. The interesting part is how I changed the structure of the code. As usual, look it over and I'll reveal all.

```
""" ants2.py
    classic counting song
    use parameters and return statements
    """


def chorus():
    output = """
...and they all go marching
down-
to the ground-
to get out-
of the rain.
Boom boom boom boom boom boom boom
"""
    return output

def verse(verseNum):
    if verseNum == 1:
        distraction = "suck his thumb"
    elif verseNum == 2:
        distraction = "tie his shoe"
    else:
        distraction = "I have no idea"


    output = """
The ants go marching %(verseNum)d by %(verseNum)d     ↵
hurrah, hurrah!
The ants go marching %(verseNum)d by %(verseNum)d     ↵
hurrah, hurrah!
The ants go marching %(verseNum)d by %(verseNum)d,
The little one stops to %(distraction)s
""" % vars()
    return output

print verse(1)
print chorus()
print verse(2)
print chorus()
```

Getting an overview of the program

It isn't always best to read a program from the beginning to the end, as you do a more
linear kind of media. I often read programs from the "outside-in." If a program is made
of functions, it makes sense to look at the road map that uses those functions before you
get up close and personal with them. This gives you an overview of how the program is
organized without worrying about the implementation details. In this version of the ant

program, I'm printing out the choruses and verses. That code actually appears at the end of the text file. Here's a pair of interesting things about the main program:

- **The functions don't print anymore.** Notice how these functions are called. Rather than saying `verse1()` as I did in the first version of the ant program, I now say `print verse(1)`. Now the function doesn't print on its own. Instead, it returns a value back — and my program does the printing. It's generally better to have programs *return* values instead of printing them, because then you can do more things with the value. For example, rather than simply printing the verse, you could save it to a file or write it to a Web page (provided, of course, I'd taught you how to do those things just yet). You've seen functions like this. For example, `raw_input()` returns a value, as do all the string-manipulation methods.

- **There's only one verse function.** In the previous `ants1.py` program, I had to write a separate `verse()` function for each verse in the program. This was especially tedious because the verses are very similar to each other. Now there's only one verse function. I include a special value in the parentheses to indicate which verse should be created.

- **The output uses a special form of interpolation**. The output string is a long text string with a lot of interpolated values. I use a special type of interpolation to clearly indicate which variable should be put into the string where.

Returning a value from a function

Look over the `chorus()` function and you'll see it hasn't changed much from the earlier version:

```
def chorus():
    output = """
...and they all go marching
down-
to the ground-
to get out-
of the rain.
Boom boom boom boom boom boom boom
"""
    return output
```

The only thing I changed from `ant1.py` is removing the `print` statement. Here's what the function does now:

1. **Creates a big variable called `output`.** This is a string variable that will contain all the information I want this function to produce.

2. **Uses a multi-line string to populate `output`.** You can assign a multi-line string to a variable just as you do an ordinary string. Remember, the triple quotes indicate a multi-line string.

3. Returns the output. The `return` statement returns the output. Whenever this function runs, it produces something (in this case, the chorus to the song) and returns it to the main program. The `return` statement is used to return a value to the main program.

 Information Kiosk

In Python, you can return anything you want from a function, including lists and multiple variables. Also, you can return any type of data, not simply the string variable I return in this example.

Passing values into a function

The `verse()` function is a little more interesting than the `chorus()`, because it has a multiple personality. It can produce one of several verses: In verse 1, the little one stops to suck his thumb. In verse 2, he stops to tie his shoe, and so on.

```
def verse(verseNum):
```

You can think of this improved `verse()` function as a "verse factory." Pass it a verse number, and it will create the corresponding verse. Functions that can work with a variety of different input values are extremely useful.

All of your functions have included parentheses, but up to now, those parentheses have been empty. When I define `verse()` I am indicating it should be called with a *parameter* — a special variable created automatically when you call the function. In this case, the parameter is called `verseNum`. When you create a function with a parameter, you're making a deal with the main program. You're requiring the program to provide some sort of value every time it invokes this function — but you're also promising to do something interesting with the value. If the program invokes `verse(1)`, the `verse()` function starts up and loads the numeric value `1` into `verseNum`.

Information Kiosk

If you're confused, run the `ant2.py` program with the debugger turned on and watch what happens. You'll see a variable called `verseNum` created whenever the program is inside the `verse()` function. As soon as the program leaves `verse()`, the `verseNum` variable is gone.

Creating a distraction based on the verse number

I'm sure I spent *way* too much time analyzing this song, but when I thought about it, I saw an interesting pattern. Each verse is nearly the same, but has a different verse number. The other difference is the distraction that causes trouble for "the little one."

This analysis points out a great way to make this song more efficient. Only two things change in each verse, the verse number and the distraction. Both can be stored in variables. The verse number is easy, because it was passed to the function in the `verseNum` variable. All we need is some mechanism for determining the distraction based on the verse number. There are a number of ways to do that. A basic `if` statement is the most straightforward technique (if not the most efficient — see the next Step Into the Real World for another option).

Each verse has a distraction that rhymes with the verse number. One obvious solution is to simply figure out what verse we're on and change the value of `distraction` accordingly. I used an `if-elif` structure for that purpose:

```
if verseNum == 1:
    distraction = "suck his thumb"
elif verseNum == 2:
    distraction = "tie his shoe"
else:
    distraction = "I have no idea"
```

This code uses `verseNum` to assign a value to the `distraction` variable. I only assigned two verses, but of course it's trivial to keep adding more verses. Notice the `else` clause used to trap for any values of `verseNum` I wasn't anticipating. If `verseNum` is anything beyond 1 or 2, it will still have a value, albeit a nonsensical one.

Creating the new verse

The verse is pretty easy to build using string interpolation techniques.

Transfer

Check Chapter 1 for a brush-up on basic string interpolation.

If you use the interpolation technique described in Chapter 1, the code will be a little tricky to read:

```
output = """
  The ants go marching %d by %d hurrah, hurrah!
  The ants go marching %d by %d hurrah, hurrah!
  The ants go marching %d by %d,
  The little one stops to %s
  """ % (verseNum, verseNum, verseNum, verseNum,
         verseNum, verseNum, distraction)
```

The string contains placeholders for six numbers (which will all contain the `verseNum` variable) and one string (for the distraction variable). While this version will work, you could argue it's not very easy to read. The long list of variable names is tedious, and it's hard to match up exactly what variable goes into what slot.

Step Into the Real World

Is there a better way to do this? The `if-elif` structure does the job, but there's a more elegant solution. If you're curious, check out `ants3.py` on the Web site. This program looks the same, but defines the distractions in a list:

```
distraction = [
    "",
    "suck his thumb",
    "tie his shoe",
    "climb a tree"
    ]
```

The first element is empty so the verses will be in their familiar 1, 2, 3 order instead of the 0, 1, 2 order the computer would prefer.

Inside the function, I can pull out the distraction from the array like this:

```
problem = distraction[verseNum]
```

I can then incorporate the problem variable into the output string. The main code is then easier to manage, because I can use a loop to control its behavior:

```
for verseNum in range(1, len(distraction)):
    print verse(verseNum)
    print chorus()
```

This has an added advantage. If I increase the number of distractions in the array, the program will automatically adapt to print out the correct number of verses.

Compare the previous version with the technique I actually use:

```
output = """
 The ants go marching %(verseNum)d by %(verseNum)d hurrah, hurrah!
 The ants go marching %(verseNum)d by %(verseNum)d hurrah, hurrah!
 The ants go marching %(verseNum)d by %(verseNum)d,
 The little one stops to %(distraction)s
 """ % vars()

 return output
```

Here's what you do:

1. Use an expanded placeholder notation.

In this revised approach, I interrupt each variable placeholder with a variable name in parentheses. For example, I replace `%d` with `%(verseNum)d`. This indicates exactly the variable I wish to use in this situation. The string is now easier to read, because the placeholders make sense.

2. **Replace the variable tuple with a call to the `vars()` function.**

In normal string interpolation, you need a list of all the variables that will be used. The `vars()` function creates a special kind of data structure containing the name and value of each variable defined in the current context (generally in the current function). When you use the `vars()` function in this context, you can use specific variable names inside your format string as I have done.

Building a Main Loop

Loops are important in Python because most programs consist of the same code being run over and over. In games, you'll often write loops meant to occur several times per second. These earlier text-based programs aren't quite as demanding, but the principle is the same. One big loop — usually called the *main loop* — is used to control the overall flow of the program.

Main loops have one special characteristic: There's often more than one way to get out of them. For example, you might exit a game by winning, losing, closing the game window, or clicking an exit button. You'll often need loops with more than one exit point. The `password.py` program shown in Figure 3-10 illustrates a simpler version of this phenomenon. The technique shown in this loop will become the foundation for main loops in all your upcoming games.

If you were asked to build a program like the `password.py` example, it might seem simple at first, but on further examination you will reach a quandary. You know that a `for` loop is best when you know how many times something should happen. The program should ask no more than three times, so this task seems like a perfect candidate for a `for` loop. However, there's another way to exit the loop: If the user enters the correct password, the loop should end immediately. This kind of behavior seems perfect for a `while` loop. So which is it to be?

Figure 3-10: The loop ends after the correct password or three errors. (Note that I ran the program twice.)

Examine the code for the `password.py` program to see one solution.

```python
""" password.py
    Ask the user for a password
    repeat until user gets it right
    or has tried three times """

keepGoing = True
correct = "Python"
tries = 3

while keepGoing:
    guess = raw_input("Please enter the password: ")
    tries = tries - 1

    if guess == correct:
        print "You may proceed"
        keepGoing = False
    else:
        print "That's not correct."

        if tries <= 0:
            print "Sorry. You only had three tries"
```

```
            keepGoing = False
        else:
            print "You have %d tries left" % tries
```

The secret to this program is the clever use of variables. Here are the steps to follow:

1. Create a Boolean variable called `keepGoing`.

The `keepGoing` variable is special because it contains only the values `True` or `False`. Variables restricted to these values are called *Boolean* variables.

Information Kiosk

Boolean variables are named after George Boole, a 19th Century mathematician who pioneered work in binary logic. He might be amazed to see how influential his work has become today!

I use the `keepGoing` variable to keep track of the user's intentions. If the program keeps going, `keepGoing` will contain the value `True`. If the loop should stop on the next pass, `keepGoing` will be given the value `False`.

2. Make a variable to keep track of the number of tries left.

The loop exits if the user tries more than three times. Somehow I need to track either the number of attempts the user has made or how many tries he has left. I decided to keep track of the number of tries left, because it's what I really care about. I initialize the `tries` variable to `3`, indicating that when the program starts, the user has three tries left.

Step Into the Real World

Variable names matter. As you look through this code, you'll see that I chose the variable names very carefully so that key phrases will be easy to read. If I had chosen some different variable names, the key line of `password.py` would have looked like this:

```
if x == egr5:
```

This code would have run correctly, but it is difficult to follow. (I'm really not exaggerating here. I see programmers write code like that all the time.)

If I'm a little more careful about my variable names (as I was in the actual code), the intent of the same line is a lot easier to follow:

```
if guess == correct:
```

Because I named my variables well, my code is pretty easy to read. Experienced programmers try to make the meaning of their code as self-evident as possible. This practice is called *self-documenting code*. You should get into the habit now as you're starting out. It will make your life a lot easier when the programs get longer and more complicated.

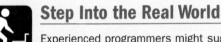

Step Into the Real World

Experienced programmers might suggest other solutions to this problem — including (for example) compound conditions and the `break` statement. Although those solutions are completely acceptable from a programming perspective (that is, they will work if you implement them correctly), neither solution is easy to understand. Using a Boolean variable makes the code a little easier to read. It's another example of self-documenting code. When possible, I prefer to make the code as easy to read as possible.

3. Make a variable to hold the correct password.

The `correct` variable holds the correct password. It doesn't seem necessary to use a variable here, but it makes the code easier to read.

4. Create the main loop.

The main loop of this program is a basic `while` loop. The condition is ridiculously simple:

```
while keepGoing:
```

Since `keepGoing` is a Boolean (`True` or `False`) value, I can use it in a condition instead of a comparison. There are two different conditions that can cause the loop to exit. The user can enter the correct password, or he can get the wrong answer three times. I'm not checking *either* of these conditions here. I'm simply looking at the Boolean variable `keepGoing` to determine its value. If `keepGoing` is `True`, the loop continues. If `keepGoing` is `False`, the loop exits.

5. Get a new guess.

Use the `raw_input()` function to get a new password guess from the user. Store this value in the variable `guess`.

```
guess = raw_input("Please enter the password: ")
```

6. Decrement the number of tries.

When the user enters a guess, he is using up one of his tries. Represent this by subtracting one from the `tries` variable:

```
tries = tries - 1
```

7. Check to see whether the guess is correct.

Now that you have a guess from the user, you can check to see whether that guess is correct. Use a basic `if` structure for this task:

```
if guess == correct:
    print "You may proceed"
    keepGoing = False
```

It's nice to provide some feedback to the user to indicate that (s)he successfully entered the password.

8. Set `keepGoing` to `False` to end the loop.

If the user has entered a correct password, set the value of `keepGoing` to `False`. Remember, the main loop continues as long as `keepGoing` is `True`. By setting this variable to `False`, you're sending a message to yourself. Next time the `while` loop checks the value of `keepGoing`, it will be `False`, and the loop will exit.

Notice that you don't immediately end the loop. You simply set up a trigger so the loop will end gracefully next time it is evaluated.

9. If guess is not correct, check the number of tries.

If the user entered the correct password, there's no need to worry about the number of tries, because the loop will exit on the next pass. If the user did not enter the correct password, the program needs to check the number of tries to see whether this should cause the loop to exit.

Take careful note of the indentation here. Since this `if` statement is inside the `else` clause of the "guess is correct" `if` statement, it will only execute when you know that the user's current guess is incorrect. In this particular situation, that's exactly the behavior I want.

My program always checked for the number of tries. This is usually fine, but in this case, suppose the user gets the password correct on the third try: The program tells the user it's okay proceed — and *then* tells the same user that no tries are left. Obviously this is confusing to the user. I only knew this was a problem because I tested my code many times. I ran the program over and over, trying to find flaws. When I got the password correct on the third try, I saw this flaw. Once I located the flaw, it was easy to fix. Moral: It's useful to try out your code from the user's point of view.

10. If the number of tries is less than or equal to zero, end the loop.

Once again, you do not exit the loop directly. Instead, you print out some feedback to the user and set the value of `keepGoing` to `False`. If the number of tries is greater than 0, provide some feedback to the user indicating how many tries he still has.

Information Kiosk

If you're having trouble visualizing how this works, don't try to do it in your head. Take advantage of the debugger! Walk through the code line by line and look at the variables. Anticipate what you think will happen before you click the "step" button — and see whether it works the way you expect.

Step Into the Real World

How do you know if your code is set up correctly? It might run without crashing but still have some sort of logical flaw. For example, in my first try at the password program, I didn't indent the second if. It looked like this instead:

```
if guess == correct:
    print "You may proceed"
    keepGoing = False
else:
    print "That's not correct."

if tries <= 0:
    print "Sorry. You only had three tries"
    keepGoing = False
else:
    print "You have %d tries left" % tries
```

Boolean variable: A variable containing either the value `True` or `False`. Boolean variables are often used to make main loops easier to follow.

condition: An expression that can be evaluated to `True` or `False`. Can be a comparison, a Boolean variable, a function that returns a Boolean value, or something else that Python can interpret as a Boolean value.

dict: A dictionary entry. This data structure allows you to associate values with strings (or other values) instead of the numeric indices used in lists and tuples. The `var()` function returns a dictionary containing the names and values of all variables in the current context.

encapsulation: The idea that functions can be used to hide detail from the main program, making the program easier to read and maintain.

equality operator: Checks to see whether two values are equal. Use the double equals sign (==) to see whether two values are equal to each other.

function: A subprogram that works in isolation to solve a particular problem.

global scope: A variable declared outside any function. The variable's value can be read from any function. Global variables are generally considered a sloppy programming practice, and should be avoided when practical.

local scope: A variable created inside a function is considered local to that function. The variable has a value only as long as the function is running. Local variables are preferred, because they are unlikely to have unintended interference with other variables in the program.

main loop: Most programs have a primary loop that controls how long the program runs. This loop is usually some form of a `while` loop. Main loops often have multiple exit points, so they are best controlled by a Boolean sentry variable.

multi-line string: A string variable denoted with triple double quotes (`"""`). Carriage returns, quote signs, indentation and single quotes are preserved.

parameters: When you define a function, you can indicate a number of variable names inside the parentheses behind the function's name. These variables become local variables when the function is called. When you call a function that has parameters, you must generally supply a value for every parameter.

self-documenting code: Code designed to be as easy to read as possible. Python encourages the development of self-documenting code through the use of docstrings. You can also make your code self-documenting by carefully choosing your variable names and making your code as straightforward as possible. In other words, avoid code that's hard to understand when a less obtuse option is available.

sentry variable: A variable which controls access to a loop. Sentry variables must be properly initialized, must be part of the condition, and must be modified inside the body of the loop.

shortcut evaluation: If you have many conditions chained together with a series of `elif` statements, Python exits the chain as soon as it finds the first `True` condition. This means the order in which you place the conditions can be very important.

variable interpolation: A technique for embedding many kinds of data into a string, which allows automatic variable conversion and formatting.

variable scope: The notion that variables only have value within some block of code. Variable scope aids in encapsulation as the programmer doesn't have to track any variables except the ones inside the function he's currently working on.

Command	Arguments	Description	Example

`if condition:`
    `block`
	condition: a comparison or Boolean expression
	block: one or more lines of indented code
		Runs block if condition is `True`.	`if answer == 42:`
			    `print "yes!"`

`elif condition:`
    `block`
	condition: a comparison or Boolean expression
	block: one or more lines of indented code
		Evaluates another condition. Always follows an `if` clause.	`if answer == 42:`
			    `print "yes"`
			`elif answer = 5:`
			    `print "huh?"`

`else:`
    `block`
	condition: a comparison or Boolean expression
	block: one or more lines of indented code
		Runs block if previous condition is `False`.	`if answer == 42:`
			    `print "yes"`
			`else:`
			    `print "no"`

`while condition:`
    `block`
	condition: a comparison or Boolean expression
	block: one or more lines of indented code
		Repeats block as long as condition is evaluated to `True`.	`guess = 99`
			`while guess != "5":`
			    `guess = raw_input`
			`("3 + 2?")`

`def fName (p1,`
`p2, ...):`
    `block`
	fName: function name
	p1, p2: parameters.
	block: one or more lines of indented code
		Creates a function called `fName` sending parameter values. Block is evaluated whenever function is called.	`def sayHi (name):`
			    `print "Hi,", name`
			`sayHi("Matthew")`
			`Hi, Matthew`

`return value`	*value*: some value that will be returned to the main program when the function is called	Returns value to the main program.	`def add(a, b):`
			    `return a + b`
			`print add(2, 3)`
			`5`

`"pattern" %`
`(values)`
	pattern: a string containing special characters
	values: values to be interpolated into the string
		Creates a new string with the values interspersed.	`print "%s is %d years`
			`old and weighs %.2f`
			`pounds." % ("Jacob",`
			`4, 46.23)`
			`Jacob is 4 years old`
			`and weighs 46.23`
			`pounds.`

Last Stop

Practice Exam

1. Name one way computers are different than most machines.

2. Why should you indent your Python code?

A) You don't have to, but it makes the code easier to read.

B) Python uses indentation to figure out how code is organized.

C) You must use tabs rather than spaces to indent code in Python.

D) If you use curly braces ({ }) you don't have to indent.

3. What's the best definition of a condition?

An _____ that can be _____ to _____ or _____

4. Which is NOT a legal comparison operator in Python?

A) ==

B) !=

C) <

D) =

5. Describe one way to make multiple comparisons in Python.

6. Why must you understand Python's shortcut evaluations?

7. When would you choose a `while` loop rather than a `for` loop?

8. Name three recommendations for avoiding endless loops:

_____

_____

_____

9. **Which is the best explanation of** *encapsulation*?

A) The process of loading an astronaut into a spacecraft.

B) Using loops and variables in your programs.

C) Using functions to hide complexity and variables from the main program.

D) Heavy use of global variables.

10. **Which would be the output of the following code:**

```
print "%s said that a circle's circumference is %d times
%.3f radians" % ("Bob", 2, 3.1415927)
```

A) "%s said that a circle's circumference is %d times %.3f radians" % ("Bob", 2, 3.1415927)

B) "2 said that a circle's circumference is Bob times 3.1415927 radians"

C) "Bob said that a circle's circumference is 2 times 3.14 radians"

D) "Bob said that a circle's circumference is 2 times 3.142 radians"

11. **True or false: A variable created inside a function is available to code outside that function.**

12. **What's the best definition of a parameter?**

13. **How do you return some value from a function?**

14. **How do you build a loop with more than one exit point?**

15. **Modify the Pig Latin program from Chapter 2 so that now it can test for vowels. Hint: Use a string function to see whether the first character is a vowel or a constant.**

16. **Write a basic adventure game. Make each "room" a function. Have the user choose from two or more choices from each room, which takes the user to other rooms. Be sure to return the new room number from each room function.**

Building a Game Foundation

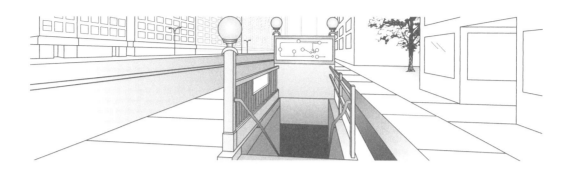

 # Enter the Station

Questions

1. How are video games different from other computer programs?

2. What is a game loop, and how do you use it as a game foundation?

3. What is SDL and how can it help you build games?

4. How do you set up a game screen?

5. How do you give the screen a background color?

6. How do you control a game's speed?

7. How do you get input from the user?

8. How do computers manage color?

9. How do you move everything around on the screen?

Solid Game-Making Fundamentals

So far you should have a pretty good grasp of how programs are written in Python. You've got all the basics, so it's time to start making graphical games. Although you'll be using the same basic programming constructs you've managed in the earlier chapters, games have some unique characteristics of their own. Games usually involve more thought about graphics, audio, user input, visual display, and timing than more traditional programs. All that may seem daunting at first, but there are many tools to help you. In this chapter, I introduce you to *pygame*, a terrific tool for writing games in Python. I also show you how to create a general structure you can use for all of your games. You learn how to put together the basic foundation that will be expanded for all games. In later chapters, you'll build on this framework to add more impressive graphics, sound effects, event handling, and more. When you finish this chapter, you'll be able to understand and build the `moveBox.py` program shown in Figure 4-1.

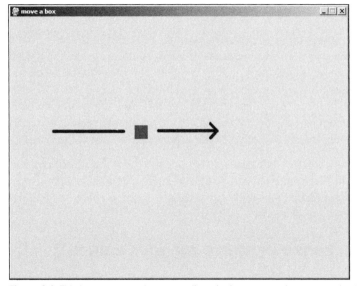

Figure 4-1: This box moves on the screen. (I put in the arrow to show you motion.)

This program won't win any gaming awards, but when you completely understand it, you will be able to expand on it to make all the remaining games in this book.

Creating a sense of time in games

Games are ultimately computer programs, but they are different from other kinds of programs in some very fundamental ways — most significant is the way they view time. Games have to run very quickly in order to approximate a fluid interactive environment.

The old mainframe computers (and even today's supercomputers) frequently work on very large problem sets that crank away for hours, days, or weeks before providing any output. Programs that reside on Web servers (as on Amazon.com) move a lot quicker than those on mainframes, but response time is still on the order of seconds or minutes between a user's interaction with the program and some sort of feedback.

Applications on individual computers (such as word processors or spreadsheets) are much quicker. Typically, the user expects feedback in less than a second. Still, much of this time, the program is sitting around waiting for input from the user, and doing very little challenging work.

Games often have to process things faster than any of these other kinds of programs. Real-time games often have to manage hundreds of calculations in a fraction of a second, and be able to repeat this process indefinitely.

The speed at which a game repeats is called the *frame rate*. If you have a high frame rate, the repeated screen updates look like fluid motion. Television has a frame rate of about 30 frames per second (in the U.S.). If your game has a frame rate less than about 10 frames per second, it will look choppy.

The more things going on in your game, the more work the computer has to do during each tiny time slice. If you have hundreds of aliens running around the screen and you need to check each possible collision, it is possible that the computer won't be able to do all the necessary calculations in the allotted time, and your game will slow down. (You've probably noticed this effect on racing games. Your frame rate sometimes slows down dramatically as you get to parts of a track that have a lot of scenery, and the display is faster and smoother when the decorations are more Spartan.)

It's important to set a frame rate that's fast enough to carry the illusion of motion and slow enough that your computer will be able to keep up. You also want to try and specify a consistent frame rate so the game doesn't seem to change speed depending on what's happening on-screen.

Creating a sense of space for your games

Games are also interesting because of they way they manage the notion of space. Games happen in a special display mode: The screen is broken into a series of dots that can each be tuned to a particular color. The screen dots are called *pixels* (for picture elements). The number of pixels used determines the screen *resolution*. Games typically run in 640×480 or 800×600 resolution. Games can also either run in a window on top of the regular operating system (as most applications do) or in *full-screen* mode. The full-screen approach stretches the pixels to take up the entire screen and completely hides all other vestiges of the underlying operating system.

The video display of a computer game is different than the one used by traditional applications. Regular programs usually rely heavily on the underlying operating system to do most of the display work, using pre-existing windows, buttons, and screen widgets.

Step Into the Real World

Of course you can write Python programs that look like traditional applications, using exactly the same widgets. In fact, Python offers a number of choices. Most installations of Python already include support for Tkinter, a variation of the TK user-interface tool set. The wx toolset is another popular library for building more traditional user interfaces. I also show how to build some basic GUI widgets using pygame throughout this book. As a game programmer, you'll still need the ability to put text and buttons on the screen, but you usually have different requirements than a traditional programmer.

Games usually rely on custom user interfaces. Game programmers require more control of how things are positioned on the screen and more precise timing than traditional user interfaces allow.

Information Kiosk

Application programmers shouldn't have to spend their time dealing directly with exactly how buttons should look; instead, they should spend their time using these tools to solve problems for the user. In traditional applications, you don't want any surprises. A button should look like a button. In a gaming environment, you don't want to remind users that they're using a computer program (most of the time). Instead, you want to transport them to a new reality. That means you'll usually need to invent your own interface rather than relying on the one that comes with your operating system or windowing toolkit. For an example, look at the `colorViewer.py` program featured later in this chapter. I whipped up my own kind of scrollbar for that program. The `gameEngine` module developed in Chapter 10 incorporates some other basic GUI widgets to get you started.

Creating a gaming loop

The basic structure of most games is the same, regardless of the type of game or programming language. This special construct is sometimes called the *animation loop* or *gaming loop*. The following shows what you should be doing at each stage in the gaming loop:

1. **Begin by setting up some resources to manipulate.**

You do this outside the gaming loop. Usually this involves creating all the characters, artwork, and music — and keeping them in memory but "off-stage" until needed. Any calculations that can be done before the loop proper starts should happen before they're needed on-screen — because processor time is at a premium once the loop begins. If you were programming the classic game

Asteroids, for example, you'd set up objects to represent all the asteroids (even the ones that aren't visible at the beginning of the round), the alien UFO, the player, and the bullets.

Transfer

If you don't remember *Asteroids*, or you want a refresher, look ahead to Chapter 10. I create a very simple version of this classic game as an illustration of the `gameEngine` module developed in that chapter. Better yet, load it up and play along.

2. **Create an almost endless loop.**

The loop will continue until one of a number of exit conditions has been met. At a minimum, check to see if the user closes the window containing the game. You may also want to check for certain button presses, or for specific winning and losing conditions. You generally use a form of the Boolean `while` loop (as described in Chapter 3) for this process.

3. **Control the amount of time inside the loop.**

It's important for each passage through the loop to take the same amount of time, or the game will speed up and slow down according to the complexity of the calculations. Pygame has some nifty built-in tools for managing the time. Most Python games run at about 30 frames per second. (Contrast this with Flash games, which normally run at 12 frames per second.)

4. **Get input from the user and system.**

Whatever the game, it usually involves getting some kind of feedback from the user. This is where you check the keyboard, mouse, or joystick for instructions. Pygame has great tools to help you read this kind of information from the user. In the *Asteroids* example, you'd check to see whether the user is pressing an arrow key. If so, you program a change in the ship's speed or direction. You also check for collisions between the player and the asteroids, and for bullet/asteroid conditions. Each kind of input may affect how the various entities are interacting.

5. **Update all your entities.**

The game objects (player, monsters, asteroids, or whatever) are essentially variables. Each of these game entities has the potential to change during each frame. In the classic game *Asteroids*, each asteroid moves slightly and rotates during each frame. The player's ship moves according to its current speed and direction, and the bullets (if there are any) keep on hurtling towards their targets (or empty space, if you play the way I do).

Information Kiosk

It's very important to note that at this stage in the animation loop *nothing has been drawn on the screen!* The things that the user sees are *not* the actual objects, but visual representations based on underlying data. You don't really change the screen directly. Instead, you change the underlying *data about* what the various objects are doing — and then (in the next step) display all the new data to the screen.

6. **Refresh the screen.**

Once you've gotten all the information you need from the system and updated all the object data, now you can use that data to draw information to the screen.

Introducing pygame

It's actually a lot more complicated to get a computer to work in a graphical mode than the text-style programs you've written so far. Essentially, all graphics work involves translating information stored in a computer's simplistic memory into a two-dimensional display on the screen. As you can guess, there are a lot of mathematics involved. This gets even more complicated when you consider the many different kinds of graphical display hardware. Back in the early days of graphics programming, you had to learn an entirely different graphics system for each graphics mode of each computer you wanted to use. Graphics programming was painstaking and challenging.

Programmers quickly realized they needed a better strategy if they were to create compelling games and graphical interfaces. They began creating reusable libraries of code called *application programming interfaces* (APIs) to handle the ugliest parts of graphics development. Today almost all graphics programming uses one of these libraries.

Graphics development in Microsoft Windows is dominated by Microsoft's DirectX API. If you've installed a game on a Windows computer, it's likely that game first checked for your version of DirectX — and required you to install a newer version if your computer was not completely up to date. The DirectX library is powerful and very common, but it has two drawbacks:

It's a proprietary technology completely owned by Microsoft. While this isn't necessarily a bad thing, it makes many people nervous that one company has so much control and can change things arbitrarily.

The larger problem is that DirectX only works on computers running Microsoft Windows. While that is undoubtedly a very large base, there still are people who prefer not to use Windows.

Step Into the Real World

Pygame and SDL   Pete Shinners is a long-time C programmer who found himself playing around with SDL and Python at about the same time in 2000. He admired both tools, and decided to build a Python interface to SDL. He succeeded admirably. It is a testament to Pete that he has dedicated this impressive work to the open-source community for free, so anyone can use it. Pygame allows you to write code that communicates with the SDL library, but it uses Python rather than C. (Python is *much* friendlier to beginners than C.) Python and pygame make a great combination. You have access to all the power of a major, cross-platform graphics API with the friendly Python programming language. All of this is completely free for you to use. (If you see Pete, you should definitely thank him for his generosity.)

Two other important libraries have popped up to challenge DirectX. These libraries are called *SDL (*Simple DirectMedia Layer*)* and *OpenGL (*Open Graphics Library*)*. Both of these APIs work on multiple platforms (including Windows) and both have completely open architecture, so anybody can view the inner workings. SDL is mainly used for 2D work, where OpenGL is used for 3D programming. (DirectX likewise has 2D and 3D components.) The open-source community has embraced SDL and OpenGL because they are more in line with the open-source ethic (multi-platform capability, open and community-based formats, with less-restrictive copyright and intellectual property barriers).

Graphics libraries are generally written in the C programming language, so they're very efficient. They are also usually designed so they can be used with multiple programming languages. The graphics library (sometimes also called the graphics *engine*) does most of the complicated math. A programmer can then write the actual logic of a game in some easier language — like Python.

Installing pygame

Of course, if you want to use pygame, you need to install it. The latest version as of this writing is pygame 1.7.1. This version is available on the Web site that accompanies this book. You might also check the pygame Web site (`www.pygame.org`) to see if there's a newer version around.

Installing pygame is pretty straightforward on Windows machines. Be sure you use the Windows installer. It's an executable file. Run the program, and it will check to see if Python is installed on your system. It will also automatically install SDL and pygame.

Watch Your Step

If you have trouble installing pygame for Windows, try downloading the Windows dependency file from the pygame main site. This installs a few other files you might need to get pygame working. Most modern computers won't need the Windows dependency file. Also, check to make sure that the version of pygame you've downloaded matches up with the version of Python on your machine. As of this writing, the latest version of pygame (1.7.1) requires a slightly out-of-date version of Python (2.4.2). It sometimes takes a few months for the pygame version to catch up with changes in Python.

If you're using a Macintosh or Linux machine, you probably won't have the simple installer that came with the Windows version. Follow the instructions at `http://pygame.org/install`. You may have to run a couple of scripts to make everything work, but just follow the directions and you'll be fine.

Transfer

Appendix C on the Web site describes how Python's installation system works, and shows you how to create your own module installers. Check there if you want more information about how to build and use installation scripts.

Here's how to make sure pygame is working:

1. Get into Python however you normally do it.

Use the command line or IDLE, but get to the Python interactive shell.

2. Import the pygame library.

Use the following command to import pygame into Python:

```
import pygame
```

If pygame is installed correctly, Python simply accepts the command. (Nothing else seems to happen.) If the pygame installation fails, you get an error message — usually referring to some library that has to be installed beforehand.

Pygame overview

Pygame provides a number of features to help programmers create games. I spend the rest of this book describing these elements in detail, but here are a few highlights:

- **Display:** The graphical display. Games often use a special display mode. The display submodule of pygame helps to control how the overall game looks and acts.

- **Surface:** A rectangular area that contains some kind of image. The screen itself is considered a surface, as are all the little objects bouncing around on it. Pygame provides an object called a `Surface` to manage these elements.

- **Rect:** An object that represents a rectangle. Since all surfaces in pygame are rectangular, each one has a rect associated with it. You use rects to help determine the size and position of objects, and to detect whether two objects collide.

- **Input modules:** Pygame supplies a number of useful tools for dealing with user input. The user can interact with pygame using a mouse, keyboard, or joystick. There is a pygame object to represent each of these input modes, with tools to help you gather data from the player.

- **Output modules:** Pygame has numerous ways to send information back to the user. The image module lets you manage a number of different image formats and convert them into surfaces for your game. Pygame also has modules for managing audio output for background music and sound effects.

- **Utility modules:** There are a few utilities which make game programming easier. These include a module for working with time, the draw interface to let you draw directly to a surface, transformation functions to let you scale and rotate images, and utilities for managing fonts and the CD-ROM drive.

IDEA/ALTER game framework overview

Building a working game isn't really that difficult, but it can be daunting — especially in a language like Python/pygame where you have to build everything from scratch. To make things easier, I've created a pair of acronyms to help you keep track of everything. These acronyms divide the game framework into two main pieces. IDEA is the overall game framework, and ALTER represents the action inside the gaming loop. It's not nearly as daunting as it seems. Take a look at the `idea.py` program shown in Figure 4-2.

I know the program doesn't look like much yet, but if you truly understand how to build this simple program, you're halfway to any game you want to write. Here's the code used to build the blue screen. Take a quick preview (especially at the comments) to see how it flows. I describe this program in detail throughout the rest of this chapter.

Figure 4-2: It's just a blue screen, but all game programming starts here.

```
""" idea.py
    simplest possible pygame display
    demonstrates IDEA / ALTER model
    Andy Harris, 5/06
    """

#I - Import and initialize
import pygame
pygame.init()

#D - Display configuration
screen = pygame.display.set_mode((640, 480))
pygame.display.set_caption("Hello, world!")

#E - Entities (just background for now)
background = pygame.Surface(screen.get_size())
background = background.convert()
background.fill((0, 0, 255))

#A - Action (broken into ALTER steps)

    #A - Assign values to key variables
clock = pygame.time.Clock()
keepGoing = True

    #L - Set up main loop
while keepGoing:
```

```
#T - Timer to set frame rate
clock.tick(30)

#E - Event handling
for event in pygame.event.get():
    if event.type == pygame.QUIT:
        keepGoing = False

#R - Refresh display
screen.blit(background, (0, 0))
pygame.display.flip()
```

 Watch Your Step

If you're using IDLE to write your code, it's best not to run pygame code directly from IDLE (with F5). IDLE tends to keep a clone of the display screen visible even after you've closed the program down, and you're liable to get confused. The best way to run pygame programs is to double-click them in the operating system or run them from the command line.

The IDEA/ALTER framework is a simple way to remember all the details that go into getting a game started. Here's an overview:

- **I — Import and Initialize:** Bring in all the libraries you'll need and start them up. This is also where you might do some other general initialization.

- **D — Display:** Set up the graphics display to the correct size or resolution and set the window caption appropriately.

- **E — Entities:** Build all the game entities you will be using. This usually includes a visual representation for the player, the playing field, and various enemies and powerups.

- **A — Action:** Create and run the animation loop. This is the part of the game the user sees. The animation loop controls the action in the game, managing time, checking for user interactions, moving things around, and updating the visual display.

The Action step is important enough that it's broken down into a number of parts. You can remember these details with another mnemonic device: ALTER (because the loop is about altering the screen).

- **A — Assign values:** You assign values to a few key variables to make sure your loop runs correctly.

- **L — Loop:** Begin the actual loop. This is almost always a `while` loop using a Boolean sentry variable.

T — Time: Manage time so you are running at a consistent frame rate.

E — Events: Capture any events from the user. Also look for system-level events like objects leaving the screen or colliding with each other.

R — Refresh Screen: Finally, you can update the visual representation of all the action and let the user know what's going on.

Initializing Your Game with the IDEA Framework

There's a lot of detail crammed into one little program. That's the bad news. The good news is, once you understand this basic framework, you'll use some variation of it in almost every game you write. Make sure you understand this program well, because you'll get a lot of mileage out of it in the long run.

I — Import and Initialize pygame

The IDEA part of the IDEA/ALTER framework is all about *initialization*, that is, setting up the environment before the game loop starts. It can be broken down into a few steps of its own.

1. **Be sure pygame is installed on your working machine.**

You installed pygame earlier in this chapter, so it should be available to your programs.

2. **Inform Python that you will be using the pygame library.**

The `import` command lets your program access a library (a collection of modules) so you can use its objects and functions in your program.

```
import pygame
```

3. **Initialize pygame.**

The pygame module has a lot of complex parts. When you start it up, it needs to turn on several subsystems that help you check the mouse and keyboard, play sounds, and set up the visual display.

```
pygame.init()
```

This function "jumpstarts" pygame and begins initializing the pygame module — as well as all the various submodules — so your game can run.

Information Kiosk

Even after you import a library, you need to include the module name to refer to the elements inside the library. For example, the `Surface` object found in pygame should always be referred to as `pygame.Surface`. While it's possible to set up Python so that you don't always need the full names, I like for beginners to start with full names until you know exactly what comes from the library and what's part of the core distribution. Full names are a little harder to type, but they make the program a little clearer (at least at first). Programmers coming from the Java language may be tempted to use `import pygame.*` to import all the pygame modules, but this will not work correctly in Python and doesn't eliminate the need to use the module name.

D — Display

Games are an extremely visual medium — so one important early job is to set up the display system. Because games are so demanding of system resources, it's common to run games in a full-screen mode. (Early systems required this, because nothing else could realistically run when a game was hogging all the system resources.) You can still run pygame games in a full-screen mode, but most programmers create their game in a window first, and then switch to full-screen mode as a final touch. (In fact, it's common in games to let the user choose between a full-screen and windowed mode.)

While there are only two lines of runnable code in this section (and a comment), they do quite a bit of work:

```
#D - Display configuration
screen = pygame.display.set_mode((640, 480))
pygame.display.set_caption("Hello, world!")
```

1. **First you create a variable to represent the display screen.**

The `screen` variable is a `pygameSurface` object. Recall that a *surface* is a place in memory that represents an image. This special surface will house the image that will eventually be displayed on the computer's monitor. Note that the `set_mode()` method creates a `Surface` object for you automatically. You'll also create your own surface directly in the Entities step coming up.

2. **Call the `pygame.display.set_mode()` function.**

This function creates the display surface according to the parameters you feed it. Notice that the function has a long but descriptive name. The `set_caption()` function is defined in the `display` module of the `pygame` module. It's nice to know the full name because this helps you get appropriate online help. If you want to know more about the display module, you can type **help("pygame. display")** in the console. You can also find more specific information about the `set_mode` function by using its full name: **help("pygame.display.set_mode")**.

3. **Determine the size or resolution of the screen.**

It's critical to specify the size of the game screen, because all the work will be done within this area. The number of pixels (dots on the screen) determines how precisely images will be displayed. If you have a large screen resolution (1280 × 1024, for example), the objects on the screen are rendered in excellent detail. The work it takes to update a screen at that resolution will cause most games to run too slowly to be fun. Turn-based strategy games that don't require real-time screen updates are often run at high resolutions, but action games are frequently set to 640 × 480 or 800 × 600.

If you run a game in a window, the window will be the specified size. For example, a 640 × 480 game screen run in a window in my normal 1280 × 1024 resolution takes up about a quarter of the screen.

If the game is run in a full-screen mode, it (obviously) takes over the full screen. The size of each pixel is expanded so the screen uses the entire display area.

I set the screen size to 640 × 480 for this game (and for most in the book) with this line of code:

```
screen = pygame.display.set_mode((640, 480))
```

You might wonder why there are two sets of parentheses around the value 640, 480. This value is a *tuple* (much like the list described in Chapter 2 but a little bit simpler and requires less memory). Tuples are enclosed in parentheses, so value must be written like this: (640, 480). The tuple that controls screen size is one parameter that can be sent to the set_mode() function. All parameters are encased in parentheses, so the outer set of parentheses indicates you are specifying function parameters, and the inner set tells that your parameter is actually a tuple containing two other values. If this is foggy to you, don't panic. Just know that you need the two parentheses in this particular situation.

Information Kiosk

640 × 480 seems ridiculously small to people with modern computers, but it's actually a very good choice. Your games will run a lot quicker on a smaller screen because there are fewer pixels to manipulate. If you create your games full-screen, most users won't be able to tell how coarse the resolution is. Standard televisions, after all, still run at 640 × 480 — and all but the very latest dedicated game consoles use this resolution. Even the newer consoles (like the Xbox 360) don't run at a full 800 × 600.

4. **Specify any other parameters.**

For now, screen size is the only parameter I send to the set_mode() function. However, you can send a number of other parameters that are useful for determining how the game will be displayed. Most important of these is the FULLSCREEN attribute, which you set by passing it as an argument to the `set_mode()` function. This is used to force pygame into full-screen mode. I won't use that mode yet because it can cause your computer to lock up if you aren't completely comfortable with setting up game-ending events. You can see some of the other options by checking in the online help, but for now you won't really need anything but the screen size.

5. **Set up the screen caption.**

If your game is in full-screen mode, you won't see any caption. If your game is in a window mode, it will have a window with a caption. You use the `pygame.display.set_caption()` function to set this caption.

Transfer

As you'll see in Chapter 5, printing text to a pygame screen is a little bit involved. It's quite easy to change the caption, so lots of pygame programmers use the caption as a quick way to print out quick information to aid in debugging.

E — Entities

At heart, 2D video games are about a bunch of things moving around on the screen and crashing into each other. Some of these things are controlled by the user, and some are controlled by the computer. The background is one of these entities (even if it's nothing more than a solid block of color). The spaceship, dancing monkey — or whatever else the user controls — is one kind of entity. The other objects that the player interacts with, kills, avoids, or does whatever with are also entities. The `idea.py` program has only one entity, the blue background screen. Of course, more interesting games will contain dozens — even hundreds — of entities.

Transfer

In Chapter 5 you'll learn how to build your own images, text, and basic shapes, and turn them into entities. Chapter 6 shows you how to expand these ideas into an extremely useful tool called a sprite.

Now let's concentrate on building a blue rectangle to place in the background:

```
#E - Entities (just background for now)
background = pygame.Surface(screen.get_size())
background = background.convert()
background.fill((0, 0, 255))
```

The background will be a big blue surface that covers the entire screen. Later you learn how to draw on the background and add images and text. To make the background, follow these steps:

1. **Create a variable called `background` to hold the background.**

The name isn't that important, but all games have some sort of backdrop, and "background" is a pretty good name for it.

2. **Use the `pygame.Surface()` constructor to build a `Surface` object.**

Surfaces (memory representing a 2D image) are a very important part of pygame. The `Surface` object is a special object whose job is to represent a surface. Like lists and strings, `Surface` objects have attributes and methods. You can look up the characteristics of the `Surface` object with the standard `help()` function — `help("pygame.Surface")` — but don't panic if you don't understand everything in the help screens. For now, all you need to know is how to *build* a `Surface` object.

```
background = pygame.Surface(screen.get_size())
```

3. **Make the background the same size as the display.**

The background will fill up the display, so it should be the same size. Use the `screen.get_size()` method to get the current screen size and send that to the `Surface` object.

4. **Convert the background to a standard color format.**

Images come in all kinds of weird formats. Pygame is smart enough to convert many formats into a version it can read easily, but the process takes a lot of time. The `convert()` method of the `Surface` object converts the object into a basic format that pygame can use efficiently. This is exactly the kind of process you want to do before the game loop starts — because your program will slow down considerably if it has to decode a graphic several times per second.

Information Kiosk

To tell the truth, this particular surface will already be in the proper format, so the `convert()` method is a bit superfluous in this example. It doesn't hurt anything, though, so until you get a feel for when it's necessary, it's smartest to just assume that every surface should be converted.

5. **Copy the converted image back to the `background` variable.**

The `convert()` method doesn't change the original surface. Instead, it creates a new surface. If you want to modify the original surface, you have to copy the converted surface back to the original:

```
background = background.convert()
```

Information Kiosk

It may seem inconvenient that the `convert()` method doesn't actually change the original object, but it's actually a pretty good idea. The `convert()` method leaves the original surface alone, but creates a new converted surface. You can do anything you want with this new surface, including copying it back to the original. You can also use this new surface in other ways, transforming or duplicating it.

6. **Change the color of the background.**

For my game I want a solid blue background. The `fill()` method of the `Surface` object is a fast and easy way to create a single-color surface:

```
background.fill((0, 0, 255))
```

7. **Specify the background color.**

You might be surprised to see that (0, 0, 255) represents the color blue, but it does. Python uses a three-number system to define colors. It's not nearly as complicated as it seems. I explain color in Python completely in the section "Controlling Your Colors in Python," later in this chapter. For now, just accept that (0, 0, 255) means "blue."

A — Action

The final part of the IDEA framework is beginning your main loop. This step isn't any harder than the others, but it does have a lot of details. To make it simpler, I created another acronym. Main loops are about changing things: changing input from the user, changing the position, direction, and speed of entities on-screen, changing scores and player status, and updating the visual display with all these changes. For this reason, the

ALTER acronym is a good way to remember what happens in the action part of the game framework.

Managing Your Main Loop with ALTER

Once you've set everything up, the heart of any game is the game loop. Almost all games use a variation of the same loop, so learn it well and you'll be able to make endless variants. As a review, here are the main aspects of the ALTER loop:

- A — **Assign values**
- L — **Loop**
- T — **Time**
- E — **Events**
- R — **Refresh Screen**

A — Assigning values to key variables

The entire program has been initialized, but you'll need to initialize at least two more variables to make a well-behaved game loop:

```
    #A - Assign values to key variables
clock = pygame.time.Clock()
keepGoing = True
```

These two variables will be used inside the loop to manage the overall behavior of the program. To set them up, here's the drill:

1. Create a clock variable.

This variable is a special object you will use within the loop to control your game's frame rate (the speed at which the game runs). The clock is an object in pygame's `time` module.

```
clock = pygame.time.Clock()
```

2. Create a Boolean variable to manage the loop.

Game loops usually have multiple exit points. The game might end because the user closed the window, pressed an "escape key," or ran out of lives. Any time you have a loop with multiple exit points, the Boolean variable solution described in Chapter 3 is a good way to go. The variable `keepGoing` will default to `True`. Any situation that should cause the game to end should set the value of `keepGoing` to `False`.

```
keepGoing = True
```

L — Creating the main loop

Finally it's time to create the main loop for your game. It's actually pretty simple:

```
    #L - Set up main loop
while keepGoing:
```

The `keepGoing` variable is preset to `True`. As long as `keepGoing` is `True`, the loop will continue. Anyplace inside the loop you want to stop the game, simply set the value of `keepGoing` to `False`. The next time the `while` statement is evaluated, program control will go to the next line past the end of the loop. Generally, that will cause the entire program to end.

T — Managing time

Time management is also pretty easy, because pygame has an object to handle time for you — and you've already created a copy of it in your game. Recall building the `clock` variable. This nifty object has a number of interesting methods, but the most useful is `tick()`. The `tick()` method effectively sets a speed limit for the game, determining its maximum frame rate. If you set the parameter of `tick()` to 30, for example, you are setting the game's target frame rate to 30 frames per second.

Information Kiosk

In this very simple program, nothing is moving, so you can't see the effect of frame rate. I'll show you how it works in the `moveBox.py` example later in this chapter. For now, know that every program needs to have a frame rate set. Here's an example:

```
#T - Timer to set frame rate
clock.tick(30)
```

This means that your main loop will run up to 30 frames per second, but no faster. If your game starts to run more quickly, pygame will automatically slow it down to reach the target frame rate.

E — Handling events

The difference between an animation and a game is the level of user control. It's not enough to build an environment with lots of things going on. Somehow the user needs to interact with that environment and make things happen. Games use all kinds of devices to allow user interaction. The player will often control your game using the keyboard, mouse or a joystick device. It's actually quite complex to handle these various input devices, but pygame simplifies the process considerably. I reproduce the entire event-handling code here, and I'll break it down into simple steps below:

```
#E - Event handling
for event in pygame.event.get():
    if event.type == pygame.QUIT:
        keepGoing = False
```

There are a number of tools for handling events, but the basic framework is presented here. Here's how to build this basic event-handling code:

1. **Get a list of events that happened during this frame.**

Pygame has a special system called an *event buffer* that keeps track of all the different kinds of user events that can happen. When one of these events occurs (the user clicks the mouse, presses a key, moves the mouse, or controls the joystick), pygame creates a special object recording the event. The following function creates a list of events that occurred during the current frame:

```
pygame.event.get()
```

 Transfer

In Chapter 7, I'll show you how to gather input from the mouse. Chapter 8 describes keyboard input.

2. **Step through each element in the event list.**

You'll analyze this list to figure out what happened. You could store the list in a variable, but you really need to look at each event in turn, so you normally build a `for` loop to look immediately at all the events:

```
for event in pygame.event.get():
```

3. **Check the event type.**

Each object in the event list has a special `type` attribute that tells you what type of event it is. Use an `if` statement to compare the event type to the various event types `pygame` supports. For now, I'm only looking for the `QUIT` event that happens when the user closes the window containing a pygame program:

```
if event.type == pygame.QUIT:
```

4. **Write code associated with the event.**

If you went through all the trouble of checking to see if an event occurred, you probably want the program to *do* something. Of course, what you want to do depends on the event and the situation, but in this particular situation (the user has chosen to close the game window), the main loop should end. This is easily (if indirectly) done by setting the value of `keepGoing` to `False`. The next time the loop checks the value of `keepGoing`, it will be `False`, and the loop will end.

```
keepGoing = False
```

R — Refreshing the display

The final step in the game loop is the most dramatic: updating the visual display so the user sees the results of all your hard work. This process uses two commands that may be new to you: blitting and display flipping.

Copying images with the blit() method

Recall that pygame relies on surface objects to manage all visual elements. You made a special surface called `screen` way back in the beginning of the program, but you haven't changed the screen yet. The easiest way to modify the screen is to copy a value onto it. Pygame uses a special function called *blitting* to copy data from one rectangular surface to another. Since the `background` is a colored rectangle that's the same size as the `screen`, you can blit (or copy) the background to the screen. This will cause the screen (which is still not displayed) to be covered with the background. Later on you will copy other images on to the screen as well, making something more interesting than a plain blue screen.

Information Kiosk

The term *blit* is an acronym for *block transfer*. The specific type of blit I show here is a *bitblit*, used to transfer rectangular blocks of image information quickly. Many modern systems have special blitting operations built into the hardware for faster image processing. The important idea here is that you frequently will copy rectangular images, and you'll use a special method called `blit()` to do it efficiently. You've learned a wonderful new vocabulary word. Try to work it into your next bit of cocktail-party conversation.

Flipping the screen

The other new technique is called *screen flipping*. This idea is related to another important idea called *double buffering*. These ideas are necessary because the process of actually displaying graphics onto the screen is relatively slow. You can modify memory very quickly — you can copy information (via the `blit()` method) very quickly as well — but if you try to update the visual display directly, your game will have a noticeable screen flicker. (If you look at older games, especially those on old gaming consoles, you'll notice a lot more flicker than on modern gaming systems. That's because the older systems could not implement double-buffering routines quickly enough.) To improve screen-refresh rates and minimize flicker, all the work is done on a non-displayed rectangle, and that rectangle gets copied to the visual display with a special version of the `blit()` method.

In pygame, the `display.flip()` method is a special kind of blitting that copies everything from the `screen` object to the actual visual display. Double buffering is the technique you're using — and the `flip()` function is how you implement double buffering in pygame.

Step Into the Real World

Don't let the idea of double buffering confuse you. Think about cooking shows. Often the host spends much of the show preparing a beautiful dish, then places it in the oven. Rather than waiting the 20 minutes for the recipe to bake, the chef reaches into the oven and immediately pulls out a version of the dish that was prepared ahead of time. To the audience, it appears that the dish was instantly ready. Working on an off-screen buffer is like preparing your food and having it already in the oven.

Performing the actual display flip

Blitting, double buffering, and display flipping all seem terribly complicated, but the code to perform all this magic is remarkably simple:

```
#R - Refresh display
screen.blit(background, (0, 0))
pygame.display.flip()
```

To actually display the screen, follow these steps:

1. **Copy the background image to the screen using the `screen.blit()` method.**

```
screen.blit(background, (0, 0))
```

This method requires two parameters. The first is the surface to copy from. In this case I want to copy the background surface onto the screen, so my first parameter is `background`. The second parameter specifies where on the primary surface (in this case, the `screen` object) to place the copy. Since `background` and `screen` are the same size, the background should be drawn at the screen's origin, which is `(0, 0)`.

 Transfer

See the section later in this chapter called "Setting up position variables" to see why `(0, 0)` is called the *origin* and why it's the upper-left corner. For now, though, just trust me that this is the right value. You've got lots of other new things to be learning at the moment.

2. **Copy any foreground images to the screen using `screen.blit()`.**

The first thing you draw to the screen will appear to be in the background; any successive images will appear to overlap images that have already been drawn. These new images can be drawn to different parts of the screen.

 Transfer

Note that my IDEA example doesn't draw anything except the background image to the screen, but very soon you'll be drawing foreground images too. Look ahead to the "Making Things Move" section of this chapter to see how an animated object can be added to your display.

3. **Flip the display.**

This function takes the finished `screen` buffer and copies it to the actual output hardware, causing the screen to update.

```
pygame.display.flip()
```

The `display.flip()` function is a special, optimized version of the `blit()` method that quickly and smoothly updates the display hardware, showing the results of all your hard work to the user.

Controlling Your Colors in pygame

The `idea.py` program shows how to draw a basic surface, but it suggests a number of questions. Earlier in the chapter I asked you to trust me that blue was represented by the value `(0, 0, 255)`. This seems like an arbitrary value, but once you understand how computers view color, it actually makes a lot of sense.

Introducing the additive color model

You're no doubt aware that you can take a few basic colors and combine them to build a large variety of new colors. In elementary school, you probably learned that the primary colors are yellow, blue, and green. This is true — when you're using crayons or paint to draw on white paper. On paper, you usually use a *subtractive* color model, which means that the paper starts out white (with lots of light reflecting off it) and you draw other colors on top, *removing* light from the reflection. As you put more paint or crayon wax on the drawing, it gets darker and darker. Computer screens use a different approach. A computer screen starts out with each dot emitting no light. Each pixel on a computer monitor can emit a variable amount of red, green, and blue light. By changing the relative amounts of these three types of light, you can specify most colors that humans can see.

Computer programs create light by specifying the amounts of color in red, green, and blue. This is called the RGB color model. To specify an RGB color, you indicate a value between 0 and 255 for red, a second value for green, and a third value for blue.

The `colorViewer.py` program shown in Figure 4-3 illustrates how computers manage colors in general, and how pygame works with color.

Here's an experiment with the Color Viewer:

1. **Run the `colorViewer.py` program.**

If you've installed Python and pygame onto your system, you should be able to run the program simply by double-clicking it.

Information Kiosk

This program was written using skills I teach later in the book. You're welcome to look at the source code and change things around if you want. Don't worry if you don't understand everything in this program yet. Just think of it as a teaser for some new skills such as keyboard access, creating `sprite` objects, and interactivity.

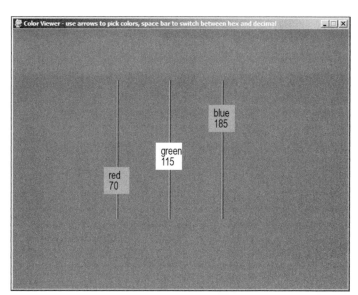

Figure 4-3: Use the arrow keys to change red, green, and blue and make new colors.

2. Use the up and down arrows on the keyboard to change the amount of red.

The red box is already highlighted when the program begins, so you can use the up or down arrow to change the amount of red being shown on the program's background. The background starts black, but as you increase the amount of red, you'll see that the background changes to a bright red color.

3. Note the minimum and maximum values.

In most computer graphic systems (including pygame), each color can have a minimum value of 0 and a maximum value of 255. This is because each color is stored in eight digits of binary code, which allows positive integers between 0 and 255.

4. Change the other colors as well.

Use the right and left arrow keys to switch to the other sliders and the up and down arrow keys to change their values. Play around until you're comfortable. Make sure you see how the various colors work. See how to make darker and lighter colors. Try making yellow, orange, and dark purple. Make a dark red. Try making brown (notoriously difficult on computer screens).

5. Press the spacebar to view hexadecimal mode.

The spacebar allows you to change the text on the bars to base-16 (hexadecimal or "hex") mode. Base 16 seems very confusing at first, but often it's an easier way to make various color combinations. If you've done any Web-design work, you may already know a few colors in hex, as the technique is often used to make more specific colors than you can refer to by using color names. Also, a great many graphics programs and Web tools provide color values in hex. If you want to use hex numbers in pygame, precede each hex number with 0x. You never have to create colors in hex, but if you're already comfortable with the technique, you're free to use it. You'll see in my examples that I often prefer hex values because they're actually easier to predict.

Setting colors in pygame

When you want to specify a color in pygame, you create a special three-value list indicating the amount of red, green and blue. For example, if you want to specify the color blue, use (0, 0, 255) or (0x00, 0x00, 0xFF). So far, the only place you've seen to specify a color is in the Surface object's fill() method. You can use this command to change the background color of your program.

Begin by modifying idea.py as follows:

1. Load **idea.py** into your editor.

Begin by examining the program.

2. Locate the **background.fill()** method.

If you haven't changed idea.py, it'll be on line 18.

3. Choose a new background color.

You can simply guess, or you can use the colorViewer.py program to choose a suitable color. You can also use a graphics program or Web editor to generate a color in RGB format.

4. Enter the new color in the parentheses after the **fill()** method.

Replace the existing color values with your new color.

5. Test your program.

There's no way to know whether you did it right until you test.

Making Things Move

You've created the basic framework, and you can manage colors. Now it's time to see something move. Remember moveBox.py I showed you at the top of the chapter.

The moveBox.py program finally shows the IDEA/ALTER structure doing an animation, where the frame rate is actually meaningful. Although idea.py used the game loop, you couldn't really see the frame rate in action, because nothing was moving. The moveBox.py program uses the IDEA/ALTER technique to actually move an object on the screen. Take a look at the code, and you'll see it's very similar to idea.py. I've highlighted the code that's been added in bold.

```
""" moveBox.py
    illustrates basic motion
    in the IDEA/ALTER framework
    moves a rect across the screen """

#Initialize
import pygame
pygame.init()

#Display
screen = pygame.display.set_mode((640, 480))
pygame.display.set_caption("move a box")

#Entities
#yellow background
background = pygame.Surface(screen.get_size())
background = background.convert()
background.fill((255, 255, 0))

#make a red 25 x 25 box
box = pygame.Surface((25, 25))
box = box.convert()
box.fill((255, 0, 0))

# set up some box variables
box_x = 0
box_y = 200

#ACTION

    #Assign
clock = pygame.time.Clock()
keepGoing = True

    #Loop
while keepGoing:

    #Time
    clock.tick(30)

    #Events
    for event in pygame.event.get():
        if event.type == pygame.QUIT:
            keepGoing = False

    #modify box value
    box_x += 5
    #check boundaries
    if box_x > screen.get_width():
        box_x = 0
```

```
#Refresh screen
screen.blit(background, (0, 0))
screen.blit(box, (box_x, box_y))
pygame.display.flip()
```

The advantage of having a framework is clear from this code. If you tried to write the moveBox.py code from scratch, it would seem an intimidating prospect. If you start with a framework, you only need to make a few changes to turn it into a new program.

Creating an animation requires a few additions to the basic IDEA code as shown in the following steps:

1. **Build the object that will move.**

This is usually done outside the game loop, in the entities section.

2. **Modify object data.**

All objects have data indicating where they belong on the screen. In this program, you create variables that indicate the box's intended x and y values. Somewhere inside the game loop, you have to update the object's position data.

3. **Check for boundaries.**

Any time you change the position of an object, you need to see whether it has moved off the screen — and act accordingly. This happens inside the game loop.

4. **Refresh the screen.**

Once you have set the object's new position, you can actually draw it to the screen. This code also is run from the game loop.

Creating the box

The first order of business is to make an object to place on the screen. You'll learn how to make several different kinds of objects later on, but for now, the Surface object is an easy way to make filled rectangles, and you've already made one for the background. Here's the code for creating a 25 × 25 pixel box:

```
#make a red 25 x 25 box
box = pygame.Surface((25, 25))
box = box.convert()
box.fill((255, 0, 0))
```

To create the small box that will move across the screen, follow these steps:

1. **Create a new pygame.Surface object.**

The Surface object creates a rectangle. This time, rather than making the surface the size of the entire screen (as you did when making the background surface) make your new surface 25 pixels × 25 pixels.

2. Convert the box's graphics format.

Once again, use the `convert()` method to ensure that your new surface uses the efficient color technique that pygame prefers.

3. Change the box color.

Now that you understand how to make colors in pygame, you can make the box whatever color you wish. I went for a red box on a yellow background, but you can choose whatever colors you want.

Setting up position variables

`Surface` objects in pygame don't have any sense of position. You determine where one goes by blitting it onto another surface. You'll need some variables to control where the box is placed on the background. I used variables called `box_x` and `box_y`, like this:

```
# set up some box variables
box_x = 0
box_y = 200
```

There's nothing magical about these variables that connects them to the box, but by giving them these names, I'm indicating that they do have something to do with the box. The box will be drawn at a particular position. Computer games normally use a variation of the *Cartesian coordinate system* from mathematics. This system uses two values — x and y — to position an object on a two-dimensional space. Computer systems usually use a modified form of the system, as you can see in Figure 4-4.

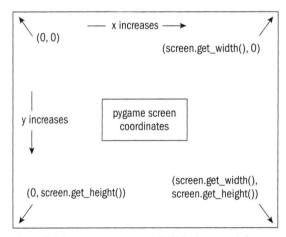

Figure 4-4: In computer systems, (0, 0) is the upper-left corner.

Study Figure 4-4 carefully, because it shows some important concepts:

● **The origin (0, 0) is not where you expect!**

In most mathematical systems, the (0, 0) point (usually called the *origin*) is either in the lower-left corner or in the center. In a computer graphics system, the origin is almost always located in the **upper-left** corner. Most display hardware works by moving from left to right, then from the top of the display to the bottom. Coordinate systems are designed to work in the same general direction.

● **X increases as you move from left to right.**

This isn't really much of a surprise. x is zero at the left side of the screen, and it increases as you move towards the right.

● **The largest value for x is `screen.get_width()`.**

Although the screen does have a numeric width (so far, all our screens have been 640 pixels wide) it's best not to rely on this number, because it may change, and it doesn't have any inherent meaning. It's much better to use the `get_width()` method of the `screen` object, to determine the actual width of the screen. Also, `screen.get_width()` is unambiguous. It's pretty clear that you're referring to the width of the screen.

● **y increases *downward!***

This is the part that confuses people. In geometry, y usually increases as you move up. Because of the way display hardware works, it's more efficient to have the zero value for y at the top of the screen, and larger values as you move downward (that is, down the screen).

● **The largest value for y is `screen.get_height()`.**

Like width, the height of the screen is best determined by a built-in method. The `screen.get_height()` method returns the maximum value for y, even if the user changes the screen size.

For the box, I store the box's x position in a (cleverly named) variable called `box_x` and the y position in another variable called `box_y`.

Transfer

It turns out that this technique of creating two variables to track an object's position becomes unwieldy when you've got a lot of objects on the screen. It's still a good idea to understand how this technique works, but in Chapter 6, I show you how to "cheat" by creating a special object called a *sprite* that can keep track of its own position.

I give box_x a default value of 0, and box_y a starting value of 200. Later, when I actually draw the box on the screen at position (box_x, box_y), it will appear at a position on the left side of the screen, not quite halfway down.

Information Kiosk

Setting the values of box_x and box_y doesn't actually move the box. They're just variables. The box will be positioned later on when I use the values of box_x and box_y in a blit() method.

Modifying the box's position

The box is created in the initial part of the program before the game loop starts. The movement happens inside the game loop, because it will happen several times per second.

```
#modify box value
box_x += 5
#check boundaries
if box_x > screen.get_width():
    box_x = 0
```

You don't actually move the box directly. Instead, you modify the variable that controls the box's position.

If you want to move the box from left to right, here's how:

1. **Add 5 to the box_x variable.**

The code box_x += 5 is just like saying box_x = box_x + 5. It's a quick way to add a value to a variable. Because this code is happening inside the game loop, box_x will increase by 5 pixels 30 times per second.

2. **Check to see if the box will leave the screen.**

If box_x gets too large, it will leave the screen. There are a number of ways to handle this situation, but for now I'll simply "wrap" the box around the screen, moving it to the left side of the screen.

Step Into the Real World

This code also points out an important principle in any kind of programming: Whenever you change a variable, consider whether it might become too large or too small. If you keep adding a value to box_x, eventually the box will leave the screen, moving off the right side, and you'll have to do something about that.

Transfer

In Chapter 8 you learn more about what to do when an object leaves the screen, including how to make an object bounce off the edge, stop at the edge, stop and slide, or wrap without ever leaving the screen. In Chapter 10 you build a custom sprite that knows how to do all these things automatically.

Use an `if` statement to check the box's progress. Recall from Figure 4-4 that the right side of the screen is `screen.get_width()`, so the box has left the screen when `box_x` is greater than `screen.get_width()`.

```
if box_x > screen.get_width():
```

3. If the box has left the screen, move it all the way to the left side of the screen.

Another look at Figure 4-4 confirms that the left side of the screen is 0, so set `box_x` to 0 and the box moves all the way to the left.

```
box_x = 0
```

4. Leave box_y alone for now.

You could also mess around with `box_y` to change the vertical position of the box, but for now, just make sure you understand how to move the box horizontally with `box_x`.

Refreshing the screen

Now your program has two entities: the background surface and the red box. When you update the screen, you must blit the background to the screen (as you did in the `idea.py` program). You must also blit the box to the screen so it appears there:

```
#Refresh screen
screen.blit(background, (0, 0))
screen.blit(box, (box_x, box_y))
pygame.display.flip()
```

Here are the steps that update this more complicated scene:

1. Copy the background to the screen.

The `blit()` method is used to copy one rectangle to another. Copy the background to the screen. Since the background is the same size as the screen, copy the background to the origin (0, 0) of the screen, and the background will take up the entire screen.

2. **Copy the box to the screen.**

The second `blit()` method is used to copy the box to the screen. Note that a new object is drawn on top of previous objects, so the box appears on top of the background.

3. **Use `box_x` and `box_y` to determine the box's position.**

The position of the box is determined by the `box_x` and `box_y` variables. Because you've adjusted these variables in other parts of the program, the `blit()` method simply takes advantage of the variables to place the box correctly.

4. **Flip the display.**

Don't forget to flip the display. This process takes the content of the `screen` object and copies it to the display hardware, causing the screen image to appear to the user.

You've Got Game!

This chapter has covered an awful lot of territory. There's a lot to learn here, but once you know it, you're well on your way to making any kind of 2D game you can imagine. The IDEA/ALTER framework is the foundation of every other program in this book, so get comfortable with it. Try writing the `idea.py` and `moveBox.py` programs on your own a few times. If you can produce the IDEA/ALTER framework from memory, you'll have a great advantage when it comes to starting any game. I've found IDEA/ALTER a great way to help me remember all the details of the basic game framework. Here's how I start a new game:

1. **Create a new file using IDLE or whatever text editor you prefer.**

2. **Write your overall documentation string first.**

Use the triple-quoted documentation string to remind yourself what the goals of this project are, what you want to accomplish, and any special techniques you will use.

3. **Write IDEA and ALTER as comments.**

Make a comment for each element in IDEA/ALTER, reminding yourself of what that letter stands for. Each comment should be on a separate line. I usually indent all the ALTER steps, as they are part of the Action step of IDEA.

4. **Flesh out each step.**

Each step requires a line or two of code. For example, the "I" stands for Import and Initialize, so you should now remember that you'll need two lines of code:

```
import pygame
pygame.init()
```

5. Don't be afraid to get help when you need it.

If you know the general command but you've forgotten details, use Python's wonderful help feature to figure it out. You can also look at working code to get details, but make sure you understand what you're doing.

6. Resist copy-and-paste.

It is tempting to start every program by simply copying from `idea.py` and pasting into your editor. This is fine as a shortcut early on, but at some point you'll want to grow beyond what's in `idea.py`. Also, you may find yourself at a new computer without access to the code. It's worth knowing how to write this code by hand.

7. Test often.

Whenever possible, stop and test your code. Write the basic IDEA/ALTER framework and test it before you move on. There's no point writing anything fancier until you know you didn't make any silly mistakes in the basic framework.

8. Enhance the framework to make something new!

Now you can go crazy adding whatever features you want, to make a game that's all your own.

In the next chapter, you'll learn how to create more interesting objects. You'll import graphics, draw onto the screen, and draw text.

additive color model: The color model used in computer display hardware. Each color is represented by three integer values between 0 and 255. The first value represents the amount of red, the second value is the amount of green, and the third value is the amount of blue.

ALTER: A second acronym explaining the details of the gaming loop: Assign values, Loop, Timing, Event handling, Refresh screen.

API (Application Programming Interface): A set of programming tools that allows you to add functionality to a programming language. DirectX, openGL, and SDL are all graphics APIs.

blit: Short for BLock Transfer, this technique for copying one surface to another is used to draw surfaces onto the screen.

DirectX: A graphics API offered by Microsoft.

display: A special pygame module used to control the screen display hardware. Usually referred to as `pygame.display`, its most important functions are `pygame.display.set_mode()` and `pygame.display.flip()`.

double buffer: All image manipulation is done on a secondary surface that resides only in memory — and the entire surface is copied onto the display screen in one special, high-speed blit. Double buffering makes the display smoother and faster. Use the `pygame.display.flip()` function to use double buffering.

event: Some kind of stimulus that the user sends to the game through the keyboard, mouse, or joystick.

event Buffer: A special list that contains all the events that have occurred during the current frame. Use `pygame.event.get()` to retrieve the event buffer.

frame rate: The basic speed of your game. Python games normally run at 30 frames per second, which is about the same speed as television.

full-screen: A display mode that takes over the entire computer display. Often the pixels are resized to fill the entire display.

game loop: Sometimes referred to as an *animation loop*, the game loop is the logical structure that manages what happens during each frame. In this book, I use the ALTER acronym to help remind myself of what happens inside the game loop.

hexidecimal (hex) notation: Color values are sometimes represented in base-16 (rather than base-10) numbers. Web programmers are often already familiar with this notation. Numbers in hex begin with 0x in Python, and hex values can contain the digits 0-9 as well as the characters A-F.

IDEA: An acronym used in this book to remember the initialization steps for the game loop: Import/Initialization, Display setup, Entities, and Action (gaming loop).

module: Python's tool for adding functionality. Python comes with several useful modules. Pygame is a special module that provides an interface to the SDL API. In order to use the tools in a module, you need to import it.

OpenGL (Open Graphics Library): A multi-platform graphics API that specializes in 3D models.

origin: In a Cartesian coordinate system, the (0, 0) point is called the origin. In most computing applications (such as Python/pygame), the origin is in the upper-left corner of the screen.

pixel: The basic graphical unit of a computer display. A pixel can produce colors by varying the amount of red, green, and blue in the light it emits.

rect: A data structure representing a rectangle. Every surface has a rect associated with it, as do many other graphical objects in pygame.

resolution: The number of pixels used in a game. Usually specified by width and height. 640 × 480 and 800 × 600 are the most common resolutions for Python games.

SDL (Simple DirectMedia Layer): A multi-platform graphics API used by pygame to simplify graphics and game programming.

surface: A pygame object that represents a rectangular image in memory.

tuple: A Python structure much like a list but with fewer capabilities. Used within pygame to manage color values and screen coordinates.

widget: A graphical element like a button or list box. Traditional programming often relies heavily on pre-built widgets in some kind of toolkit, but game programmers usually create their own widgets to fit the feel of the game.

Command	Arguments	Description	Example
`import module`	`module`: module to import (pygame)	Makes a module available to the program.	`import pygame`
`pygame.init()`	\<none\>	Initializes pygame module and submodules.	`pygame.init()`
`pygame.display.set_mode(size)`	`size`: a tuple containing height and width integers	Sets the screen size and mode.	`pygame.display.set_size((640, 480)`
`pygame.display.set_caption(caption)`	`caption`: the string to display in window caption	Sets the caption if not in full-screen mode.	`pygame.display.set_caption("hello, world!")`
`pygame.Surface(size)`	`size`: a tuple containing height and width integers	Creates a surface of the given size.	`background = pygame.Surface(screen.get_size())`

continued

 *continued*

Command	Arguments	Description	Example
`surface.convert()`	*surface*: a pygame Surface object	Converts `surface`'s graphics mode to an efficient system.	`background = background.convert()`
`surface.fill (color)`	*surface*: a pygame Surface object *color*: a tuple containing red, green, and blue values	Fills in the surface with the given color.	`background.fill ((255, 255, 0))`
`surface.get_ size()`	*surface*: a pygame Surface object	Returns the size of the surface as a tuple.	`screenSize = screen.get_size()`
`pygame.time. Clock()`	<none>	Creates a new `Clock` object to control game speed.	`clock = pygame. time.Clock()`
`clock.tick (framerate)`	*clock*: a pygame Clock object *framerate*: target game speed in frames per second	Sets the game's maximum speed to the `framerate`. Called inside the game loop.	`clock. tick(30)`
`pygame.event.get()`	<none>	Returns a list of events that have happened in the current frame.	`eventList = pygame. event.get()`
`event.type`	*event*: a pygame Event object	Returns the type of event that occurred.	`if event.type == pygame.QUIT: print "bye!"`
`surface1.blit (surface2, position)`	*surface1*: image that will be drawn *surface2*: canvas that *surface2* is drawn to *position*: coordinates on *surface2* where *surface1*'s upper-left corner will be placed	Draws *surface1* onto *surface2* at *position*.	`screen.blit(box, (100, 100))`
`pygame.display. flip()`	<none>	Copies everything on the screen object to the actual display hardware.	`pygame.display. flip()`
`surface.get_ height()`	*surface*: a pygame Surface object	Returns the height of the surface in pixels.	`print screen. get_height()`
`surface.get_ width()`	*surface*: a pygame Surface object	Returns the width of the surface in pixels.	`print screen. get_width()`

Practice Exam

1. Why do most games use a graphics API?

_____

_____

2. Which is NOT a graphics API?

A) OpenGL

B) Python

C) DirectX

D) SDL

3. The speed of a game is called its _____ _____.

4. What's the name of one dot on the screen?

A) A pixel

B) A dot

C) A frame

D) An origin

5. Which action is NOT normally part of a gaming loop?

A) Checking for user events

B) Initializing pygame

C) Updating object variables

D) Refreshing the screen

6. How is pygame related to SDL?

A) They are the same thing.

B) SDL is a special version of pygame.

C) pygame is a wrapper that gives Python programmers access to SDL.

D) pygame actually uses DirectX because SDL only works on Windows machines.

7. Please summarize the steps in IDEA:

I _____

D _____

E _____

A _____

8. Please summarize the steps in ALTER:

A _____

L _____

T _____

E _____

R _____

9. Briefly describe double buffering.

_____

_____

10. Build a variation of `idea.py` from memory.

11. Make a program that moves a box from right to left. (Tip: you'll have to change the boundary checking.)

12. Make a program that moves a box from top to bottom. (Tip: you'll have to change boundary checking again.)

13. Make a box that moves in a diagonal path.

14. Make a program with four different boxes going in four different directions.

Drawing and Events

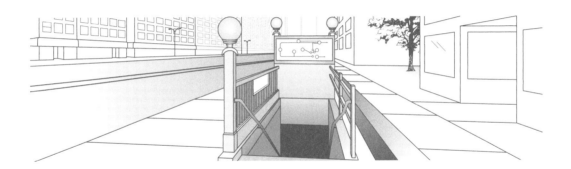

Enter the Station

Questions

1. Why do many Python programs have a `__name__ == "__main__"` condition in them?

2. How can a dedicated Python editor make it easier to write Python programs?

3. How can you draw basic shapes on the screen?

4. How do you save and load images?

5. How do you put text messages on a pygame screen?

6. How do you respond to mouse events?

7. How does pygame know which key has been pressed?

Introducing Graphics

By this point, you know how to build a basic graphical program. Now that you can use the IDEA/ALTER structure to build the foundation of your games, you're probably eager to draw something more interesting than a rectangle. Python supports several kinds of images. In this chapter, you learn how to deal with several basic ways to get visual elements on the screen. You also learn how to manage the basic mouse and keyboard events. Along the way, you'll build a basic-but-functional painting program like the one shown in Figure 5-1.

Figure 5-1: You can make your own painting program with Python!

The painting program is just a start, but it does have a number of interesting features:

- **You can draw with the mouse.** When you move your mouse over the painting with the left button down, you can draw. Not a revolutionary innovation, but necessary for a painting program.

- **The keyboard accepts commands.** The title bar shows a series of commands the user can access through the keyboard. Various keys allow the user to change the drawing color, set the line width, save or load a graphic, and quit.

- **The program provides rudimentary feedback.** Labels on the screen tell the user the current status of the pen (color and width).

- **The user can save and load a picture.** The program provides a very basic form of file management that allows the user to save or load a picture. As it stands, the program always saves and loads `painting.bmp` in the same directory as the program.

Pygame supports three main ways to draw something on the screen:

- **Drawing functions.** Pygame has a module called `draw` with a number of drawing functions. These functions allow you to draw lines and shapes directly onto a surface.

- **Loading pre-existing images.** The most common approach to graphics is to create an image object based on a digital image file. You can make an image with a graphics program, and use that image inside your game.

- **Using text to make labels.** In pygame, you don't display text directly on the screen. If you want text to appear on-screen, you'll make a special element called a *font* and use it to create a surface displaying your message. You can then manipulate this surface just like any other.

In your games, you'll likely use a combination of all three techniques. The `paint.py` program uses a drawing command to draw the lines. It has the capability to save and load an image (using the image-loading technique), and it makes an image from text to build the label describing the pen color and width.

Building More Complex Programs

By this point, you are starting to write longer, more sophisticated programs. As you do so, you will need to consider ways to support more complex programs. Two significant techniques are the use of a main function to prevent certain side-effects and the use of a more sophisticated programming editor than IDLE.

Using a main function

You learned how to use functions back in Chapter 3. In that chapter I explained that functions make long programs easier to create and maintain. This is equally true of graphical programs. In Chapter 4, I introduced graphical programs without functions, so you could focus on the basic IDEA/ALTER model. Of course, you can and should use functions in your pygame programs. Any code written outside a function is considered to have *global scope*. It's considered bad form (and a little sloppy) to leave a lot of code in the global scope. Whenever possible, your code should be tucked into functions. When your code is inside functions, the scope mechanism (discussed in Chapter 3) protects your variables from inadvertent changes and collisions with other variables with the same names — making your code more robust and easier to maintain. Figure 5-2 shows a familiar-looking program last seen in Chapter 4, modified to use functions.

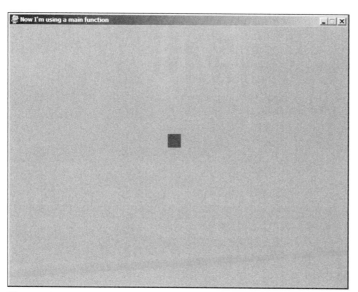

Figure 5-2: This program looks familiar, but has a little better code design.

The user can't see it, but the design of the `mainFunc()` program features an improved design:

```python
""" mainFunc.py
    illustrate using the main function
    """
#I - Import and init - still in global scope
import pygame
pygame.init()

def main():
    #D - Display now part of main function
    screen = pygame.display.set_mode((640, 480))
    pygame.display.set_caption("Now I'm using a main
function")

    #E - Entities part of main function
    background = pygame.Surface(screen.get_size())
    background.fill((0, 255, 255))

    square = pygame.Surface((25, 25))
    square.fill((255, 0, 0))

    #Action also part of main function
    clock = pygame.time.Clock()
    keepGoing = True
    while keepGoing:
```

```
        for event in pygame.event.get():
            if event.type == pygame.QUIT:
                keepGoing = False

        screen.blit(background, (0, 0))
        screen.blit(square, (300, 200))

        pygame.display.flip()

#Run main if this is the primary program
if __name__ == "__main__":
    main()
```

The basic IDEA layout is still in place, but this time I've moved most of the code into a special function called main().

 ## Information Kiosk

Unlike many languages (such as C or Java) there's nothing magical about the function name main(). It could be called anything, but programmers in most languages call the primary function main(). It's a good tradition, and it makes your code predictable, so I'll continue the trend.

Converting your pygame code to use functions requires three steps:

1. Do a little setup work outside the main() function. The "I" step (Import and Initialize pygame) still happens at the global scope (that is, outside the main() function). This is because you will generally have other functions in your program that will need access to the pygame module. If you have other functions (and you usually will), you'll also define them before you define main().

2. Write the main() function. The main function is the remainder of the IDEA code (everything except the "I" step you already did). This code won't run until you call the main() function explicitly (which you'll do in the next step).

3. Call the main() function only when this is a stand-alone program. The last chunk of code looks a little weird:

```
#Run main if this is the primary program
if __name__ == "__main__":
    main()
```

Every language has its quirks, and this is one of Python's little gems. Still, once you understand it, this code makes a certain amount of sense. Here's what's going on . . .

Every Python program you create is considered a module. Modules can be programs that stand on their own or programs meant to be imported into other programs (like you've been importing pygame).

Transfer

You build your own basic module in Chapter 6. In Chapter 10, you create a much more complete module that simplifies writing games.

Sometimes (like when you use an editor with syntax completion or documentation features) a module will be imported when you don't expect it. Whenever that happens, whatever code is in that module's global scope will run, but code inside functions will not. For this reason, Python programmers generally put all of their code inside functions.

To prevent unwanted side-effects of this process, you need a mechanism that prevents code from running accidentally, but that allows it to run when you want. Python provides exactly such a mechanism. Every module has a special attribute called __name__. If this value is equal to the string literal "__main__", then the module is being run as a program (not as a side-effect of some other tool or process). Normally you call the main() method (which calls all the rest of the module's code) only when the module is being deliberately run as a program. That's what the __name__ == "__main__" business is all about.

Using a more sophisticated editor

The IDLE editor is perfectly sufficient for basic Python, but you may be wishing you had something with a little more horsepower. There are many terrific free editors out there. This may be a good time to try one. My personal favorite among dedicated Python editors is called Stani's Python Editor, or SPE. Figure 5-3 shows SPE in action.

Figure 5-3: Stani's Python Editor showing a list of possible functions.

This tool has a number of really great features:

- **Syntax completion.** When you type in some text, SPE provides a list of valid completions. For example, when you start working with the `pygame.draw` commands later in this chapter, if you type **pygame.draw**, SPE generates a list of all the functions available in the `pygame.draw` module, so you don't have to memorize them.

- **Syntax hints.** As you're calling a built-in function, SPE pops up a dialog box to explain how that function works and what parameters it expects. Figure 5-4 shows an example. This makes learning new modules like pygame a *lot* easier.

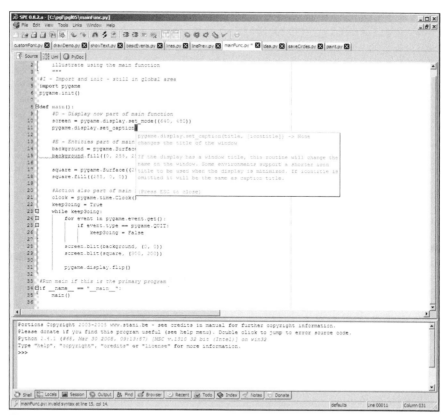

Figure 5-4: SPE gives you syntax help when you call a function.

Smart overview. SPE automatically creates an index of your programs, listing all the functions and (as you learn to create them) classes in your program. You can even put special markers in your code so you can make it easier to get to any particular part of your program you want.

Multiple document support. Soon enough your programs will involve more than one file. SPE lets you have several files open at once.

Advanced features. SPE has numerous advanced features you can explore, including a very powerful debugger, a nice syntax-checking feature, and an automatic documentation feature.

Information Kiosk

The author of SPE has generously released this great program to the public for free. If you like it, I encourage you to visit his Web page at `http://stani.be/python/spe/blog/` and donate a few dollars for a PDF version of the manual. Note that you'll also need to install the wxWidgets library to get SPE working correctly, but it's worth it.

Drawing Commands

The drawing commands are a basic way to get visual information on your display. Each of the commands is stored in the pygame.draw module. As always when encountering a new module, it might be wise to run help("pygame.draw") in your interpreter to see some of the features of this tool. Figure 5-5 is a simple program illustrating a number of drawing commands.

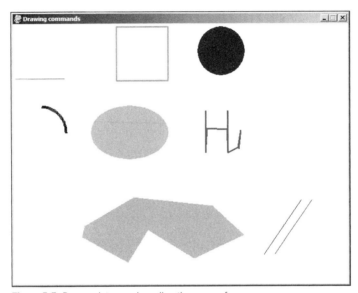

Figure 5-5: Pygame lets you draw directly on a surface.

The main drawing functions in pygame are illustrated in this code. Look it over first, and then I'll explain each of the commands.

```
""" drawDemo.py
    demonstrate using the drawing
    features in pygame"""

import pygame, math
pygame.init()

def drawStuff(background):
    """ given a surface, draws a bunch of things on it """

    #draw a line from (5, 100) to (100, 100)
    pygame.draw.line(background, (255, 0, 0), (5, 100), ↩
(100, 100))

    #draw an unfilled square
```

```
      pygame.draw.rect(background, (0, 255, 0),              ↩
((200, 5), (100, 100)), 3)

      #draw a filled circle
      pygame.draw.circle(background, (0, 0, 255),            ↩
(400, 50), 45)

      #draw an arc
      pygame.draw.arc(background, (0, 0, 0), ((5, 150),      ↩
(100, 100)), 0, math.pi/2, 5)

      #draw an ellipse
      pygame.draw.ellipse(background, (0xCC, 0xCC, 0x00),    ↩
((150, 150), (150, 100)), 0)

      #draw lines,
      points = (
         (370, 160),
         (370, 237),
         (372, 193),
         (411, 194),
         (412, 237),
         (412, 160),
         (412, 237),
         (432, 227),
         (436, 196),
         (433, 230)
      )
      pygame.draw.lines(background, (0xFF, 0x00, 0x00),      ↩
False, points, 3)

      #draw polygon
      points = (
         (137, 372),
         (232, 319),
         (383, 335),
         (442, 389),
         (347, 432),
         (259, 379),
         (220, 439),
         (132, 392)
      )
      pygame.draw.polygon(background, (0x33, 0xFF, 0x33),    ↩
points)

      #compare normal and anti-aliased diagonal lines
      pygame.draw.line(background, (0, 0, 0), (480, 425),    ↩
(550, 325), 1)
```

```
        pygame.draw.aaline(background, (0, 0, 0),          ↵
(500, 425), (570, 325), 1)

    def main():
        screen = pygame.display.set_mode((640, 480))
        pygame.display.set_caption("Drawing commands")

        background = pygame.Surface(screen.get_size())
        background = background.convert()
        background.fill((255, 255, 255))

        drawStuff(background)

        clock = pygame.time.Clock()
        keepGoing = True
        while keepGoing:
            clock.tick(30)
            for event in pygame.event.get():
                if event.type == pygame.QUIT:
                    keepGoing = False
                elif event.type == pygame.MOUSEBUTTONUP:
                    print pygame.mouse.get_pos()
            screen.blit(background, (0, 0))
            pygame.display.flip()

    if __name__ == "__main__":
        main()
```

The code may seem involved, but as you look at it more closely, you'll see that much of the code is the now-familiar IDEA/ALTER framework, and the drawing commands are all relatively similar to each other.

Information Kiosk

Until you're fluent in the IDEA/ALTER framework, you may want to continue writing comments for that part of your code first and then flesh it out. I decided not to show the comments used to build the framework, so that the comments relating to the new ideas are easier to spot.

Beginning with the IDEA/ALTER framework

Every pygame program begins with the IDEA/ALTER framework, so begin by writing that into your editor and testing. At first you should just create a program that fills the background screen, displays itself, and ends when the user closes the program.

Watch Your Step

It's tempting to write that initial IDEA/ALTER code and keep bang-ing away at new code before you test your program. Resist the temptation! Test your code at every opportunity. Begin with the most basic IDEA/ALTER framework that will run. There's no point writing other code if the framework is broken. Each time you add a new element to your program, test again. This way, when things break (and they will), you'll know when it was last working — and you'll have a good idea which code caused the problem.

In this program, all your drawings will occur in the *entities* step of IDEA. You'll see examples later in this chapter where you might run drawing commands in the game loop, but if something is going to just sit there, it's best to draw it once outside the loop. Code should go in the game loop only if it needs to be run 30 times a second, or you'll slow your game down unnecessarily. Also, I put all the drawing commands in one function. The main code simply calls that function to handle the drawing. Because the drawing commands all refer to the background object, I'm passing that object to the drawStuff() function.

Transfer

All the drawing commands require coordinates. Review the "Setting up position variables" section from Chapter 4 on the computer coordinate system if you need a refresher. It's much easier to work with drawing commands if you've already planned out your coordi-nates on graph paper.

Importing the math module

Don't get anxious, but some of the drawing commands use some mathematical opera-tions (specifically the value pi). Import the math module to give your program access to this important library of functions and constants. You can do this in the same line that imports pygame if you want.

```
import pygame, math
```

Drawing a line

The most basic drawing command is the line, as shown in this bit of code:

```
#draw a line from (5, 100) to (100, 100)
pygame.draw.line(background, (255, 0, 0), (5, 100),    ←
(100, 100))
```

To draw a line, just follow these steps:

1. **Determine where the line will go.**

Use graph paper to sketch out your line. You'll need to know the starting and ending points, as well as the line thickness and color.

2. **Use the `pygame.draw.line()` function to set up the line.**

As always, check the online help if you need some assistance remembering the various parameters.

3. **Specify the surface you are drawing on.**

You can't just draw in thin air. You'll need to draw on a surface. Usually if you want some of your drawing to stay the same throughout the program, you'll draw on the background surface. If you want to animate the drawing, you'll have to put the drawing code inside the game loop, and you'll probably draw directly on the screen surface.

4. **Choose a line color.**

The color is a three-element tuple as described in Chapter 4. The three numbers specify amounts of red, green, and blue. If you're comfortable with the hex color system used in Web design, you can use hex codes by preceding each value with `0x`.

5. **Specify the beginning and end points.**

The beginning and ending points are specified using *tuples*. Recall that a tuple is a non-changeable set of values encased in parentheses. If you remember ordered pairs from math class, it's exactly the same thing. My line begins at (5, 100) and ends at (100, 100).

 Transfer

If you are drawing a lot of lines that will touch each other, look ahead in this chapter to the section called "Drawing a series of lines." Also, see the section called "Exploring anti-aliased lines" to learn how you can make smoother-looking lines.

Drawing a rectangle

You can draw filled and unfilled rectangles and squares easily with the `pygame.draw.rect()` function:

```
#draw an unfilled square
pygame.draw.rect(background, (0, 255, 0), ((200, 5),    ↩
(100, 100)), 3)
```

The rectangle requires a similar (but not identical) set of parameters. Here's how you do the coding:

1. Use the `pygame.draw.rect()` function.

2. Determine the surface to draw on.

Again, I'm drawing directly on the background, because this drawing won't change.

3. Choose a color.

The color is determined with a three-element tuple as usual.

4. Specify the `Rect` object.

It's possible to get a little confused here. A pygame `Rect` is not simply a rectangle. A `Rect` is a special object in pygame that describes a rectangular space. `Rect`s are incredibly important in pygame, and if you look it up in the online help with `help("pygame.Rect")`, you'll see how many methods (behaviors) and attributes (data) this object has. You don't need to know all of them here. It's enough now to know how to specify a `Rect`. The way I've done that here is to specify two ordered pairs. The first (200, 5) is the position of the rectangle's upper-left corner. The second pair (100, 100) is the size of the rectangle. These two pairs themselves go into a tuple, so the `Rect` is defined as ((200, 5), (100, 100)). This tells Python to create a 100 by 100 square with the upper-left corner at (200, 5). The lower-right corner of this square will be (200 + 100, 5 + 100), or (300, 105). Pygame uses these two tuples to create a `Rect` object and draw it on the screen.

5. Choose a border width.

The last parameter determines how wide the line defining the rectangle will be in pixels. If you set the width to zero, pygame will draw a filled-in rectangle.

 Information Kiosk

You can also draw a filled rectangle by creating a surface, filling it in, and blitting it in place. That's how you made the square in the `moveBox.py` program back in Chapter 4.

Drawing a circle

Circles require a center point, a radius, and a color. The circle-drawing command obliges:

```
#draw a filled circle
pygame.draw.circle(background, (0, 0, 255), (400, 50), 45)
```

Step Into the Real World

If you look carefully at my code, you'll see I completely skipped the line-width parameter for the circle command. You might wonder how I knew I could leave out the line width. Take a close look at the specification for the `pygame.draw.circle` command from the online help:

```
pygame.draw.circle(Surface, color, pos, radius, width=0)
```

Notice especially the part that says `width=0`. Some parameters (like width) are set up with default values. If you don't specify the width, it will be set to zero. If a parameter has a default value listed in the online help, you can skip it. Any parameters that do not have a default value must be filled in.

Here's how you draw a circle:

1. **Use the `pygame.draw.circle()` function.**

As always, check it out to see what parameters the function takes.

2. **Choose the drawing surface.**

Like every drawing command in this section, I'm drawing to the background.

3. **Specify a color.**

Again, no surprises here.

4. **Pick the center point.**

This tuple indicates where the center will go.

5. **Indicate the radius.**

The radius is the distance from the center point. Remember, the circle will be twice as tall and twice as wide as the radius, so if you want a circle to be 100 pixels tall, you should specify a radius of 50.

6. **Specify the line width.**

If you want an outlined circle, describe how wide (in pixels) this line should be. If you set the line width to 0 (or don't specify it at all), the circle will be filled in.

Drawing an ellipse

An ellipse is an oval shape. Pygame allows you to draw an ellipse by specifying its *bounding rectangle* — the smallest rectangle that will contain the ellipse — as shown here.

```
#draw an ellipse
pygame.draw.ellipse(background, (0xCC, 0xCC, 0x00),        ↩
((150, 150), (150, 100)), 0)
```

The ellipse is drawn much like the other shapes, but it uses a rectangle to describe its shape. Here's how you do it:

1. **Decide where you want to draw the ellipse.**

I use the background, as always. The `pygame.draw.ellipse()` function is used to create an ellipse.

2. **Choose a color.**

This time I used a little imagination. I wanted a dark tan, so I started with yellow (255, 255, 0) and decided to make it a few shades darker. This is actually easier to do in hex than in base 10, so I made my new shade (0xCC, 0xCC, 0).

3. **Describe the bounding rectangle.**

You don't actually have to determine the ellipse formula mathematically. (Good thing, too . . . I'd be digging through your sophomore geometry text now, looking for it. Or maybe you'd just give up.) All you have to do is describe an imaginary rectangle. The computer will draw the largest possible ellipse that will fit in that rectangle.

Step Into the Real World

It doesn't seem logical that base 16 would be easier to work in than base ten, but it's true, especially if you use an old Web developer's trick. Back in the ancient days of the Internet, Web browsers could be counted on to handle only a few colors well. These colors all mapped to hex values that followed a very specific pattern. Each color value could be only 00, 33, 66, 99, CC, or FF, with 00 being the darkest possible value and FF being the brightest for each color. With this system, FF0000 is a standard red color. The next shade darker would be CC0000, and the next shade lighter is FF3333. Even though the Web has long moved beyond this "Web-safe palette," these numbers are easy enough to work with that many programmers still use them as a starting place and then tweak them when necessary. That's why I wrote this color in hex.

Truth be known, you can actually use color names like "red" and "bisque." (I have no idea what color "bisque" is. My design disability appears again.) Use `pygame.color.Color("red")` for red. If you want to see all the color names pygame supports and their corresponding RGB values, type the following code into your IDE (after importing pygame):

```
for colorName, value in pygame.color.THECOLORS.items():
    print colorName, value
```

If you must know, pygame indicates several versions of bisque. Standard bisque is (255, 228, 196). I plugged those values into `colorViewer.py` and got a sort of creamy pink. This is exactly why I tend to use numeric values. Okay, (255, 228, 196) isn't very charming, but it's unambiguous. Come to think of it, I'd have to use burlywood2 (238, 197, 145) instead. At least it sounds a little more manly.

With `colorViewer.py` and an understanding of RGB colors, you can make any color you want, and modify it as you need. Since the `pygame.color.Color` trick creates RGB values anyway, you might as well create them directly.

4. **Choose the line width.**

As usual, specify a width of 0 to fill in the shape or any other value to determine the width of the line in pixels. (Truthfully, the width has a default parameter, so I could have left it out, but I decided to explicitly set the width.) A width of 0 causes a filled shape.

 Information Kiosk

If you use a square as the bounding rectangle, your ellipse will actually be a circle. Use this technique if it's easier for you to build a circle with a bounding box than it is to use the center-and-radius technique.

Drawing an arc (portion of a circle)

An *arc* is a curved segment of a circle or ellipse. Think of it as building an ellipse, but then drawing only a portion of the ellipse.

```
#draw an arc
pygame.draw.arc(background, (0, 0, 0), ((5, 150),
(100, 100)), 0, math.pi/2, 5)
```

1. **First you choose a drawing surface and a color (but you knew that by now).**

Use the `pygame.draw.arc()` function as the foundation of your arc.

2. **Build the bounding rectangle.**

This is actually just a bit tricky. You're not building the bounding rectangle of the arc, but of the entire ellipse (or circle) the arc will be selected from. Start by thinking about the entire ellipse.

3. **Specify starting and ending points.**

Pygame does most of its angle measurements the math way, using radians rather than degrees. If this is unfamiliar to you, I'll explain in more detail in Chapter 9. Radians are almost always expressed as fractions of *pi*, a mathematical constant roughly equivalent to 3.14159. For example, 7 pi / 4 means seven times pi divided by 4. Radians are usually measured counterclockwise from the rightmost point of the circle. Figure 5-6 shows some common measurements in radians:

4. **Use the built-in `math.pi` constant.**

Pi itself is a little awkward, which is why mathematicians simply use the π symbol or word *pi* to specify it. To avoid working with the awkward decimal values, use the special `math.pi` constant included in Python's `math` module. You'll need to import the `math` module to use this constant. Look at the beginning of the program (where I usually import pygame) and you'll see that I also imported `math`.

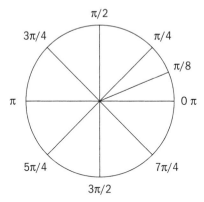

Figure 5-6: Some common angle measurements in radians.

Drawing a series of lines

You might want to draw a series of connected lines, with the endpoint of one line acting as the starting point of the next. The `pygame.draw.lines()` function works a lot like the `pygame.draw.line` function, except rather than requiring a single line, it expects a list of points:

```
#draw lines,
points = (
    (370, 160),
    (370, 237),
    (372, 193),
    (411, 194),
    (412, 237),
    (412, 160),
    (412, 237),
    (432, 227),
    (436, 196),
    (433, 230)
)
    pygame.draw.lines(background, (0xFF, 0x00, 0x00),          ↩
False, False, points, 3)
```

Here's how you create a series of lines:

1. Create a tuple full of points.

It's easiest to do this before you call the `draw.lines` function. You can use graph paper to determine the points. After you know how to get information from the mouse, you can easily write a program to retrieve coordinate points from the screen. The `pointList` is a tuple containing other tuples. Each element of the list is a coordinate pair, which is another tuple.

2. Start the `pygame.draw.lines()` function.

3. Specify the drawing surface in the usual way.

4. Pick a color as you have done for the other drawing commands.

5. Decide whether the lines should be closed with a Boolean value.

If you put `True` here, pygame will automatically draw a line from the end of the group back to the beginning, making a closed-off shape.

6. Specify the point list.

You've already created a point list in Step 1, so it's easy to make a reference to it in this step.

7. Determine the line width.

Set the line width in pixels. You cannot fill in the shape with a value of `0`. (If you want a filled-in shape, use the `pygame.draw.polygon` command described next).

Drawing a polygon

You create polygons using a command almost identical to `pygame.draw.lines()`. A polygon is always closed, and can be filled in. Here's what that code looks like:

```
#draw polygon
points = (
  (137, 372),
```

```
    (232, 319),
    (383, 335),
    (442, 389),
    (347, 432),
    (259, 379),
    (220, 439),
    (132, 392)
)
pygame.draw.polygon(background, (0x33, 0xFF, 0x33), points)
```

If you understand `draw.lines`, `draw.polygon` is even easier, as you'll see in the following steps:

1. **Create a point list.**

Graph paper or a program-driven system are good ways to generate lists of points.

2. **Determine the drawing surface and color.**

There's nothing new about these requirements.

3. **Set the point list.**

Polygons require point lists, just like line sets.

4. **Determine the line width.**

The line width can be set to a number of pixels. If you choose to leave the line width out or set the width to zero, the polygon will be filled in.

Exploring anti-aliased lines

The term *anti-aliasing* refers to a graphics trick used to make diagonal lines look smoother on a computer screen. Pygame includes a number of commands that allow you to turn anti-aliasing on, including anti-aliased versions of the `line` and `lines` commands. The best way to explain this illusion is through an illustration. I've added two diagonal lines to the `drawDemo.py` program:

```
#compare normal and anti-aliased diagonal lines
pygame.draw.line(background, (0, 0, 0), (480, 425),      ↩
(550, 325), 1)
pygame.draw.aaline(background, (0, 0, 0), (500, 425),    ↩
(570, 325), 1)
```

 Watch Your Step

The final parameter of `pygame.draw.aaline()` isn't the line width, as it has been in nearly every other `pygame.draw` function. Instead, this parameter describes whether the line should be blended with the background. You will almost always want the blending behavior if you're using anti-aliasing, so the typical value is 1. You can leave out the final parameter, and pygame will set it to one for you.

The `pygame.draw.line()` function draws a normal (non-anti-aliased) line, and the `pygame.draw.aaline()` function uses the anti-aliasing trick. When you look at the `drawDemo.py` program at its normal resolution in the lower-right corner of Figure 5-7, the second line (the one on the right) looks smoother. Note that I've darkened most of the image so you can concentrate on the diagonal lines discussed in this section.

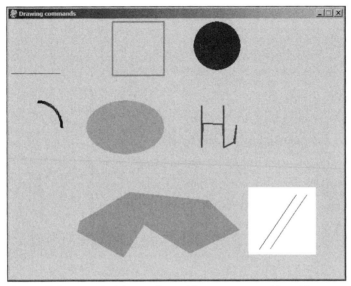

Figure 5-7: The second of the two diagonal lines uses a smoothing trick.

To see what's going on, take a look at Figure 5-8, which is an extreme close-up of the relevant part of the `drawing.py` output screen.

Step Into the Real World

Anti-aliasing sounds pretty great, but it's got a couple of serious drawbacks. First, in pygame you can't set the width of an anti-aliased line. Your line has to be 1 "virtual pixel" wide — which will actually be about 3 – 5 pixels wide, depending on the angle of your line. Also, anti-aliased lines can be a lot slower to draw, because the computer has to do a lot more work. One more issue is common in painting applications, but not as much in the real-time drawing of pygame: The shading pixels are combined with the background color. If you anti-alias a black line on a white background, but then change the background to blue, you'll see a white "halo" around your line, and the illusion is completely broken. I'm amazed how often I see graphics with this little halo effect on the Web.

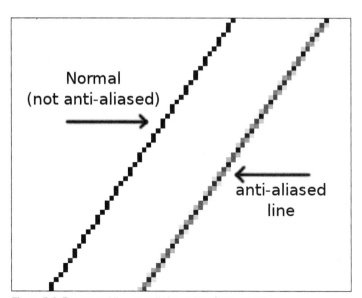

Figure 5-8: The second line actually has a lot of gray pixels!

Figure 5-8 reveals the secret of anti-aliasing. The ordinary line looks jagged because it is. Most display hardware actually generates rectangular pixels. If a line is absolutely vertical or horizontal, the line looks perfectly smooth, but diagonal lines ultimately have a "stairstep" look to them. If you use anti-aliasing, the computer calculates the background color and generates "in-between" colors. In this case, I drew a black line on a white surface, so pygame used various values of gray to draw a thicker line. When you view the line at a normal scale, your eye is tricked into thinking the line is smooth when it really isn't.

Getting mouse data

Drawing in pygame requires a lot of coordinate pairs. (No wonder I've suggested using graph paper throughout the chapter.) If you're writing a program that uses a lot of drawing commands, graph paper will really help you out. Of course, you can also use some functions of pygame to get useful information. I actually used a dirty trick: I added some code to have pygame tell me where various places on the screen are. If you look at the event-handling code for drawDemo.py, you'll see that I added some very handy commands:

```
for event in pygame.event.get():
    if event.type == pygame.QUIT:
        keepGoing = False
    elif event.type == pygame.MOUSEBUTTONUP:
        print pygame.mouse.get_pos()
```

In the normal IDEA/ALTER loop, you've checked for only the `pygame.QUIT` event, but pygame can respond to a lot of other events as well. I give much more complete coverage of mouse events later in this chapter, but here's a little preview. When you click the screen of `drawDemo.py`, Python prints out the current screen coordinates in the console. Figure 5-9 illustrates the program running with a few coordinates being displayed.

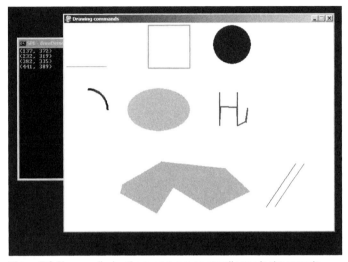

Figure 5-9: You can display the current mouse coordinates in the console.

Here's how to do it:

1. Write the normal event-handling routine.

Every pygame program has an event-handling routine, so you're simply going to modify the basic routine you already wrote for IDEA/ALTER.

2. Check for the MOUSEBUTTONUP event.

Use an `elif` command to see whether the user has released the mouse button. (Normally you don't check for mouse presses, but mouse releases. This is actually the behavior the user is expecting.)

3. Get the current coordinate of the mouse.

The `pygame.mouse.get_pos()` function returns the current position of the mouse as a coordinate pair.

4. Print the mouse position to the console.

Even though it's not part of the pygame screen, you can still use the `print` command to send output to the console just like you did in the first three chapters.

Saving and Loading Images

It's nice to know how to draw your own images in Python, but much of the time you'll use some other program to create your images and load them into pygame surfaces. It's important to know how to load images from a graphic file, and how to save the images your program creates to the hard drive.

Importing images

The most common way to get images into your games is to generate the image in some other graphical tool and import it into pygame as a surface. Figure 5-10 shows a program with a picture of me.

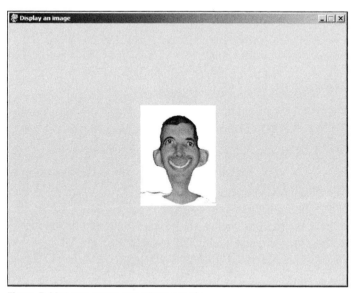

Figure 5-10: I look almost this silly in real life.

The code for `face.py` is a simple variant of the IDEA/ALTER model with an image surface:

```
""" face.py
    draw an image on the screen"""

import pygame
pygame.init()

def main():
    screen = pygame.display.set_mode((640, 480))
    pygame.display.set_caption("Display an image")

    background = pygame.Surface(screen.get_size())
    background = background.convert()
    background.fill((255, 255, 0))

    face = pygame.image.load("andy.jpg")
    face = face.convert()

    clock = pygame.time.Clock()
    keepGoing = True
    while keepGoing:
        clock.tick(30)
        for event in pygame.event.get():
            if event.type == pygame.QUIT:
                keepGoing = False

        screen.blit(background, (0, 0))
        screen.blit(face, (250, 150))

        pygame.display.flip()

if __name__ == "__main__":
    main()
```

Getting a basic image to work in pygame is very simple:

1. Prepare the image.

Think carefully about images you use in your games. Don't use any images that you do not have the right to work with. It's also important that the image is an appropriate size for the game, and is in a useable format. (All the most common image formats — including GIF, BMP, PNG, and JPG — work just fine.)

2. Put the image in the code directory.

To simplify things, put your image in the same directory as your program if you can. This means you won't have to write a complex path for retrieving your image.

3. **Make standard IDEA/ALTER code.**

Begin the framework code as always, choosing a background color. Make sure your basic framework is working right before you add the image code.

4. **Add the image with the `pygame.image.load()` function.**

This function creates a pygame surface displaying the image.

```
face = pygame.image.load("andy.jpg")
```

Load the image in the "Entities" part of the IDEA sequence, because the image will become one of the entities you will manipulate.

5. **Convert the image with the `convert()` method.**

You already learned to convert surfaces into pygame's native color format. This is much more important with image surfaces, because each image format has its own way of storing image data.

Watch Your Step

If you don't convert the image once before the loop begins, pygame will do automatic conversion, dramatically reducing your game's performance characteristics.

6. **Blit the image.**

Just like any surface, you can use the `blit()` method to copy the image onto the screen:

```
screen.blit(background, (0, 0))
screen.blit(face, (250, 150))
```

Watch Your Step

If you want the image to be displayed over the background, you must blit the background first and *then* blit the image. All blits are done in order; newer blits will overwrite older ones, and will appear to be in front of them.

Transfer

I'll talk a lot more about images in Chapter 8, when you learn how to add transparency to images, make animated images, and do other fun stuff with image files.

Saving images

Python also includes a neat feature for saving images. The pygame..image.save() function allows you to save an image in a number of standard formats. All you need to supply is a surface and a filename. The following simple program doesn't have its own graphical display at all! Instead, it creates a Surface object with an interesting image — and saves it to a file called circles.bmp.

```
""" saveCircles.py
    builds a simple pattern of circles and
    saves the result as "circles.bmp" """

import pygame
pygame.init()

def main():
    #no display!
    background = pygame.Surface((640, 480))
    background.fill((0, 0, 0))

    for i in range(1, 320, 3):
        pygame.draw.circle(background, (0xFF, 0x00,      ↩
0x00), (i, i), i, 1)
        pygame.draw.circle(background, (0x00, 0x00,      ↩
0xFF), (640 - i, i), i, 1)
        pygame.draw.circle(background, (0x00, 0x00,      ↩
0xFF), (i, 480 - i), i, 1)
        pygame.draw.circle(background, (0xFF, 0x00,      ↩
0x00), (640 - i, 480 - i), i, 1)
        pygame.draw.circle(background, (0xFF, 0xFF,      ↩
0xFF), (320, 240), i, 1)

    #save the background
    pygame.image.save(background, "circles.bmp")

    #no need for a main loop here!
    print "look in current directory for circles.bmp"

if __name__ == "__main__":
    main()
```

The drawCircles.py program doesn't have any graphical output of its own, but when you run it, you'll find an image like Figure 5-11 in the current directory. (It looks a lot better in color . . .)

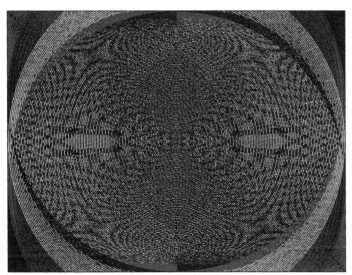

Figure 5-11: `drawCircles` created this interesting drawing called `circles.bmp`.

Using Text

Pygame treats text as a special kind of surface. To make a text display on the screen, you first create a special element called a *font* and use it to *render* a specific phrase. The render process creates a surface you can blit just like any other surface.

Watch Your Step

The term *font* here is a little misleading, because many people use this term to describe the various letter-shape files in their computer. Technically, the thing most of us call a font is actually a *typeface*, and a font is a particular combination of a specific typeface at a specific size (for example, 10-point Arial). As you'll see, the `pygame.font.Font` object actually comes closer to the original meaning of a font than the more common uses of the word do. I'll use the word *font* when I'm talking about the files on your computer that describe how letters look, and I'll use `pygame.font.Font` (or `pygame.font.SysFont`) when I'm talking about the actual pygame objects.

Pygame actually supports several kinds of fonts. The two most commonly used are

System fonts: These are the fonts already installed on your computer system. The advantage of using a system font is that it reduces the file size of your program. If the user already has the font installed on his system, you don't have to include it in your program. Of course, if the user *doesn't* have the font you've specified, it will be replaced by a generic font, which may or may not look as you intended. If you know all your users have Windows XP installed, you can freely use any of the fonts commonly installed with that system. Just remember that anybody using a Mac or Linux machine will get a default font instead.

Custom fonts: You can also specify a particular font you want pygame to use in your game. This font doesn't have to be installed on the user's machine, but it must be included in your application. The great thing about this is it allows you to use all kinds of fonts in your applications. The downside is you must obtain permission for that font. Fortunately, lots of really great free fonts are out there. The www.pygame.org resources site has links to several outstanding sources of free fonts.

Information Kiosk

I've discovered that system fonts don't travel very well. If you want your program to work on a wide variety of platforms, it's much safer to use the custom font technique. This is doubly true when you create executable versions of your program, as shown in Appendix C on the Web site.

Using a system font

The system font technique allows you to create a surface from one of the fonts installed on your PC. Figure 5-12 illustrates such a font using the Comic Sans MS font installed in Windows XP.

Figure 5-12: Text is fun and very useful.

showText.py creates a system font and then renders a surface using that font:

```python
""" showText.py
    illustrates basic text manipulation
    in pygame: making a font and rendering
    it to make text surfaces """

import pygame
pygame.init()

def main():
    screen = pygame.display.set_mode((640, 480))
    pygame.display.set_caption("display some text")

    background = pygame.Surface(screen.get_size())
    background = background.convert()
    background.fill((0, 0, 0))

    myFont = pygame.font.SysFont("Comic Sans MS", 30)
    label = myFont.render("Text is Fun!!!", 1,  ↩
(255, 255, 0))

    clock = pygame.time.Clock()
    keepGoing = True
    while keepGoing:
        clock.tick(30)
        for event in pygame.event.get():
            if event.type == pygame.QUIT:
                keepGoing = False

        screen.blit(background, (0, 0))
        screen.blit(label, (100, 100))

        pygame.display.flip()
if __name__ == "__main__":
    main()
```

Here's how to build a texture using a system font:

1. **Begin with the standard framework.**

I *told* you this would come in handy.

2. **Create a SysFont object.**

The pygame.font.SysFont() function creates a font object based on the system fonts built into the machine. It requires two parameters: the font name and the font size in pixels.

```python
myFont = pygame.font.SysFont("Comic Sans MS", 20)
```

Information Kiosk

If you want to know which fonts are installed on a particular computer, you can get a list of the fonts via the `pygame.font.get_fonts()` function. However, just because a font exists on one computer doesn't mean it will exist on others. The `SysFont` function is predictable only if you use a standard font *and* you know your users are using the same setup and have that font installed.

3. **Render some text using the newly created `SysFont` object.**

Once you've defined a font object, you can use its `render()` method to create text surfaces.

```
    label = myFont.render("Text is Fun!!!", 1, (255,
255, 0))
```

The `render()` method generates a new surface object you can manipulate just like an image.

4. **Specify the text you want to display.**

The first parameter is the text you wish to display on the screen.

5. **Determine if you want to anti-alias the text.**

Anti-aliasing causes the text to look smoother, but it can slow down your program. Use 1 to turn on anti-aliasing or 0 to turn it off.

6. **Set the text color.**

Specify a color in the normal way.

7. **Store the results of the `render()` method to a variable containing a `Surface` object.**

The `render()` method doesn't draw anything onto the screen. All it does is create a variable — a `Surface` object that you can draw on-screen by using a `blit()` method (just as you can for any other surface).

8. **Blit the surface to the screen.**

Use the `blit()` method to draw the surface to the screen. The blit is how you specify where the text should be drawn.

Information Kiosk

If you specify a font that doesn't exist on the remote system, pygame will choose its default font, which looks fine but isn't anything special. The user will still see the text, but not necessarily as you expected. If you really want the generic font, just use None for the font name.

Using a custom font

System fonts are great for testing, because it's easy to know what fonts are on your own system. However, they'll cause you problems when you give programs to other people, because there's no way to be certain what font a user has installed. Fortunately, it's very easy to use custom fonts within pygame. You can include a font file with your game and have pygame use that file whether the font is installed or not.

Watch Your Step

Font manipulation in pygame depends on the `SDL_ttf` extension. This is usually available, but if you have problems with fonts, check to see that this module is available.

The `customFont.py` program featured in Figure 5-13 demonstrates use of an external font file.

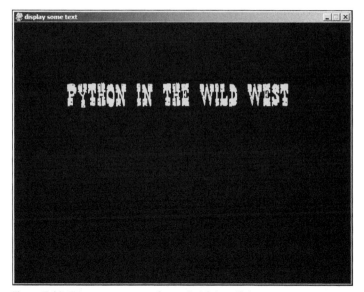

Figure 5-13: This program uses a font called Gringo Nights.

I found the font used in Figure 5-13 by doing a Web search. This particular font's called Gringo Nights by Jakob Fisher. (If you like this font, you can find a huge number of other great fonts at his Web site: `www.pizzadude.dk`.)

The Python code for a custom font is very similar to the system font technique:

```
""" customFont.py
    use of a customized font """

import pygame
pygame.init()

def main():
    screen = pygame.display.set_mode((640, 480))
    pygame.display.set_caption("display some text")

    background = pygame.Surface(screen.get_size())
    background = background.convert()
    background.fill((0, 0, 0))

    myFont = pygame.font.Font("GringoNights.ttf", 40)
    label = myFont.render("Python in the Wild West", 1, ↩
(255, 255, 0))

    clock = pygame.time.Clock()
    keepGoing = True
    while keepGoing:
        clock.tick(30)
        for event in pygame.event.get():
            if event.type == pygame.QUIT:
                keepGoing = False

        screen.blit(background, (0, 0))
        screen.blit(label, (100, 100))

        pygame.display.flip()

if __name__ == "__main__":
    main()
```

The main difference between ordinary fonts and system fonts is ensuring you have the font available, and using the `pygame.font.Font()` object rather than the `pygame.font.SysFont()` object.

1. **Acquire the font you wish to use.**

Pygame requires `.ttf` font files. These files are readily available on the Internet.

 ## Watch Your Step

Fonts are protected by the same kinds of copyright laws as other resources. Make sure you have the right to use and distribute the font. Fortunately, there are a lot of generous font authors who are glad to let you use their fonts for free as long as you give them credit. Of course, if you see a really great shareware font, you should use it and pay the (usually very reasonable) fee to support the author.

2. **Place the font in your program's main directory.**

As you're starting out, keep all files in the same directory as your main program so your file-management code doesn't get too complex.

3. **Use the `pygame.font.Font()` command to build a `Font` object.**

The `Font` object works just like the one you made with `SysFont`.

Watch Your Step

If you specify a font file that doesn't exist, you'll get an error message and the program will break.

Responding to Basic Events

You've got to have interaction if it's going to be a game, so it's important to know how to handle user events. You built the basic framework for event handling in Chapter 4, but now you're ready to look at how to deal with basic mouse and keyboard input. Figure 5-14 shows a very simple program that demonstrates these basic events.

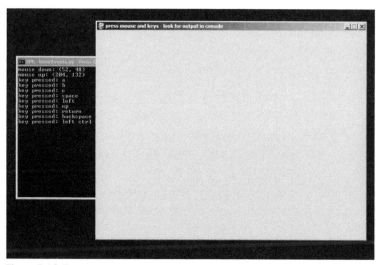

Figure 5-14: The console shows when the user presses a key or clicks the mouse.

Information Kiosk

Notice that the output for Figure 5-14 doesn't happen on the main screen, but on the console. This is a useful debugging trick, because it allows you to send a message without having to create a font and render it.

The basic event-handling structure in pygame is very straightforward. Inside the main loop, you collect events with the pygame.event.get() function. You then check each event to see what type it is, and then do work based on the event type. So far, you've mostly been checking for the event type pygame.QUIT. Of course, pygame supports a lot of other event types too. basicEvents.py illustrates a standard way to read the keyboard and mouse:

```
""" basicEvents.py
    demonstrate essential
    mouse and keyboard events"""

import pygame
pygame.init()

def main():

    screen = pygame.display.set_mode((640, 480))
    pygame.display.set_caption("press mouse and keys -  ↩
look for output in console")

    background = pygame.Surface(screen.get_size())
    background = background.convert()
    background.fill(pygame.color.Color("yellow"))

    keepGoing = True
    clock = pygame.time.Clock()

    while keepGoing:
        for event in pygame.event.get():
            if event.type == pygame.QUIT:
                keepGoing = False
            elif event.type == pygame.KEYDOWN:
                keyName = pygame.key.name(event.key)
                print "key pressed:", keyName
                if event.key == pygame.K_ESCAPE:
                    keepGoing = False
            elif event.type == pygame.MOUSEBUTTONDOWN:
                print "mouse down:",
                pygame.mouse.get_pos()
            elif event.type == pygame.MOUSEBUTTONUP:
                print "mouse up:", pygame.mouse.get_pos()

        screen.blit(background, (0, 0))
        pygame.display.flip()

if __name__ == "__main__":
    main()
```

The `basicEvents.py` program is a standard IDEA/ALTER structure with some new pieces built into the event-handler. Here's how to set it up:

1. **Start with the IDEA/ALTER structure.**

Even though I'm not going to display anything on the screen but the background, the event-handling mechanism is tied to the display timing, so I still need to create a basic display.

2. **Check for all events using the `for event in pygame.event.get()` structure.**

Remember, this sets up a loop of all events that happen in the current frame. Each time through the loop, the current event is contained in the variable `event`.

```
for event in pygame.event.get():
```

3. **Check for `pygame.QUIT` as usual.**

Event types are tied to constants in the pygame module. If you look up pygame on the online help, you'll see a list of the event constants after the label "DATA."

 Information Kiosk

Constants are something like variables, but their values are not meant to change during the run of a program. Normally, programmers use constants to describe some value by giving it a name, so it's easier to remember. All the event values are really integers, but it's much easier to remember `pygame.QUIT` than 12 (the integer that pygame uses internally to represent the `quit` command). By convention, constant names are rendered in all uppercase.

If the user chooses to quit (by closing the pygame window), set `keepGoing` to `False`:

```
if event.type == pygame.QUIT:
    keepGoing = False
```

4. **Check for keyboard input.**

Of course, `QUIT` isn't the only event pygame can read. If the user pressed a key on the keyboard, `event.type` will be equal to `pygame.KEYDOWN`:

```
elif event.type == pygame.KEYDOWN:
```

5. **Determine which key was pressed.**

If pygame registered a keyboard event, the event will also have a `key` attribute that tells you which key was pressed. Each key on the keyboard has an integer assigned to it. `event.key` returns that integer.

6. **Print out the key name.**

In this example, I want to print something to the console each time a key is pressed, and I want to include the name of the key that was pressed. Pygame includes a function that allows me to convert from a key integer to a human-readable name:

```
keyName = pygame.key.name(event.key)
```

`event.key` returns the integer code corresponding to the key that was pressed. `pygame.key.name()` converts that integer to a human-readable form.

```
print "key pressed:", keyName
```

7. **Look for the Escape key.**

The most common thing you'll do with keyboard input is check if certain keys have been pressed. In this case, I want to close the program when the user presses the Escape key.

```
if event.key == pygame.K_ESCAPE:
    keepGoing = False
```

Note that this code is inside the `event.type` `if` statement, so first I check to see whether the current event is a keyboard event, and then do something (print out the key name) for *all* keyboard events. Now I'm checking the event to see whether the key is a specific key (in this case, the Escape key).

Pygame has a constant for every key on the keyboard. Use `help("pygame")` in the console to see the list of keyboard constants. Each of these constants begins with `K_`. Even the special keys (function keys, arrow keys, shift keys, spacebar, and so on) have constants associated with them.

8. **Check for a `mouse` `down` event.**

Mouse events are much like keyboard events. You can actually check for several different kinds of mouse events, but in this program I'm looking only for when the mouse button is pressed and when it is released.

```
elif event.type == pygame.MOUSEBUTTONDOWN:
    print "mouse down:", pygame.mouse.get_pos()
```

If a mouse button is down, pygame will create an event with the `MOUSEBUTTONDOWN` type. You can find out where the mouse is by evaluating the `mouse.get_pos()` function.

Step Into the Real World

In a typical game, you might use an `if-elif` structure to check for each key in your game. For example, you might handle what will happen with the left, right, up, and down keys, and the spacebar.

Transfer

I'm showing you only the most basic event handling here so you can get your painting program working. Look ahead to Chapter 9 for some more advanced techniques, like real-time keyboard reading.

Making a Line-Drawing Program

Before you make the full-blown paint program featured at the beginning of this chapter, combine your knowledge of events and drawing commands by building a simpler drawing program that makes straight lines. Figure 5-15 shows such a program, called `lines.py`.

Figure 5-15: Drag the mouse to draw a line on the screen.

Begin a line by clicking the mouse button and dragging. When you release the mouse, the program draws a line between the point where the mouse button was pressed and where it was released.

The actual program combines the `line` command with some basic event handling:

```
""" lines.py
    combine event handling and
    drawing commands to build
    a prototype drawing program """

import pygame
```

```
pygame.init()

def main():
    screen = pygame.display.set_mode((640, 480))
    pygame.display.set_caption("Draw lines with the mouse")

    background = pygame.Surface(screen.get_size())
    background.fill((255, 255,255))

    clock = pygame.time.Clock()
    keepGoing = True
    while(keepGoing):
        clock.tick(30)

        for event in pygame.event.get():
            if event.type == pygame.QUIT:
                keepGoing = False
            elif event.type == pygame.MOUSEBUTTONDOWN:
                lineStart = pygame.mouse.get_pos()
            elif event.type == pygame.MOUSEBUTTONUP:
                lineEnd = pygame.mouse.get_pos()
                pygame.draw.line(background, (0, 0, 0),  ↩
lineStart, lineEnd, 3)

        screen.blit(background, (0, 0))
        pygame.display.flip()

if __name__ == "__main__":
    main()
```

Begin, as usual, with the IDEA structure — and flesh it out like this:

1. **Build a functioning IDEA program.**

As always, test the basic framework before you add anything new.

2. **Test for a mouse button press in the event handler.**

As part of the event-handling process, check to see whether the user is pressing any mouse key. If so, the event type will be `pygame.MOUSEBUTTONDOWN`.

```
            elif event.type == pygame.MOUSEBUTTONDOWN:
```

Information Kiosk

The previous condition tests to see whether any mouse buttons are currently pressed, but doesn't distinguish between the various buttons. To find out which button has been pressed, you'll need the `mouse.get_pressed()` function. I explain this function later in this chapter.

> ## Step Into the Real World
>
> Truthfully, most drawing programs do draw a preview version of the line as you're moving the mouse. I want to keep this example simple to make sure you've got the basic ideas. If you want to see a version of this program with a preview line, take a look at linePrev.py on the Web site that accompanies this book.

3. Determine the current position of the mouse.

The mouse module has a handy function called get_pos() that is used exactly for this purpose. It returns a tuple (ordered pair) describing where the mouse currently is on the screen.

4. Store the mouse position to lineStart.

This variable is the starting point of the line you will eventually draw. Notice that you can easily store a tuple to a variable:

```
lineStart = pygame.mouse.get_pos()
```

5. Check to see when the mouse is released.

You won't actually draw the line until the mouse button has been released. The event type will equal pygame.MOUSEBUTTONUP when this has occurred:

```
elif event.type == pygame.MOUSEBUTTONUP:
```

6. Determine the line's ending position.

Use the pygame.mouse.get_pos() function again to get the mouse's current condition. Store this value to the lineEnd variable:

```
lineEnd = pygame.mouse.get_pos()
```

7. Draw the line.

The only time you want to draw a line in this program is when the user has released the mouse button. If he has released the button, he must have also pressed it, so you will have meaningful values for the beginning and end of the line (lineBegin is where the user clicked the mouse, lineEnd is where he released it).

```
pygame.draw.line(background,                    ↵
(0, 0, 0), lineStart, lineEnd, 3)
```

> ## Information Kiosk
>
> I chose to draw the line directly on the background, because I want the drawing to last beyond one frame. If you draw on the screen, the drawing will disappear as soon as you blit the background on the next frame. Drawing to the background makes the image part of the background; it becomes more permanent.

Creating the Painting Program

You now have all the skills you need to build the painting program that debuted at the beginning of this chapter. Although this code is slightly more involved than the other programs you've seen, it's still closely related to the IDEA framework, with only a few new wrinkles thrown in. Get an overview of the code here, and then I'll show you the details.

```
""" paint.py
    a simple paint program"""

import pygame

def checkKeys(myData):
    """test for various keyboard inputs"""

    #extract the data
    (event, background, drawColor, lineWidth, keepGoing) = myData

    if event.key == pygame.K_q:
        #quit
        keepGoing = False
    elif event.key == pygame.K_c:
        #clear screen
        background.fill((255, 255, 255))
    elif event.key == pygame.K_s:
        #save picture
        pygame.image.save(background, "painting.bmp")
    elif event.key == pygame.K_l:
        #load picture
        background = pygame.image.load("painting.bmp")
    elif event.key == pygame.K_r:
        #red
        drawColor = (255, 0, 0)
    elif event.key == pygame.K_g:
        #green
        drawColor = (0, 255, 0)
    elif event.key == pygame.K_w:
        #white
        drawColor = (255, 255, 255)
    elif event.key == pygame.K_b:
        #blue
        drawColor = (0, 0, 255)
    elif event.key == pygame.K_k:
        #black
        drawColor = (0, 0, 0)

    #line widths
    elif event.key == pygame.K_1:
        lineWidth = 1
    elif event.key == pygame.K_2:
        lineWidth = 2
    elif event.key == pygame.K_3:
        lineWidth = 3
    elif event.key == pygame.K_4:
        lineWidth = 4
```

```
        elif event.key == pygame.K_5:
            lineWidth = 5
        elif event.key == pygame.K_6:
            lineWidth = 6
        elif event.key == pygame.K_7:
            lineWidth = 7
        elif event.key == pygame.K_8:
            lineWidth = 8
        elif event.key == pygame.K_9:
            lineWidth = 9

        #return all values
        myData = (event, background, drawColor, lineWidth, keepGoing)
        return myData

    def showStats(drawColor, lineWidth):
        """ shows the current statistics """
        myFont = pygame.font.SysFont("None", 20)
        stats = "color: %s, width: %d" % (drawColor, lineWidth)
        statSurf = myFont.render(stats, 1, (drawColor))
        return statSurf

    def main():
        pygame.init()
        screen = pygame.display.set_mode((640, 480))
        pygame.display.set_caption("Paint:  (r)ed, (g)reen, (b)lue, (w)hite,   ↵
blac(k), (1-9) width, (c)lear, (s)ave, (l)oad, (q)uit")

        background = pygame.Surface(screen.get_size())
        background.fill((255, 255, 255))

        clock = pygame.time.Clock()
        keepGoing = True
        lineStart = (0, 0)
        drawColor = (0, 0, 0)
        lineWidth = 3

        while keepGoing:
            clock.tick(30)

            for event in pygame.event.get():
                if event.type == pygame.QUIT:
                    keepGoing = False
                elif event.type == pygame.MOUSEMOTION:
                    lineEnd = pygame.mouse.get_pos()
                    if pygame.mouse.get_pressed() == (1, 0, 0):
                        pygame.draw.line(background, drawColor, lineStart,   ↵
lineEnd, lineWidth)
                    lineStart = lineEnd
                elif event.type == pygame.KEYDOWN:
                    myData = (event, background, drawColor, lineWidth, keepGoing)
                    myData = checkKeys(myData)
                    (event, background, drawColor, lineWidth, keepGoing) = myData

            screen.blit(background, (0, 0))
            myLabel = showStats(drawColor, lineWidth)
            screen.blit(myLabel, (450, 450))
```

```
        pygame.display.flip()

if __name__ == "__main__":
    main()
```

Overview of paint.py

Paint.py lets the user draw images onto the screen and save them to the disk. Like any other program, paint.py is centered around data. Here are the main variables of the painting program:

- **background:** All of the pygame programs have featured a background surface, but the background in this program is especially important, because it represents the actual drawing.

- **event:** Since much of the program revolves around figuring out what event just occurred, the event object is especially important in this program.

- **drawColor:** This variable represents what color the user wants to draw with. When the user chooses another color, he is really changing the value of drawColor.

- **lineWidth:** This variable represents the width of the drawing line. The user is actually changing the value of this variable when she chooses a new line width with the number keys.

- **lineBegin:** The program works by drawing a series of small lines. Because these lines are very close together, they appear to be curved. These lines work much like the ones in the lines.py program, but this time a line is drawn every time the mouse moves (as long as the button is down).

- **lineEnd:** This variable keeps track of the end of the line. It is regenerated each time the mouse is moved, but the line is drawn only when the left mouse button is pressed.

You can break down the paint.py program into three functions, each with different responsibilities:

- The checkKeys() function checks the keyboard for all the various commands, and changes variables as necessary.

- The showStats() function creates a text label to tell the user the status of the paintbrush.

- The main() function is much like any other IDEA/ALTER program. It does all the primary work common to any Python game.

The primary job of the paint program is to receive input and use that input to create a drawing on the screen. Here are the various kinds of input that `paint.py` can receive.

- **Quitting commands.** In addition to checking for the regular `pygame.QUIT` `event`, a game with this much keyboard input should have another mechanism for exiting. If the user presses the Q key, the program will end.

- **Mouse events.** A typical drawing program is reliant on mouse motion. After all, the program should draw things on the screen when the mouse is moving. The status of the mouse buttons is also important, because the program should draw only when the left mouse button is down.

- **Color commands.** Several foreground colors can be chosen by selecting keys from the keyboard. Ordinary characters (like R for "red") are used for this purpose.

- **Line-width commands.** The numbers 1–9 are used to indicate the line width in pixels.

- **Utility commands.** A few other commands are used to save and load images, and to clear the screen.

Because there are so many keyboard events to manage, `paint.py` has a special function called `checkKeys()` dedicated to managing the keyboard.

The paint.py main initialization

The `main()` function of `paint.py` is not much more difficult than any other program you've made. For the most part, it is an ordinary IDEA model. The most interesting thing about the `main()` function is how it calls other functions to handle some of the work. Build the `main()` function like this:

- **Build the basic framework as always.** It's nice to have a consistent starting point. Write all the standard IDEA/ALTER code including the basic event handling, and then come back to add other features.

- **Skip over `checkKeys()` and `showStats()` for now.** Even though the `checkKeys()` and `showStats()` functions come first in the code listings, these functions are meant to help the main program, so they don't mean much until you have a context. Generally, you'll write these functions after you've got the `main()` function working, even though they come earlier in the code listing.

- **Display help in the window caption.** The easiest place to put a basic help system is in the window caption. There are more elegant ways to do this, but the caption is not in the viewing area, so it won't interfere with the painting.

```
pygame.display.set_caption("Paint:  (r)ed, (g)reen,  ↵
(b)lue, (w)hite, blac(k), (1-9) width, (c)lear,  ↵
(s)ave, (l)oad, (q)uit")
```

Step Into the Real World

The other functions must be placed before the `main()` function, because `main()` refers to them. If you define `main()` first, Python will choke when it gets to a reference for another function because it doesn't know what that function is yet. Some languages automatically look for functions later in the code — or use techniques like function prototyping to allow you to write your functions in any order — but Python requires you to be somewhat careful about this. The `main()` function will usually be written first, but will be placed last in your code listing.

Information Kiosk

The `display.set_caption` function takes up three lines in the code listing here, but it can fit on one line of the actual program, because there is no artificial limit to the width of a logical line. I broke the line up here to make it fit on the printed page.

Set up default variables. The variables that drive the painting program have to be initialized before the main loop runs:

```
background = pygame.Surface(screen.get_size())
background.fill((255, 255, 255))

clock = pygame.time.Clock()
keepGoing = True
lineStart = (0, 0)
lineEnd = (0, 0)
drawColor = (0, 0, 0)
lineWidth = 3
```

The background is an ordinary white surface. `lineStart` and `lineEnd` are the points that will make up the line. For now you can initialize them both to (0, 0). The `drawColor` and `lineWidth` variables are used to determine how the line will be drawn. I start with a three-pixel black line.

Adding events to the painting program

Once you've set up the basic framework, it's time to add new event code. The code to handle mouse manipulation is fairly simple, so I kept it in the main loop.

```
elif event.type == pygame.MOUSEMOTION:
    lineEnd = pygame.mouse.get_pos()
    if pygame.mouse.get_pressed() == (1, 0, 0):
        pygame.draw.line(background, drawColor, lineStart,  ↵
lineEnd,    lineWidth)
        lineStart = lineEnd
```

The paint program works a lot like the earlier `lines.py`, but rather than drawing a long line, `paint.py` calculates a tiny line every time the mouse is moved. It paints the line only if the mouse button is currently down. Here's what you do:

1. **Check for mouse motion.**

   Check to see whether the mouse has been moved on every frame by comparing `event.type` to `pygame.MOUSEMOTION`.

   ```
   elif event.type == pygame.MOUSEMOTION:
   ```

2. **Copy the current mouse position to `lineEnd`.**

   The current mouse position will become the current value of `lineEnd`.

3. **Check the status of the mouse buttons.**

   The painting program always calculates values for `lineBegin` and `lineEnd`, but it draws the line only if the left mouse button is currently pressed. The `pygame.mouse.get_pressed()` function returns a tuple of three numbers, representing the status of the three buttons on a typical mouse. If the value is (0, 0, 0), none of the buttons are currently down. (1, 0, 0) means only the left button is down.

4. **Draw the line using the standard `pygame.draw.line()` function.**

   All the parameters of this function are variables you have set elsewhere in the program.

   ```
   pygame.draw.line(background, drawColor, lineStart, lineEnd, lineWidth)
   ```

 Information Kiosk

The code that draws the line is the heart of this program. Everything else in the entire program supports this one line. It's important to see that almost everything in the line is a variable. The purpose of the `checkKeys()` function is to provide a mechanism for changing these variables.

5. **Copy `lineEnd` to `lineStart`.**

   Regardless of whether the mouse button is down, make the end of the current line the beginning of the next.

Updating the screen

The screen update is much like any other IDEA program, except you have two surfaces. The first is the background, which the user has been drawing with the various events. The second surface is a label indicating the pen color and width.

```
screen.blit(background, (0, 0))
myLabel = showStats(drawColor, lineWidth)
```

```
screen.blit(myLabel, (450, 450))
pygame.display.flip()
```

Here's how you manage the screen update in `paint.py`:

1. **Blit the background to the screen first.**

Remember, things you blit first will appear behind anything that is blitted later. To make sure the label appears over the background, blit the background first.

```
screen.blit(background, (0, 0))
```

2. **Create a stats label.**

The `showStats()` function (which I'll describe later in this chapter) will create a surface with text describing the pen color and width. It doesn't really matter at this point how it works, as long as you know what inputs it needs (the current drawing color and line width) and what output it will create (a surface containing the appropriate text).

```
myLabel = showStats(drawColor, lineWidth)
```

3. **Blit the label to the screen.**

If the label is blitted after the background surface, it will appear on top of the background.

```
screen.blit(myLabel, (450, 450))
```

4. **Flip the display to display the current screen.**

Calling the checkKeys() function

The paint program is interesting because you can use the keyboard to change its behavior. Keyboard management is easy, but there is a lot of it to do in this program. Whenever a task starts to take up a lot of space in your program, you should think about moving it to a function. Keyboard management is a perfect candidate for being its own function, because it:

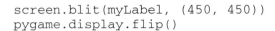 **Performs one particular task.** A function should do one job and do it well.

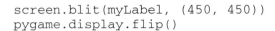 **Works with a defined set of data.** The keyboard commands are used to change the drawing color, line width, and background image. This information can be passed to the function for manipulation and then transferred back to the `main()` function.

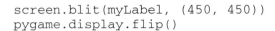 **Encapsulates details out of the way.** The `main()` function is concerned with the big picture. When you're working on the `main()` function, you don't have to be concerned about exactly how keyboard handling works. You can compartmentalize that problem into a function.

When you break your code into functions, you must think about how you will transfer data between functions. You could simply make all your data global, but that's considered a sloppy practice. It's safer to just have functions able to manage the data they need and nothing else. Just as you'd put items together in a box before you ship them, I used a special tuple to send data to and from the checkKeys() function:

```
elif event.type == pygame.KEYDOWN:
    myData = (event, background, drawColor, lineWidth, keepGoing)
    myData = checkKeys(myData)
    (event, background, drawColor, lineWidth, keepGoing) = myData
```

Here's how the data-passing works:

1. Check for a key press in the ordinary way.

2. Store relevant variables in **myData.** This variable is simply a tuple that holds all the variables.

```
myData = (event, background, drawColor, lineWidth, keepGoing)
```

I could have made a more complicated version of the function with several parameters, but storing the data into one tuple has its advantages, as you'll see.

Information Kiosk

You might wonder how I knew which data I'd need to send to the function. The truth is, I didn't. As I wrote the function, I looked at the information I needed. Each time I discovered I needed something else, I added it to myData.

3. Call the **checkKeys()** function, using the **myData** tuple as an argument.

Since all the data is compressed into one tuple, you can send that tuple to the checkKeys() function. Each of the variables in the tuple has the potential to be changed. For example, the user might have pressed the B key, which means checkKeys() should change the value of drawColor to (0, 0, 255). The checkKeys() function extracts all the data from myData, manipulates it as necessary, packs it back into myData, and returns it to the main() function. myData is used to ship relevant variables to the function and back again.

```
myData = checkKeys(myData)
```

4. Place returned values back in **myData.**

The checkKeys() function returns a tuple containing new values for each variable in myData. Copy the results of checkKeys() back to myData to update myData with any values that have changed.

Step Into the Real World

Pass by reference or value?   If you've programmed in other languages, you've probably wrestled with the notion of passing arguments by reference or by value. Python passes everything by reference, but some values (strings and tuples, especially) are *immutable*. This means they can't be changed on the fly. You can change their values only by re-assigning something to them. There are a couple of ways to get your information where it needs to go. If you have just a few values, pass them as parameters and return them. (You can return more than one value in a Python function.) If you have a large number of parameters — as I do in the `checkKeys()` example — you can pack them up in a tuple for cleaner transport.

5. **Copy values from `myData` back to original variables.**

While `myData` is a useful mechanism, what we really need is those values that were stored into `myData`. Unpack the tuple back to the individual variables with this line:

```
(event, background, drawColor, lineWidth, keepGoing) = myData
```

This is the only place where you can have more than one variable on the left side of an assignment statement. The number of variables on the left has to match the number of values on the right.

Information Kiosk

If you're a little confused about this `myData` thing, keep on reading. The purpose of this object is to facilitate communication between the `main()` function and `checkKeys()`. Once you see how the data is used and returned by `checkKeys()`, it will probably make a lot more sense.

Checking the keyboard

The hardest part of the `checkKeys()` function is figuring out how to get data into and out of the function. The function itself is remarkably simple:

```python
def checkKeys(myData):
    """test for various keyboard inputs"""

    #extract the data
    (event, background, drawColor, lineWidth, keepGoing) = myData
    #print myData

    if event.key == pygame.K_q:
        #quit
        keepGoing = False
    elif event.key == pygame.K_c:
        #clear screen
        background.fill((255, 255, 255))
```

```
elif event.key == pygame.K_s:
    #save picture
    pygame.image.save(background, "painting.bmp")
elif event.key == pygame.K_l:
    #load picture
    background = pygame.image.load("painting.bmp")
elif event.key == pygame.K_r:
    #red
    drawColor = (255, 0, 0)
elif event.key == pygame.K_g:
    #green
    drawColor = (0, 255, 0)
elif event.key == pygame.K_w:
    #white
    drawColor = (255, 255, 255)
elif event.key == pygame.K_b:
    #blue
    drawColor = (0, 0, 255)
elif event.key == pygame.K_k:
    #black
    drawColor = (0, 0, 0)
#line widths
elif event.key == pygame.K_1:
    lineWidth = 1
elif event.key == pygame.K_2:
    lineWidth = 2
elif event.key == pygame.K_3:
    lineWidth = 3
elif event.key == pygame.K_4:
    lineWidth = 4
elif event.key == pygame.K_5:
    lineWidth = 5
elif event.key == pygame.K_6:
    lineWidth = 6
elif event.key == pygame.K_7:
    lineWidth = 7
elif event.key == pygame.K_8:
    lineWidth = 8
elif event.key == pygame.K_9:
    lineWidth = 9

#return all values
myData = (event, background, drawColor, lineWidth, keepGoing)
return myData
```

The checkKeys() function grabs the myData tuple, unpacks it by assigning each
element to an individual variable, checks the event to see what key was pressed, packs
the data back into myData, and then returns it to the main() function. Here's how
you put the checkKeys() function into play:

1. **Accept one tuple as a parameter.**

   The function definition determines how many parameters will be sent to the
   function. I have several, but I packaged them all into the tuple myData. This is
   a relatively common practice in Python when you send a large number of
   parameters to a function.

2. Break the `myData` value into the constituent data variables.

In order to do its job, checkKeys() needs to know the value of event. As the user presses various keys, the program will respond by making changes to background, drawColor, lineWidth, and keepGoing. I extract these values from the myData tuple into the appropriate variables:

```
(event, background, drawColor, lineWidth, keepGoing) = myData
```

3. Check for the `quit` command.

If the user presses Q, he is indicating a desire to quit, so write a condition to handle that eventuality:

```
if event.key == pygame.K_q:
    #quit
    keepGoing = False
```

Information kiosk

The keyboard technique I'm using doesn't distinguish between uppercase and lowercase letters. It simply checks to see if the indicated key has been pressed.

4. Handle clearing the screen.

The C key indicates the user wants to clear the screen. The fill() method is the easiest way to do this.

```
elif event.key == pygame.K_c:
    #clear screen
    background.fill((255, 255, 255))
```

Information Kiosk

Note that I filled the background, not the screen. That's because the background *is* the actual drawing in this case, and it is relatively permanent. The screen is much more volatile, because it is being redrawn every single frame. Of course, the screen always shows the background, so screen and background appear to be the same thing to the user.

5. Manage `save` and `load` commands.

The pygame.image.save() and pygame.image.load() functions are very useful tools for managing image files. The save() function needs a surface name and a filename. The load() function needs only a filename, and loads the file into the specified surface object.

```
elif event.key == pygame.K_s:
    #save picture
    pygame.image.save(background, "painting.bmp")
```

```
elif event.key == pygame.K_l:
    #load picture
    background = pygame.image.load("painting.bmp")
```

Information Kiosk

The `save()` function stores data in several standard formats. The `load()` function can accept these and a number of other image formats. The latest version of pygame (1.8) can save to BMP, JPG, PNG, GIF, TGA, and other formats. For now, just go with `.bmp` because it's relatively universal, and works with the older versions of pygame. I'm not going to worry about filenames for now, but always assume the paint program will refer to an image called `painting.bmp`.

6. **Change the drawing color.**

Several keyboard commands are used to change the drawing color. This is actually a very simple operation: Just check the key and set `drawColor` accordingly. Note how the comments help the programmer figure out what is supposed to be happening. This is handy — especially if you make a mistake. If the R key is making yellow, you can easily find the spot in the code that was supposed to be making red, and check the color value.

```
elif event.key == pygame.K_r:
    #red
    drawColor = (255, 0, 0)
elif event.key == pygame.K_g:
    #green
    drawColor = (0, 255, 0)
elif event.key == pygame.K_w:
    #white
    drawColor = (255, 255, 255)
elif event.key == pygame.K_b:
    #blue
    drawColor = (0, 0, 255)
elif event.key == pygame.K_k:
    #black
    drawColor = (0, 0, 0)
```

7. **Change the line width.**

Line width is also pretty easy. Each number is associated with a corresponding line width. The `lineWidth` variable is used in the drawing command, so changing the value of this variable changes the way the line is drawn.

```
#line widths
elif event.key == pygame.K_1:
    lineWidth = 1
elif event.key == pygame.K_2:
    lineWidth = 2
elif event.key == pygame.K_3:
```

```
        lineWidth = 3
    elif event.key == pygame.K_4:
        lineWidth = 4
    elif event.key == pygame.K_5:
        lineWidth = 5
    elif event.key == pygame.K_6:
        lineWidth = 6
    elif event.key == pygame.K_7:
        lineWidth = 7
    elif event.key == pygame.K_8:
        lineWidth = 8
    elif event.key == pygame.K_9:
        lineWidth = 9
```

8. **Return the data to the `main()` program.**

Once all the other commands have changed the data variables around, stuff them back into the `myData` variable and return them to the `main()` function.

```
#return all values
myData = (event, background, drawColor, lineWidth, keepGoing)
return myData
```

Creating the status label

One task remains in the paint program, and that is creating a label to display the pen status. The `showStats()` function performs this task:

```
def showStats(drawColor, lineWidth):
    """ shows the current statistics """
    myFont = pygame.font.SysFont("None", 20)
    stats = "color: %s, width: %d" % (drawColor, lineWidth)
    statSurf = myFont.render(stats, 1, (drawColor))
    return statSurf
```

There isn't anything new in the `showStats()` function. It simply uses ideas you already know to perform a specific task for you.

1. **Accept the drawing color and line-width variables.**

These are the two stats I want to display, so I'll need to pass the appropriate variables as arguments to the function.

2. **Create a suitable font.**

I chose the standard default font. By using a `SysFont` and setting the font name to `"None"`, I tell Python to use the standard font built into pygame. It won't be especially fancy, but it will work.

```
myFont = pygame.font.SysFont("None", 20)
```

Watch Your Step

You might argue that it isn't necessary to create the font inside the main loop, where it will be re-created 30 times per second, but since I'm not having any speed problems, I decided to leave it alone. If I'd made the font outside the loop, I'd have had to pass it in as an argument or make it a global variable. Sometimes simplicity trumps performance.

3. Create the `stats` string.

I used the string-interpolation operator to build a suitable output string. Note that Python automatically converts the `drawColor` tuple to a string.

```
stats = "color: %s, width: %d" % (drawColor, lineWidth)
```

4. Render a surface displaying the stats.

Use `myFont`'s `render()` method to create a surface displaying the `stats` string. As an added feature, draw the stats in the current drawing color. This allows the user to hide the stats if desired by placing a solid color in the lower-right corner and changing the drawing color to that color before saving.

5. Return the surface.

The whole point of this function is to return a `Surface` object, so send the surface back to the main program, which can use it to draw the text on the screen. The stat label is blitted onto the display after the background so the stat label will overwrite whatever the user paints.

The painting program is a pretty impressive piece of work for this early in your programming journey. It's fun in its own right, but even more important is how the key ideas you learned here will relate to other games. Almost every game involves creating visual elements on the screen and responding to user events. In the next chapter, you learn how to build very powerful objects called *sprites,* which finally let you make objects that the user can control. See you then!

anti-aliasing: A technique that uses shading between the foreground and background color to trick the eye into believing a line is smoother than it is.

bounding rectangle: The smallest rectangle with vertical and horizontal sides that can be drawn around a shape. Used in the `ellipse()` and `arc()` drawing functions. Also used in collision detection, as described in Chapter 6.

constant: A variable that is not meant to change as the program runs. Constants are often used for convenience and clarity. Most constants are written entirely in uppercase.

font: Formally, a combination of typeface with size. Often used in computing to refer to a file containing typeface information. Also, pygame has an object for this purpose (called the `Font` object), which can be created using the `pygame.font.Font()` or `pygame.font.SysFont()` function.

global scope: Any code or variables that exist outside a function are said to have global scope. It's best to place as much code as possible *inside* functions. Placing code and variables inside functions makes it easier to avoid certain side effects.

immutable: Certain data types (notably strings and tuples) are immutable. This means assignment is the only way to change them. This is important when you want to pass data to a function.

keyboard constants: A series of keyboard names stored in the pygame module. They all begin with *K* and contain the letter or key name, for example: `pygame.K_SPACE` or `pygame.K_a`.

pi: A constant used in angle measurement. Angles measured in radians are almost always expressed as fractions of pi.

radian: The length of a circle's radius inscribed on the circumference of the circle. A standard mathematical unit of angle measurement. Math operations involving angles usually require the angles to be in radians first. See Chapter 9 for more information about the relationship between degrees and radians.

typeface: The characteristic shapes of whole sets of letters. What most people call a *font* is more properly called a typeface.

Command	Arguments	Description	Example
`pygame.draw.line(Surface, color, start_pos, end_pos, width=1)`	`Surface`: drawing surface `color`: color value `start_pos`, `end_pos`: endpoints of line `width`: line width	Draws a line on the surface with the given values.	`pygame.draw.line( background, (0, 0, 0), (0, 0), (100, 100), 3)`

T**⊙**KENS

Command	Arguments	Description	Example

`pygame.draw.rect(Surface, color, Rect, width=0)`	`Surface`: drawing surface
	`color`: color value
	`Rect`: rectangle to draw
	`width`: drawing width
		Draws the given rectangle on the surface.
		
		Width value of zero (default) fills in the rectangle.
			`pygame.draw.rect(`
			`background,`
			`(0, 0, 0),`
			`((0,0),(100,100)),`
			`1)`

`pygame.draw.circle(Surface, Color, pos, radius, width=0)`	`Surface`: drawing surface
	`color`: color value
	`pos`: center of circle
	`radius`: radius of circle
	`width`: drawing width
		Draws the given circle on the surface.
		
		Width value of zero fills in the circle.
			`pygame.draw.`
			`circle(background,`
			`(0, 0, 0),`
			`(100, 100),`
			`50,`
			`1)`

`pygame.draw.ellipse (Surface, color, Rect, width=0)`	`Surface`: drawing surface
	`color`: color value
	`Rect`: bounding rectangle of ellipse
	`width`: drawing width
		Draws the largest ellipse that fits in the given rectangle.
		
		Width value of zero fills in the ellipse.
			`pygame.draw.`
			`ellipse`
			`(background,`
			`(0, 0, 0),`
			`((0,0),(200,100)),`
			`1)`

`pygame.draw.arc(Surface, color, Rect, start_angle, stop_angle, width=1)`	`Surface`: drawing surface
	`color`: color value
	`Rect`: bounding rectangle of ellipse containing arc
	`start_angle`: beginning of arc in radians
	`stop_angle`: end of arc in radians
	`width`: drawing width
		Generates an ellipse inside bounding rectangle, then uses `start_angle` and `stop_angle` to determine portion of arc to draw. Draws this arc on the surface.	`pygame.draw.arc(`
			`background,`
			`(0, 0, 0),`
			`((0,0),(200,100)),`
			`0,`
			`math.pi`
			`1)`

`pygame.draw.lines(Surface, color, closed, pointlist, width=1)`	`Surface`: drawing surface
	`color`: color value
	`closed`: makes polygon if `True`
	`pointList`: tuple of vertex points
	`width`: width of line
		Uses `pointlist` to generate a series of connected lines. See `draw.polygon` for a filled polygon.	`pointList = (`
			`(0,0),(0,10),`
			`(10,10), (10,0))`
			`pygame.draw.`
			`lines(`
			`background,`
			`(0, 0, 0),`
			`True,`
			`pointList,`
			`1)`

continued

 *continued*

Command	Arguments	Description	Example

`pygame.draw.aaline(Surface, color, startpos, endpos, blend=1)`	`Surface`: drawing surface
	`color`: color value
	`start_pos`, `end_pos`: endpoints of line
	`blend`: if set to 1 (`True`), blends drawing color with background color
		Draws lines that appear smoother but cannot be wider than one pixel.	`pygame.draw.`
			`aaline`
			`(background,`
			`(0, 0, 0),`
			`(0, 0),`
			`(100, 100),`
			`1)`

`pygame.draw.polygon (Surface, color, pointList, width =0)`	`Surface`: drawing surface
	`color`: color value
	`closed`: makes polygon if `True`
	`pointList`: tuple of vertex points
	`width`: width of line
		Draws a closed polygon using `pointList` as vertices.	`pointList = (`
			`(0,0),(0,10),`
			`(10,10), (10,0))`
			`pygame.draw.`
			`polygon(`
			`background,`
			`(0, 0, 0),`
			`True,`
			`pointList,`
			`1)`

`pygame.mouse.get_pos()`	`<none>`	Returns the mouse's position as a tuple.	`print pygame.` `mouse.get_pos()`

`pygame.mouse.get_pressed()`	`<none>`	Returns the button status as a three-number tuple.	`if pygame.`
			`mouse.get_pressed`
			`== (0,0,1):`
			`    print "right`
			`button clicked"`

`pygame.image.load(filename)`	`filename`: name of image file to load	Returns a surface containing the image.	`face =`
			`pygame.image.`
			`load("face.gif")`

`pygame.image.save(Surface, filename)`	`Surface`: surface object to create image from
	`filename`: name of image file to save
		Creates a file called filename from `Surface`.	`pygame.image.`
			`save(background,`
			`"myImage.jpg")`

`pygame.font.Font( filename, size)`	`filename`: name of TrueType font (.ttf) file
	`size`: size of font in pixels
		Generates a font from a given .ttf file.	`myFont =`
			`pygame.font.Font(`
			`"arial.ttf",`
			`20)`

`pygame.font.SysFont( fontName, size, bold=False, italic=False)`	`fontName`: the font name (must be an installed system font)
	`size`: font size
	`bold`, `italic`: Booleans for font style
		Creates a pygame font based on the named system font, if possible.	`myFont =`
			`pygame.font.`
			`SysFont("Comic`
			`Sans MS",`
			`20)`

![TOKENS logo]

Command	Arguments	Description	Example

`fontObj.render(`
`text,`
`aa,`
`color,`
`background =None)`
	`fontObj`: a font created with `Font` or `SysFont` commands
	`aa`: antialiasing (0 means off, 1 means on)
	`text`: text to render
	`color`: foreground color
	`background`: background color
		Returns a surface with the text rendered according to `fontObj`.	`myFont.render(`
			`"Hello, World!",`
			`1,`
			`(0, 0, 0))`

`event.key`	`Event`: an event object
	`key`: keycode describing which key was pressed
		If a keyboard event occurred, `event.key` is used to determine which key was pressed.	`if event.key`
			`== pygame.K_q:`
			`keepGoing = False`

`pygame.key.name`
`(keyCode)`
	`keyCode`: a keyboard code value	Returns a human-readable name corresponding to `keyCode`.	`print pygame.`
			`key.name(`
			`event.key)`

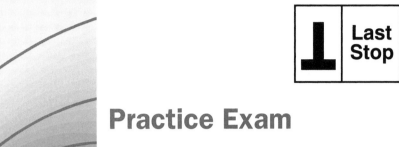

Practice Exam

1. Which is NOT a common feature of an advanced programming editor?

A) Syntax completion

B) Integrated debugging

C) Code translation

D) Syntax highlighting

2. Why is it best to put most of your code in functions?

_____

_____

3. True or false: The `__name__ == "__main__":` business prevents your code from running accidentally.

_____

4. What's the general strategy for drawing basic shapes in pygame?

A) You can't. You have to import them as graphics.

B) Use the `pygame.draw` module.

C) Use the various drawing methods of the `Surface` object, like `surface.drawCircle()`.

D) There are special pygame objects called `Line`, `Circle`, `Ellipse`, and so on.

5. How do you load an image into pygame?

_____

_____

6. What does `event.key` return?

A) A numeric code corresponding to a key that was pressed

B) The name of the key that was pressed

C) A list of keys that have been pressed since the last call to `event.key`

D) The coordinates on the keyboard of the key

7. What's the downside of using a system font?

A) There's no downside. They're great!

B) What's installed on your system may not be on your users'.

C) There are never very many system fonts installed.

D) You can use only the default font.

8. If your game uses a standard `pygame.font.Font` command, you'll also need to supply _____.

9. Create a program that draws a simple figure on the screen. Be sure to use at least one circle, ellipse, rectangle, and line.

10. Write an image marker program that loads up an image, writes some text to it, and saves it.

CHAPTER

6

Audio and Basic Sprites

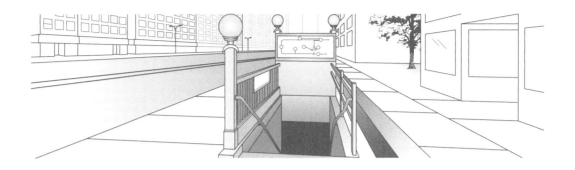

Enter the Station

Questions

1. Why do you need a special way to organize your game objects?

2. How do you incorporate audio effects into your games?

3. How can you ensure a `Sprite` object acts on its own?

4. How can you tell if two game elements have collided?

5. How can you re-use and improve objects you build?

Using Sprites and Audio for Games

Throughout this book you've been building basic games. You've learned how to write basic commands and use variables. You learned how to put commands together to build functions, and how to group data in lists and tuples. You also learned how to use built-in objects that combine data and instructions into one powerful tool. Now you're ready to take a really important step. It's time to make your own objects! In particular, you learn in this chapter how to build your own `Sprite` objects, which are the key elements of almost every 2D game made.

The best news is, there isn't really that much new to learn. Once you figure out how sprites are wired, you can use them in the same IDEA framework you've been using all along — and you'll have a lot more power without much more work.

Before working on sprites, though, there's another important aspect of video games you're ready to take on: Sound effects. Sound is actually pretty easy in pygame, so you'll learn how to build your own sound objects and use them to add all the crashes and bangs you can imagine.

Incorporating Audio

Sound effects add tremendously to the gaming experience. There are two main facets of audio work: creating the audio files, and using them in your game. It might surprise you that getting pygame to play sounds is trivial. The hard part is creating quality sounds in the first place. Fortunately, there's some great free software to make that job a lot easier.

Using the Ogg Vorbis format

The pygame library is capable of working with several audio formats, including WAV and MP3, but most Python programmers prefer a third format called *Ogg Vorbis*. There are several reasons for this:

Ogg is a completely free format. The WAV and MP3 formats both have some parts that are considered proprietary. Because various companies own parts of the technology, there are legal ramifications of what can be done with the files. Python programmers generally prefer to use open-source formats where possible. The Ogg Vorbis format is an open-source standard, and it's free to use.

Watch Your Step

I'm talking about the *format* here, not the content. Copyrighted material is copyrighted whatever the storage technique, and you need to respect the artists and laws. What's free about Ogg is the method of compression and storage.

- **Ogg is technically sound.** Ogg Vorbis compresses audio files at least as well as the standard MP3 format, and makes high quality files generally a tenth the size of the same file in a WAV format. Ogg uses a *lossy* compression algorithm (like MP3) but (also like MP3 format) the lost information is the stuff that doesn't factor into human perception, so it usually sounds very good at 1/10th of the size of the raw data.

- **Ogg works better with Python/pygame.** There are documented problems with pygame's support for MP3 files (especially under Windows), but I've never had any trouble at all with Ogg.

- **There are plenty of free tools to help.** If you already have a sound file in another format, you can easily convert it to Ogg Vorbis. You can also readily record your own audio files into .ogg format.

Creating sound effects with Audacity

There are two main ways to obtain audio:

- **Obtain sound effects from somewhere else.** Sound effects CDs are easy to get your hands on. Some are extremely inexpensive (but sometimes you get what you pay for). Be sure if you purchase sound effects that you are also getting the rights to use these sound effects in your games. Normally this involves seeking royalty-free sound effects.

- **Record your own.** This sounds a little bit frightening if you've never done any audio work before, but it's actually a pretty good way to go, because you don't have to worry about copyright issues, and you can do a lot with a cheap microphone, free software, and a little imagination.

Watch Your Step

Be wary of using audio you find on the Internet. The "free audio" sites are often rife with content of questionable legal status, including copyrighted works. It's tempting to use some of this material, but doing so can complicate legally reproducing your work. It's better to make your own and avoid the hassle.

The Audacity program shown in Figure 6-1 is an incredible cross-platform open-source tool for creating and modifying audio files.

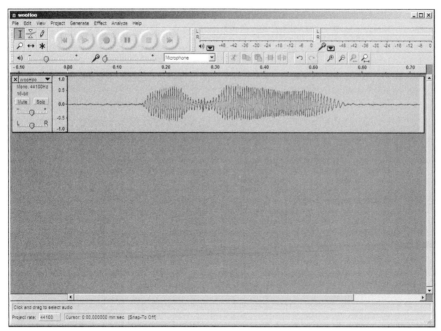

Figure 6-1: Audacity is a useful tool for creating and modifying sound files.

Audacity has many interesting features, but the following are the most useful for game programmers:

- **Saves and loads Ogg Vorbis natively.** Audacity can handle its own internal format as well as the industry-standard MP3, WAV, and Ogg Vorbis formats. This means you can load an audio file, modify it, and save it in Ogg Vorbis format for easy use in Python.

Information Kiosk

If you want to use Audacity to work with MP3 files, you'll have to locate a copy of a plug-in called LAME. Unfortunately, Audacity cannot ship with MP3 support built in and still remain free. Do a search for the LAME encoder, and you should be able to find it.

- **Allows direct recording.** You can plug a microphone into your computer and record sounds instantly. I created all the sound effects for the mail pilot game in the next chapter using a $20 headset. You can use the microphone that's built into your machine, if you have one, or any other inexpensive mike. You don't need a fancy microphone (although if you have one, you can get even better results).

Offers nifty editing features. You can record multiple tracks and mix them to create interesting audio. You can make sounds play backwards, change the volume, and pan sounds from the left to the right ear. You can also add echo and reverberation effects easily.

Costs nothing. Free is good. If it *works really well* and it's free, that's even better.

A copy of Audacity is included on the Web site that accompanies this book. You can also download Audacity from `http://audacity.sourceforge.net`.

Creating a sound is a pretty easy thing to do with Audacity:

1. Record or import a sample.

Either begin with a sound or record something new. For the `soundDemo.py` program I build through this section, I simply spoke into the microphone.

2. Keep your sample short if possible.

Sound can take up a lot of space, making your programs unnecessarily bloated. Keep in mind you can loop sounds indefinitely in pygame. For example, I wanted an engine sound for a game in the next chapter. The original effect is only four seconds long. I had Python loop the sound as long as the game is in action, so a short sound can sound much longer.

3. Apply any special effects.

Select your clip by clicking on the clip's label. You can then apply any of the tools in the Effect menu.

4. Try multiple tracks.

You can build some really neat features with multiple tracks. For example, to make the airplane sound, I recorded my voice humming into the microphone. I copied it to a new track and played the second track backwards. I then set the pan so the original track plays in the left ear and the second track (the one in reverse) plays in the right.

5. Normalize your audio.

Before saving your audio clip, use Normalize from the Effect menu to set the volume to a standard level. This makes all your sound effects begin at roughly the same level. You can adjust the relative levels of the various sound effects through your Python code.

6. Export the file in `Ogg Vorbis` format.

Audacity has built-in support for Ogg Vorbis. When you're happy with the sound you've created, export the file to your program's directory as an Ogg file.

7. **Save in the native Audacity format, too.**

It's a good idea to also save your files in Audacity's native format, because the Ogg file will not have all the original detail. If you want to reconfigure the file, it's best to work with the raw data rather than a compressed copy. Also , the Audacity format preserves all the tracks individually, where the Ogg Vorbis format combines all tracks into one.

Creating a sound object

Once you've created an Ogg file, you can make a program to play it. Figure 6-2 shows the `playSound.py` program in action.

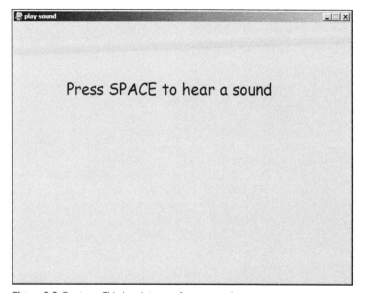

Figure 6-2: Trust me. This is a lot more fun on a real computer.

You create sound effects in pygame with a special built-in module called `pygame.mixer`. The `playSound.py` program illustrates the process:

```
""" playSound.py
    demonstrates playing an ogg sound
    on demand """

import pygame
pygame.init()
pygame.mixer.init()

def main():
    screen = pygame.display.set_mode((640, 480))
```

```
pygame.display.set_caption("play sound")

#create background
background = pygame.Surface(screen.get_size())
background = background.convert()
background.fill((255, 255, 0))

#create label
myFont = pygame.font.SysFont("Comic Sans MS", 30)
label = myFont.render("Press SPACE to hear a sound", ↩
1, (0, 0, 255))

#create sound
wooHoo = pygame.mixer.Sound("wooHoo.ogg")

keepGoing = True
clock = pygame.time.Clock()

while keepGoing:
    for event in pygame.event.get():
        if event.type == pygame.QUIT:
            keepGoing = False
        elif event.type == pygame.KEYDOWN:
            if event.key == pygame.K_SPACE:
                wooHoo.play()
            elif event.key == pygame.K_ESCAPE:
                keepGoing = False

    screen.blit(background, (0, 0))
    screen.blit(label, (100, 100))
    pygame.display.flip()
if __name__ == "__main__":
    main()
```

The steps for playing a sound are actually pretty straightforward:

1. **Begin with a standard framework.**

   The program begins with a standard IDEA framework.

2. **Initialize the mixer module.**

   You don't have to import the mixer module explicitly (because it's automatically imported as a part of pygame), but you must initialize it.

```
pygame.mixer.init()
```

 Information Kiosk

If the mixer initialization fails, `mixer.init()` returns the value `False`.

3. Create a `Sound` object.

Pygame uses a special object called `Sound` to manage sound effects. Make a `Sound` object by specifying the filename of the Ogg Vorbis file you created earlier.

```
#create sound
wooHoo = pygame.mixer.Sound("wooHoo.ogg")
```

 Information Kiosk

It's easiest for now to keep all resources for a game in the same directory as the game. Later, I show you how to manage directories in a way that works across platforms.

4. Play the sound.

The most fun thing to do with a sound is to play it.

```
elif event.type == pygame.KEYDOWN:
    if event.key == pygame.K_SPACE:
        wooHoo.play()
```

In this program, I chose to play the sound when the user pressed the space bar. Of course, you can play sounds in a lot of other situations in your games. The optional `loops` parameter of the `play()` method lets you specify how many additional times to play the sound. A `loops` value of minus one (–1) repeats the sound indefinitely.

 Watch Your Step

If you loop a sound indefinitely, you have an obligation to stop the sound somewhere. Use the sound's `stop()` method for this purpose.

5. Modify the `Sound` object.

Once the sound is stored in an object, you can do several things with it. You can set the sound's volume, fade the sound out, and get the length of the sound in seconds. See `pygame.mixer.Sound` in the online help for specific details.

 Watch Your Step

Headphones are a good way to save your marriage or relationship. When you're testing your sound effects, you'll end up playing the blood-curdling screech hundreds of times in a row. My kids always know when I'm doing sound effects for my games, because they hear all kinds of strange repetitive noises coming out of the office.

Building a Sprite

Arcade games are about things moving around on the screen. Some of these things are under user control, and some are controlled by the computer. The game ultimately comes down to the interaction between these things. The idea of visual elements is so important to video games that the early gaming hardware had special support for game elements wired into the system. These special objects were called *sprites*. Nowadays, modern computers can manage visual elements on the screen without requiring any special hardware, but the term *sprite* has stuck, and now it represents a discrete game object. Regardless of the programming environment, a game sprite should have a number of qualities:

- **A visual representation.** You need to be able to see a sprite on the screen, at least sometimes. It usually has some sort of graphic attached to it. Some sprites have several graphics attached, but for now we'll stick to one.

- **Attributes representing position and size.** Each sprite has a particular size and a position on the screen.

- **The ability to move.** A sprite should be able to move (although they might also remain stationary).

- **The ability to recognize collisions.** If sprites are moving around, they're bound to bump into each other. Most of the interesting things in video games happen when sprites crash into each other. A sprite has to know when it's hit something else.

- **Dynamic birth and death.** The program should be able to create and destroy sprites as needed. Think of the rocks in the classic *Asteroids* game.

- **Be reasonably self-contained.** A sprite should "know" how to do these things. You shouldn't have to write a lot of code to tell sprites what to do. The sprites should be little robots with their own programming, and your game code concentrates on the interactions between sprites and larger game dynamics.

Sprites and object-oriented programming

It turns out the characteristics of a sprite match almost perfectly with one of the most important ideas in computing: Object-oriented programming (OOP). Objects are a special way of thinking about programming, which are a natural extension of what you've already learned. Variables are a powerful way of looking at data, but a group of variables in a list or a tuple is even more powerful. Likewise, programming statements are powerful, but they're even more useful when they're grouped into functions.

What if you could build something that contains both multiple data elements and multiple functions? You'd have something pretty cool. That's what OOP is all about.

Typically, an object (in any language) has these elements:

 Properties. These are characteristics or attributes of the object. They're like adjectives in grammar. They describe something about an object. A `cow` object might have a `breed` property, a `gotMilk` property, and a `sleeping` property. Properties in Python generally map to variables associated with an object.

Methods. These are things the object knows how to do. A method is like a verb. It's a behavior or action the object can take. A `cow` object would have methods like `giveMilk()` or `moo()`. Methods are simply functions attached to an object.

Events. These are stimuli the object responds to. The best grammar analogy would be an interjection: "Hey!" or "He's touching me!" In pygame, you generally use the special `update()` method of a sprite as a big event handler.

A constructor. This is a special method that is called when the object is first created. The constructor contains code for starting the object up and giving it initial values.

You've been using objects all along, in one sense. Think about this code:

```
myString = "Jacob"
print myString.upper()
```

This code works because strings in Python are actually objects. `myString.upper()` is actually calling the `upper()` method of the string object `myThing`.

Information Kiosk

Actually, the Python string object called `str`. `String` is a module that's no longer being supported.

Pygame has a special object called `Sprite`. This object has all the basic features a sprite needs. However, the `Sprite` object itself isn't very useful. It's just a foundation. To make useful sprites for your games, you'll need to make new objects based on the `Sprite` class.

The `basicSprite.py` program displayed in Figure 6-3 looks a lot like the `moveBox.py` program from Chapter 4, but `basicSprite.py` uses a sprite to control the box.

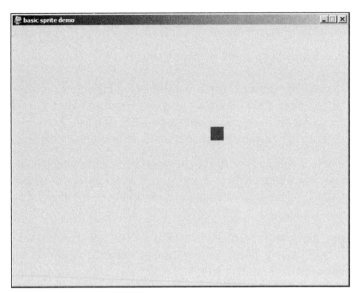

Figure 6-3: This box is actually a sprite.

As usual, I give you the code up front and then I'll explain the relevant pieces as we go.

```
""" basicSprite.py
    works just like moveBox.py
    from chapter 4,
    but now uses a sprite """

import pygame
pygame.init()

screen = pygame.display.set_mode((640, 480))

class Box(pygame.sprite.Sprite):
    def __init__(self):
        pygame.sprite.Sprite.__init__(self)
        self.image = pygame.Surface((25, 25))
        self.image.fill((255, 0, 0))
        self.rect = self.image.get_rect()
        self.rect.centerx = 0
        self.rect.centery = 200
        self.dx = 10
        self.dy = 0

    def update(self):
        self.rect.centerx += self.dx
        if self.rect.right > screen.get_width():
            self.rect.left = 0

def main():
```

```
        pygame.display.set_caption("basic sprite demo")

        background = pygame.Surface(screen.get_size())
        background = background.convert()
        background.fill((255, 255, 0))
        screen.blit(background, (0,0))

        box = Box()
        allSprites = pygame.sprite.Group(box)

        clock = pygame.time.Clock()
        keepGoing = True
        while keepGoing:
            clock.tick(30)
            for event in pygame.event.get():
                if event.type == pygame.QUIT:
                    keepGoing = False

            allSprites.clear(screen, background)
            allSprites.update()
            allSprites.draw(screen)

            pygame.display.flip()

if __name__ == "__main__":
    main()
```

There are two main parts of working with sprites: building the `Sprite` classes, and using them in a sprite group.

Pygame Sprite objects

Pygame has a built-in `Sprite` object that is a useful template for your own sprites. It isn't meant to be used on its own. It's designed entirely as a base class you can build your own sprites with. The built-in `Sprite` object has some features your other sprites will need.

Built-in sprite attributes

The built-in sprite has two primary attributes: `image` and `rect`. The `image` attribute is a surface indicating the graphical representation of the sprite.

Transfer

In Chapter 8 you learn how to attach multiple images to a sprite so it can animate and turn.

The most common way to give a sprite an image is to use the `pygame.image.load()` function to load the surface from a graphic you have already created directly to the sprite's `image` attribute. You can also use any other pygame surface, including a `Surface` object (as I have done in the box example) or the result of a font render (illustrated later in this chapter).

Watch Your Step

Although pygame expects every sprite to have `image` and `rect` attributes, there is nothing enforcing this behavior. If you create a sprite without an image or a rect, you will get an `AttributeError` exception.

The `rect` attribute is the most powerful part of the pygame sprite. This is an ordinary pygame `Rect` object, but manipulating this object manipulates the position of the sprite. Table 6-1 gives some useful attributes and methods of the `sprite.rect` object.

Table 6-1   Sprite rect Attributes

Attribute	Description	Use
`top`, `bottom`, `left`, `right`	Single value determining the x or y position of the rectangle sides.	Tests to see whether the object is still on the screen.
`topleft`, `midtop`, `topright`, `midleft`, `center`, `midright`, `bottomleft`, `midbottom`, `bottomright`	(x,y) coordinate of various points on rectangle.	Positions a box according to a corner or other point.
`centerx`, `centery`	x and y values of rectangle center.	Positions a box according to the center of its rectangle.
`size`	x, y values describing the size of the `rect`.	
`height`	Height of the box.	
`width`	Width of the box.	
`colliderect(rect2)`	Collision with another rect.	Determines collision between two rectangles.
`collidepoint(point)`	Collision with a point.	Tests to see whether a point is inside the `rect`.
`inflate(x,y)`	Changes the size of the `rect`.	Sometimes used to tweak collision routines.
`move(dx, dy)`	Moves by the dx and dy values.	Sometimes used to move a sprite.

If you want to find out information about a sprite's size and position, you can examine its `rect` attributes. For example, if you have a sprite called `myThing` and you want to know how wide it is, you can use `myThing.rect.width` to discover its width. You can also use the position properties to move a sprite. For example, to position an object so its center point is (100, 100), you can say `self.rect.center = (100, 100)`. If you want to leave the object's vertical position alone and simply set its horizontal position to 100, you can say `self.rect.centerx = 100`.

Watch Your Step

You can freely access `rect` values from outside the class, but you shouldn't directly manipulate the class from the outside. Instead, use the `update` method to change the class, or create a special class method or attribute to manage the update. I'll introduce both techniques later in this chapter.

Custom sprite attributes

In addition to the attributes that are already built into the `Sprite` object, you will often want to add your own attributes. The most important of these add-on attributes are `dx` and `dy`. These two special variables are used to determine the sprite's speed and direction of travel. (I describe how to use `dx` and `dy` in much more detail throughout this and other chapters.) You will often add other custom *attributes* — attached variables — to your `Sprite` objects.

Built-in sprite methods

`Sprite` objects almost always have at least two methods. These two methods are `__init__(self)` (which acts as the object constructor) and `update(self)`. The `__init__` method is called when your object is created. The constructor is used to give the sprite its initial values. Typically you'll use the `__init__` method to establish the `image` and `rect` attributes for the sprite. This is also where you create any custom attributes. The `update()` method will be called once per frame. Anything that causes the sprite to move around or change its status, you'll put code in `update()`.

Watch Your Step

If you want to be truly technical, Python's `__init__()` method isn't truly a constructor. Still, this method is used to initialize a sprite and set up any parameters. If you want to think of `__init__()` as a constructor, I won't tell anybody otherwise.

Custom sprite methods

Of course, you don't have to stick with the built-in methods. You can add as many methods as you want. Each method represents something the sprite can do. For example, you might have methods called `moveRight()` and `moveLeft()` that allow the sprite to move. You might have a `checBorders()` method that checks to see whether the sprite has strayed off the screen. You might have a `checkCollisions()` method that checks to see whether the sprite has crashed into any other sprites.

Creating the Sprite object

The first task in `basicSprite.py` (and any other program using sprites) is to create the `Sprite` object. This actually happens outside the main code, because the sprite is really a separate object from the rest of the program. Here's what it looks like:

```
class Box(pygame.sprite.Sprite):
    def __init__(self):
        pygame.sprite.Sprite.__init__(self)
        self.image = pygame.Surface((25, 25))
        self.image.fill((255, 0, 0))
        self.rect = self.image.get_rect()
        self.rect.centerx = 0
        self.rect.centery = 200
        self.dx = 10
        self.dy = 0

    def update(self):
        self.rect.centerx += self.dx
        if self.rect.right > screen.get_width():
            self.rect.left = 0
```

Creating a sprite requires a few basic steps.

Defining the sprite

There's a little bit of overhead required to build the class itself. It's not too difficult, and you'll find it's pretty much the same for every sprite you make. Here's how to do it:

1. Define the sprite as a new class.

In the object-oriented programming you've done so far in this book, you've made *instances* of existing classes. In other words, you've made new cookies from an existing recipe. Making a sprite is different, because you're making a new *class* (that is, a new recipe). The `class` keyword tells Python you're defining a new class. My new class will be called `Box`.

Information Kiosk

It's traditional to capitalize the name of classes and to start instance names in lowercase. With all the objects I create, I will follow that convention. Unfortunately, Python/pygame is not consistent in this matter. Some of the important classes (such as `Sprite`) begin with an uppercase value, while others (such as `list`) do not. Thanks for that little inconsistency, guys.

2. **Base the sprite on the existing `pygame.sprite.Sprite` class.**

If you're building police cars, you probably wouldn't start with a pile of metal. Instead, you'd take a suitable sedan from a sedan factory, and build a second factory that handles those changes that turn a large sedan into a cop car. You don't build something from scratch if you can simply improve on an existing design. In object-oriented programming, this idea is called *inheritance*. It's a really great idea. The `Sprite` class built into pygame doesn't do anything useful on its own. Instead, it's designed to be used as the foundation of whatever kind of sprite you want to make. To make a class that inherits from an existing class, simply indicate the existing class name in parentheses:

```
class Box(pygame.sprite.Sprite):
```

3. **Create an initializer for the class.**

Objects have a special method called the *initializer*. The constructor is automatically called when you create an instance of a class. It is used to help you set up the class and make sure it's ready to do its job. In Python, an object's constructor is a special method called __init__():

```
def __init__(self):
```

4. **Incorporate the `self` parameter.**

All object methods in Python require the special variable `self`. This parameter refers to the object itself. As you'll see shortly, the `self` variable is a handy way to refer to an object inside its methods.

5. **Call the `pygame.sprite.Sprite()` constructor.**

This new `Box` class you are creating is based on the `Sprite` class that comes with pygame. `Sprite` has some neat features of its own. To ensure that the sprite is properly initialized, you need to call the constructor of the `pygame.sprite.Sprite()` class as well.

```
pygame.sprite.Sprite.__init__(self)
```

Setting the sprite attributes

Once you've got the basic sprite definition underway, use the __init__() method to initialize the sprite's attributes. You'll almost always want to set the sprite's image, rect, dx, and dy attributes in the __init__() method. (The dx and dy attributes will be used to manage the sprite's motion.) Here's how you set the attributes:

1. **Create the sprite image.**

Each sprite needs an image attribute. Usually (though not always) this is set up in the __init__() method. In this simple case, I'm simply making a pygame surface like this:

```
self.image = pygame.Surface((25, 25))
self.image.fill((255, 0, 0))
```

Information Kiosk

Notice that the image variable is actually self.image. This helps Python (and the programmer) understand that image is not simply a variable, but an attribute of the current object. When you define an attribute as part of a class, you will always attach it to the self object. Attaching a variable to the object with the self keyword also makes that variable accessible outside the class definition.

2. **Create the sprite rect.**

Pygame also expects each sprite to have a rect attribute. Generally you extract the rect from the image, like this:

```
self.rect = self.image.get_rect()
```

If you create the rect from the image, you are certain that the rect is the same size as the image (although you can make it a different size if you want, to make collisions easier or harder, for example).

3. **Give the sprite an initial position.**

You don't move the sprite directly. Instead, the sprite's position is related to its Rect object. Here I've set the starting position of the box by setting the rect.centerx and rect.centery attributes. You will see many other ways to determine the position of a sprite, but I tend to use this technique, because it allows for a great deal of control.

```
self.rect.centerx = 0
self.rect.centery = 200
```

4. **Set dx and dy attributes to determine the sprite's direction and speed.**

The pygame Sprite object doesn't include dx and dy attributes, but you'll almost always put them in yourself — at least for sprites that will move on their own. These attributes are used to determine how much the sprite should move in the horizontal (dx) and vertical (dy) axes during each frame.

```
        self.dx = 10
        self.dy = 0
```

I'll explain shortly how dx and dy work, but for now, just accept that I'm going to move the sprite 10 pixels to the right every frame, and the sprite will have no vertical movement.

Building an update() method

If __init__() is where your sprite is born, update() is its heartbeat. The update() method defines what the sprite does every frame. Follow these steps:

1. Build an update() method.

The update() method is simple, but it's really the heart of any sprite.

```
def update(self):
    self.rect.centerx += self.dx
    self.rect.centery += self.dy
    if self.rect.right > screen.get_width():
        self.rect.left = 0
```

The update() method will be called once per frame (generally 30 times per second).

2. Move the sprite by dx and dy.

On each pass, I add the value of self.dx to self.rect.centerx and self.dy to self.rect.centery. If dx is a positive value, the sprite will move to the right dx pixels each frame. If dx is negative, the sprite moves to the left. Likewise, if dy is positive, the sprite moves downward. If dy is negative, the sprite moves upward.

```
    self.rect.centerx += self.dx
    self.rect.centery += self.dy
```

 Information Kiosk

Of course, this is a very simple example. You'll often have more complex movement, but we'll keep it straightforward for now.

3. Check for boundaries.

In this simple example, dx is 10 and dy is zero, so the box will only move from left to right. I need to check for a boundary condition. It's possible (in this case inevitable) that the box will move off the right side of the display screen. I need to test for this condition and respond appropriately:

```
    if self.rect.right > screen.get_width():
        self.rect.left = 0
```

What I really want to know is if the sprite is about to leave the screen on the right side. This is where the `sprite.rect` attributes are really handy. Even though I moved the sprite by manipulating its `centerx` attribute, I can check to see where the sprite's right edge is by examining the `right` attribute. If the `self.rect.right` value is larger than the screen's width (determined by the cleverly named `screen.get_width()` method), I know the sprite is about to leave the screen, and I need to wrap it to the left side of the screen.

Transfer

I'm keeping the boundary-checking really simple here, so you can focus on how sprites work. Look ahead to Chapter 8 for more information on what to do when a sprite leaves the stage, and how to make it bounce, slide, or stop.

4. **If the sprite leaves on the right, enter stage left.**

It's an easy matter to place the sprite on the left side of the stage. Simply assign 0 to its `rect.left` attribute.

Using a sprite group with the IDEA framework

Although sprites are very powerful, they aren't any harder to use than the IDEA framework you already know.

Building and grouping sprites

Sprites are actually perfect for the E step (Entities), because they are far more powerful than the basic surface entities you've seen before. Simply put the following code in the Entities step to make a sprite-enabled IDEA program:

```
box = Box()
allSprites = pygame.sprite.Group(box)
```

Here's how it works:

1. **Create an instance of your new Box sprite.**

Remember that when you define an object by writing a class definition, you aren't actually cooking. You're writing a recipe. Now that you have created a recipe for the `Box` sprite, you need to cook one up. When you use this line:

```
box = Box()
```

you are creating an instance of the `Box` class, and calling that instance `box`.

Watch Your Step

You might think that `box` and `Box` are the same thing, but they aren't. Remember that Python is case-sensitive (it treats uppercase and lowercase letters differently). Object-oriented programmers tend to capitalize class names but not instance names. In other words, `Box` is a recipe. I can use it to make new instances of this special `Box` type. When I make one of them, I call it `box`. I could have named it something else, but honestly, it's a box. Calling it something else like `myBox` wouldn't really add much to the program. As long as you understand the difference between classes and instances it really isn't that confusing.

2. **Create a sprite group.**

`Sprite` objects are not meant to act on their own. If you want a pygame sprite to do anything, you have to put it in a *sprite group*. This is a special object that lets you control one or more sprites.

Information Kiosk

Pygame actually has several different kinds of sprite groups, but starting with pygame 1.8, the basic `pygame.sprite.Group` object has all the features you will normally need. If you are using an earlier version of pygame, your code will not run correctly because the ordinary `Group` object was not as sophisticated in ancient times. If possible, upgrade to pygame 1.8 or later to get the more sophisticated behavior. If you can't upgrade (because you're not the system administrator, for example) use the `pygame.sprite.RenderUpdate` class where I use `pygame.sprite.Group` in my code.

3. **Add the box object to the group.**

If you have already created all the sprites you need (as I have in this example), you can simply pass them to the group constructor, and the group will contain those sprites.

4. **Assign the group to a variable.**

You won't generally control the sprites individually. It's more efficient to let the `Group` object manage all your sprites. Give the group a name so you can refer to it later:

```
allSprites = pygame.sprite.Group(box)
```

Updating your sprites

When you use sprites, you don't have to blit them to the screen by hand the way you do with surfaces. The sprite group will call each sprite's update() method, and the sprite will update itself. Take a look at the main loop code and you'll see it's been changed a little bit to handle sprites:

```
screen.blit(background, (0,0))

box = Box()
allSprites = pygame.sprite.Group(box)

clock = pygame.time.Clock()
keepGoing = True
while keepGoing:
    clock.tick(30)
    for event in pygame.event.get():
        if event.type == pygame.QUIT:
            keepGoing = False

    allSprites.clear(screen, background)
    allSprites.update()
    allSprites.draw(screen)

    pygame.display.flip()
```

The sprite-enabled loop isn't any harder than the old-fashioned loop, but it's slightly different. Here's a look at the changes:

Blitting the background one time before the loop begins. In the previous examples, I copied the entire background onto the screen during every frame. This is a computationally expensive process; there are a *lot* of pixels to copy. The group object supports a more efficient kind of updating that doesn't require the entire background to be drawn every frame. You must blit the background one time, so it's in place, but then you'll use a special trick so that only the parts of the background that were changed in the last frame are cleared in the current frame.

```
screen.blit(background, (0,0))
```

Clearing the sprites. The sprite group has a special method called clear(). This method clears off all the sprites that were drawn in the *previous* frame, and replaces them with the appropriate part of the background. The clear() method requires the drawing surface (usually screen) and the background surface (usually background) as arguments.

```
allSprites.clear(screen, background)
```

Updating the sprites. The sprite group has another handy method called `update()`. This method calls the `update()` method of every sprite in the group. (That's why Sprite subclasses you define need an `update()` method.)

```
allSprites.update()
```

Information Kiosk

The sprite group's `update()` method does not update the screen! It simply passes control back to the sprites and tells them to run their own `update()` methods. Once the sprites have updated themselves, their images and `rect`s may have changed, so when the `draw()` step comes next, they will be drawn in their new places.

Drawing the sprites. The sprite group's `draw()` method automatically blits all the sprites onto the screen in the appropriate places, according to each sprite's `rect` attribute. There's no need to blit each sprite to the screen by hand. The `draw()` method requires a drawing surface (usually `screen`) as its only argument.

```
allSprites.draw(screen)
```

Information Kiosk

Call me Mr. Mnemonic. I had trouble remembering the order these group commands come in, so I think of a cow chewing its cud. Get it? C = Clear, U = Update, D = Draw. (Maybe you have a better memory than mine; I think I'm getting old. I need this kind of trick or I get lost.)

Flipping the display as usual. You don't have to blit each surface any more (because the sprite group takes care of that for you now) but you still have to flip the display to tell pygame you're ready to update the actual graphics hardware.

Information Kiosk

You might be wondering if all this sprite stuff is really worth it. After all, this `basicSprite` program isn't any shorter than the `box.py` in Chapter 4 that does exactly the same thing. For small programs like this, the object-oriented stuff doesn't buy you much. The real advantage comes when you have a lot of sprites running around and crashing into each other. Stick with me, and you'll see how handy sprites can be.

Making Sprite Variations

The basic sprite is pretty easy. It's common to make a few variations in the basic pattern. I show you here how to build a `Circle` sprite that follows the mouse automatically, as well as a square that creates itself in a random spot in a particular color, and a very handy `Label` sprite that lets you write text to the screen. Later I put all these sprites in an external module — and then put them together to demonstrate collision handling.

Building a mouse-following sprite

Sprites are interesting when they move around and crash into things, so the next few example programs show several variations of the basic `Sprite` objects and how they can work together. The first variation is the `moveCircle.py` program illustrated in Figure 6-4.

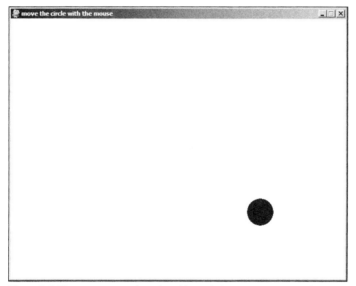

Figure 6-4: The mouse cursor is replaced by a circle you can move on the screen.

The `Circle` sprite automatically follows the mouse as it moves. Here's all the code, but I'll break it up into steps, as usual:

```
""" moveCircle.py
    create a blue circle sprite and have it
    follow the mouse"""

import pygame, random
```

```
pygame.init()

screen = pygame.display.set_mode((640, 480))

class Circle(pygame.sprite.Sprite):
    def __init__(self):
        pygame.sprite.Sprite.__init__(self)
        self.image = pygame.Surface((50, 50))
        self.image.fill((255, 255, 255))
        pygame.draw.circle(self.image, (0, 0, 255),      ↩
(25, 25), 25, 0)
        self.rect = self.image.get_rect()

    def update(self):
        self.rect.center = pygame.mouse.get_pos()

def main():
    pygame.display.set_caption("move the circle with      ↩
the mouse")

    background = pygame.Surface(screen.get_size())
    background.fill((255, 255, 255))
    screen.blit(background, (0, 0))

    circle = Circle()
    allSprites = pygame.sprite.Group(circle)

    #hide mouse
    pygame.mouse.set_visible(False)
    clock = pygame.time.Clock()
    keepGoing = True
    while keepGoing:
        clock.tick(30)
        for event in pygame.event.get():
            if event.type == pygame.QUIT:
                keepGoing = False

        allSprites.clear(screen, background)
        allSprites.update()
        allSprites.draw(screen)

        pygame.display.flip()

    #return mouse
    pygame.mouse.set_visible(True)

if __name__ == "__main__":
    main()
```

Creating the circle sprite

The player controls the circle by moving the mouse. The `Circle` sprite class itself is pretty easy to understand:

```
class Circle(pygame.sprite.Sprite):
    def __init__(self):
        pygame.sprite.Sprite.__init__(self)
        self.image = pygame.Surface((50, 50))
        self.image.fill((255, 255, 255))
        pygame.draw.circle(self.image, (0, 0, 255),      ↩
(25, 25), 25, 0)
        self.rect = self.image.get_rect()

    def update(self):
        self.rect.center = pygame.mouse.get_pos()
```

Design the `Circle` class like this:

1. Create a 50 × 50 surface.

The image will start as a square, 50 pixels on a side.

```
        self.image = pygame.Surface((50, 50))
```

2. Fill in the background with white.

The white background will blend in with the screen's white background.

```
        self.image.fill((255, 255, 255))
```

3. Draw a circle on the surface.

The shape will look like a circle to the user even though it's actually drawn onto a square surface (this is important later).

```
        pygame.draw.circle(self.image, (0, 0, 255), (25, 25), 25, 0)
```

4. Extract a `rect` from the `image` object.

The sprite needs a `rect`. The typical way to get one is through the image object's `get_rect()` method:

```
        self.rect = self.image.get_rect()
```

5. Add a basic `update()` method.

The circle will be capable of moving every frame, so it needs an `update()` method to tell it how to move.

```
    def update(self):
```

6. Attach the circle position to the mouse.

The easiest way to make the sprite follow the mouse pointer is to copy the mouse pointer's position to the center of the `rect`, like this:

```
        self.rect.center = pygame.mouse.get_pos()
```

Using the circle in a program

Of course, a `Sprite` object by itself isn't much fun. You have to give it an environment to play in, and that's what the main program is for. This program is pretty typical, but it has one new twist: If the circle will replace the mouse pointer, you need the mouse pointer to go away. You also need to return it at the end of the program. That's pretty easy to do; the `moveCircle.py` program's `main()` function works like this:

1. **Don't forget to blit the background outside the main loop.**

I often blit the background right after I create it, so I don't forget it:

```
screen.blit(background, (0, 0))
```

2. **Make an instance of the `Circle` class and add it to a sprite group.**

Sprites don't do anything interesting until they're part of a group.

```
circle = Circle()
allSprites = pygame.sprite.Group(circle)
```

3. **Hide the mouse cursor.**

Pygame has a really obvious technique for this:

```
pygame.mouse.set_visible(False)
```

The cursor will be hidden only inside the game window. It will be available to other programs outside the game window.

4. **Use the group methods to handle screen updating**.

Updating the screen becomes consistent, no matter how the `Sprite` objects work. It doesn't matter that this sprite is following the mouse rather than incrementing x. You update in exactly the same way:

```
allSprites.clear(screen, background)
allSprites.update()
allSprites.draw(screen)

pygame.display.flip()
```

5. **Make the mouse cursor visible again after the main loop is over.**

When Python exits, the mouse cursor will reappear. Still, if you turned the mouse cursor off, you should turn it back on again.

```
pygame.mouse.set_visible(True)
```

Understanding how "dirty rect" updating works

The `pygame.sprite.Group` object's `update()` method uses a trick called "dirty rect" updating. To see how it works, I temporarily removed the line that blits the white background onto the screen in `moveCircle.py`. Figure 6-5 shows what happens after I move the mouse around.

Figure 6-5 illustrates well how the dirty `rect` update works. As I move the sprite, the update method grabs the appropriate part of the background (which is all white) and draws it wherever the sprite was in the previous frame. The sprite is then redrawn in its current position. This is more efficient than re-drawing the entire background every frame. Of course, if you forget to draw the background ahead of time, the screen will be its default black color — you'll only see the intended background after the sprite has visited that particular part of the screen.

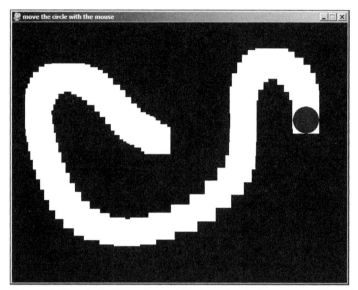

Figure 6-5: If you forget the background, it's drawn in a trail as you move the sprite.

Building a basic label

Often you'll find yourself wanting to place text on the screen. You learned in Chapter 5 how to build a `Font` object and use its `render()` method to draw text on the screen. Putting the text in a `Sprite` object makes it easier to maintain and re-use. Figure 6-6 shows a program with three labels on the screen.

Two labels just sit there on the screen, but the center label dynamically changes based on your input activities. That is, it tells you the status of the mouse and whether a key has been pressed. This illustrates how you can make a dynamic label that's easy to change.

The `labelDemo.py` program shown in Figure 6-6 could have been built without sprites, but you'll see how creating a custom `Sprite` object makes it easier to build and maintain text elements on the screen. You can also see how easy it is to make more than one instance of a class:

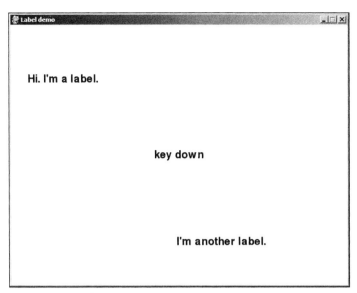

Figure 6-6: Each of these labels is actually a sprite.

```
""" labelDemo.py
    creating a basic label sprite"""

import pygame
pygame.init()

screen = pygame.display.set_mode((640, 480))

class Label(pygame.sprite.Sprite):
    """ Label Class (simplest version)
        Attributes:
            font: any pygame Font or SysFont object
            text: text to display
            center: desired position of label center (x, y)
    """
    def __init__(self):
        pygame.sprite.Sprite.__init__(self)
        self.font = pygame.font.SysFont("None", 30)
        self.text = ""
        self.center = (320, 240)

    def update(self):
        self.image = self.font.render(self.text, 1,        ↩
(0, 0, 0))
        self.rect = self.image.get_rect()
```

```
                self.rect.center = self.center

    def main():
        pygame.display.set_caption("Label demo")

        background = pygame.Surface(screen.get_size())
        background.fill((255, 255, 255))
        screen.blit(background, (0, 0))

        label1 = Label()
        label2 = Label()
        labelEvent = Label()
        allSprites = pygame.sprite.Group(label1, label2,    ↩
labelEvent)

        label1.text = "Hi. I'm a label."
        label1.center = (100, 100)

        label2.text = "I'm another label."
        label2.center = (400, 400)

        clock = pygame.time.Clock()
        keepGoing = True
        while keepGoing:
            clock.tick(30)

            for event in pygame.event.get():
                if event.type == pygame.QUIT:
                    keepGoing = False
                elif event.type == pygame.MOUSEMOTION:
                    (mouseX, mouseY) = pygame.mouse.get_pos()
                    labelEvent.text = "mouse: (%d, %d)" %
(mouseX, mouseY)
                elif event.type == pygame.MOUSEBUTTONDOWN:
                    labelEvent.text = "button press"
                elif event.type == pygame.KEYDOWN:
                    labelEvent.text = "key down"

            allSprites.clear(screen, background)
            allSprites.update()
            allSprites.draw(screen)

            pygame.display.flip()

    if __name__=="__main__":
        main()
```

Creating the Label class

To make labels, begin with a new kind of sprite class specialized for displaying text:

```python
class Label(pygame.sprite.Sprite):
    """ Label Class (simplest version)
        Attributes:
            font: any pygame font object
            text: text to display
            center: desired position of label center (x, y)
    """
    def __init__(self):
        pygame.sprite.Sprite.__init__(self)
        self.font = pygame.font.SysFont("None", 30)
        self.text = ""
        self.center = (320, 240)

    def update(self):
        self.image = self.font.render(self.text, 1,     ↵
(0, 0, 0))
        self.rect = self.image.get_rect()
        self.rect.center = self.center
```

The `Label` class still does the same job as any other sprite, but the image of this class is actually text. Because the text could change during any frame, the `image` and `rect` attributes are re-created during each frame in the `update()` method. `Label` also introduces two custom attributes — `text` and `center`. When you create an instance of the `Label` class, your program can change these attributes of the sprite.

Here's what you do to make the `Label` class work:

1. Begin with a basic sprite.

Label is a subclass of `pygame.sprite.Sprite`, so it needs all the standard features; an `__init__()` method, a call to `Sprite` class's `__init__()` method, and an `update()` method.

2. Write a documentation string for the sprite.

It's smart to write a quick docstring explaining any key features of the object. In this case, the attributes are the most important features of the label object, so I write a quick note explaining how they work. When another programmer tries to use my sprite (or I try to use it again in five minutes), it will be clear what the sprite does and how to change it.

3. Create a `font` attribute for the `Label` class.

Use one of the techniques described in Chapter 5 to build a Font object for the class.

```
self.font = pygame.font.SysFont("None", 30)
```

4. Determine starting text for the `Label` class.

Create a `text` attribute. The initial value of this attribute is not important, because it will be changed later so I use an empty string — just two quotation marks with nothing inside. The important thing to do in the __init__() method is establish that the attribute exists.

5. Create a `center` attribute for the `Label` class.

During update, you'll actually change the center attribute of the `rect` to set the position of the sprite. It's easier for the external program to manage things if your sprite has its own center attribute. I give my sprite a default center position of (320, 240), because that's the center of a 640×480 display.

```
self.center = (320, 240)
```

6. Write an `update()` method for the class.

The sprite has the potential to change each frame. Specifically, the program that uses the sprite might change any of its attributes. During each frame, it's possible that the sprite font, text, or center has been changed by the main program. The update() method accepts these changes and builds the text appropriately based on the current situation.

7. Build the sprite's image by rendering the text.

The image attribute of a label should be the label's text rendered by the label's font.

```
self.image = self.font.render(self.text, 1, (0, 0, 0))
```

Information Kiosk

As the Label sprite stands right now, it always renders in black. Of course, you could make another attribute so the font can be rendered in whatever color you want. (Gosh, that sounds like a *peachy* end-of-chapter exercise . . . .)

8. Move the sprite to the specified center.

The `center` attribute doesn't do anything by itself. The actual position of the label is determined by the `rect.center`. Copy the custom `center` attribute to the built-in `rect.center` and you've made a label with its own `center` attribute and your programs never have to deal directly with the `rect`.

```
self.rect.center = self.center
```

Adding Label instances to your program

Once you've created the `Label` class, you can put it to work in your program. Sprites become really handy when you use more than one in your program: You think once about how to make a general case work (as you define the class), and then you can make as many instances as you want — and they'll all work the same way without any additional code.

You can build as many instances of `Label` as you want using the `Label()` constructor:

```
label1 = Label()
label2 = Label()
labelEvent = Label()
allSprites = pygame.sprite.Group(label1, label2,      ↩
labelEvent)

label1.text = "Hi. I'm a label."
label1.center = (100, 100)

label2.text = "I'm another label."
label2.center = (400, 400)
```

Step Into the Real World

If you've used another OOP language (especially Java), you may be horrified at the cavalier way Python allows you to simply create class attributes. Many OOP languages use special, protected variables and access methods to protect the data inside objects. That sort of thing is possible in Python, but is rarely done. The technique I show you here is fine for the kind of work we'll be doing, and is a more typical Python idiom. Technically, the special protected version is referred to as "properties," and variables attached to a class as we've done are called "attributes." Because they are used in basically the same way, I tend to use the terms interchangeably in Python.

Once you've made custom `Sprite` objects, they're pretty easy to use:

1. **Create the objects with the `Label()` constructor.**

Remember, `Label()` calls the `__init__()` method of the `Label` class and returns a new instance you can assign to a variable.

```
label1 = Label()
label2 = Label()
labelEvent = Label()
```

2. **Put all the labels in a group.**

Sprites are easiest to use when they're in a group. I made a simple group called `allSprites`.

```
allSprites = pygame.sprite.Group(label1, label2, labelEvent)
```

3. **Change `label` attributes as you wish.**

All the label instances have a default center of (320, 240), so if I don't move them, they'll all be on top of each other. Also, labels aren't very interesting without some text, so I add text to `label1` and `label2`.

```
label1.text = "Hi. I'm a label."
label1.center = (100, 100)

label2.text = "I'm another label."
label2.center = (400, 400)
```

The third label (`labelEvent`) will be dynamically updated, just so you can see that the label can be preset at the beginning of the program (as I do with `label1` and `label2`) or during the event loop.

4. **Modify a label inside the main loop.**

I can change the label every frame if I want. Look inside the event handler of the main loop, and you'll see that's exactly what I've done:

```
        for event in pygame.event.get():
            if event.type == pygame.QUIT:
                keepGoing = False
            elif event.type == pygame.MOUSEMOTION:
                (mouseX, mouseY) = pygame.mouse   ↵
.get_pos()
                labelEvent.text = "mouse: (%d, %d)" ↵
% (mouseX, mouseY)
            elif event.type == pygame.MOUSEBUTTONDOWN:
                labelEvent.text = "button press"
            elif event.type == pygame.KEYDOWN:
                labelEvent.text = "key down"
```

All I did here was trap for various events, and send appropriate text to the `labelEvent` object.

Making sprites with parameters

Most of the time, when you build a sprite, you'll have some sort of default behavior to set. Fortunately, you can create a sprite with parameters that work just like the function parameters you've already used. Figure 6-7 shows `boxes.py` with a lot of boxes on the screen.

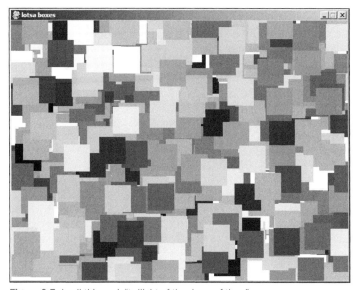

Figure 6-7: I call this work "twilight of the dawn of time."

```
""" boxes.py
    demonstrate multiple boxes,
    adding parameters """

import pygame, random
pygame.init()

screen = pygame.display.set_mode((640, 480))

class Square(pygame.sprite.Sprite):
    """ makes a box with a random starting
```

```
                position and the given color.
                To make a red square, use
                redSquare = Square((255, 0, 0))

                requires screen be predefined and import random """

        def __init__(self, color):
            pygame.sprite.Sprite.__init__(self)
            self.image = pygame.Surface((50, 50))
            self.image.fill(color)
            self.rect = self.image.get_rect()
            self.rect.centerx = random.randrange(0,            ↩
screen.get_width())
            self.rect.centery = random.randrange(0,            ↩
screen.get_height())

    def main():
        pygame.display.set_caption("lotsa boxes")

        background = pygame.Surface(screen.get_size())
        background.fill((255, 255, 255))
        screen.blit(background, (0, 0))

        boxes = []
        for colorName in pygame.color.THECOLORS:
            boxes.append(Square(pygame.color.Color(colorName)))

        allSprites = pygame.sprite.Group(boxes)

        keepGoing = True
        clock = pygame.time.Clock()
        while (keepGoing):
            clock.tick(30)
            for event in pygame.event.get():
                if event.type == pygame.QUIT:
                    keepGoing = False

            allSprites.clear(screen, background)
            allSprites.update()
            allSprites.draw(screen)

            pygame.display.flip()

    if __name__ == "__main__":
        main()
```

Step Into the Real World

Take a careful look at the part of the code that copies the mouse position to the label:

```
(mouseX, mouseY) = pygame.mouse.get_pos()
labelEvent.text = "mouse: (%d, %d)" %(mouseX, mouseY)
```

I wrote this code in two steps for clarity, but I could have combined them. In the first line, I extract the mouse position, determined by the function `get_pos()`, into a tuple. In the second line, I use that tuple in a string interpolation (check Chapter 1 if you need a refresher on interpolation). Of course, I could also have used the result of the function directly, like this:

```
labelEvent.text = "mouse: (%d, %d)" % pygame.mouse.get_pos()
```

It doesn't matter that much which technique you use, as long as it works, and you can understand what's going on. I generally tend towards readability when I can.

Building the Square class

The `Square` sprite featured in this program is an extremely basic extension of the basic `Sprite` class. I don't intend this sprite to move or change at all, so it doesn't need an `update()` method. The other interesting feature of `Square` is how it uses a parameter in its constructor.

```
class Square(pygame.sprite.Sprite):
    """ makes a box with a random starting
        position and the given color.
        To make a red square, use
        redSquare = Square((255, 0, 0))

        requires screen be predefined and import random """

    def __init__(self, color):
        pygame.sprite.Sprite.__init__(self)
        self.image = pygame.Surface((50, 50))
        self.image.fill(color)
        self.rect = self.image.get_rect()
        self.rect.centerx = random.randrange(0,          ↵
screen.get_width())
        self.rect.centery = random.randrange(0,          ↵
screen.get_height())
```

1. **Begin with a basic sprite.**

Because this sprite doesn't require motion, it doesn't even need an `update()` function.

2. **Incorporate a second parameter in the __init__() method.**

Remember, all methods include the `self` parameter. If you add another parameter to a class's constructor, you can create the class with a parameter. This allows you to create instances of the class with many variations. In this simple case, I can feed any color tuple to the `Square()` constructor and the program will create a square of that color.

```
def __init__(self, color):
```

3. **Include documentation.**

Any time you build a new class, you should incorporate documentation so you'll remember how to use the class.

4. **Create a 50 x 50 surface.**

This basic surface will be filled with the color:

```
self.image = pygame.Surface((50, 50))
```

5. **Fill the surface with the given color.**

Use the `fill()` method to incorporate the color parameter's value:

```
self.image.fill(color)
```

6. **Place the square in a random spot on the screen.**

Use the `randrange()` function to generate appropriate random x and y values for the square:

```
self.rect.centerx = random.randrange(0, screen.get_width())
self.rect.centery = random.randrange(0, screen.get_height())
```

Watch Your Step

If you use `randrange`, you'll need to import the `random` `import random` module. It's an easy thing, but it's also easy to miss.

Using the Square class to make boxes

You'll use the `Square` class again in another example, but for now, just see how it can be used to make the image shown in Figure 6-7 with all the colored boxes. Sprites are extremely useful when you want to make a lot of similar things. The `boxes.py` program takes advantage of the `pygame.color.Color()` structure to build a square in every color built into Python. Here are the steps:

1. **Make an empty list to contain the boxes.**

This can be done before the main loop runs.

```
boxes = []
```

2. **Step through every value in pygame.color.THECOLORS.**

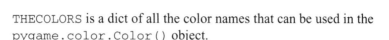

THECOLORS is a dict of all the color names that can be used in the pygame.color.Color() object.

```
for colorName in pygame.color.THECOLORS:
```

Transfer

THECOLORS is another example of the dict structure introduced in Chapter 3.

3. **Make a square of each color and add that color to the boxes list.**

```
boxes.append(Square(pygame.color.Color(colorName)))
```

4. **Add all the boxes to the allSprites group.**

This is where the sprite-group concept really pays off. Python will create 657 boxes. (Extra point if you can write a one-line command to prove that!) All of the sprites are packaged in the boxes list, and that list is dropped into the allSprites group. All the rest of the program works exactly the same whether there is one or 657 sprites. If I want all the sprites to move around, all I have to do is change the Sprite class definition, and it will happen automatically for all 657 sprites.

```
allSprites = pygame.sprite.Group(boxes)
```

Managing Collisions

The three specialty sprites (Label, Circle, and Square) I've been showing you are useful for proving a couple of other important points. First of all, I'm going to use all these sprites in the next few examples — so I need a way to store them and re-use them without having to copy and paste. Once I've got the sprites in a handy library, I use them to show a number of aspects of collision detection.

Making a class module

Now I've made three really interesting objects. They are so useful, I think I might use them in other programs. It would be great if you could store them in one place and bring them back when you want. Of course, this is easy to do once you know about a little thing called a class module. Here you go: Take a look at the code for collisionObjects.py:

```
""" collisionObjects.py
    A class library of objects used in the collision demos
    in chapter 6"""

import pygame, random

class Square(pygame.sprite.Sprite):
```

```
""" makes a box with a random starting
    position and the given color.
    To make a red square, use
    redSquare = Square((255, 0, 0), screen)

    requires screen be predefined and import random """

def __init__(self, color, screen):
    pygame.sprite.Sprite.__init__(self)
    self.image = pygame.Surface((50, 50))
    self.image.fill(color)
    self.rect = self.image.get_rect()
    self.rect.centerx = random.randrange(0,          ↩
screen.get_width())
    self.rect.centery = random.randrange(0,          ↩
screen.get_height())

class Circle(pygame.sprite.Sprite):
    """ makes a blue circle that
        follows the mouse. """

def __init__(self):
    pygame.sprite.Sprite.__init__(self)
    self.image = pygame.Surface((50, 50))
    self.image.fill((255, 255, 255))
    pygame.draw.circle(self.image, (0, 0, 255),      ↩
(25, 25), 25, 0)
    self.rect = self.image.get_rect()

def update(self):
    self.rect.center = pygame.mouse.get_pos()

class Label(pygame.sprite.Sprite):
    """ Label Class (simplest version)
        Attributes:
            font: any pygame font object
            text: text to display
            center: desired position of label center (x, y)
    """
def __init__(self):
    pygame.sprite.Sprite.__init__(self)
    self.font = pygame.font.SysFont("None", 30)
    self.text = ""
    self.center = (320, 240)

def update(self):
    self.image = self.font.render(self.text, 1,      ↩
(0, 0, 0))
    self.rect = self.image.get_rect()
    self.rect.center = self.center
```

This code has some interesting characteristics:

- **It doesn't do anything!!** If you run this code, it seems like it doesn't do anything. That's because this code is not meant to run on its own, but to be used by other programs. There is no main loop, and no code at all outside the object definitions.

- **The objects are very familiar.** All the objects are taken from the examples in this chapter. The only difference is the `Square` class. I added a second parameter so I can send the object a reference to the screen. (More on that next.)

- **The square is a little different.** It's good to start breaking things up into several files as I'm doing here, but sometimes you find some new problems. Recall that the `Square` instance needs to know the size of the screen so it can place itself randomly on-screen. In the `boxes.py` program, the screen was defined globally before I defined the `Square` class or made instances of it, so the `Square` instances knew what the screen was. When I moved the class definitions to their own file, I had to add some mechanism so the square will know what the screen is. Now the square takes two parameters. The first is a color (just like before) but the second parameter is the screen, so the square can figure out its boundaries.

Re-using your classes

Once you've stored your classes into a separate file, you can use the `import` statement to include those classes the same way as you can import a built-in module. To illustrate, take a look at the `useCOL.py` program in Figure 6-8.

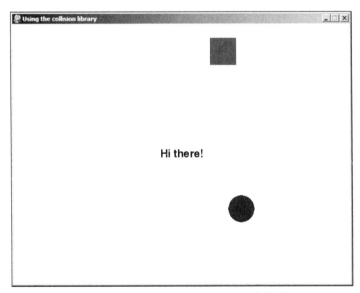

Figure 6-8: This program is simple because it uses a pre-built library.

As you can see, useCol.py combines all the objects. The program itself is pretty simple, because all the details are packed away in the object definitions.

```
""" useCOL.py
    demonstrate using the collisionObjects Library
    """

import pygame, collisionObjects
pygame.init()

screen = pygame.display.set_mode((640, 480))

def main():
    pygame.display.set_caption("Using the collision    ↵
library")

    background = pygame.Surface(screen.get_size())
    background.fill((255, 255, 255))
    screen.blit(background, (0, 0))

    label = collisionObjects.Label()
    label.text = "Hi there!"
    circle = collisionObjects.Circle()
    square = collisionObjects.Square((255, 0, 0), screen)

    allSprites = pygame.sprite.Group(circle, square, label)

    clock = pygame.time.Clock()
    keepGoing = True
    while keepGoing:
        for event in pygame.event.get():
            if event.type == pygame.QUIT:
                keepGoing = False

        allSprites.clear(screen, background)
        allSprites.update()
```

```
        allSprites.draw(screen)

        pygame.display.flip()

if __name__ == "__main__":
    main()
```

The great thing about useCOL.py is how it returns to the IDEA framework. The program isn't really much more complicated than anything else you've done in the last couple of chapters. The new things are all stored in the sprites, which are hidden off in their own file. Encapsulation is grand!

Here's how I made it:

1. **Import the object library.**

I saved my object library as collisionObjects.py. I can import that library just like any other module, and my program has access to it.

```
import pygame, collisionObjects
```

 Watch Your Step

The file is called collisionObjects.py but the import statement doesn't use the .py extension. It's an easy mistake to make. The script file ends in .py but the module created by the script does not have the .py extension.

2. **Make instances of the objects.**

Now that I have access to the classes, I can make instances of them for my program.

```
label = collisionObjects.Label()
label.text = "Hi there!"
circle = collisionObjects.Circle()
square = collisionObjects.Square((255, 0, 0), screen)
```

3. **Add text to the label.**

The label isn't interesting without words and stuff, so I added some text to it.

4. **Make the square with a reference to the screen object.**

I've modified the Square class so that it requires a surface parameter (screen). When I create an instance of the new Square object, I have to send it both of the arguments it expects: a color and the screen surface.

5. **Add the sprites to a group in the normal way (as described in the "Using a sprite group with the IDEA framework" section earlier in this chapter).**

I make a sprite group called allSprites and add stuff to it.

```
allSprites = pygame.sprite.Group(circle, square, label)
```

Checking for sprite-on-sprite collisions

Arcade games are all about things bonking into each other. It's no surprise that collision detection is an important part of game programming. There are many ways to handle collisions. Start with the simplest form that simply checks to see whether two rectangles overlap. The `Rect` object has a `colliderect()` method which accepts another `Rect` as a parameter. If the two `rects` are overlapping, the method returns the value `True`. The `spriteSprite.py` program in Figure 6-9 illustrates this technique in action:

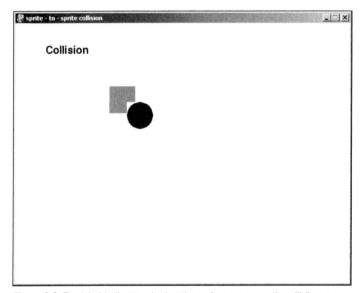

Figure 6-9: The label indicates whether the sprites are currently colliding or not.

In Figure 6-9 the square is placed randomly on the screen, and the circle moves with the mouse. The program is pretty simple, because it uses the objects from `collisionObjects.py`. The only thing new is the collision code inside the event handler. I've marked that section of the code in boldface so you can find it easily.

```
""" spriteSprite.py
    demonstrates a simple sprite - sprite
```

```
              collision using rect's collision method"""

   import pygame, collisionObjects
   pygame.init()

   def main():
       screen = pygame.display.set_mode((640, 480))
       pygame.display.set_caption("sprite - to - sprite     ↩
   collision")

       background = pygame.Surface(screen.get_size())
       background.fill((255, 255, 255))
       screen.blit(background, (0, 0))

       lblOutput = collisionObjects.Label()
       lblOutput.center = (100, 50)
       lblOutput.text = "Hi"

       circle = collisionObjects.Circle()
       square = collisionObjects.Square((0, 255, 0), screen)

       allSprites = pygame.sprite.Group(square, circle,      ↩
   lblOutput)

       keepGoing = True
       clock = pygame.time.Clock()
       pygame.mouse.set_visible(False)
       while keepGoing:
           clock.tick(30)
           for event in pygame.event.get():
               if event.type == pygame.QUIT:
                   keepGoing = False

           if circle.rect.colliderect(square.rect):
               lblOutput.text = "Collision"
           else:
               lblOutput.text = "No collision"

           allSprites.clear(screen, background)
           allSprites.update()
           allSprites.draw(screen)

           pygame.display.flip()
       pygame.mouse.set_visible(True)

   if __name__ == "__main__":
       main()
```

To check for collisions between sprites, follow these steps:

1. Build the sprites.

In this case that's easy because I'm re-using the `collisionObjects` library I already wrote. I made one instance each of the circle, square, and label:

```
lblOutput = collisionObjects.Label()
lblOutput.center = (100, 50)
lblOutput.text = "Hi"

circle = collisionObjects.Circle()
square = collisionObjects.Square((0, 255, 0), screen)

allSprites = pygame.sprite.Group(square, circle, lblOutput)
```

 Transfer

If you don't understand how I set up any of these variables, refer back to the section in this chapter called "Re-using your classes."

2. Check for a collision between the circle and the square.

The `colliderect` method of the `rect` attribute does that for me.

```
if circle.rect.colliderect(square.rect):
```

3. Update the label accordingly.

There's really not much to it! Four lines:

```
if circle.rect.colliderect(square.rect):
    lblOutput.text = "Collision"
else:
    lblOutput.text = "No collision"
```

See how great objects are?

Colliding with multiple objects

When you have a lot of objects on the screen, you'll have a *lot* of potential collisions to check. Pygame gives you some tools to manage collisions a little better. You can make more than one sprite group and check to see whether an object is colliding with any member of a group. Figure 6-10 shows one circle with a group of squares, and reports if the circle is touching any square.

The `spriteGroup.py` program uses 10 squares. If each square were in a separate group, you'd have to use 10 different collision checks to see whether the circle is colliding with each of the squares. If you put all the squares into the same group, you can use one `pygame.sprite.spritecollide()` function to look for all the possible collisions between a sprite and all the other sprites in a group.

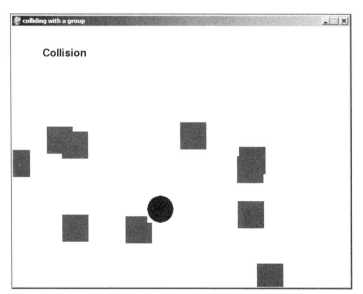

Figure 6-10: The circle checks for a collision with all squares using only one command.

```
""" spriteGroup.py
    shows how to check for a
    collision between a sprite and
    a group"""

import pygame, collisionObjects
pygame.init()

def main():
    screen = pygame.display.set_mode((640, 480))
    pygame.display.set_caption("colliding with a group")

    background = pygame.Surface(screen.get_size())
    background.fill((255, 255, 255))
    screen.blit(background, (0, 0))

    lblOutput = collisionObjects.Label()
    lblOutput.text = "Hi"
    lblOutput.center = (100, 50)

    circle = collisionObjects.Circle()
    squares = []
    for i in range(10):
        square = collisionObjects.Square((255, 0, 0),    ↩
screen)
        squares.append(square)

    basicSprites = pygame.sprite.Group(circle, lblOutput)
```

```
        squareGroup = pygame.sprite.Group(squares)

        keepGoing = True
        clock = pygame.time.Clock()
        while keepGoing:
            clock.tick(30)
            for event in pygame.event.get():
                if event.type == pygame.QUIT:
                    keepGoing = False
            if pygame.sprite.spritecollide(circle,          ↩
squareGroup, False):
                lblOutput.text = "Collision"
            else:
                lblOutput.text = "No collision"

            squareGroup.clear(screen, background)
            basicSprites.clear(screen, background)

            squareGroup.update()
            basicSprites.update()

            squareGroup.draw(screen)
            basicSprites.draw(screen)

            pygame.display.flip()

    if __name__ == "__main__":
        main()
```

The only truly new element here is the `spritecollide()` function. This function takes three parameters:

- **A sprite.** Normally you'll be checking one sprite against a group of other sprites. The single sprite is the first parameter. For this discussion, I call this sprite the *primary* sprite.

- **A sprite group.** This is the group of sprites the primary sprite might collide with.

- **A Boolean value for killing the collided sprite.** The last value is a Boolean. If the value is `True`, the object in the sprite group is automatically killed. It actually still exists in the computer's memory — but removed from its group so it will no longer be updated or displayed.

If there was no collision between the sprite and the group, the `spritecollide()` function returns an empty list. If there was a collision, the function returns a list of all the sprites in the group that collided with the primary sprite. If you want to know which sprite the primary sprite collided with, you can extract it from the returned list.

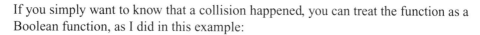

If you simply want to know that a collision happened, you can treat the function as a Boolean function, as I did in this example:

```
if pygame.sprite.spritecollide(circle, squareGroup, False):
    lblOutput.text = "Collision"
else:
    lblOutput.text = "No collision"
```

Understanding collisions better

Collision detection is pretty easy to do, but you do need to know a couple of things about collision in pygame:

- **All sprites are rectangular.** Even the circle is really a rectangular sprite with a circle drawn on it. Take a look at Figure 6-11, which is a closeup of a collision between a circle and a square: That white corner missing from the rectangle on the left is actually the leading corner of the rectangle with the circle drawn on it on the right.

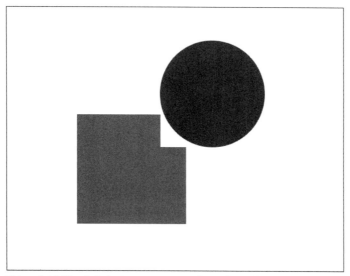

Figure 6-11: The circle is drawn on a rectangle, so the collision is still between two rectangles.

- **Pygame uses bounding-box collision detection.** If you're checking for collisions between two rectangles, everything works fine, but the standard collision routines use a bounding rectangle (the smallest rectangle with vertical and horizontal sides that can contain the shape) to describe the size of each object.

Improving on a class

The circle's white corner (shown in Figure 6-11) is distracting but there's a simple way to make it go away: Modify your classes to add a form of transparency.

I want to make this simple addition to the `Circle` class without changing the original `Circle` class. Fortunately, you can use one of the primary ideas of object-oriented program to do exactly that.

The `colorkey.py` program shown in Figure 6-12 creates a new variation of the circle with transparent corners.

Figure 6-12: Now the circle overlaps neatly with the rectangle.

It's pretty clever code, as you can see:

```
class TransCircle(collisionObjects.Circle):
    """ extended colisionObjects circle with
        colorkey transparency. """

    def __init__(self):
        collisionObjects.Circle.__init__(self)
        self.image.set_colorkey((255, 255, 255))
```

Because the `TransCircle` is almost exactly like the `Circle` object I already built, I can simply extend the existing circle — and make a new variation with the new features I want to add. Here's the drill:

1. **Create the `TransCircle` class just like you'd create any other class.**

2. **Extend the `Circle` class rather than the `Sprite` class.**

   The `TransCircle` will be a variation of the `Circle` class — which is, in turn, an extension of the `Sprite` class. If you extend `Circle`, you are in effect also extending the `Sprite` class. This code assumes I've imported the `collisionObjects` library.

   ```
   class TransCircle(collisionObjects.Circle):
   ```

3. **Build an `__init__()` constructor.**

   The `TransCircle` class needs a constructor to get itself situated.

4. **Call the `collisionObjects.Circle()` constructor.**

   Most of what you want this class to do is already taken care of by the `Circle` constructor, so call it first, to get the advantage of all its behavior:

   ```
   collisionObjects.Circle.__init__(self)
   ```

5. **Set the image's `colorkey` to white.**

   The `Surface` object's `colorkey` is a color that pygame treats as transparent. Because I filled the background of the original circle with white — and there's no other white in the circle — I can tell pygame to treat the color white as a *transparent* color in the sprite. That is, any white pixels are not drawn — but whatever is underneath the sprite is drawn instead. TV newscasters and movies use essentially the same idea with blue or green screens.

   ```
   self.image.set_colorkey((255, 255, 255))
   ```

6. **Don't add `update()` — you don't need it.**

   Amazingly enough, you don't need to add an `update()` method, because `Circle`'s `update()` method already does everything you need. The `TransCircle` class inherits the `update()` method from `Circle`.

Watch Your Step

The `Circle` sprite might not *look* like a rectangle any more, but it still is one. *All* sprites are rectangles, even when you use transparency to make them look like something else. This has important consequences when you check for collisions.

Understanding the nature of bounding rectangles

To understand how bounding rectangles can affect your games, take a look at Figure 6-13.

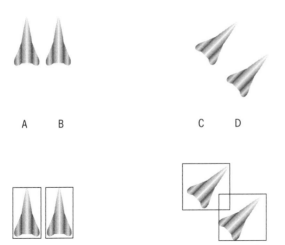

Figure 6-13: Although A and B appear to be closer than C and D, only C and D are colliding.

The top illustrations in Figure 6-13 illustrate how the user sees objects. Often you go to great lengths as a programmer to make your objects look like they are not rectangles, when in fact they are. I used transparency to make the rockets all appear rocket-shaped. At the bottom of the diagram, I drew bounding rectangles around each of the objects so you can see them the way pygame sees them.

A and B appear to be very close to each other, but because they are nearly vertical, they have narrow bounding boxes, and can approach each other very closely without the bounding boxes overlapping.

C and D are exactly the same size as A and B, but because they are diagonal, they occupy much larger bounding boxes. As you can see, the bounding boxes for C and D overlap even though the ships are relatively far apart.

Transfer

I'll show you numerous ways to mitigate the bounding-box effect as we go. For now it's sufficient to understand that it exists. Check Chapter 7 for one approach that simply decreases the size of the bounding box, and Chapter 9 for a technique that essentially makes a bounding circle.

Getting to Games

You've learned some very important ideas in this chapter. Now you've got the most critical tool of the game programmer, the sprite. It's time to make a complete game! You start that process in the next chapter.

attribute: A characteristic of an object. In Python classes, attributes are usually defined with `self.attributeName` in the classes' `__init__()` method.

bounding box: The smallest possible box with horizontal and vertical sides that surrounds a sprite. Used in collision detection. In pygame, the sprite's `rect` attribute is its bounding rectangle.

class: A template or definition for creating instance objects.

class module: A file containing a series of class definitions. Can be loaded with the `import` statement.

color key: A color that is designated as transparent. Any pixels that are this color will not be drawn, and the background will be shown instead.

constructor: A special method called when an object is created. In Python, use the the initializer `__init__()` to act as a constructor.

dirty `Rect` updating: A performance-enhancing technique that only updates the part of the screen that was changed (dirtied) during the previous frame.

encapsulation: Hiding details inside objects, methods, or functions.

event: A stimulus (such as an action on the part of a user). In pygame, the `update()` method acts as an event handler.

inheritance: Making a new class based on a previously defined class. Can provide powerful families of objects efficiently.

initializer: The `__init__()` method of an object is the initializer. It acts much like a constuctor in other OOP languages.

instance: The actual objects made from a class.

lossy compression algorithm: A technique for compressing information that throws away perceptually less-important information. Ogg Vorbis uses lossy compression.

Ogg Vorbis: A free and efficient audio compression format. Preferred audio format in pygame.

sprite: An object that represents an entity in a game. In pygame, sprites are special objects.

sprite group: A special object containing sprites. Has special methods for managing sprites.

Command	Arguments	Description	Example
pygame.mixer.Sound(*filename*)	*filename*: a sound file (usually Ogg Vorbis format) you want to play	Loads *filename* into a sound object.	mySound = pygame.mixer.Sound("whee.ogg")
sound.play(*loop*)	*sound*: sound object *loop*: extra repetitions, default is zero; -1 is indefinite	Plays sound stored in sound object.	mySound.play(-1)
sound.stop()	*sound*: sound object	Stops playing the sound.	mySound.stop()
sound.set_volume(*level*)	*sound*: sound object *level*: A float between 0 (silent) and 1.0 (maximum)	Sets the play volume for this sound.	mySound.set_volume(.5)
class *className*(*parentClass*):	*className*: name of a class you want to define *parentClass*: class you are inheriting from	Defines a new class based on the parent class.	class myClass(pygame.sprite.Sprite):
self	*<none>*	Within a class definition, a special name referring to the current object.	self.rect = self.image.get_rect()
pygame.sprite.Group(*sprites*)	*sprites*: sprites you want to add to the group	Creates a group containing sprites.	myGroup = pygame.sprite.Group(sprite1, sprite2)
group.clear(*screen*, *background*)	*group*: a sprite group *screen*: the drawing surface *background*: the background surface	Clears any sprites that were drawn during the last frame.	myGroup.clear(screen, background)
group.update()	*group*: a sprite group	Calls the update() method of every sprite in the group.	myGroup.update()
group.draw(*screen*)	*group*: a sprite group *screen*: the drawing surface	Draws each sprite onto the screen.	myGroup.draw(screen)

Command	Arguments	Description	Example
group.add(sprites)	group: a sprite group sprites: sprites to add to the group	Adds one or more sprites to the group.	myGroup.add (sprite3)
group.remove (sprites)	group: a sprite group sprites: sprites to remove from the group	Removes one or more sprites from the group.	myGroup.remvoe (sprite3)
group.has(sprites)	group: a sprite group sprites: sprites to check	Checks to see whether sprites are in the group. (All sprites mentioned must be present for the method to return True.)	if myGroup.has (sprite3): print "it's there"
group.sprites()	group: a sprite group	Returns a list of sprites in the group.	print myGroup. sprites()
rect1.colliderect (rect2)	rect1, rect2: two Rect objects (can be the rect attributes of sprites)	Returns True if the rects are overlapping.	if car.rect. colliderect (tree.rect): print "Your insurance just went up"
pygame.sprite. spritecollide(sprite, group, kill)	sprite: a sprite object group: a sprite group kill: if True, removes the hit objects from group	Checks for a collision between a sprite and a group.	if pygame.sprite. spritecollide(car, trees, False): print "uh, oh"
surface.set_colorkey (color)	surface: a surface (often a sprite image) color: color to be changed to transparent	Specifies a color on the surface to treat as.	myImage.set_ colorkey (255, 255, 255)

Last
Stop

Practice Exam

1. **Which is the best audio format for pygame programming?**

A) MP3

B) aup

C) Ogg Vorbis

D) wav

2. **Why do we use `Sprite` objects?**

A) They attach all the sprite's characteristics to the sprite.

B) They use encapsulation.

C) They are easy to re-use.

D) All of the above.

3. **Name three components of objects:**

_____

_____

_____

4. **True or false: Inheritance refers to hiding code details.**

_____

5. **Why would you inherit a class rather than build a new class?**

_____

6. How do you create a class initializer in Python?

A) `def __init__(self):`

B) `def init(self)`

C) `def __constructor__(self)`

D) `pygame.sprite.Sprite.__init__(self)`

7. What is a class most like?

A) A cake

B) A recipe

C) A fish

D) A banana

8. What is an instance most like?

A) A cake

B) A recipe

C) A fish

D) A banana

9. Why might you create a class library?

_____

10. What is a color key used for?

A) To unlock a color

B) To choose a primary key

C) To determine a transparent color

D) Color keys are not used in pygame.

11. Create your own sprite, using an image you've created.

12. Make your custom sprite (created in question 11) capable of following the mouse pointer.

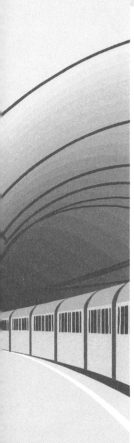

13. Make a variation of the `Label` class that allows you to set and change the font color.

14. Add the capability to change the background color to your custom `Label` class.

15. Make a variation of the `Box` class that lets the box move in a random direction. (Hint: Set random values for `dx` and `dy`, and add `dx` and `dy` to the `rect.center` on each frame.) You'll also need to handle screen boundaries. Wrap the box off the screen when it hits the edge.

16. Write a program to see whether your box program works correctly.

CHAPTER

7

Building a Working Game

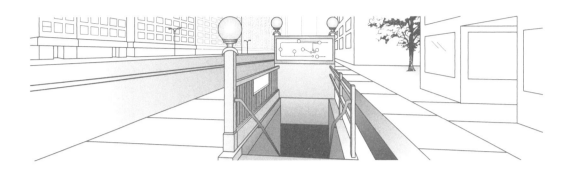

Enter the Station

Questions

1. How do you begin writing a game?

2. What should you know about each object in your game?

3. How do you build a scrolling background?

4. How do you automate scorekeeping?

5. How do you manage a multi-state program?

6. How do you build an instruction screen?

Introducing the Mail Pilot Game

It's finally time! You've learned all the basic skills to get a pygame environment up and running. You can handle basic events and generate visual elements. You know how to build sprites and create a sprite-based framework. It's time to start writing actual games that look like games. In this chapter, you create a full-fledged arcade game from beginning to end. Figure 7-1 shows the startup screen for the Mail Pilot game:

Figure 7-1: This game looks easy enough . . .

The introduction screen shows you the primary control (the airplane) and gives you basic instructions. The goal is to fly over the islands without hitting any clouds. If you touch a cloud, your plane is struck by lightning (the clouds are really testy in this part of the world). You can take only five lightning strikes before the game ends.

The user uses the mouse to control the airplane's side-to-side motion. The ocean, islands, and clouds move down the screen to give the illusion that the plane is moving upward. The clouds move in a random speed and direction. (See Figure 7-2.)

The game has a lot of interesting features that may not be apparent from the figures:

- **Sound effects.** The plane engine hums along as the game is playing. You hear a (cheesy) thunder sound when you crash into a cloud and a (cheesier) "Yay" sound when you fly over an island and successfully deliver the mail to the island dwellers.

- **Lots of moving objects.** There's a lot of stuff flying around on the screen. Of course, the plane is controlled by the user, but the program also moves an island, three clouds, and the ocean. All this moving flotsam and jetsam gets organized as sprites, which really simplifies the programming.

- **A scrolling graphic.** The ocean seems endless, but it's not. I introduce a sneaky way to make an apparently endless ocean from a basic graphic.

- **Collisions.** If you've got things moving on the screen, sooner or later they'll bump into each other.

- **An introduction screen.** Games usually have a main screen where the game action takes place and another screen or two to handle some of the administrative duties, like showing high scores and providing instructions.

- **A basic scorekeeping mechanism.** The game keeps track of your previous game's score for this playing session. This simple feature gives the game a lot more replay value, because you'll be drawn to beat your previous score.

- **Lots of room for improvement.** The game is playable now, but once you know how it's made, you'll have plenty of ideas for improving it. For example, you can simply change the graphics to make a different theme. You might also add extra lives, or make the game speed up after the player achieves a certain score.

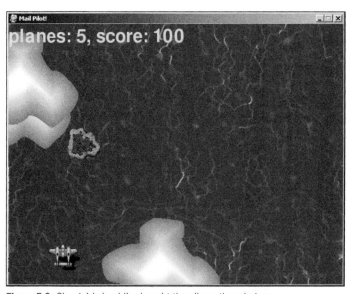

Figure 7-2: Clouds! I should've bought the all-weather airplane.

Interestingly enough, there are almost no new commands to learn in this chapter. You know most of the programming concepts you need. Now we're focusing more on how to write games.

Preparing the Mail Pilot Game

Games are fun to write, but they are complex things. Mail Pilot seems like a really simple game. It is, but there's still a lot of details to worry about. Think about how you would write the game now, and then read ahead. You might be surprised how many details there are in a simple game like this. When the games have more elements than this one (and they will), they require even more planning — so get into the planning habit now.

If you want to make a game like Mail Pilot, you need to do a little bit of preparation, or you'll get frustrated and never finish. Designing a game is fun, but if you aren't disciplined about it, you'll never get anything working the way you want. The worst thing you can do is jump right into code. If you do that, you'll end up with *something*, but it won't be what you want. A little planning will make things a lot more fun down the road.

Planning the game

Most of my games are designed long before I turn the computer on. I usually think about them in the car or while I'm mowing the lawn. (Of course, I drive and mow carefully while I'm thinking about game ideas.) As you're getting started, keep these things in mind:

A game needs some kind of environment. Games are really a form of storytelling. When you create a game, you're building a virtual environment. The player is a character in that environment. In a sense, he's playing against you, the programmer. You're building a platform for the user's imagination. Think through the background story. It can be simple (you're a round little man who lives in a maze, eating dots and avoiding ghosts) or complex (you have to assemble a team, break into a castle, and defeat a dragon after several sub-quests).

The player needs a goal. An important part of the story is the player's goal. Somehow the player needs to be motivated to do something. Classic arcade games simply had the player rack up a high score. (It's a little depressing, but the Space Invaders always won.) An adventure game calls for a more sophisticated goal.

- **Place obstacles in the player's way.** Something's got to stand in the player's way. It can be puzzles, opponents, barriers. The player wants to be challenged.

- **It should be the appropriate level of difficulty.** A game should be hard to beat, but the player should win most of the time. This seems like a contradiction, but it's the key to writing a game that people want to play. If a game is too easy, the player will lose interest. If a game is too hard, the player gets frustrated and quits. If the player can usually win, but not always, the game is motivating and fun. This is why many games have multiple layers of difficulty. It's also why arcade games usually start out simple and get more challenging.

- **You'll need artwork, music, and other assets.** The game will most likely involve some artwork, music, and sound effects. Think about how you're going to attain these things. You should think about the style of your game, because this will affect all your media. Is the game realistic? Cartoon-like? Retro?

- **You'll have to write this thing at some point.** The great thing about dreaming up games is you have no limitations. You can think of anything you want. Of course, eventually, you'll need to be able to write the game, so you should keep in mind your current abilities and tools. Start simple. Things that seem easy for you to do right now are probably a lot harder than you think.

 ## Watch Your Step

The number-one mistake of beginning game programmers is starting out way too big. If you're thinking about taking up carpentry as a hobby, your first project probably won't be a multi-story office building. It takes well-led teams of experienced professionals years to plan and build that kind of structure. If you're a beginning carpenter, you should start with something less ambitious, like a chair or a table. You'll be able to get the job done and have success while learning skills you might use on the office building. Game programmers often want to begin by writing the next sequel to *Quake*. That sort of program is the game-programming equivalent of a multi-story office building. If you're a beginning game programmer, start with a relatively simple game like Mail Pilot. It's challenging enough that you'll learn a lot, but it's also small enough that you can really finish it.

Making a game sketch

For arcade games, I like to begin with a sketch of the game action. Figure 7-3 shows my sketch of the Mail Pilot game:

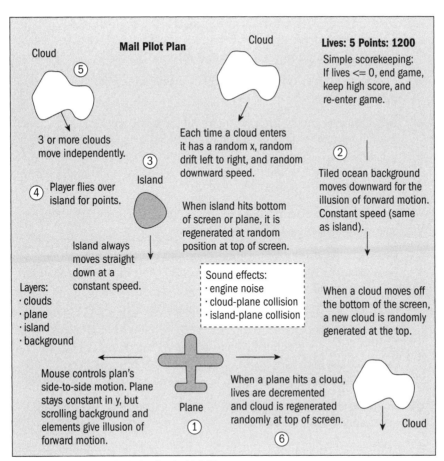

Mail Pilot Plan

Cloud

Cloud

Lives: 5 Points: 1200
Simple scorekeeping:
If lives <= 0, end game,
keep high score, and
re-enter game.

⑤

3 or more clouds
move independently.

Each time a cloud enters
it has a random x, random
drift left to right, and random
downward speed.

③ Island

② |

Tiled ocean background
moves downward for the
illusion of forward motion.
Constant speed (same
as island).

④ Player flies over
island for points.

When island hits bottom
of screen or plane, it is
regenerated at random
position at top of screen.

Island always
moves straight
down at a
constant speed.

Layers:
· clouds
· plane
· island
· background

Sound effects:
· engine noise
· cloud-plane collision
· island-plane collision

When a cloud moves off
the bottom of the screen,
a new cloud is randomly
generated at the top.

Mouse controls plan's
side-to-side motion. Plane
stays constant in y, but
scrolling background and
elements give illusion of
forward motion.

Plane

①

When a plane hits a cloud,
lives are decremented
and cloud is regenerated
randomly at top of screen.

⑥

Cloud

Figure 7-3: Here's my initial plan for the Mail Pilot game.

For a relatively simple game like Mail Pilot, you can capture most of the primary concepts of the game in one drawing. Your first full game should be something you can capture in one main drawing, or you will have trouble finishing it. Take a look at the image and you'll see the amount of detail that went into producing the drawing. Here are some notes about making the game plan.

- **It's not a computer program.** Planning doesn't happen in your text editor. It usually doesn't even happen at the computer. I actually drew the plan on paper first. (I also like whiteboards.) Then I re-created it in a drawing program because you shouldn't have to be forced to read my crummy handwriting. You'll probably have to try several times before you pin down what you really want.

- **Draw a picture of the user's experience.** I drew a crude view of what the user sees. In this case, it's the ocean backdrop, clouds, an island, and an airplane.

Don't bother with pretty drawings here. Don't put any work into the visual beauty of this drawing. Nobody will see it but you. Make rough sketches of the things you want to see, but don't make them perfect.

Label everything. Write a little label by everything on the screen and say what it does.

Describe everything interesting about each object. This is the hardest and most important part. Think about each object on the screen. How does it move? What happens when it leaves the screen? What happens if it collides with the other objects? Can it die? Can it be regenerated? If it's controlled by the player, what are the controls?

Plan for sound effects. Make a list of sound effects you will need, and when they will occur (usually during collisions).

Draw arrows if they help you understand the flow of the game. In the Mail Pilot game, the direction that things travel is important, so I added arrows to help me explain.

Describe the relative depth of objects. If objects are allowed to overlap, which one should appear to be on top? Consider making a list of layers, so you can visualize the depth of the elements on the screen. For example, the clouds should be the highest element, so they should overlap the plane, which should overlap the island, and the ocean background should be at the bottom.

Describe scorekeeping and end-of-game conditions. What causes the player to get points, win, or lose? Describe how this works.

Write everything down. You don't need to write a book (although professional game design documents *are* essentially books). You do need to describe all these details. The point is to think about everything you need *before* you start programming, so you can make decisions about what specific tasks need to be accomplished. You'll keep this paper in front of you as you write your game, and it will help you.

Guidelines for Mail Pilot

As I made the sketch for the Mail Pilot game, I did a first draft on paper, and then I transferred it to the whiteboard in my office. I scribble all over my whiteboard, making notes and comments as I plan, and I constantly refer to it as I program. Here's the main points I decided on for the Mail Pilot game (note these are numbered the same as the callouts in Figure 7-3):

1. **The player controls an airplane with the mouse.** The sprite that represents the player is sometimes called an *avatar*. This is the player's alter ego in the game's world. In Mail Pilot, the avatar is the airplane that the player controls with the mouse. The plane will stay near the bottom of the screen, but will move side to side based on the mouse position. The plane will appear to be moving upward because all other elements will be moving downward. This is a classic technique called *scrolling* that allows the game world to seem very large when in fact it's the size of the screen.

2. **The ocean background will seem to scroll forever.** At first, I won't bother with a graphic for the background, because it isn't important to game play. When I do decide to add it, I want it to appear to scroll forever, even though there is no such thing as an infinitely large graphic. I'll show you an easy way to make a seemingly endless background later in this chapter.

3. **An island moves down the screen.** The island object appears at a random spot at the top of the screen and moves straight down at a constant speed. When the island reaches the bottom of the screen or hits the plane, it regenerates at the top of the screen — in a new, randomly generated x position — and begins the journey down the screen again.

4. **If the plane hits the island, a "success" sound (audio feedback that something good has happened) is played, and the player gets 100 points.** (In arcade games, you never get just *one* point for anything. Grade inflation — okay, point inflation — is a part of the tradition.) The plane stays in the same place, but the island is regenerated at the top of the screen.

5. **Clouds are somewhat random.** Clouds float from the top of the screen to the bottom, just like the island, but they're less predictable. They will move at a speed that varies. They also don't always move straight down the screen. They may drift to the left or the right. When clouds hit the bottom of the screen, they regenerate at the top with a new speed, position, and direction of motion.

6. **Cloud-plane collisions are bad.** When the plane collides with any cloud, the cloud is reset, the player loses a life, and a "bad" sound is played.

Planning in segments

Even a simple game like the Mail Pilot game is reasonably complex. (My final version is 230 lines long.) There's no way you can get there immediately. Instead, you should do what mountain climbers do. Set up a series of base camps, or intermediate goals. Pick each part of the problem from the diagram, and add one at a time. Test each part as you go, so if something goes wrong, you have a fall-back position. I gave myself nine major tasks, each of which has a number of sub-tasks:

1. **Build the basic plane sprite.**

   Create the plane image, get the core IDEA framework together, and get the user control in place.

2. **Make a sprite for the island.**

   Build a graphic for the island, build a sprite, handle its movement, and manage it when it leaves the stage.

3. Build a single cloud sprite.

Although I will eventually have three (or more) clouds, it's best to get one working first. Once I have one working, I can add more pretty easily.

4. Manage the collisions and sound effects.

Build the sound effects and then implement them in code. The sound effects play mainly when things collide, so this is also a good place to put collision detection.

5. Create the scrolling ocean background.

This is the last (and least important) of the primary sprite objects. The programming isn't hard, but there is some conceptual and graphic work involved in building this type of sprite.

6. Make the change to multiple clouds.

This involves reorganizing the sprite groups. It isn't difficult but it does require some attention.

7. Add a scorekeeping mechanism.

Figure out a way to keep track of good things (when the plane runs over an island) and bad things (when the plane hits a cloud). Also have a mechanism for displaying this information to the player.

8. Build an intro screen, and manage the game states.

Most games have more than one *state*. (A state is a particular condition or activity within the game.) Of course, there's the Game state where the player is actively participating in the game, but there's also often another state, which gives the player instructions, reports on high scores, and so on. This game has two states: the Intro state and the Game state.

9. Tune up and run final tests.

You'll be testing every stage, but even when everything seems to be working, there's always more to add.

There's always more you can do to improve a game. At a minimum, you need to play your game many times to see whether it's reasonably fun. You may have to tweak certain variables and change some options before you're ready to have other people play it.

 ## Information Kiosk

There are other right ways to set this game up. This is the way I wrote it, but you could choose another route. The main thing is to write your game in small, attainable chunks.

The filenames in parentheses indicate the name of the file corresponding to that step. The first version of the program is called `mpPlane.py`, because it only includes the basic airplane sprite. The next version (`mpIsland.py`) still has the plane, but it adds the island as well. In a sense, these are not separate programs, but different cumulative steps on the path to the main program. If you want, you can simply open `mailPilot.py` to see all the code in the chapter, but it can be overwhelming. Take a look at each of the smaller programs in turn to see how it grew from a very simple program to the complete game.

As you move throughout this chapter, you'll see that all the sections after "Building the Plane and Framework" correspond to a particular version of the game.

Creating the media

Some people like to create all the needed media files ahead of time. I generally make the graphics and audio as I need them, because they require a kind of thinking that's different from programming, and I find that breaks up my work sessions and keeps my mind refreshed. Even if you aren't very good at graphics or audio (I'm certainly no expert), you can still make the media for your games. I'll show you some tricks as I go. Even if you'll have somebody else do graphics and sound for you, you'll need to make something as a placeholder until you get the final material in place.

Building the Plane and Framework

The first thing to do is to get something started to build around. I chose to begin with the airplane sprite. It's a relatively easy place to start and provides a central character for the rest of the game to build upon.

Preparing the airplane graphic

The airplane is the central character in this game, so it needs to look good. I'm not a great artist, so I like to borrow work from others when I can do so legally. Fortunately, there's some great free artwork available. A super guy named Ari Feldman has released a bunch of professional game graphics — free for anyone to use — called SpriteLib GPL. (GPL — which stands for General Public License — is a particular software license that gives the user great freedom in how he uses the work.) I've included a copy of SpriteLib on the Web site so you can look it over and use it for your own games. You can also download it directly from `www.flyingyogi.com/fun/spritelib.html`. SpriteLib is a series of directories, each containing several useful image files for your games. Figure 7-4 shows a graphic full of images for a remake of the classic arcade game *1945*.

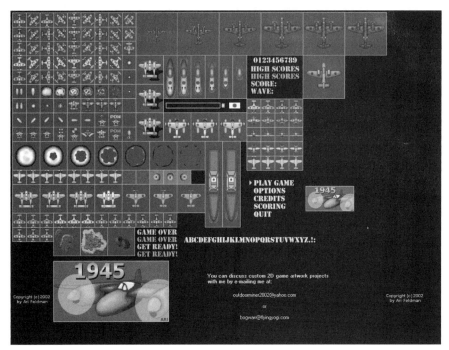

Figure 7-4: There are lots of great airplane images here.

I'll use the central green plane with the shadow.

ℹ Information Kiosk

Feldman wrote an excellent book on creating game graphics. Although it's now out of print, he has made it available for free on his Web site: `www.flyingyogi.com/fun/`.

The book is well worth the download. Even people without a lot of graphics skill can use it to learn how to make super game graphics.

There are a couple of ways to isolate the image you want, but the easiest is to use a graphics editor. Any high-end graphics program will do, but I like the GIMP (if you really must know, that stands for GNU Image Manipulation Program), because it's powerful and free. (Of course, I've included it on the companion Web site to this book, but if you want to look for the newest version or a version for your OS, go to `http://gimp-app.sourceforge.net/.`) If you know how to use GIMP or some other graphics tool, use it to crop out the plane image you need and add transparency.

Information Kiosk

If you need some help with the specifics of graphics editing in GIMP, please see the complete instructions for making the airplane graphic in Appendix D on the Web site.

Building an airplane sprite

The class defining the plane sprite is pretty easy to make. Creating the necessary `Plane` class is actually a lot like the `Circle` class you made in the last chapter:

```
class Plane(pygame.sprite.Sprite):
    def __init__(self):
        pygame.sprite.Sprite.__init__(self)
        self.image = pygame.image.load("plane.gif")
        self.rect = self.image.get_rect()

    def update(self):
        mousex, mousey = pygame.mouse.get_pos()
        self.rect.center = (mousex, 430)
```

There is very little new in the `Plane` class, but here's the basic rundown of what you do along the way:

1. Initialize the sprite as usual.

The `Plane` class is a subclass of `Sprite`, so it needs to call the sprite `__init__()` method.

2. Use `plane.gif` as the image.

The plane image you prepared in the last section becomes the image attribute of the sprite.

```
        self.image = pygame.image.load("plane.gif")
```

3. Extract the sprite's `rect` from its `image` as usual.

The easiest way to initialize the `rect` attribute is to extract it from the image.

4. In the `update()` method, get the mouse's current position.

Note that since the position is a two-value tuple, I can extract it into two variables:

```
        mousex, mousey = pygame.mouse.get_pos()
```

5. Make the sprite follow the mouse on the x axis.

Copy the `mousex` value to the `rect.centerx` attribute. This makes the sprite always follow the x value of the mouse.

6. Leave the sprite's y value constant.

I want the plane to always stay near the bottom of the screen, so I set the center's y value always at 430.

Building the main loop

This main loop will be typical of the ones you've made throughout the book. Figure 7-5 shows the `mpPlane.py` program, with an airplane under user control (and not much else).

Figure 7-5: The plane moves under mouse control.

In one sense, the `main()` function will be very simple — all it has to do is test the airplane. In another sense, it's quite important because it will be the foundation of the entire game. It's still pretty easy.

> ### Information Kiosk
>
> Throughout this chapter, I am continuously modifying a large and complex program. I don't repeat every line of code for every version of the program in the printed listing. Instead, I show you the relevant parts of each iteration of the program and point you to the code listing on the Web site where you can see the listing in its entirety. (You should be running the programs anyway, because a static book just can't do a moving interactive game justice.)

```python
def main():
    screen = pygame.display.set_mode((640, 480))
```

```
        pygame.display.set_caption("Mail Pilot! mpPlane.py - ↵
creating the Plane sprite")

        background = pygame.Surface(screen.get_size())
        background.fill((0, 0, 255))
        screen.blit(background, (0, 0))

        plane = Plane()

        allSprites = pygame.sprite.Group(plane)

        clock = pygame.time.Clock()
        keepGoing = True
        while keepGoing:
            clock.tick(30)
            pygame.mouse.set_visible(False)
            for event in pygame.event.get():
                if event.type == pygame.QUIT:
                    keepGoing = False

            allSprites.clear(screen, background)
            allSprites.update()
            allSprites.draw(screen)

            pygame.display.flip()

        #return mouse cursor
        pygame.mouse.set_visible(True)

if __name__ == "__main__":
    main()
```

The program is a very standard IDEA program with a sprite. Here are the highlights
of what you do at each step of the program:

1. **Initialize pygame as usual.**

   Set things up like you normally do, importing and initializing pygame and setting up the screen and the caption.

2. **Build the background and blit it into place.**

   With sprite-based programs, I often blit the background into place as soon as I
   build it, because the background doesn't need to be drawn during every screen.
   You'll use a more elaborate background in a later iteration of this game, but
   make the standard one now.

   ```
   background = pygame.Surface(screen.get_size())
   background.fill((0, 0, 255))
   screen.blit(background, (0, 0))
   ```

3. Make a plane and put it in a group.

Make an instance of the `Plane` class, and put it in a standard sprite group for now.

```
plane = Plane()
allSprites = pygame.sprite.Group(plane)
```

4. Build a basic main loop.

The `event` loop will be typical of the ones in the last chapter. The only event you need to track right now is the `pygame.QUIT` event. You'll add other events later.

```
for event in pygame.event.get():
    if event.type == pygame.QUIT:
        keepGoing = False
```

5. Use the sprite group to manage screen updates.

Use the standard `clear/update/draw` mechanism (from Chapter 6) to draw the plane to the screen.

```
allSprites.clear(screen, background)
allSprites.update()
allSprites.draw(screen)

pygame.display.flip()
```

6. Save and test the program.

Make sure this version of the program is working before you move on to anything else. Right now all that should happen is the program should run, the plane should appear near the bottom of the screen, and the plane should follow the mouse as it moves left and right.

Adding an Island

The island is easy to add, but it does a lot for the game, because it uses a standard trick of 2D games: To make the player think the plane is moving up the screen, leave the plane alone and move everything else *down* the screen. You need to know a couple of things to make this trick work:

- **The things moving down the screen all must be nearly the same speed.** Once I add a water texture, it needs to move at the same speed as the island, or the illusion will be broken.

- **There needs to be a steady stream of things moving down.** The objects moving down are key to the illusion. If they all disappear at once, the illusion is killed. This is why many games of this type (including this one, later on) have a constantly moving background.

Building the island graphic

You make the island graphic in much the same way as you make the plane. There are actually three different island images on the *1945* bitmap (or of course you can draw your own). Regardless, keep these things in mind when creating an image that will serve as a target:

Size is very important. Larger targets are easier to hit (and harder to avoid) than smaller targets. If your target is something you want to hit (like islands in this game), making the image larger makes the game easier, and smaller islands make the game harder. When you make images the player is trying to avoid (such as the clouds in this game), smaller is easier and larger is harder.

Crop as close as possible to the image. The sprite's `rect` will be the size of the image (at least by default), so don't have a lot of padding around your image.

Use transparency to give the illusion of a non-rectangular shape. The actual collision area of a sprite is always a rectangle, but clever use of transparency lets you make other visual shapes.

Don't use too much transparency. The transparent parts of the image will still register collisions. Players will get frustrated if the sprite images clearly do not look like they touch but they're still charged for a collision. Try to minimize the amount of transparency if you can.

If you can't make it perfect, just get something. If you're an ace graphic artist, you can come up with any graphic your game might need. If not, don't panic. Get something close, so you can at least explain to an artist the size and general shape of your image. You might also choose a cartoon-like style for your game to disguise any lack of artistic skill. You wouldn't be the first game programmer to use that trick.

Building the island sprite

The island sprite is a basic sprite but has some special behaviors:

The island sprite moves down the screen at a constant speed, to give the illusion of forward motion to the plane.

The island sprite has no side-to-side motion. There will be no need to calculate changes in x for every frame, just for the changes in y.

The sprite resets itself after leaving the screen. When the island leaves the screen, it jumps back to the top of the screen. While there appear to be many islands, in fact there's only one that I'm recycling over and over.

The island sprite needs to reset itself after a collision, too. The island will also need to reset each time it collides with the plane. There are a lot of situations that will cause the island to reset. Since many places in the island's code may need to know how to reset, it makes sense to give the `Island` class a `reset()` method. That way you have to write the resetting code only once, and you can use the same method whether the island hits a plane or a screen boundary.

■ **The starting position is somewhat random.** When the island begins each journey, its top is at the top of the screen, but its y position is a random point on the screen. I'll need a random-number generator to pick a random y value for the island.

The code for the `Island` class is straightforward, but I've added a new wrinkle. Look it over, and then I'll explain why I wrote it this way.

```python
class Island(pygame.sprite.Sprite):
    def __init__(self):
        pygame.sprite.Sprite.__init__(self)
        self.image = pygame.image.load("island.gif")
        self.rect = self.image.get_rect()
        self.reset()

        self.dy = 5

    def update(self):
        self.rect.centery += self.dy
        if self.rect.top > screen.get_height():
            self.reset()

    def reset(self):
        self.rect.top = 0
        self.rect.centerx = random.randrange(0,        ↵
screen.get_width())
```

Information Kiosk

All the code for this section is in the file called `mpIsland.py` on the Web site.

There's nothing shocking about the `Island` class, but it has a few interesting features as outlined in the following steps:

1. You begin with a typical sprite.

The `Island` class extends the `pygame.sprite.Sprite` class as usual, has `__init__()` and `update()` methods, and sets up the `image` and `rect` attributes in the normal way.

2. Call the `reset()` method to set up the sprite's initial position.

When the game begins, you'll want the island to be at a random x position at the top of the screen. This is exactly what the `reset()` method does, so I just call that method (which I'll make in a moment).

3. Add a `dy` attribute.

The `dy` attribute stands for "delta Y" or "difference in Y." This special attribute tells me how many pixels the island will move in the Y axis (that is, up and down) each frame. The `dy` attribute is used in the `update()` method to control the island's motion. Since y values increase downward, adding a positive value to the sprite's y value will cause the island to move down the screen:

```
self.dy = 5
```

4. Update the position of the island.

Most objects that move do so by adding dy to the y attribute and dx to the x attribute. The island doesn't move in x, so I need to worry only about y:

```
self.rect.centery += self.dy
```

5. Check for the edge of the screen.

If the sprite leaves the bottom of the screen, it should be reset back at the top. Fortunately, the `reset()` method will take care of the details:

```
def update(self):
    self.rect.centery += self.dy
    if self.rect.top > screen.get_height():
        self.reset()
```

6. Create the `reset()` method that positions the island at the top of the screen with a random x position.

```
def reset(self):
    self.rect.top = 0
    self.rect.centerx = random.randrange(0,       ↩
screen.get_width())
```

Step Into the Real World

When you're working on a multi-stage program like the Mail Pilot game, it makes a lot of sense to change the name of the program periodically as I have done. Each layer builds on the previous layer, but if something goes terribly wrong, you can always go back to the last successful program and start the new step over again without losing everything. As you get more serious about your coding, you might also consider using a source-control system such as CVS or Subversion, which automates the process.

Watch Your Step

Note that the `reset()` method uses the `random.randrange()` function. Be sure to import Python's `random` module before using this function, or you will have problems.

Incorporating the island with the plane

Once the island sprite has been designed, it's pretty easy to modify the code to include the island. I call this new version `mpIsland.py`, and you can see it in Figure 7-6.

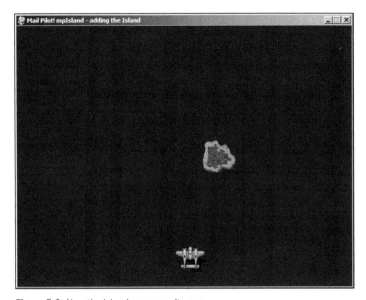

Figure 7-6: Now the island moves on its own.

Since all the real work happens in the `Island` class, the only change I make to the `main()` function is to add another sprite (the island in this instance) to the `allSprites` group:

```
plane = Plane()
island = Island()

allSprites = pygame.sprite.Group(island, plane)
```

Encapsulation is a wonderful thing. You'll see this pattern repeat. I'll keep adding sprites, each with more capabilities, but almost all the action happens in the sprite classes. The only time I make major changes to the main() function is when I'm dealing with interactions between sprites (collision detection).

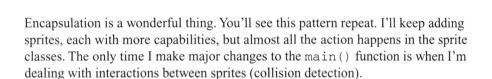

Information Kiosk

Since the main() function of mpIsland.py is very much like the main() function in mpPlane.py, I'm not going to repeat it here. Throughout this chapter, I'll focus on changes to the code rather than showing every line of the program. Please refer to the actual source code on the Web site.

Adding a Cloud Sprite

Most games involve an avatar, a goal, and an enemy. In the Mail Pilot game, the plane serves as the avatar. The island is the goal, so you need an enemy character. The clouds will serve that purpose. The plan calls for three clouds, but it's easier to start with one. If you can get one to work well, it's easy to add more later. Don't worry about the complexity of multiple clouds until you can get your first one to do what you want. Figure 7-7 shows mpCloud.py with a basic cloud sprite.

The cloud is similar to the island, but it's a little more devious:

- **Clouds move at a random speed.** Clouds can move down the screen faster than the island or at the same speed as the island.

- **Clouds have some side-to-side motion.** Each cloud has the ability to move slightly to the left or right each frame. This makes the cloud's motion predictable as long as it's on the screen, but each time the cloud is regenerated, it will be moving in a different direction. When you add multiple clouds, you should get the illusion of a swirling thunderstorm.

- **There's no cloud image in SpriteLib! You'll have to make your own.** You can't have everything for free. Fortunately, clouds are pretty easy to make in a drawing program even if you don't have any particular graphics skill. If you want to see how I did it, check the step-by-step instructions in Appendix D on the Web site.

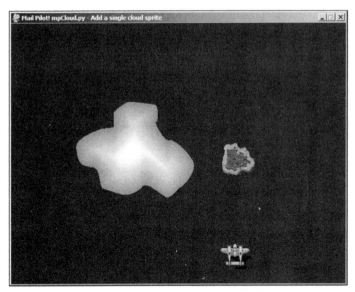

Figure 7-7: Now there's a cloud to avoid.

Creating the cloud sprite

The cloud sprite is much like the island, except its behavior is a little more random. Here's the code for creating the Cloud class:

```
class Cloud(pygame.sprite.Sprite):
    def __init__(self):
        pygame.sprite.Sprite.__init__(self)
        self.image = pygame.image.load("Cloud.gif")
        self.image = self.image.convert()
        self.rect = self.image.get_rect()
        self.reset()

    def update(self):
        self.rect.centerx += self.dx
        self.rect.centery += self.dy
        if self.rect.top > screen.get_height():
            self.reset()

    def reset(self):
        self.rect.bottom = 0
        self.rect.centerx = random.randrange(0,          ↵
screen.get_width())
        self.dy = random.randrange(5, 10)
        self.dx = random.randrange(-2, 2)
```

Like the `Island` class, the `Cloud` class has three methods: `__init__()`, `update()`, and `reset()`. Each of the `Cloud` class methods acts much like the same method in the `Island` class — but with a few new twists.

The cloud is built much like the island, as follows:

1. You initialize the sprite.

The `Cloud` class's `__init__()` method is much like the `Island` class's `__init__()`. Call the sprite initializer, load up the cloud image, get a `rect`, and call `reset()`.

2. Update the sprite.

The island always moves straight down the screen, but the cloud has some side-to-side drift. For this reason, you need to add `dy` to the cloud's y position and `dx` to the cloud's x position.

```
self.rect.centerx += self.dx
self.rect.centery += self.dy
```

3. Handle boundary conditions.

Don't worry about clouds that leave the side of the screen. They'll give the player some breathing space. If a cloud moves off the bottom of the screen, reset it at the top. Since clouds move only downward, it's not necessary to check for collisions with the top of the screen.

```
if self.rect.top > screen.get_height():
    self.reset()
```

4. Write the `reset()` method.

The cloud will move at a random speed and direction (within constraints, as described in steps 7 and 8). Each time the cloud is reset, its position, `dx`, and `dy` attributes have to be changed.

Step Into the Real World

Both the `Island` and `Cloud` classes have a `reset()` method, but the two objects reset differently. This points out another important characteristic of object-oriented programming: *polymorphism*. This term can be used to describe how one object does things in different ways, or two different objects can do the same thing in different ways. The `reset()` example is the latter type of polymorphism. `Birthday_Present`, `Garage_Door`, and `Banana` objects might all have `open()` methods, but the way you open these objects is very different.

You already saw the other kind of polymorphism at work with default parameters in Chapter 4. If a method or function has a default parameter, you can call it with or without the parameter, and it will act appropriately in either case.

5. Move the cloud to the top of the screen.

Set the `self.rect.bottom` attribute to 0. This moves the entire cloud off the screen so it appears to drift in from above the screen:

```
self.rect.bottom = 0
```

6. Set the center to a random value on the screen.

Use the `randrange()` function to generate a random integer between zero and the screen width. Set the sprite's center x to this random value:

```
self.rect.centerx = random.randrange(0, screen.get_width())
```

7. Choose a random speed downward.

The island always moves downward at a speed of 5. Make the clouds move at the same speed or faster. With some experimentation, I determined that a downward speed between 5 and 10 is best:

```
self.dy = random.randrange(5, 10)
```

Information Kiosk

The downward speed of the island and clouds is an important variable for determining the difficulty of the game. You might note this for later consideration — especially for when you're thinking about how to make difficulty levels in your game.

8. Pick a random side-to-side speed.

After some experimenting, it seems to me that a random `dx` (which controls side-to-side speed) between positive 2 and negative 2 provides the most interesting cloud motion.

```
self.dx = random.randrange(-2, 2)
```

Incorporating the cloud into the game

Now it's time to build on the `mpIsland.py` program constructed in the previous section, and modify it to include the cloud sprite. (I'm still in the `mpCloud.py` program.) Here's how you do it:

1. Create an instance of the cloud.

Build an instance of the cloud sprite just like you made the others:

```
plane = Plane()
island = Island()
cloud = Cloud()
```

2. Add the cloud to the sprite group.

Add the cloud to the sprite group so its `update()` method will be automatically called, and so it will be drawn with the other sprites:

```
allSprites = pygame.sprite.Group(island, plane, cloud)
```

Information Kiosk

Remember, the order in which you add sprites to the sprite group matters. The sprites will be drawn in the order they are listed in the group. I want the cloud to be drawn over the plane, which should be drawn over the island, so I put them in order from the lowest to the highest.

Watch Your Step

There is no guarantee that sprites will be displayed in the order they are placed in the group. Although the order in which you put sprites in the group seems to work fine for Windows and Mac machines, the display system seems to work differently on Linux computers.

There are two easy ways to solve this problem. If you're having problems with sprite overlaps, place your sprites in the `pygame.sprite.OrderedUpdate` in place of `pygame.sprite.group`. This variation of the sprite group guarantees to draw its elements in the order they are listed.

When you break sprites into multiple groups, as I describe later in this chapter, you can specify the order each group is displayed, which also eliminates the problem.

3. **Make no other changes!**

Once again, the power of the sprite/sprite group combination becomes clear. Once you've created a sprite and dropped it into a group, everything else is pretty much automatic. The code you wrote for `mpPlane.py` still works fine, even though there are now three different sprites in the group.

Adding Sound and Testing Collisions

Sound and collisions are natural companions. Many collisions involve a sound effect, so you may want to add audio and collision testing as part of the same step, the way I did. This step doesn't involve creating a new sprite; you just modify an existing sprite and make some changes to the main loop. The `mpCollision.py` program illustrates how to add both features.

Planning the sound effects

My favorite tools for sound effects are my own voice (not because I truly like the sound of my own voice, but because it's free) and the open-source program Audacity.

I'm going for a kind of cartoon-like atmosphere for this game, so I recorded some goofy sounds. Looking back at my notes, it was clear I needed three sound effects:

- **A happy noise when the plane overflies an island.** I simply recorded my voice saying a somewhat bored "Yay" sound.

- **A thunder noise when the plane and a cloud collide.** I made a suitable noise in my microphone and added some echo to make it more menacing.

- **An engine noise rumbling in the background.** The engine noise is a little different from the other sounds; it needs to run all the time. Sound effects can be very large files, so I'll design this sound carefully so it can be a small file that's repeated. Also, because the image is a two-engine plane, I want a slightly different sound in each ear. This simple effect greatly improves the atmosphere of the game.

Creating the audio files

I chose to record my own audio to prevent copyright conflicts (and because it's fun and easy to do). See Appendix D on the Web site for specific instructions on how to create the sound effects needed for the game. Even if you know how to edit audio files already, you may want to check out the site for how to build the engine sound, which is intended to loop indefinitely.

Adding the sounds to the plane sprite

Now that you have your sound effects in place, move the resulting OGG Vorbis files to your testing directory and write some code to incorporate the sound effects.

There are a couple of ways to add sounds. In this game, I think all the sounds really "belong" to the plane, because all the sounds happen in response to something the plane is doing. I made all the sound effects attributes of the `Plane` class by adding some code to the `Plane` class's `__init__()` method.

```
class Plane(pygame.sprite.Sprite):
    def __init__(self):
        pygame.sprite.Sprite.__init__(self)
        self.image = pygame.image.load("plane.gif")
        self.image = self.image.convert()
        self.rect = self.image.get_rect()

        if not pygame.mixer:
            print "problem with sound"
        else:
            pygame.mixer.init()
            self.sndYay = pygame.mixer.Sound("yay.ogg")
            self.sndThunder =pygame.mixer.Sound("thunder.ogg")
            self.sndEngine = pygame.mixer.Sound("engine.ogg")
            self.sndEngine.play(-1)
```

If you want to attach sound effects to an object, follow these steps:

1. **Check to see that the mixer module is working.**

Sometimes a user will have problems with the mixer module (for example, it may not be installed properly). It's a good idea to ensure that the module is in place, and at least tell the user what's wrong if the mixer is not available:

```
if not pygame.mixer:
    print "problem with sound"
```

2. **Initialize the mixer.**

If the mixer is available, turn it on. Unlike most parts of pygame, the mixer module requires a separate initialization. It isn't automatically initialized during `pygame.init()`.

```
else:
    pygame.mixer.init()
```

3. **Create a `pygame.mixer.Sound` object for each sound effect.**

```
self.sndYay = pygame.mixer.Sound("yay.ogg")
self.sndThunder = pygame.mixer.Sound("thunder.ogg")
self.sndEngine = pygame.mixer.Sound("engine.ogg")
```

Transfer

Check back in Chapter 6 if you need a refresher on how to create an object for a sound effect.

4. **Start the engine immediately.**

The engine noise will keep going continuously throughout the game. Use the `play()` method to begin this sound effect immediately. Use a repeat parameter of –1 to indicate the sound should repeat indefinitely. As soon as a `Plane` instance is created, it will start playing its engine sound.

```
self.sndEngine.play(-1)
```

It isn't necessary to start the other sounds yet, as they should play only during certain circumstances (coming up in the next section).

Information Kiosk

When you test your sound effects, you might find that they're not balancing properly. For example, the engine might overpower the other sounds. You have two options. If the sound is way too loud or way too soft, use your audio editor to amplify or quiet the clip. If you need a finer adjustment, you can use the `Sound` object's `set_volume()` method to tune the volume. This method takes one argument — a floating-point number — to set the sound from silent (0) to maximum (1).

5. **Stop the engine sound at the end of the game.**

When you create a sound that loops, you should write code somewhere to turn it off. I put this code right after the end of the main loop (still in mpCollision.py):

```
while keepGoing:
    clock.tick(30)

    # .... code deleted for clarity

    allSprites.clear(screen, background)
    allSprites.update()
    allSprites.draw(screen)

    pygame.display.flip()
plane.sndEngine.stop()
```

Note the indentation carefully. The sound effect shutdown happens outside the `while` loop — so as long as the main loop is repeating, the engine sound keeps on playing. As soon as the user has indicated a desire to stop playing, the loop ends, and the next line (turning off the sound effect) is run.

Checking for collisions

The collision-checking routine is really pretty easy. Just use the single-sprite collision method (described in Chapter 6) to see whether the plane collides with the cloud or the island. Following is the modified main loop with a collision-detection routine built in:

```
while keepGoing:
    clock.tick(30)
    pygame.mouse.set_visible(False)
    for event in pygame.event.get():
        if event.type == pygame.QUIT:
            keepGoing = False

    #check collisions
    if plane.rect.colliderect(island.rect):
        plane.sndYay.play()
        island.reset()
    if plane.rect.colliderect(cloud.rect):
        plane.sndThunder.play()
        cloud.reset()

    allSprites.clear(screen, background)
    allSprites.update()
```

```
allSprites.draw(screen)

pygame.display.flip()

plane.sndEngine.stop()
```

Checking for collisions doesn't require a whole lot of effort, because the sprite objects can do most of the work for you. Here's what you do:

1. First you look for a collision between the plane and island.

Compare the `rects` of the two objects to see whether they're colliding:

```
if plane.rect.colliderect(island.rect):
```

2. Play the "Yay" sound if the plane is hitting the island.

When the plane hits the island, it's supposed to be a happy occasion. Play the "Yay" sound. This is also where scorekeeping will go.

```
plane.sndYay.play()
```

Information Kiosk

If you're having trouble with the sound effects, you might want to check to see whether the collisions are working without worrying about the sounds. You can use the `print` statement to debug your collisions and make sure they're working right, like this:

```
if plane.rect.colliderect(island.rect):
    print "plane-island collision"
    island.reset()
if plane.rect.colliderect(cloud.rect):
    print "plane-cloud collision"
    cloud.reset()
```

3. Reset the island.

As soon as two sprites collide, you need to move them apart from each other. If you allow them to continue moving closer to each other, they will register a collision on the next frame, and on all subsequent frames until they're no longer overlapping. In this game, as soon as the plane collides with an island, the island is reset so they will not collide on the next frame:

```
island.reset()
```

4. Check for a plane-cloud collision.

Repeat the process if the plane is colliding with the cloud.

```
if plane.rect.colliderect(cloud.rect):
    plane.sndThunder.play()
    cloud.reset()
```

Because the cloud has a large transparent area, it's possible you'll run into the rectangle collision problem I mentioned earlier. You can get a more precise collision with a neat trick: Use the `Rect.inflateIP()` method to shrink the collision rectangle around one or more of your objects. Take the following code, for example:

```
Cloud.rect.inflate_ip(-5, -5)
```

This method changes the cloud image's rectangle from being 226 × 178 (its default size) to 221 * 173 (decreases the `rect`'s x and y values each by 5). The cloud will still display at exactly the same size it did before, but the `rect` used for collisions and boundary calculations will be smaller, and your player will be less frustrated by "false collisions."

Building the Scrolling Background

The Mail Pilot game uses a standard arcade trick: simulating an endless map. The ocean seems to go on forever. Of course, you don't have an infinitely long bitmap in your computer. You have a couple of possible ways to make this happen, but I'll show you one of the simplest techniques in the mpOcean.py program.

Making an illusion of infinity

In Mail Pilot's seemingly endless map, the ocean is actually a sprite the same width as the screen but three times as tall. The ocean sprite moves downward at the same speed as the island, supporting the illusion that the plane is moving forward. Figure 7-8 illustrates how the illusion works.

The secret behind the illusion is in the way the background is built:

The background image is three times the height of the screen. It can be taller, but it should be at least three times as tall as the screen. For a 640 × 480 game, you'll need a background image that's 1440 pixels tall.

Information Kiosk

The background can be shorter if you're really tight for space, but I find it easier to make the graphic look seamless (that step is coming up) if you have some room to play. Also, a three-screen-tall background has twice as much information on it as a two-screen image, so it's less repetitive — and more likely to fool the user.

The background has a suitable image drawn on it. Since this is an ocean game, you need some kind of image that represents water viewed from above. I'll show you shortly how to build water. It's easiest if the pattern has some randomness.

The top and bottom of the image must be identical. Notice the letters in Figure 7-8. The bottom of the background image (the part that's visible to the screen when the game first starts) is marked A. An exact copy of A must be at the top of the tall background image. (Don't worry yet about exactly how you'll do this; just understand the theory for now.)

The background moves down. As the background moves down, it gives the illusion that the player is looking through a camera following the plane's forward motion. The background must always feel like it's moving down; the moment at which it recycles must not be obvious.

Eventually, the background has gone as far as it can. When the background is finished moving down, the top region (which is an exact copy of the bottom region) is visible.

Move the image back to its original position. If both regions marked A are identical, it will be very difficult for the user to tell that the image has suddenly moved dramatically. This is why the bottom and top screen areas must be identical.

Repeat as long as the game continues. This process will continue indefinitely. If you watch very carefully, you will probably be able to see the swap, but the typical user will be focusing on the game elements (you hope) and will never see the sleight-of-hand.

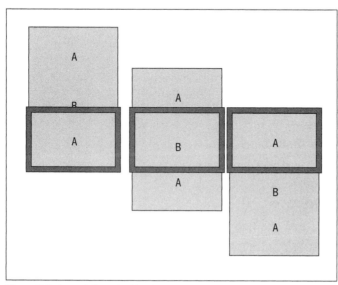

Figure 7-8: A carefully crafted background can seem infinite.

Building the ocean graphic

Now that you understand the basic principle, it's time to build the graphic. Of course, there are many ways to do this. The specific technique I used in GIMP is described in Appendix D on the book's companion Web site.

Building a background sprite

Creating the graphic is the hardest part. Making it into a sprite is pretty routine, as you can see here in the code and the steps that follow:

```
class Ocean(pygame.sprite.Sprite):
    def __init__(self):
        pygame.sprite.Sprite.__init__(self)
        self.image = pygame.image.load("ocean.gif")
        self.image = self.image.convert()
        self.rect = self.image.get_rect()
        self.dy = 5
        self.reset()

    def update(self):
        self.rect.bottom += self.dy
        if self.rect.top >= 0:
            self.reset()

    def reset(self):
        self.rect.bottom = screen.get_height()
```

1. Build a standard `sprite` object.

The `ocean` sprite starts out like any other sprite. Set the image to `"ocean.gif"` and extract the `rect` from the image as usual.

```
class Ocean(pygame.sprite.Sprite):
    def __init__(self):
        pygame.sprite.Sprite.__init__(self)
        self.image = pygame.image.load("ocean.gif")
        self.rect = self.image.get_rect()
```

2. Set the sprite's `dy` to 5.

This will cause the ocean sprite to move down 5 pixels per screen, at the same speed as the island.

3. Reset the sprite.

Like most sprites in scrolling games, this one has a `reset()` method that initializes the position.

4. **Update the sprite.**

The ocean sprite has a typical `update()` method, except for one thing. Since this sprite is larger than the screen, it doesn't reset when its bottom touches the bottom of the screen. Instead, it has to reset when the *top* of the ocean sprite is 0 or greater (which means the ocean sprite is about to move down on the screen, exposing the default background underneath).

```
if self.rect.top >= 0:
    self.reset()
```

5. **Build the `reset()` method.**

The `reset()` method has only one new twist. To get the effect illustrated in Figure 7-14, I need to reset the ocean graphic so the bottom of the ocean sprite is aligned with the bottom of the screen:

```
def reset(self):
    self.rect.bottom = screen.get_height()
```

6. **Add the sprite to the group.**

The ocean sprite should be added to the beginning of the sprite group, so it will appear underneath all the other sprites:

```
ocean = Ocean()

allSprites = pygame.sprite.Group(ocean, island, plane, cloud)
```

7. **You no longer need to clear the sprite group!**

I'm using a very large sprite as a background, which means the background surface will never be visible. The user will never see anything but sprites, so there's no need to use the `group.clear()` method. In fact, this method just slows things down without any benefit, so I've used a comment character (#) to tell Python not to run that line of code. I left it in place just in case I needed it again, and to remind myself that the omission of this line was deliberate and not a mistake.

```
#allSprites.clear(screen, background)
allSprites.update()
allSprites.draw(screen)
```

Watch Your Step

Using a large background sprite is easy and effective — but it's definitely not efficient. If you're using an older computer, you might find that the program gets sluggish when using a large sprite — especially as your games get more complex. Turning off the `clear()` method will definitely help, as will using a smaller background image.

Using Multiple Clouds

The game is really coming together now. All the main pieces are in place, but the game is too easy. More clouds are in order. This is relatively easy to do, because you've already created a cloud sprite. Figure 7-9 shows the `mpMultiClouds.py` program running with several clouds at once.

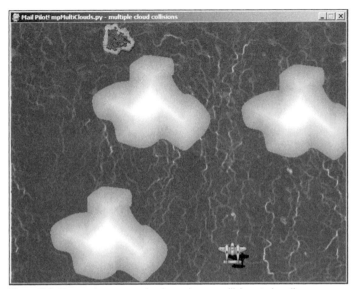

Figure 7-9: Now we have more clouds, and more collisions to handle.

With more clouds comes more collisions. The best way to handle these potential collisions is to make several clouds and put them in a separate cloud group, like so:

1. **Make no changes to the `Cloud` class.**

You've already tested the `cloud` sprite, so there is no need to change its behavior.

2. **Build several instances of the `Cloud` class.**

You now want several clouds, so simply make a bunch of them:

```
cloud1 = Cloud()
cloud2 = Cloud()
cloud3 = Cloud()
```

Information Kiosk

Since all the clouds are the same kind of thing, it would be easier to work with them if they're in the same grouping structure
(like a list). In a moment, I'm going to be putting them all into a
`pygame.sprite.Group()`, which has all the benefits of a list plus added
features like the ability to do collision checking and other game-specific
tools.

3. Split the sprites into two groups.

Now that I have several clouds, the collision detection will be a lot easier if I
use the group collision method (see Chapter 6 for a refresher on this). All the
clouds go into a group called `cloudSprites` and the other sprites go into
another group called `friendSprites`.

```
friendSprites = pygame.sprite.Group(ocean, island, plane)
cloudSprites = pygame.sprite.Group(cloud1, cloud2, cloud3)
```

4. Modify the collision routine to incorporate the cloud group.

You no longer need to check for a single collision between the plane and a
cloud, but you should still check for a basic plane-island collision:

```
if plane.rect.colliderect(island.rect):
    plane.sndYay.play()
    island.reset()
```

**5. Determine whether the plane has hit any member of the `cloudSprite`
group.**

The `pygame.sprite.spritecollide()` function returns an empty list if
there are no collisions between the given sprite and group. If there are any collisions, `spritecollide()` returns a list of sprites in the group (usually only
one) that the primary sprite collided with in this frame. The `hitClouds` variable will therefore contain either an empty list (which will cause the `if` statement in the next step to test as `False`) or a list with at least one item in it
(which will cause the `if` statement to test as `True`).

```
hitClouds = pygame.sprite.spritecollide(plane, cloudSprites, False)
```

6. If the plane hit any clouds, play the thunder sound.

Something bad has happened, so indicate this with a sound effect:

```
if hitClouds:
    plane.sndThunder.play()
```

7. Reset any clouds that were hit.

`hitClouds` is a list of sprites that were hit in this frame. Step through that list
and reset any cloud in it.

```
for theCloud in hitClouds:
    theCloud.reset()
```

8. Update and draw both sprite groups in your main loop:

```
friendSprites.update()
cloudSprites.update()
friendSprites.draw(screen)
cloudSprites.draw(screen)
```

The order in which you draw the sprites really matters here. You want the clouds to appear after the other stuff, so the cloud sprites need to be drawn later. Also, remember that you don't need the clear step here because the ocean sprite will cover the entire background anyway.

Information Kiosk

Now that the various objects are in their own groups, you're less likely to have problems with layering (islands floating on top of the airplane). You can't be 100 percent certain which items *within* a group will render (unless you use `OrderedUpdates`). You can be sure that each group will be drawn in the order specified in the code.

Adding a Scorekeeping Mechanism

As I test the game so far, I'm feeling really good about it. Things are working together well, and I'm actually getting into the game. In fact, I really want to know how well I'm doing! That's a great sign, because it means your users will probably want to play the game as well — and know how well they're doing. So the next step is to add a basic scorekeeping mechanism. In a simple arcade game like this, you usually have two kinds of scores. You count the number of good collisions (with islands) and the bad collisions (with clouds). Generally, the game ends when a certain number of bad collisions is reached. It's important to put a mechanism in place to handle this information. You also need some way to tell the user what's going on. The `mpScore.py` version of the code incorporates these changes.

Building the Scoreboard class

I'll handle the scorekeeping by building a new class called `Scoreboard`. This class will hold the scoring information (number of lives left and points) and will have a label for displaying that information to the user. It will be another sprite, so it can be displayed the same way as any other sprite in the main loop.

Here's the code for the `Scoreboard` class definition:

```
class Scoreboard(pygame.sprite.Sprite):
    def __init__(self):
        pygame.sprite.Sprite.__init__(self)
        self.lives = 5
```

```
        self.score = 0
        self.font = pygame.font.SysFont("None", 50)

    def update(self):
        self.text = "planes: %d, score: %d" %          ↩
(self.lives, self.score)
        self.image = self.font.render(self.text, 1,    ↩
(255, 255, 0))
        self.rect = self.image.get_rect()
```

It's very much like the label sprites you built in Chapter 6, except it also has attributes for handling the scoring. Here's how to put it together:

1. Begin like an ordinary sprite.

The general sprite definition should be very familiar to you by now.

2. Create attributes for lives and score.

The `lives` attribute indicates how many hits are remaining on the plane. This will start at 5 and decrease each time the plane hits a cloud. The `score` attribute starts at 0 and increases each time the player hits the island.

```
        self.lives = 5
        self.score = 0
```

3. Create a font for displaying the score.

I created a basic generic font because I'll need it when I use the `font.render()` method to display the scorekeeping information later.

4. Create an `update()` method for the `Scoreboard` class.

As in most label-style sprites, the image and `rect` are created in the `update()` method, because they're rendered in real time from the font.

5. Create a text message describing the current status.

I used string interpolation (see Chapter 1) to create text that describes the number of airplanes and the current score:

```
        self.text = "planes: %d, score: %d" % (self.lives, self.score)
```

6. Render the text.

Use the `font.render()` method to turn the message into a surface you can display.

```
        self.image = self.font.render(self.text, 1, (255, 255, 0))
```

7. Extract the `rect` from the surface.

Whenever you create or modify a sprite's `image` attribute, you have to extract the `rect` so the sprite knows its current size.

```
        self.rect = self.image.get_rect()
```

Adding the scoreboard to the game

The scoreboard is a sprite, so you use the same technique to make it visible as you would for any other sprite: put it in a group, and then clear, update, and render the group. The problem here is which group to put the scoreboard in. Clearly it's not a cloud, so it shouldn't go into the `cloudSprites` group. You also want it to appear higher than the clouds, so it shouldn't go into the `friendSprites` group, either (the clouds are drawn on top of that group). The solution is to give it a separate group of its own:

```
scoreboard = Scoreboard()

friendSprites = pygame.sprite.Group(ocean, island,  ↵
plane)
cloudSprites = pygame.sprite.Group(cloud1, cloud2,  ↵
cloud3)
scoreSprite = pygame.sprite.Group(scoreboard)
```

Of course, this group must be updated and rendered (but not cleared, because of the way I've used the ocean sprite), so now the sprite-updating code looks like this:

```
friendSprites.update()
cloudSprites.update()
scoreSprite.update()

friendSprites.draw(screen)
cloudSprites.draw(screen)
scoreSprite.draw(screen)
```

Updating the score

The scoring parameters are changed when the plane hits a cloud or the island. Modify the collision code so it looks like this:

```
#check collisions

if plane.rect.colliderect(island.rect):
    plane.sndYay.play()
    island.reset()
    scoreboard.score += 100

hitClouds = pygame.sprite.spritecollide(plane,  ↵
cloudSprites, False)
    if hitClouds:
        plane.sndThunder.play()
        scoreboard.lives -= 1
        if scoreboard.lives <= 0:
```

```
            print "Game over!"
            scoreboard.lives = 5
            scoreboard.score = 0
    for theCloud in hitClouds:
            theCloud.reset()
```

Here's what you do along the way:

1. **If the plane hits the island, increment the score.**

You don't have to do anything but change the value of `scoreboard.score`. The scoreboard sprite will handle updating the display for you. Of course, no self-respecting arcade action scores only one lousy point. Give 'em a *hundred* points for delivering the mail. There is no maximum score, so you don't have to worry about the score getting too high.

2. **If the plane hits a cloud, decrement the number of lives.**

Decrease `scoreboard.lives` by one each time the plane hits a cloud.

3. **Check to see whether the game should end.**

There's a limit to the number of times the plane can be hit. If the number of lives becomes 0 or less, the game will end.

4. **Indicate the game is over.**

I'll describe in some detail how to handle game-ending conditions in the next section; for now, it's enough to simply indicate the game is over.

```
            print "Game over!"
```

5. **Reset the score variables.**

Set the number of lives back to the starting value (5) and the score back to 0.

```
            scoreboard.lives = 5
            scoreboard.score = 0
```

Adding the Introduction State

So far you've concentrated on how the game plays, which is certainly important. Note, however, that when you play a game, you don't usually start right in. There's usually some sort of introduction screen that sets the stage, gives you some basic instructions, and prepares you for the game. Figure 7-10 shows the intro screen for Mail Pilot, which makes its debut in `mpIntro.py`.

An introduction screen will have some mechanism for beginning the game. The game will continue until it ends. (Ooh, that's profound!) In essence, however, the game has multiple personalities, or *states*. When the player loses the game, the program usually leaves the Game state and goes to one of two other states: a summary screen (describing how the player did) or back to the introduction.

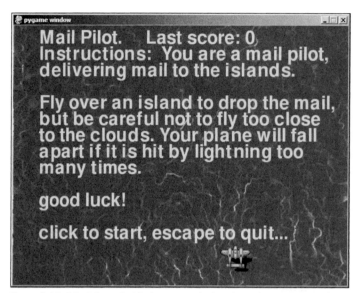

Figure 7-10: It isn't fancy, but it shows you what's going to happen.

Introducing state transition diagrams

Computer scientists have long used a technique called the *state transition diagram* to describe how a program or object can have multiple states, and how it transitions between these states. Figure 7-11 shows a basic state transition diagram for the Mail Pilot game.

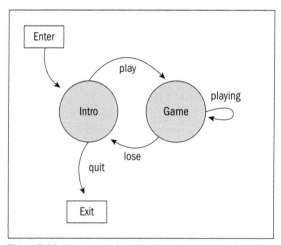

Figure 7-11: A state transition diagram gives an overview of the game's flow.

This particular state diagram consists of two primary states (the circles,) entry and exit points (the rectangles), and paths between states (the arcs). Here's how you read it:

1. **The user enters the program.**

   Beginning the program takes you immediately to the Intro state.

2. **There are two ways out of the Intro state.**

   Two arrows leave the Intro state. The labels on these arrows indicate what will cause the state to change. In this case, the user can choose either to quit or to play the game.

3. **The user can choose to play the game.**

   This will cause the program to shift into the Game state. The Game state is the part of the program you've already written. It's the main part of the program, with all the game-play elements.

4. **The game can continue for some time.**

   The playing label indicates the game can keep repeating.

5. **Eventually, the game ends.**

   It's a depressing fact of arcade games: The player rarely wins. The best she can hope for is to die slowly. Eventually, the dark forces will overcome, and the game returns to the Intro state. Note that switching between states isn't always a matter of the user making some conscious choice (as it was in the transition from Intro to Game); sometimes it's triggered by other circumstances, such as the player running out of lives.

6. **Losing the game takes the user back to the Intro state, where the same choices are available.**

   The user encounters an existential crossroad, where s/he can either play the game again or quit.

7. **If the player decides to quit, she exits the entire system.**

Step Into the Real World

The state transition diagram for Mail Pilot is pretty simple, because it has only two states. Certain kinds of games (especially point-and-click adventure games) are characterized by huge state diagrams. The fun of this sort of game is wandering around between states and figuring out how to unlock new states. Arcade games with multiple levels (like *Pac-Man*) often have multiple states. You'll also learn in the next chapter how an individual sprite can have more than one state.

A state transition diagram can be a useful way to visualize the big picture of a game. It can be used to clarify how the game-play elements can be incorporated into a finished game.

Implementing the state transition diagram

The process for making a multi-state program in pygame is actually pretty simple:

1. **Break each state into a function.**

   The finished game will have three primary functions: one to represent each of the two game states, and one to control transition between states.

2. **Build the Game state.**

   What has been the main() function of the game will now be the game() function. It will be responsible for implementing the Game state.

3. **Build the Intro state.**

   The intro() function will essentially be a new pygame program. Fortunately, it will be very easy to build because most of the necessary sprites and techniques have already been developed in the main game.

4. **Control the states with the main() function.**

   Up to now, the main() function has been about game play. Back when that was the only thing the program could do, that was fine. Now that the program has multiple states, however, the main() function is about controlling the states.

Creating the game() function

If you look over the code for mpIntro.py (and you really should), you will see that everything that was in the main() function is now in the game() function. I haven't shown the entire code for a while, so here it is:

```
def game():
    pygame.display.set_caption("Mail Pilot! mpIntro -    ↵
Add intro and game states")

    background = pygame.Surface(screen.get_size())
    background.fill((0, 0, 0))
    screen.blit(background, (0, 0))
    plane = Plane()
    island = Island()
    cloud1 = Cloud()
    cloud2 = Cloud()
    cloud3 = Cloud()
    ocean = Ocean()
```

```
        scoreboard = Scoreboard()

        friendSprites = pygame.sprite.Group(ocean, island,  ↵
plane)
        cloudSprites = pygame.sprite.Group(cloud1, cloud2,  ↵
cloud3)
        scoreSprite = pygame.sprite.Group(scoreboard)

        clock = pygame.time.Clock()
        keepGoing = True
        while keepGoing:
            clock.tick(30)
            pygame.mouse.set_visible(False)
            for event in pygame.event.get():
                if event.type == pygame.QUIT:
                    keepGoing = False

            #check collisions

            if plane.rect.colliderect(island.rect):
                plane.sndYay.play()
                island.reset()
                scoreboard.score += 100

            hitClouds = pygame.sprite.spritecollide(plane,  ↵
cloudSprites, False)
            if hitClouds:
                plane.sndThunder.play()
                scoreboard.lives -= 1
                if scoreboard.lives <= 0:
                    keepGoing = False
                for theCloud in hitClouds:
                    theCloud.reset()

            friendSprites.update()
            cloudSprites.update()
            scoreSprite.update()

            friendSprites.draw(screen)
            cloudSprites.draw(screen)
            scoreSprite.draw(screen)

            pygame.display.flip()

        #turn off engine noise
        plane.sndEngine.stop()
        #show mouse cursor
        pygame.mouse.set_visible(True)
        return scoreboard.score
```

There are only a couple of things about the `game()` function that make it different from `main()` in all the previous programs, as you'll see in the following steps:

1. **It is now called `game()`.**

   I know, that's obvious, but it's important, because all the functions in a program must have unique names. All you have to do to rename the function is change the `def` statement to reflect the new name.

2. **It still has a `keepGoing` loop.**

   The general operation of the function hasn't changed at all. `keepGoing` still controls whether the function continues or not. The only difference is what happens when the user leaves this function (because s/he's either closed the screen or lost). In either case, the program doesn't end immediately, but control reverts back to the new `main()` function.

3. **It returns the score.**

   My intro screen actually does double duty. It serves as both the introduction and a summary after each game. To do that job, the `game()` function must report the current high score back to the `main()` function, where it will be passed to the intro.

   ```
   return scoreboard.score
   ```

Understanding the instructions() function

The Intro state is implemented in the `instructions()` function. This function has a few main jobs:

- **Set the stage.** This is the first screen the player sees, so it needs to introduce the basic idea of the game, and set the general tone. I do this by re-using the plane and ocean sprites (which already know how to act, so they require no additional code). In this way, the instruction screen introduces the primary characters and even allows the player to practice the controls.

- **Tell the user how to play.** Some kinds of instructions are necessary, even for the simplest games. I don't want to mess with a custom label class for this, so I'll put the instructions in a tuple and render them onto the screen.

- **Provide feedback.** The player will return to this screen after finishing the game, so there should be some feedback on the previous game. I chose to incorporate the previous score into the instructions.

Let the user choose between playing and quitting. The most important job of this function is to determine whether the player wants to play the game or quit. The mechanism for doing these things must be clearly indicated to the player.

Creating the instructions() function

If you look at the `instructions()` function on its own, it looks like a new IDEA/ALTER framework (which is exactly what it is):

```python
def instructions(score):
    plane = Plane()
    ocean = Ocean()

    allSprites = pygame.sprite.Group(ocean, plane)
    insFont = pygame.font.SysFont(None, 50)

    instructions = (
    "Mail Pilot.    Last score: %d" % score ,
    "Instructions:  You are a mail pilot,",
    "delivering mail to the islands.",
    "",
    "Fly over an island to drop the mail,",
    "but be careful not to fly too close",
    "to the clouds. Your plane will fall ",
    "apart if it is hit by lightning too",
    "many times.",
    "",
    "good luck!",
    "",
    "click to start, escape to quit..."
    )

    insLabels = []
    for line in instructions:
        tempLabel = insFont.render(line, 1, (255, 255, 0))
        insLabels.append(tempLabel)

    keepGoing = True
    clock = pygame.time.Clock()
    pygame.mouse.set_visible(False)
    while keepGoing:
        clock.tick(30)
        for event in pygame.event.get():
            if event.type == pygame.QUIT:
                keepGoing = False
```

```
                    donePlaying = True
        if event.type == pygame.MOUSEBUTTONDOWN:
            keepGoing = False
            donePlaying = False
        elif event.type == pygame.KEYDOWN:
            if event.key == pygame.K_ESCAPE:
                keepGoing = False
                donePlaying = True

    allSprites.update()
    allSprites.draw(screen)

    for i in range(len(insLabels)):
        screen.blit(insLabels[i], (50, 30*i))

    pygame.display.flip()

plane.sndEngine.stop()
pygame.mouse.set_visible(True)
return donePlaying
```

The `instructions()` function acts like a completely separate pygame program, but it uses some pre-existing sprite objects and ideas.

Here's what you do at each step in the program:

1. Begin with a new IDEA framework.

Each state is a nearly independent IDEA framework. (Well, almost. You have to import and initialize pygame only once, and the display has already been set up, so I guess each state is really a new EA framework. Still, it's best to think of each state as a somewhat independent entity, like a state inside a country.)

2. Build ocean and plane sprites.

It's very easy to re-use the ocean and plane sprites, to keep the look and feel of the game going:

```
plane = Plane()
ocean = Ocean()

allSprites = pygame.sprite.Group(ocean, plane)
```

The text is handled a little differently than you've seen before, so skip it for now. I describe how to incorporate the text in the next section.

3. Manage the events.

The `instructions()` function has two primary events it's checking: If the user presses the Escape key, she wants to completely exit the program. If he clicks the mouse, he wants to exit the instruction screen but move on to the Game state.

```
for event in pygame.event.get():
    if event.type == pygame.QUIT:
        keepGoing = False
        donePlaying = True
    if event.type == pygame.MOUSEBUTTONDOWN:
        keepGoing = False
        donePlaying = False
    elif event.type == pygame.KEYDOWN:
        if event.key == pygame.K_ESCAPE:
            keepGoing = False
            donePlaying = True
```

There are two Boolean variables in action here. keepGoing acts like it always has. It controls the current event loop (in the instructions() function). As long as keepGoing is True, the current event loop will continue running, and the user will continue to see the instructions screen. When keepGoing is False, this event loop will end, and program control will revert to the main() function, which will send control on to the game() function or exit the game.

The donePlaying variable has a different but related job. When this variable is True, it indicates that the player is finished playing the game and wants to return to the operating system.

When the user presses the Escape key or closes the window, he really wants the game to end. In this case I set keepGoing to False and donePlaying to True. If the user clicks the mouse button, he wants this screen to end, but not the entire game. I set keepGoing to False (so the Instruction state ends) and donePlaying to False (because the user wants to continue playing).

4. **Return the value of donePlaying to the main() function.**

The last line of code in the function returns the value of donePlaying so the main() function knows whether to quit or keep playing.

Step Into the Real World

It's no accident that I made it physically easier to start the game than to quit. The user already has a hand on the mouse, and it's really easy to click again. Each time our user friend encounters the instruction screen, he or she has to decide what to do. Playing again is almost reflexive, but quitting requires more activity (pressing the Esc key). If you make it really easy to play again, your game will be perceived as more addictive. That's a good thing. Trust me.

Managing the text

The text in instructions() is a little unique. There are multiple lines of text. It won't save a lot of effort to build a sprite for this, so I just use old-fashioned Surface objects to draw the text onto the screen, as you can see in the following steps:

1. **Create a Font object.**

Text is a prominent part of the instructions() screen, so I need a Font object for displaying that text:

```
insFont = pygame.font.SysFont(None, 50)
```

2. **Make a tuple of strings for the instructions.**

The instructions are simply text. Note that I used string interpolation to incorporate the latest score, and I included empty strings for formatting purposes.

3. **Make an empty list of surfaces to hold the instructions.**

The text won't appear on-screen on its own. Each line has to be rendered into a surface, and then the surfaces need to be placed on the screen. To begin this process, build a list to contain the surfaces:

```
insLabels = []
```

4. **Render each line of instructions.**

Step through each element of the instructions tuple and render that line into a temporary Surface object.

```
for line in instructions:
    tempLabel = insFont.render(line, 1, (255, 255, 0))
```

5. **Add the temporary surface to the insLabels list.**

I made insLabels a list rather than a tuple so I could add elements to it on the fly. After you render a line, add the newly created surface to insLabels.

```
insLabels.append(tempLabel)
```

6. **Blit the label objects onto the screens.**

The labels aren't sprites, so I have to manually draw them onto the screen. Since I want them to appear above the ocean, I use a quick loop to display the graphics after the sprite updates:

```
allSprites.update()
allSprites.draw(screen)

for i in range(len(insLabels)):
    screen.blit(insLabels[i], (50, 30*i))
```

The loop draws each label in turn, keeping track of the label's index (position in the list) with the variable i. Notice how I multiplied the Y value by 30 (the text height) to make sure each label is on its own line.

Writing the main() function

The main() function is actually pretty easy to write. All it does is manage the states:

```
def main():
    donePlaying = False
    score = 0
    while not donePlaying:
        donePlaying = instructions(score)
        if not donePlaying:
            score = game()
```

Here's what you do, step by step:

1. Initialize **donePlaying** to **False**.

When the program begins, assume the user is not done playing.

2. Initialize the score to 0.

Since this is the first time through the program, set the initial score to 0.

3. If the user is not done playing, make a loop that controls everything in the whole program:

```
while not donePlaying:
```

4. Run the **instructions** function and store the result in **donePlaying**.

Send the score to instructions() (so it can display the current score) and copy the value of donePlaying (returned from instructions() to the donePlaying variable).

```
donePlaying = instructions(score)
```

5. Play the game, if required.

When the instructions() function has finished, donePlaying will be True if the user is finished or False if he wants to play the game. If donePlaying is False, send control to the game() function. game() will return a new value for score, which will be useful when the instructions() function runs again.

```
if not donePlaying:
    score = game()
```

Tuning Up the Program

At this point, you have a completely functional game! It's a lot of fun (if I do say so), but it still has a lot of potential to be more fun, exciting, and challenging. Here are some suggestions:

- **Change the theme.** It's really easy to turn this into a totally different game simply by changing the graphics and sprite names. The basic framework could be used for a racing game, skiing game, or many others.

- **Allow more control.** How would the game play be different if the user could move the plane vertically as well as horizontally?

- **Gradually speed things up.** Make a constant for the game speed. Set the island's dy, ocean's dy, and cloud's minimum dy to this value. Speed the game up after each ten islands.

- **Add powerups.** Create some sort of object that gives you special powers after you touch it. For example, if you click the mouse, you're automatically teleported to a random part of the screen.

- **Add extra lives.** At a certain score, time, or when you hit a certain powerup, reward the player with an extra life.

- **Tweak the collisions.** When I tested the game with non-programmers, they all complained about the collisions. They don't know anything about bounding rectangles, so it seems that a collision should occur only when the *visible* parts of the sprites touch each other. Look up the Rect.inflate() method for a way to make the collision rectangle smaller than the actual bounding box. This can make the game seem a bit more fair to the player.

- **Package it into an executable.** You can give this game to your friends right now if you want, but they can *play* it only if they have a copy of Python and pygame installed. Look to Appendix C on the Web site for instructions on how to create a standalone program so Windows users can run your game even if they don't have Python or pygame installed.

You've done it! You have a game! In the next chapter, I show you how to extend these skills to more interesting sprites that can go in different directions and have different behaviors.

alpha channel: A tool in a graphics program for controlling the amount of transparency in a pixel. You must explicitly add an alpha channel to some graphics to incorporate transparency.

avatar: The sprite controlled by the user. The user's alter ego within the game world.

game sketch: A diagram used to illustrate all the primary objects in a game, how they behave, and how they interact.

normalize (audio): A technique for making the volume of an audio recording predictable. If you normalize all audio clips, you will have an easier time balancing them within your game.

polymorphism: A characteristic of object-oriented programming whereby different objects can do a similar thing in different ways, or the same method can act differently in different circumstances.

scrolling: A game graphics technique using a continuously moving background to give the illusion of an endless world.

state: A particular condition or activity. The finished Mail Pilot game has two states: Intro and Game.

state transition diagram: A technique for illustrating the various states in a program or object — and the mechanism for transitioning between those states.

Command	Arguments	Description
`rect.inflate(x, y)`	*rect:* a `pygame.Rect` object *x, y:* How much to inflate in each direction	Allows you to change the size of a `rect`. Positive values make the `rect` larger, negative make it smaller. Deflate a sprite's `rect` to simulate smaller bounding rectangles.

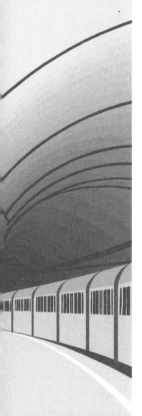

Practice Exam

1. Name at least two techniques to make a game more appealing.

_____

_____

2. What information should go into the game sketch?

A) The player's view of the game

B) All the sprites

C) Behaviors and collisions

D) All of the above

3. Why should you break a game plan into smaller goals?

A) So you have a series of achievable goals.

B) To conform with rules of the game programmers' union.

C) Python won't let you write long code in one session.

D) It's really not a good idea to have smaller goals.

4. True or false: Collision detection and sound effects are often implemented together.

_____

5. How do you design a graphic for use as a scrolling background?

A) Larger than the screen

B) With no visible seams

C) Duplication at the top and bottom of the image

D) All of the above

6. **Why did I make a sprite for the scoreboard?**

    A) I just love sprites.

    B) It allows me to combine the scores with the mechanism to display them.

    C) I didn't. The scoreboard isn't a sprite!

    D) What's a scoreboard?

7. **Why is the notion of state important to game programmers?**

    A) You pay different tax rates depending on the state you live in.

    B) All games have exactly three states.

    C) The idea of state helps you design the overall flow of your game.

    D) Every function in a game is represented by a state.

8. **What characteristics should be included in a state transition diagram?**

_____

_____

_____

_____

9. **Build your own variation of Mail Pilot with your own theme, sprites, and background.**

10. **In your version of Mail Pilot, incorporate one or more of the suggestions from the section of the chapter called "Tuning Up the Program."**

Making Animated Sprites

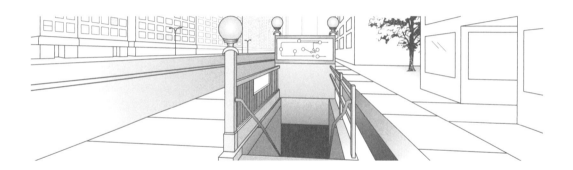

Enter the Station

Questions

1. When might you choose to stop a sprite when it hits the edge of the screen?

2. How do you make a sprite bounce off a screen boundary?

3. How do you animate a sprite so it acts like a little movie?

4. How do you control the speed of a sprite's animation?

5. How can you dynamically change the rotation and size of an image?

6. How do you combine sprite animation with motion?

7. How do you make a sprite move in eight directions?

Building More Interesting Sprites

So far, the sprites you have created move in basically two directions: side-to-side and top-to-bottom. The sprites also have been single images that don't change much. In this chapter you build sprites with more personality. You start off with animating sprites with a sequence of images. Next you learn a couple of ways to build sprites that face in multiple directions. You'll also learn how to move sprites in the eight basic directions, and learn many ways to handle collisions with the screen boundaries. You finish the chapter with a program that smoothly animates a cow walking around the screen in eight directions under user control. Although the program seems simple, it requires 64 different images to do its job. You will learn how to manage that much data in a way that makes it easy to use.

Checking for Boundaries

When a sprite can move, it can get out of bounds. You've already had several experiences with basic boundary checking, but more sophisticated motion techniques call for more variety in boundary handling. There are five main strategies for handling a sprite that collides with the screen boundary:

- **Scrolling.** The sprite stays on the screen, but the screen background moves so the sprite appears to move in the opposite direction. You used a simple form of this behavior in the Mail Pilot game in Chapter 7. This technique is used to create virtual worlds that are larger than the display screen. It usually involves some kind of very large background.

- **Wrapping.** When a sprite leaves the screen, it reappears on the opposite side of the screen. This is used in two major ways: In Mail Pilot, you used wrapping to reuse the same island sprite to feel like an infinite number of islands. When you wrap the player sprite, you create the illusion of an infinitely large world. This is especially effective against a relatively repetitive background such as space or water.

- **Bouncing.** When the sprite encounters a screen boundary, it appears to bounce off the screen and return in the opposite direction. This technique is used to indicate a tight space. For example, you might have bullets bounce off the walls. The classic game *Pong* relied on bouncing.

- **Stopping.** You might want a sprite to stop when it encounters a boundary. This technique also indicates a small space. It is often used in racing or action games to limit the size of the playing field.

- **Hiding.** When the sprite leaves the screen, it either dies completely or (more often) hides off-stage until it's needed again. This technique is often used for bullets and missiles that usually disappear as soon as they hit a screen boundary.

Of course, there are many combinations of these basic techniques. For example, the game *Civilization II* allows players to wrap around the left and right sides of the map, but stops them at the top and the bottom. This makes the map feel more like a spherical planet. (Of course, it's really more like a cylindrical planet, but who am I to argue with one of the best games of all time?) When you know how to implement the standard techniques, you'll be able to combine them in all kinds of interesting ways.

Creating a boundary-checking example

So far, you've used wrapping quite a bit. It's a common technique because it's easy to understand and implement, and it makes the screen feel larger than it is. Figure 8-1 shows a ball that wraps around the screen.

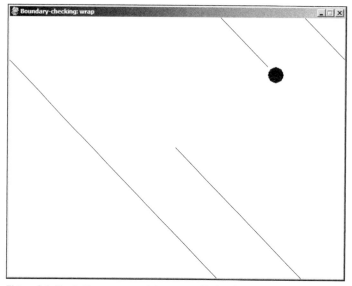

Figure 8-1: The ball wraps around the screen. Notice the trail it left behind.

I build a special sprite for this demonstration (as well as the next few). This sprite is a simple ball that moves on the screen, but it also draws a path. You should really run these programs on your own computer to see how it works, but I added the path so you can see on the figures how it works. I captured the figure a few seconds after the program began. The thin line shows where the ball has been since the beginning of the program run.

Step Into the Real World

Drawing the path is a handy little trick, even if you don't end up keeping the path in your final game. I often have my sprites draw a trail so I can see how motion is working — particularly if my sprites aren't doing what I want. This helps me see where exactly things are going wrong.

Although you've done some wrapping already, take a careful look at the wrap.py program featured in Figure 8-1 so you can see how it works with the drawing turned on:

```
""" wrap.py
    demonstrate screen wrap boundaries
"""

import pygame
pygame.init()

class Ball(pygame.sprite.Sprite):
    def __init__(self, screen, background):
        pygame.sprite.Sprite.__init__(self)
        self.screen = screen
        self.background = background

        self.image = pygame.Surface((30, 30))
        self.image.fill((255, 255, 255))
        pygame.draw.circle(self.image, (0, 0, 255), (15, 15), 15)
        self.rect = self.image.get_rect()

        self.rect.center = (320, 240)

        self.dx = 5
        self.dy = 5

    def update(self):
        oldCenter = self.rect.center
        self.rect.centerx += self.dx
        self.rect.centery += self.dy
        pygame.draw.line(self.background, (0, 0, 0), oldCenter,
            self.rect.center)

        self.checkBounds()

    def checkBounds(self):
        """ wrap around screen """

        if self.rect.centerx > self.screen.get_width():
            self.rect.centerx = 0
```

```
            if self.rect.centerx < 0:
                self.rect.centerx = self.screen.get_width()
            if self.rect.centery > self.screen.get_height():
                self.rect.centery = 0
            if self.rect.centery < 0:
                self.rect.centery = self.screen.get_height()

def main():
    screen = pygame.display.set_mode((640, 480))
    pygame.display.set_caption("Boundary-checking: wrap")

    background = pygame.Surface(screen.get_size())
    background.fill((255, 255, 255))
    screen.blit(background, (0, 0))

    ball = Ball(screen, background)
    allSprites = pygame.sprite.Group(ball)

    clock = pygame.time.Clock()
    keepGoing = True

    while keepGoing:
        clock.tick(30)
        for event in pygame.event.get():
            if event.type == pygame.QUIT:
                keepGoing = False

        allSprites.clear(screen, background)
        allSprites.update()
        allSprites.draw(screen)

        pygame.display.flip()

if __name__ == "__main__":
    main()
```

Building the ball sprite

The ball sprite is nothing new, except it leaves a "trail of breadcrumbs" on the screen so you can see what it does when it hits the boundaries. Here are the highlights:

The ball sprite needs to know the screen size. The `Ball` class requires that the screen be sent as an argument when the `ball` instance is created. There are other ways of sending this information, but passing the screen as an argument is probably the most direct and easiest to understand. Any sprite with boundary-checking should accept the screen as an argument. Assign the screen parameter as an attribute so your other `class` methods can also have access to the screen.

```
def __init__(self, screen, background):
    pygame.sprite.Sprite.__init__(self)
    self.screen = screen
    self.background = background
```

The ball sprite will also need the background. Because this particular sprite will draw on the background surface, that surface needs to be sent to the sprite as an argument as well. The only time you need to do this is when your sprite will be modifying the background, as it is in these examples.

Information Kiosk

If you're clever (and I know you are, if you've gotten this far), you might be wondering why I'm passing both the screen and the background to the sprite constructor. After all, they're both the same size, so I should be able to get the screen size from the background size. That's true in this example, but it's not always true. Sometimes the background is much larger than the screen. The more important idea here is the logic: If your object is going to check for screen boundaries, you should pass the screen as an argument.

The sprite image is a simple circle. My sprite image could be anything, but I simply created a white surface (same color as the background) and added a blue ball to it:

```
self.image = pygame.Surface((30, 30))
self.image.fill((255, 255, 255))
pygame.draw.circle(self.image, (0, 0, 255), (15, 15), 15)
self.rect = self.image.get_rect()

self.rect.center = (320, 240)
```

The ball sprite will move using dx and dy attributes. Like most moving sprites, the Ball class has dx and dy attributes that indicate how much the ball should move in each axis during each frame. For now I've set both dx and dy to 5, indicating that the ball will move down and to the right. Of course, you can (and should) change these values to anything you want, so long as they ensure that the algorithm still works regardless of the ball's direction and speed.

Information Kiosk

Remember, dx means "difference in x" and it indicates how much the sprite will move along the x (horizontal) axis in the current frame. dy is "difference in y" and indicates how much the sprite will move in the y (vertical) axis in the current frame. dx and dy when taken together are one way to determine a sprite's speed and direction, which is also called its *motion vector*.

Updating the ball

The ball has a normal `update()` method, except it incorporates the tail-drawing functionality by drawing a line on the background surface that goes from the previous position to the new position during each frame. Here's how you do it:

1. Save the current center.

Determine where the ball is before moving it, and store this value into the `oldCenter` variable.

```
oldCenter = (self.rect.centerx, self.rect.centery)
```

2. Update the ball's position with dx and dy.

Use the `dx` and `dy` attributes to change the position of the ball.

```
self.rect.centerx += self.dx
self.rect.centery += self.dy
```

3. Draw a line from the previous center to the current one.

Use the `pygame.draw.line()` function to draw a line on the background from the ball's previous center to its current center.

```
pygame.draw.line(self.background, (0, 0, 0),
oldCenter, self.rect.center)
```

 Transfer

Check back to Chapter 5 if you need a refresher on the drawing commands.

4. Check for boundaries.

Boundary-checking can go directly into the sprite class's `update()` method, but I often prefer to put it in a separate method, which I call from within `update()`. The `update()` method can get pretty cluttered when you add in all the stuff that can happen in a game frame, so I like to encapsulate details like boundary-checking and keep them out of the way.

```
self.checkBounds()
```

Wrapping around the screen

When a sprite wraps around the screen, its speed and direction do not change, only its position. Normally when you wrap a sprite, you check to see which boundary it is crossing, and move it to the opposite edge. That is, if a sprite moves off the top of the screen, you reposition it at the bottom. If the sprite is at the bottom, you reposition it at the top. The `checkBounds` method handles the wrapping:

```
def checkBounds(self):
```

```
""" wrap around screen """
if self.rect.centerx > self.screen.get_width():
    self.rect.centerx = 0
if self.rect.centerx < 0:
    self.rect.centerx = self.screen.get_width()
if self.rect.centery > self.screen.get_height():
    self.rect.centery = 0
if self.rect.centery < 0:
    self.rect.centery = self.screen.get_height()
```

Here are a few things to note about wrapping algorithms:

Examine the sprite's position. *Position* is a single point, but a sprite is a rectangular shape. You must choose a point on the sprite to determine exactly what part of the sprite crossing a screen boundary constitutes a collision with the boundary. When I'm wrapping a sprite, I like to use the sprite's center. This causes a smooth transition because the sprite doesn't simply pop on or off, but seems to make a smooth transition to the other side of the screen. I compare the sprite's `rect.centerx` and `rect.centery` attributes to the screen boundaries.

Information Kiosk

As you'll see shortly, you will test for other parts of the sprite crossing the screen boundaries when you use other kinds of collision checks. For example, if your ball is bouncing off the screen boundary, you don't want it to change direction when its center hits the screen boundary; instead you want the ball to change direction when the edge closest to the screen boundary hits the edge.

Examine the screen boundaries. The left and top boundaries of the screen will always be 0. Use `screen.get_height()` to find the bottom of the screen, and `screen.get_width()` to determine the right edge of the screen. This is why a position-checking sprite usually takes the screen as an argument.

When the sprite crosses a boundary, move it. If a sprite crosses a boundary, move it accordingly. Each boundary causes a slightly different movement. For example, if the sprite moves off the right side of the screen (`screen.get_width()`), it needs to be moved to the left side of the screen (0).

```
if self.rect.centerx > self.screen.get_width():
    self.rect.centerx = 0
```

Check all necessary boundaries. If a sprite can move in only one direction, then you only need to check for one boundary. For example, the island in the Mail Pilot game only moved straight down, so the only boundary it could cross was the bottom of the screen. If the sprite can move in more than one direction, you'll probably need to have some code in place to handle all boundaries.

Writing the main program

All the interesting stuff in this program (and the next few examples) happens in the sprite. The main loop is nothing new. The only modification to the basic IDEA/ALTER code is remembering that this sprite requires two arguments, the screen and the background:

```
ball = Ball(screen, background)
allSprites = pygame.sprite.Group(ball)
```

Bouncing

Sometimes it makes more sense to have a sprite bounce off of a side of the screen or some other sprite. When you bounce a sprite, you don't change its position. Instead, you reverse the dx or dy. Figure 8-2 shows bounce.py, which is exactly like wrap.py except it uses a different checkBounds method:

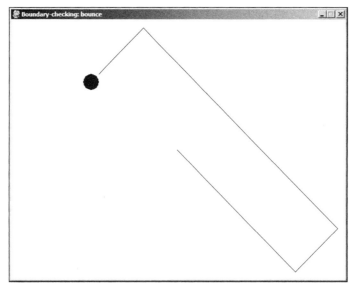

Figure 8-2: This ball bounces off the screen boundaries.

Here is how you change checkBounds to produce the bouncing behavior:

```
def checkBounds(self):
    """ bounce on encountering any screen boundary """

    if self.rect.right >= self.screen.get_width():
        self.dx *= -1
    if self.rect.left <= 0:
        self.dx *= -1
    if self.rect.bottom >= self.screen.get_height():
        self.dy *= -1
    if self.rect.top  <= 0:
        self.dy *= -1
```

Bouncing off each wall causes a slightly different result:

- **If the sprite hits the right wall,** it must be moving towards the right, so its dx value is positive. Make it move towards the left by multiplying dx by -1. If dx was 5, it will now be -5, causing the sprite to move to the left at the same speed.

- **If the sprite hits the left wall,** it is moving towards the left, and dx is negative. Multiply this negative number by –1 to move the ball in a positive dx, or back toward the right. (-5 * -1 = 5)

- **If the sprite hits the bottom wall,** dy is positive, so multiply dy by –1 to move back upward.

- **If the sprite hits the top wall,** dy is negative (since the sprite is moving up). Multiply by -1 to make dy positive and move the sprite downward.

- **Check for collisions on the edges of the sprite.** If you check for collisions between the center of the sprite and a wall (the way you did for wrapping), the sprite will appear to move halfway off the screen before it bounces back. Fortunately, the rect object has attributes you can use to determine the location of the top, bottom, left, and right of the sprite. Use these attributes to make the sprite bounce as soon as its leading edge touches a boundary. If you're testing for a collision with the top of the screen, for example, check to see if the sprite's top is less than 0, and the sprite will appear to bounce as soon as it hits the top of the screen.

Step Into the Real World

Any time something bounces in reality, it loses a little energy. If you want to simulate this, simply multiply by a smaller negative number, such as –.95 rather than –1. This will cause the sprite to slow down a little each time it hits a wall.

Stopping

You can also stop a sprite when it encounters a screen boundary. Once again, I modified the `wrap.py` program's `checkBounds()` method to show how this can be accomplished. Figure 8-3 shows the `stop.py` program in action.

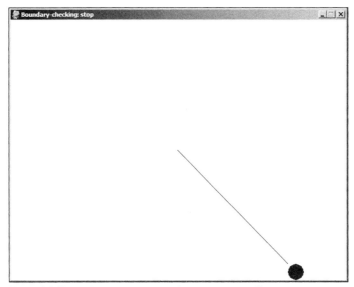

Figure 8-3: The sprite stops as soon as it encounters a wall.

The mechanism for stopping the sprite is simplicity itself. Whenever you encounter any wall (it doesn't matter which one), simply stop the sprite by setting both its `dx` and `dy` attributes to `0`. The sprite will no longer move in any direction. Here's the `checkBounds` code:

```
def checkBounds(self):
    """ stop on encountering any screen boundary """

    if self.rect.right >= self.screen.get_width():
        self.dx = 0
        self.dy = 0
    if self.rect.left <= 0:
        self.dx = 0
        self.dy = 0
    if self.rect.bottom >= self.screen.get_height():
        self.dx = 0
        self.dy = 0
    if self.rect.top <= 0:
        self.dx = 0
        self.dy = 0
```

Stopping a sprite is pretty easy. There are a few cautions and variations.

- **If you stop it, you should be able to start it again.** Things that are just sitting there aren't very interesting. Typically the only sprites you stop are user-controlled sprites that the user can get moving again.

- **A sudden stop might cause damage.** In a racing game, hitting a wall can cause damage to the car. Often a stop will also incur some sort of penalty in the game — a great opportunity to keep play from getting too easy.

- **You can cause something to slide along the wall.** You don't have to completely stop your sprite. Instead you could stop it only along the axis that matters. For example, Figure 8-4 shows `wallSlide.py`.

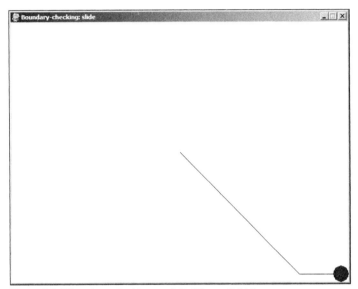

Figure 8-4: When the sprite hits a wall, it slides until it hits a corner.

I accomplished this with the following variation in `checkBounds`:

```
def checkBounds(self):
    """ begin slide on encountering any screen
        boundary """

    if self.rect.right >= self.screen.get_width():
        self.dx = 0
    if self.rect.left <= 0:
        self.dx = 0
    if self.rect.bottom >= self.screen.get_height():
        self.dy = 0
    if self.rect.top <= 0:
        self.dy = 0
```

Collisions with the right and left walls cause dx to be 0, so the ball stops moving to the right or left, but its vertical motion remains, so it slides along the wall until it hits a corner. Likewise, collisions with the top and bottom walls zero out the dy attribute, but allow the sprite to continue moving horizontally until it eventually hits a corner.

Animating a Sprite with Multiple Frames

You can move sprites around the screen, but it's also nice to animate a graphic so it seems to be moving in place. As an example, take a look at the cowMoo.py program featured in Figure 8-5.

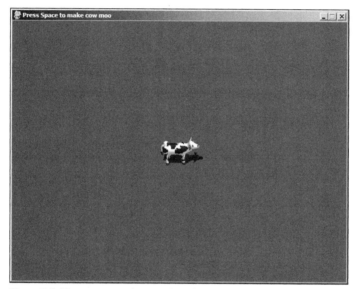

Figure 8-5: When you press the spacebar, the cow moos.

The mooing effect is quite a bit more complex than it seems. Of course, it involves a sound effect (which you already know how to add). When the cow moos, it doesn't just stand there, but tips up its head. It actually follows the series of images shown in Figure 8-6. It also takes advantage of color key techniques to make the original brown background transparent so it looks like the cow is on a green (if digital) pasture.

Transfer

Turn to Chapter 6 if you need a refresher on creating sound effects. You'll find the details on color key transparency in that chapter as well.

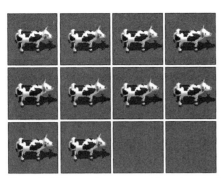

Figure 8-6: The mooing cow goes through each of these frames in sequence.

So far all your sprites have had one image. The cow actually has 11! The default Standing state is one image and the mooing sequence takes up another ten. The secret to animation is to store all the extra images in a way they can be swapped to the screen quickly. The user is fooled into thinking it's one animated image rather than a sequence of individual images.

> ## ℹ Information Kiosk
>
> If you're a talented artist (or know one who accepts bribes), you can generate your own animated artwork. If not, there are still some great options. Ari's SpriteLib (mentioned in the last chapter) has some terrific animations available for free. The cow images come from another great site, Reiner's Tilesets. Reiner Prokein has created thousands of images that anyone can use for free. He has hundreds of objects available, most with many images. I'm including the cow images on the companion Web site for this book, but be sure to explore his site at `http://reinerstileset.4players.de/englisch.htm` for many more terrific images. Thanks, Reiner!

Basic image-swapping

The key to animation is to create a list of images and swap through them. Figure 8-7 shows `cowMooFast.py`, which demonstrates the simplest form of image-swapping.

The `cowMooFast.py` program is centered on an object called `Cow`:

```
class Cow(pygame.sprite.Sprite):
    def __init__(self):
        pygame.sprite.Sprite.__init__(self)

        self.loadImages()
        self.image = self.imageStand
        self.rect = self.image.get_rect()
        self.rect.center = (320, 240)
```

```
            self.frame = 0

    def update(self):
        self.frame += 1
        if self.frame >= len(self.mooImages):
            self.frame = 0
        self.image = self.mooImages[self.frame]


    def loadImages(self):
        self.imageStand = pygame.image.load          ↵
("cowImages/stopped0002.bmp")
        self.imageStand = self.imageStand.convert()
        transColor = self.imageStand.get_at((1, 1))
        self.imageStand.set_colorkey(transColor)

        self.mooImages = []
        for i in range(10):
            imgName = "cowImages/muuuh e000%d.bmp" % i
            tmpImage = pygame.image.load(imgName)
            tmpImage = tmpImage.convert()
            transColor = tmpImage.get_at((1, 1))
            tmpImage.set_colorkey(transColor)
            self.mooImages.append(tmpImage)
```

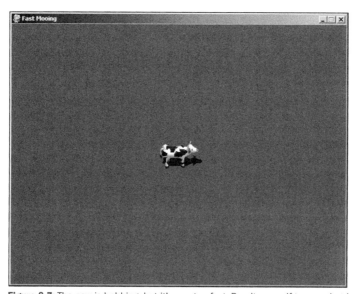

Figure 8-7: The cow is bobbing, but it's way too fast. Run it yourself to see what I mean.

This is a fairly standard sprite, but it has a few new attributes:

- **self.image:** The image currently being displayed. Previous sprites had only one image. The cow will have several images. To make a particular image visible, it will be copied over to self.image.

- **self.imageStand:** The image of the cow standing still and pointing east. I used it to test the basic framework before I added the other images. The cow is initialized to this standing image, but as soon as the other images are loaded in, they will cycle (at least in this version of the program), and you won't see the standing image. It's still worth having because I'll use it again in later versions of the program.

- **self.mooImages:** Once the for loop runs, this list of images contains the ten images in the mooing sequence.

- **self.frame:** A number that denotes the current position in the self.mooImages sequence. If self.frame is 0, the program will show self.mooImages[0].

Information Kiosk

I didn't include the main loop code for cowMooFast in this chapter, because there's nothing at all new there. Be sure to look at the entire file on the Web site to see how I incorporate the Cow class into a standard IDEA loop.

Preparing the images

The way your images are organized on the disk can have an effect on how they are loaded. In this case, I'm using some images from Reiner's Tilesets, so I'll go with the format they already have. Here's how I prepared the images:

1. Locate the images you want.

I looked through the online tile sets to find the cow images. On Reiner's site, each image is stored as a separate BMP file, with all the images for a particular sprite stored in one large ZIP file.

2. Store the images in an accessible place.

The complete cow tile set has a whopping 232 images in it! I created a subdirectory of my game directory called cowImages and unzipped all the images into that directory.

3. Examine the filenames of the images you need.

The filenames are usually set up to help you determine what each image contains. Usually in a multi-image package (such as the cow images) the filenames will have numbers to indicate where in the sequence they belong. Look over all the images to make sure you understand the file-naming convention.

4. **Check for transparency**.

Some image formats (particularly GIF and PNG) have built-in support for transparency. Most formats do not. If your images do not have a transparent background, they will usually have a solid-colored background. You can use a color key in your code to make this color transparent. The cow images I downloaded all have a brown background, which I made transparent so my green background was visible instead.

5. **Modify images if necessary.**

Sometimes your images will require some tweaking in an image editor. This may involve changing the size, doing rotations, modifying colors, or trimming excess space from the edges. You may also need to change filenames to make the files work on multiple platforms.

Loading the images

The Cow class's loadImage() function loads up all the images for you:

```
def loadImages(self):
    self.imageStand = pygame.image.load
("cowImages/stopped0002.bmp")
    self.imageStand = self.imageStand.convert()
    transColor = self.imageStand.get_at((1, 1))
    self.imageStand.set_colorkey(transColor)

    self.mooImages = []
    for i in range(10):
        imgName = "cowImages/muuuh e000%d.bmp" % i
        tmpImage = pygame.image.load(imgName)
        tmpImage = tmpImage.convert()
        transColor = tmpImage.get_at((1, 1))
        tmpImage.set_colorkey(transColor)
        self.mooImages.append(tmpImage)
```

Step into the Real World

If I were distributing this game for real (not to illustrate programming principles), I wouldn't include all 232 images, just the ones I needed. There's no need to make the user download stuff the game won't use.

If you do use some of Reiner's work, be sure to give him credit. He's very generous, and will allow you to use his excellent graphics even in commercial work. Give him a tag line, and send him a copy of your game. (While you're at it, send me a copy too. You don't have to give me any credit though... Just let my family stay at your beach house sometime if one of your games makes you a millionaire.)

Here's what you have to do to make the Cow class load up imageStand() and the list of mooing images:

1. **Load imageStand() in the ordinary way.**

```
        self.imageStand = pygame.image.load        ↩
("cowImages/stopped0002.bmp")
```

I'm loading up a normal (non-mooing) image first for a couple of reasons. First, I'm going to need it eventually, when the cow has a Standing state and a Mooing state. Secondly, the standing image is a single image, and it's a lot easier to test than the sequence of images I'll get when I'm mooing. Build the simple case first, then add complexity.

Watch Your Step

Since my image is in a subdirectory of the main program directory, I'm using the forward slash (/) character to indicate the subdirectory. Windows usually uses the backslash (\) character to indicate subdirectories, but in Python the forward slash will work on all major operating systems. If this makes you uncomfortable, import Python's os module and use the os.join() function to determine the path separator in a cross-platform manner.

2. **Convert the image so it's in the efficient pygame format.**

```
        self.imageStand = self.imageStand.convert()
```

Remember, the convert() method converts an image from its original format (BMP, GIF, JPG, or whatever) to a consistent internal pixel format optimized for processing speed. (The pixel format must be the same as the display surface's format to make blitting to the screen as efficient as possible.) If you don't do the conversion yourself, pygame will have to do the conversion on the fly, and this process will slow down your game considerably.

3. **Find the color of the pixel in the upper-left corner.**

The cow images are bitmaps with no transparency. They have a consistent brown background color. Rather than trying to figure out exactly what color the background is, I simply find the color of pixel (1, 1) and store that in transColor:

```
        transColor = self.imageStand.get_at((1, 1))
```

4. **Set a colorkey value for transparency.**

The transColor value is then set as the sprite's color key. Whenever Python encounters this color in the sprite, it ignores the color and shows the background instead:

```
        self.imageStand.set_colorkey(transColor)
```

5. **Make an empty list for `mooImages`.**

You won't have anything in this list yet.

```
self.mooImages = []
```

6. **Start a loop.**

The images we need have all the same name, but a different number embedded in them. A `for` loop is a natural way to add all these files to the list. This way you only have to write one file-loading line and repeat it within the loop. Since I'll be using images from 0 to 9, I made a loop with ten elements.

```
for i in range(10):
```

```
for i in range(10):
```

 Information Kiosk

If you look at the images, they actually go from 0 to 10, but that last image makes the loop a little more complex than needed. I determined through experimentation that the animation looks fine without it, so I just skipped it.

7. **Determine the image name from a pattern and the image number.**

I used string interpolation to create each image name in turn. For example, when `i` is 3, the program will load up `cowImages/muuuh e0003.bmp`:

```
imgName = "cowImages/muuuh e000%d.bmp" % i
```

Transfer

Turn back to Chapter 1 if you need a refresher on string interpolation.

8. **Load the image into a temporary variable, converting the image and adding transparency just as you did with the default standing image.**

Here's what that looks like:

```
tmpImage = pygame.image.load(imgName)
tmpImage = tmpImage.convert()
transColor = tmpImage.get_at((1, 1))
tmpImage.set_colorkey(transColor)
```

9. **Add the image to the list.**

Use the list's `append()` method to add the image to the list:

```
self.mooImages.append(tmpImage)
```

Step Into the Real World

The filenames in Reiner's Tilesets have spaces in them. This works fine on Windows and Mac OS machines, but it might cause you problems on Linux or Unix machines. You can modify each filename by hand, or look up Python's file-manipulation functions in the `os` module and write your own program. For now, I've left the files alone and I'm simply working in Windows.

Updating the sprite

To make the animation, you simply swap the sprite image each frame in the sprite's `update()` method:

```
def update(self):
    self.frame += 1
    if self.frame >= len(self.mooImages):
        self.frame = 0
    self.image = self.mooImages[self.frame]
```

The process is pretty easy as shown in the following steps:

1. Increment the **frame** attribute.

This attribute determines which frame the animation is currently on. It was initialized to 0 in the `___init()___` method. Each time the `update()` method occurs, the value of `self.frame` will be incremented by one.

```
        self.frame += 1
```

Watch Your Step

It's very tempting to use a `for` loop here, because you're stepping through the elements of a list. Remember, the `update()` function is happening at 30 frames per second. You don't want to go through the entire animation that fast (in fact, your computer probably can't — and if it could, most people couldn't see it). During each update, you simply want to move to the next frame of the animation. (You'll see when you run the program that even this is probably too fast.)

2. Check for boundaries.

Any time you increment or decrement a variable, you should check for possible overflow conditions. In this case, the frame numbers should correspond to the indices in the list, so use the `len()` function to determine how many elements are in the list:

```
        if self.frame >= len(self.mooImages):
```

Checking for Boundaries **351**

3. Reset the frame counter if necessary.

If the frame number has become too large (equal to or greater than the number of images in the list), simply reset its value to 0:

```
self.frame = 0
```

4. Copy the current list element to `self.image`.

The list elements are never visible to the user. They're just a storage place. To make a particular frame visible to the user, copy it over to `self.image`:

```
self.image = self.mooImages[self.frame]
```

Adding a delay to your animation

The cow animation shown in `cowMooFast.py` works well enough, but it has a couple of problems: It isn't happening under user control, and the head is bobbing so fast it doesn't look like mooing at all. Instead it looks like some sort of head-banging punk cow. (I'll have to work that idea into a game sometime!) The problem is the frame rate. The program is running at 30 frames per second, and the cow animation is processing during every frame. At that speed, the cow bobs its head three times a second. You can never make an animation faster than the game's frame rate, but you can make it slower, and you usually need to. `cowMooDelay.py` slows down the animation so a complete moo cycle takes about one second. There's no point in showing a figure, because the critical difference between this and `cowMooFast` is the animation speed. Load `cowMooDelay.py` onto your own machine and verify that now the cow's head is bobbing at a more reasonable speed.

Initializing animation attributes

To slow down an animation, you need to add two additional attributes (in addition to the `frame` attribute you're already using to determine which frame of the head-bob animation you're currently showing) to the sprite class:

- **Delay:** This attribute tells how many game frames to skip between each animation. If you set the `delay` to 3, the animation will swap every third game frame (after you add the code to the `update()` method to make this work, of course).

- **Pause:** This is a counter that increments every frame. As soon as `pause` is equal to `delay`, I'll reset `pause`. So if `delay` is equal to 3, `pause` will count 0, 1, 2, and 3. When `pause` gets to 3, the image will be swapped and `pause` will be reset to 0.

In `cowMooDelay.py`, I add these two attributes to the `Cow` class's `__init__()` method:

```
self.frame = 0
self.delay = 3
self.pause = 0
```

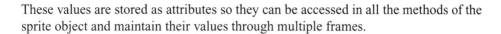

These values are stored as attributes so they can be accessed in all the methods of the sprite object and maintain their values through multiple frames.

Updating the sprite with a delay

The key to a delayed animation is to not advance the animation frame during each game frame. The improved `update()` method limits the cow animations so they occur less frequently:

```
def update(self):
    self.pause += 1
    if self.pause >= self.delay:
        #reset pause and advance animation
        self.pause = 0
        self.frame += 1
        if self.frame >= len(self.mooImages):
            self.frame = 0
        self.image = self.mooImages[self.frame]
```

Here's how the `update()` method incorporates a delay:

1. The **update()** method increments the pause counter by one.

The `pause` counter determines how many game frames have happened in the current animation frame.

2. Then **update()** checks to see if **pause** is equal to the **delay** attribute.

If `self.pause` is smaller than `selfdelay`, no frame animation needs to happen here. If `pause` is larger than or equal to `delay`, it's time to update the animation.

3. If **pause** is equal to **delay**, it's time to do the animation swap.

4. **update()** resets **pause** to **0** so the pause counter can reset for the next frame.

5. Next **update()** increments the frame counter so that the next frame of the animation can be loaded.

6. Finally **update()** loads the animation image to **self.image** just as you did in the **cowMooFast.py** version of the program.

Step Into the Real World

You might wonder why I went to all this trouble to make the cow move more slowly. I could have just used the `clock.tick()` function to make the whole program run at only ten frames per second. That would have been a lot easier. That's true, but not everything in a game will run at exactly the same speed. You may want the overall game engine to run at 30 frames per second, but your cow to run at ten frames per second, and a fly to run at 20 frames per second. Make your overall game loop fast, and use a delay technique to make any other sprites move at whatever slower speed you wish.

Adding states to your sprite

The cow now has an animation, and the animation is working at a controllable speed. The next thing is to give the user control. Normally the cow should just stand there. When the user presses the spacebar, the cow will tip back its head and deliver a plaintive moo. The version of the cow in cowMoo.py has two *states*.

- **Standing:** The cow just stands there, making no noise, and facing east.

- **Mooing:** The cow is still facing east, but now the mooing animation plays the appropriate sound.

Initializing the multi-state cow object

You've done most of the groundwork with the previous versions of the cow program. It just takes a little more effort to add states. Here's the cow's __init__() method after all the changes so far:

```
class Cow(pygame.sprite.Sprite):
    def __init__(self):
        pygame.sprite.Sprite.__init__(self)

        self.STANDING = 0
        self.MOOING = 1

        self.loadImages()
        self.image = self.imageStand
        self.rect = self.image.get_rect()
        self.rect.center = (320, 240)
        self.frame = 0
        self.delay = 3
        self.pause = 0
        self.state = self.STANDING
        pygame.mixer.init()
        self.moo = pygame.mixer.Sound("moo.ogg")
```

Most of the code in this method has been described earlier in the chapter. Here's the new stuff:

- **Create state constants.** Computers prefer working with numerical values. People like words. Use constants as a compromise. I added these constants to the cow object's __init__() method.

    ```
    self.STANDING = 0
    self.MOOING = 1
    ```

The programmer can now refer to self.STANDING and self.MOOING, and these values are translated into integers that are easy for the computer to use. The programmer doesn't have to remember if STANDING is 0 or 1, and it's easy to add new states by adding new constants.

Set the current state to `self.STANDING`. The `self.state` attribute will hold an integer corresponding to the current state. Your other methods can query this attribute to determine what state the cow is currently in, and then change the attribute to indicate that the cow should be in a new state:

```
self.state = self.STANDING
```

Information Kiosk

You could set the state attribute directly to 0 instead of `self.STANDING`, but the constant is preferred because it's easy to understand. When you look at this code again in a week or two, you'll probably be able to figure out that you're trying to make sure the cow is standing now. If you set the state to 0, it wouldn't be so clear what your intentions were. Whenever possible, write your code so it is easy to read.

Initialize the mixer module. The cow will now have a sound effect, so it's important to turn on the mixer module.

Load a moo sound as an attribute of the `cow` object. The moo sound is just an Ogg file I created by mooing into a microphone and changing the pitch in Audacity. Of course, I happened to be working on this chapter in a public library. (If only you could see the look I got from the librarian when I was mooing in the library while recording the audio effect.)

Managing events

So far I haven't shown you any of the main loops in the cow programs, because they're so basic. This version (`cowMoo.py`) of the cow program has some event handling, but it's nothing too dramatic:

```
while keepGoing:
    clock.tick(30)
    for event in pygame.event.get():
        if event.type == pygame.QUIT:
            keepGoing = False
        elif event.type == pygame.KEYDOWN:
            if event.key == pygame.K_SPACE:
                cow.state = cow.MOOING
                cow.moo.play()

    allSprites.clear(screen, background)
    allSprites.update()
    allSprites.draw(screen)

    pygame.display.flip()
```

The event handling relegates most of the work to the `cow` object. Here's how to implement that:

1. **Check to see if the spacebar is pressed.**

Use the normal event-handling procedure for this task:

```
elif event.type == pygame.KEYDOWN:
    if event.key == pygame.K_SPACE:
```

2. **Set the cow's state to MOOING.**

The cow itself will do most of the work, but you have to indicate to the cow that its status should change:

```
cow.state = cow.MOOING
```

3. **Play the moo sound.**

It's easiest to play the sound as the state changes:

```
cow.moo.play()
```

Update the sprite according to the current state

The update() method is modified to handle the two possible states. The cow will behave in one way if the cow is in its STANDING state, and will have another behavior in the MOOING state.

```
def update(self):
    if self.state == self.STANDING:
        self.image = self.imageStand
    else:
        self.pause += 1
        if self.pause > self.delay:
            #reset pause and advance animation
            self.pause = 0
            self.frame += 1
            if self.frame >= len(self.mooImages):
                self.frame = 0
                self.state = self.STANDING
                self.image = self.imageStand
            else:
                self.image = self.mooImages[self.frame]
```

The basic strategy is to break the update() method into two distinct behaviors based on the state of the sprite. Here's how you do it.

1. **Determine whether the cow is standing by checking the state attribute.**

```
if self.state == self.STANDING:
```

2. **If the cow is standing, set the sprite's primary image to the standing image.**

No other work is required in the standing mode, as it has only one frame in its animation.

```
self.image = self.imageStand
```

3. **If the cow is not standing, it must be mooing.**

Since this sprite has only two states, the `else` clause will activate when the cow is not standing.

4. **When the mooing animation is complete, reset the state to STANDING.**

```
if self.frame >= len(self.mooImages):
    self.frame = 0
    self.state = self.STANDING
    self.image = self.imageStand
```

5. **If the animation is still in effect, copy the current image to the primary image.**

The sprite animation is nearly the same as it was in the `cowMooDelay.py` program. Simply copy the value indicated by `self.frame` from `self.mooImages` to `self.image`.

```
else:
    self.image = self.mooImages[self.frame]
```

Using a combined image

The images from Reiner's Tilesets come in a series of small images. Other tile sets, like the ones in SpriteLib, combine many sprites onto one image file. For example, Figure 8-8 shows `heli.bmp` from Ari's SpriteLib package.

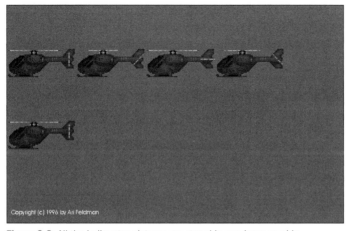

Figure 8-8: All the helicopter pictures are stored in one large graphic.

Of course you could use an image editor to break the image into several smaller files, but the single file format is a lot easier to work with than hundreds of smaller files. Actually you already have a tool that allows you to copy a segment of one image to another — in this case, a portion of a surface — and that tool is none other than the `blit()` command. You can make an animated sprite by loading in one master image, making a list of smaller surfaces, and copying the appropriate sections of the master image onto the image list. That's exactly what I do in `chopper.py`, featured in Figure 8-9.

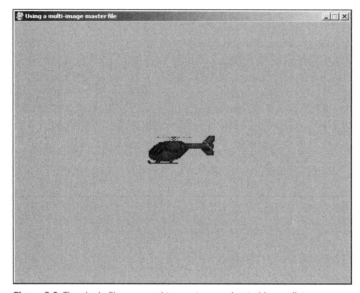

Figure 8-9: The single file was used to create an animated image list.

Analyzing the original image

In order to copy parts of the original image to individual pygame surfaces, you have to know where on the original each smaller picture is — and exactly how large each sub-image is. It's easiest to do this with an image-editing program. Regardless of the specific program you use, here are the general steps to analyze the image:

1. **Open the original image in an editor.**

I usually use a wonderful free tool called IrfanView (www.irfanview.com) for this task, because it loads faster than GIIMP and I don't really need to manipulate the image, just examine it closely. It doesn't matter which image viewer you use, as long as you have some way to determine what size things are in the image, and where they are.

2. **Determine the size of each sub-image.**

The selection tools of most image editors can tell you the size of the current selection. Usually each object will be pretty close to the same size. Often the width and height values of the sprite will be powers of two. In this case, all the chopper images were 128 pixels wide by 64 pixels tall. Drag your selection tool around the smaller image, and usually you'll get an indicator somewhere what the size and position of the selection are within the larger image. Write down this size, as you'll need it later.

3. **Determine the upper-left corner of each image.**

Write down the upper-left corner of each image.

4. **Make a chart with all the relevant information.**

My chart for the chopper image looks like Table 8-1.

Table 8-1   Size and Position of Chopper Images

Image #	Left	Top	Width	Height
0	2	78	128	64
1	134	78	128	64
2	266	78	128	64
3	398	78	128	64

All the chopper images are the same size. The only thing different about them is their positions. This chart gives you all the information you'll need to make the image list from this primary image. It's not unusual to see some numeric relationships in this chart, which might help you later. For example, the top, width, and height of each image are the same in this particular situation, so the left value is the only thing I'll need to worry too much about.

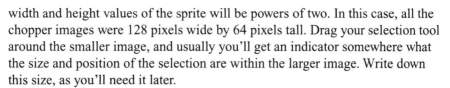

Information Kiosk

I skipped the last image because it appears to be the same as image 0. The animation works well enough with the four images, so I didn't bother adding one more.

Extracting a subsurface from an image

The way you've used the `blit()` method so far, it copies a complete surface to another surface. There's a variation of the `blit()` method that extracts just a portion of one surface to another. If you give the `blit()` method a rectangle as a third parameter, it copies only that section of the original image. This version of the `blit()` method looks like this:

```
surfaceB.blit(surfaceA, position, (offset, size)
```

Here's what all the parameters mean:

- **surfaceA:** The surface you're copying *from*.
- **surfaceB:** The surface you're copying *to*.
- **position:** The position on surfaceB where you want the copy to go. Since you'll be filling up all of surfaceB, this position will be (0, 0).
- **offset:** The position of the image you want to extract from surfaceA. It will be an (x, y) coordinate pair.
- **size:** The size of the image you are copying from surfaceA.

Building the sprite

The general structure of the Chopper sprite is pretty familiar. The only thing that's really different is the loadImages() method. Rather than loading several separate images from a lot of little files as you've done in the past, this program loads up one large image file and makes several separate surfaces from it. Here's what that looks like:

```
def loadImages(self):
    imgMaster = pygame.image.load("heli.bmp")
    imgMaster = imgMaster.convert()

    self.imgList = []

    imgSize = (128, 64)
    offset = ((2, 78), (134, 78), (266, 78), (398, 78))

    for i in range(4):
        tmpImg = pygame.Surface(imgSize)
        tmpImg.blit(imgMaster, (0, 0), (offset[i],  ↩
imgSize))
        transColor = tmpImg.get_at((1, 1))
        tmpImg.set_colorkey(transColor)
        self.imgList.append(tmpImg)
```

The method takes advantage of the blit() command with the offset and uses some special variables to make things easier. Here's how you do it:

1. **Load the master image into a local variable using the normal technique, and convert the image to the pygame pixel format.**

```
imgMaster = pygame.image.load("heli.bmp")
imgMaster = imgMaster.convert()
```

2. **Create an empty list.**

This variable will contain the list of images when the method is complete.

```
self.imgList = []
```

3. **Place the image size in a variable.**

All the sub-images are the same size (128, 64), so I'll put this value in a variable to make my code easier to manage.

```
imgSize = (128, 64)
```

4. **Create a list of positions.**

The `blit()` method create new images by copying segments of the original image. Each new image requires its own `blit()` method, but the details of these blits are nearly identical. The only thing that's different in each case is the image number and the offset. Take the offset values from your previous chart and put them in a fancy tuple.

```
offset = ((2, 78), (134, 78), (266, 78),    ↵
(398, 78))
```

Watch Your Step

Make sure you put the offsets in the correct order. The offset for image 0 should come first, followed by the one from image 1, and so on. There should be the same number of offsets as there will be images in the final animation.

5. **Make a `for` loop.**

I'm creating four images, here, so I'll do the image-creation code four times:

```
for i in range(4):
```

6. **Create a temporary `Surface` object of the needed size.**

You've already stored the size in the `imgSize` variable.

```
tmpImg = pygame.Surface(imgSize)
```

7. **Blit a sub-image of `imgMaster` to the temporary image.**

Get the image offset from the `offset` tuple, and the image size from the `imgSize` variable:

```
tmpImg.blit(imgMaster, (0, 0),           ↵
(offset[i], imgSize))
```

8. **Set the color key of the temporary image.**

Use the `get_at()` and `set_colorkey()` methods you've already learned to add transparency to the temporary image:

```
transColor = tmpImg.get_at((1, 1))
tmpImg.set_colorkey(transColor)
```

9. **Add the temporary image to the image list.**

Now that the temporary image is ready to go, add it to the image list for later use.

The rest of the `Chopper` class works just like any other animated sprite. The `chopper.py` program is available on the Web site if you want to look it over and make changes.

Rotating Sprites

Often your sprites will be capable of moving in multiple directions. In one sense, the direction a sprite is pointing is just another kind of state the sprite can be in. Most sprites have some way of indicating the direction they're pointing — and sprites tend to go in the direction they're facing. There are two aspects to adding direction to the sprite. The first is the visual element. The second is adding the actual motion. Learn how to rotate the visual part of an image, and then you can move it in the indicated direction.

Rotating a sprite with transformations

If you have images that point in all eight directions, you can simply load these images in as you did other sprite animations. If you have a top-down image, you can use the functions in a special module called called `pygame.transform` to rotate the image. This means you can make all the images you need from only one master image.

Figure 8-10 shows `rotate.py`. This program takes a single ship image and uses transformation functions to rotate the ship when the user presses the left or right arrow keys.

Notice that in the game, the ship is pointing to the Northwest. This is interesting, because the game has only one ship image, which is pointing to the East. Somehow, I used one image to create all the rotated images I needed.

Directions in Python

Before going too much further into doing rotation, it's important to discuss how Python views angles and rotations. Python uses a mathematically grounded system for working with angles, which is different from the navigational system you may be more familiar with. Figure 8-11 illustrates the difference.

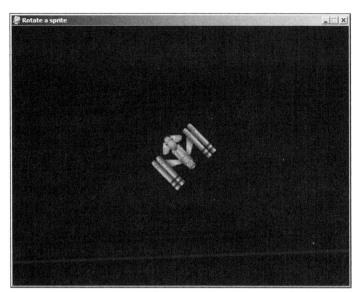

Figure 8-10: Only one image is used to create eight distinct directions.

The system used in navigation has 0 degrees facing up (usually North). Angles increase in a clockwise direction, with 360 degrees in the full circle. Mathematicians measure angles differently. 0 degrees is usually placed along the X-axis, which means it points to the right (or east). Angles increase as you move around the circle counterclockwise.

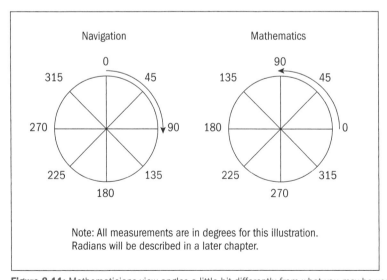

Figure 8-11: Mathematicians view angles a little bit differently from what you may be used to.

Step Into the Real World

Truthfully, mathematicians rarely use degrees at all, because they're an arbitrary unit of angle measurement. I'll stick with degrees for now, but in the next chapter you'll see how to use radians, which are usually preferred in mathematical applications.

Preparing an image

If you want to use a single image that will be dynamically rotated, here are a few key tips to keep in mind:

- **The element needs to be viewed from directly above.** The dynamic rotation trick will only be believable if the object appears to be viewed from a camera directly above it.

- **The object shouldn't have obvious shading or shadows unless the apparent light source is also directly above.** If the object appears to be shaded from the upper left, for example, the light source will also appear to move as the object rotates. This can destroy the illusion. If you want to incorporate shading or shadows, you'll need to have separate images for each direction to keep the apparent light source consistent.

- **The object should be relatively small.** The computer will have to do some heavy computation to rotate the object in real time. Large objects may be difficult to rotate quickly enough to keep the frame rate going.

- **The default orientation should be to the East.** This last point isn't absolutely critical, but it is helpful, because it makes the math easier.

Use your image editor to prepare an image for use. Figure 8-12 shows `ship.bmp`, an image I modified for this purpose.

Figure 8-12: The original image is pointed East. Other rotations will be created through code.

Information Kiosk

The ship image comes from an older version of Ari's SpriteLib package. He actually included all the rotations in his image, but I just cropped it to one image and rotated it myself to illustrate the process.

The basic idea behind rotation is pretty simple, but there's a wrinkle: When you rotate a sprite, you will often change the object's shape. This is because bounding rectangles don't rotate with the image. Figure 8-13 shows the ship image with the bounding rectangles drawn over it.

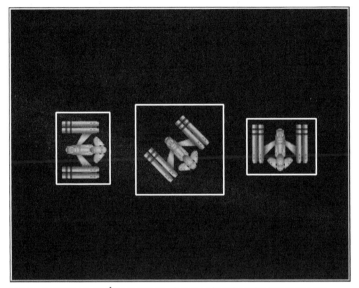

Figure 8-13: The bounding rectangle changes size when the image rotates.

Information Kiosk

To create Figure 8-13, I wrote a program called `drawBounds.py` that draws the bounding rectangle on the sprite as it rotates. I ran `drawBounds.py` several times and created a composite image so you can easily compare the bounding rectangle sizes. I've included `drawBounds.py` on the Web site so you can run it yourself and see what happens to the bounding rectangle as you rotate the image.

You can see from these images that the bounding rectangle changes sizes as it rotates. This will have some side effects that you will have to manage as you rotate your images.

Transfer

One of the problems with the change in bounding rectangle size occurs with collision-detection. Diagonal objects generally have a larger bounding rectangle than the vertical or horizontal version. Use the `rect.inflate_ip()` method shown in Chapter 7 or the distance calculation trick shown in Chapter 9 to overcome this problem.

Building the sprite

The sprite object is very ordinary. This code is show in `rotate.py`.

```
def __init__(self):
    pygame.sprite.Sprite.__init__(self)
    self.imageMaster = pygame.image.load("ship.bmp")
    self.imageMaster = self.imageMaster.convert()
    self.image = self.imageMaster
    self.rect = self.image.get_rect()
    self.rect.center = (320, 240)
    self.dir = 0
```

Notice that the sprite loads up an image called `imageMaster`. The `dir` attribute holds the sprite's current direction.

 Information Kiosk

Each time you transform an image, you lose some quality. This will quickly become troublesome if you transform the same image many times. To prevent this, keep one master image and transform that same, pristine image each time.

Updating the sprite

The `update()` method acts a bit differently than those you've seen before. The `update()` method doesn't change the position of the sprite, but instead it replaces the image with a new image that is rotated appropriate to the current direction. Here's what the code looks like:

```
def update(self):
    oldCenter = self.rect.center
    self.image =
pygame.transform.rotate(self.imageMaster, self.dir)
    self.rect = self.image.get_rect()
    self.rect.center = oldCenter
```

The rotation requires a few steps:

1. Copy the current rectangle's center into a temporary variable.

When the object is rotated, it might change size and position. Storing the center helps to ensure that the sprite doesn't move when it changes size and shape.

2. Rotate the image.

The `pygame.transform` module contains a series of functions for manipulating surfaces. `pygame.transform.rotate()` turns an image. Use it to rotate the `imgMaster` image `dir` degrees:

```
self.image = pygame.transform.rotate(self.imageMaster, self.dir)
```

3. Re-calculate the rectangle.

When an image rotates, its object changes. The bounding rectangle can change sizes dramatically. Each time you change the image size, you need to recalculate the rectangle, or the image will appear to move across the screen.

```
self.rect = self.image.get_rect()
```

4. Re-center the image.

When the image is rotated, it might change sizes. This can cause the center to move. Copy the center value you stored earlier in this process back to the object's `rect.circle` attribute.

Turn the sprite

The sprite object can now rotate itself according to its `dir` attribute. Of course, you need an opportunity to change the direction. I do this through two functions:

```
def turnLeft(self):
    self.dir += 45
    if self.dir > 360:
        self.dir = 45

def turnRight(self):
    self.dir -= 45
    if self.dir < 0:
        self.dir = 315
```

These functions are used to change the direction. Here's how they work — and what you do at each step:

1. Add 45 degrees to the `dir` attribute.

Remember from Figure 8-11 that angles increase in a counterclockwise manner. Adding 45 degrees to the angle will cause the sprite to appear to rotate to the left:

```
self.dir += 45
```

2. Check for an upper boundary.

If the angle gets larger than 360 degrees, it should be reset to a smaller number:

```
if self.dir > 360:
```

3. Reset the direction to 45 degrees.

As soon as the angle is larger than 360 degrees, it needs to go to the next position, which will be 45 degrees:

```
self.dir = 45
```

4. Repeat the process for turning left.

Turning left works almost the same, except you subtract 45 degrees from the current angle, and reset the value to 315 when it becomes smaller than 0.

Moving in eight directions

You can point a ship in any of the eight directions, but it takes a little more effort to make the ship actually *move* in the direction it's pointed. Figure 8-14 shows `move8dir.py`. This program modifies the `rotate.py` program to make the ship move in the direction it's pointed.

Figure 8-14: The ship moves under user control.

The ship moves at various speeds and in all eight directions. The arrow keys are used to rotate the sprite, and to change its speed.

Initializing the ship

The sprite class has the basic attributes of any sprite, but a few new attributes to handle motion:

- **dir.** The `dir` attribute indicates the direction the sprite is facing. In this program, the `dir` value will be stored in degrees.

- **speed.** This attribute indicates how many pixels the ship will move per frame in the `dir` direction.

- **dx and dy.** These values are used to determine how the object will change positions in x and y. The `speed` and `dir` will be used to set up the values of `dx` and `dy` during each frame.

x and y. Although `ship.rect.centerx` and `ship.rect.centery` can be used to position the ship, there are some problems with this approach. (I'll explain later why I use these x and y attributes to make the sprite move correctly.)

The entire process for managing the sprite's motion is summarized in Figure 8-15.

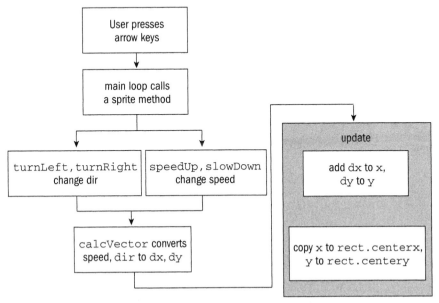

Figure 8-15: This figure illustrates the process used to animate the sprite.

The Figure 8-15 diagram shows how the various variables are connected, and how data flows through the program.

Information Kiosk

Don't worry if you don't completely understand Figure 8-15 right now. It's an overview of the process described throughout this section. I just want to give you an overview of how things will work before you see all the details.

The `__init__()` method sets initial values to all the variables and does other typical startup tasks.

```
class Ship(pygame.sprite.Sprite):
    def __init__(self, screen):
        pygame.sprite.Sprite.__init__(self)
```

```
            self.screen = screen
            self.imageMaster = pygame.image.load("ship.bmp")
            self.imageMaster = self.imageMaster.convert()
            self.imageMaster = pygame.transform.scale          ↩
(self.imageMaster, (30, 30))

            self.image = self.imageMaster
            self.rect = self.image.get_rect()
            self.rect.center = (320, 240)

            self.x = self.rect.centerx
            self.y = self.rect.centery
            self.dir = 0
            self.speed = 0
            self.dx = 0
            self.dy = 0
```

Here's the way you create this sprite:

1. **Pass the screen as an argument.**

The sprite will move and require boundary checking, so it will need access to the `screen` object. The screen parameter is copied to an attribute so it can be re-used within the class.

2. **Load the master image.**

Load the primary image as `imageMaster`.

3. **Resize the image.**

Use the `transform.scale()` method to resize the `ship` sprite to 30×30 pixels.

```
        self.imageMaster = pygame.transform.scale(self.imageMaster, (30, 30))
```

4. **Set the attributes.**

This object will need all the attributes mentioned before. I initialize all of them, which looks like this:

```
            self.image = self.imageMaster
            self.rect = self.image.get_rect()
            self.rect.center = (320, 240)

            self.x = self.rect.centerx
            self.y = self.rect.centery
            self.dir = 0
            self.speed = 0
            self.dx = 0
            self.dy = 0
```

Updating the sprite

The update() method manages all the tasks that need to be handled during each frame:

```
def update(self):
    oldCenter = self.rect.center
    self.image = pygame.transform.rotate          ↩
(self.imageMaster, self.dir)
    self.rect = self.image.get_rect()
    self.rect.center = oldCenter

    self.calcVector()
    self.x += self.dx
    self.y += self.dy
    self.checkBounds()
    self.rect.centerx = self.x
    self.rect.centery = self.y
```

The update() method rotates the image, determines how the sprite should be positioned, and moves the sprite appropriately as follows:

- **The image is rotated.** The update() method rotates the image by saving the center, using the pygame.tranform.rotate() method to rotate the image, and re-centering the sprite.

- **The sprite's new dx and dy attributes are calculated.** The calcVector() method (which I'll detail shortly) has a very important job. It translates the object's speed and direction to dx and dy attributes. Right now I simply call the calcVector() method to manage this detail.

    ```
    self.calcVector()
    ```

- **self.dx is added to self.x and self.dy is added to y.** Note that I don't directly update the self.rect.centerx and self.rect.centery variables; instead, I update the new attributes self.x and self.y. The centerx and centery attributes are predefined as integers. If you try to change the integer rect attributes directly, the decimal part gets truncated — causing the sprite to move incorrectly at slow speeds. Adding dx and dy to the floating-point x and y attributes, and then transferring the values of these attributes to `self.rect.centerx` and `self.rect.centery` eliminates this problem.

```
self.x += self.dx
self.y += self.dy
```

The **update()** method checks for boundary conditions. If the sprite leaves the screen it should wrap. Delegate this behavior to the `checkBounds()` method.

```
self.checkBounds()
```

Finally, the update() method copies x and y attributes to self.rect. The `update()` method works on the floating-point `x` and `y` attributes internally, but in order to move the sprite, the data must be transferred to `self.rect` as a last step.

```
self.rect.centerx = self.x
self.rect.centery = self.y
```

Calculating new dx and dy variables

As the user plays this game, he uses the arrow keys to turn the sprite right or left, speed it up, and slow it down. These actions call sprite methods — which in turn change the `dir` and `speed` attributes. The sprite needs to translate `dir` and `speed` into `dx` and `dy` values, so it knows how much to move the sprite along each axis in the current frame. Table 8-2 illustrates the eight basic directions, and how they relate to `dx` and `dy`.

Table 8-2   Math Representations of Directions

Direction	Angle	dx	Dy
East	0	1	0
Northeast	45	.7	-.7
North	90	0	-1
Northwest	135	-.7	-.7
West	180	-1	0
Southwest	225	-.7	.7
South	270	0	1
Southeast	315	.7	.7

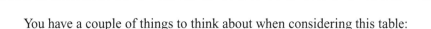

You have a couple of things to think about when considering this table:

Degrees are calculated in the mathematical way. Remember, Python calculates angles using the mathematical technique, with 0 degrees meaning East and angles increasing counterclockwise.

dx and dy are calculated to move the sprite 1 pixel in each direction. Look at the cardinal directions (North, South, East, and West) and you'll see that one of the values (dx or dy) is 0, and the other is 1. This means the sprite will move 1 pixel directly on one of the axes.

Transfer

Movement in 1 pixel is called a *unit vector*. I explain more about motion vectors in Chapter 9. The important idea here is this: If you know the dx and dy values to move the sprite 1 pixel per frame, you can multiply these values by a speed value to calculate the appropriate dx and dy for any speed.

Diagonals have strange values. It might surprise you that the values for southeast are (.7, .7) rather than (1, 1). This is done because you want the sprite to travel approximately 1 pixel in each direction. If you move the sprite 1 pixel on the x axis, it is moving 1 pixel per frame. If you move it 1 pixel in x and one in y, the sprite will actually move about 1.4 pixels. Then, when you incorporate speed into your equations, this would cause the sprite to move much more quickly in diagonal directions than in the cardinal directions. If the diagonals are variations of .7 (on the other hand), the total distance traveled will still be about 1 pixel. Figure 8-16 illustrates the mathematical principle at work here.

$$a^2 + a^2 = 1^2$$

$$2a^2 = 1$$

$$a^2 = 1/2$$

$$a = \sqrt{1/2}$$

$$a \approx 0.7$$

Figure 8-16: You can use the Pythagorean theorem and a little algebra to get the .7 diagonal value.

Information Kiosk

If you're not quite following the math here, don't worry. In the next chapter, I'll show you a more complete way to handle directions. For now, it's important to understand that the .7 values make the sprite go at the same speed regardless of the direction it's pointing.

Writing the calcVector method

The dx and dy values are used to actually move the sprite. These values can be considered the *motion vector* of the sprite. A motion vector is a data structure that indicates how the sprite will move.

Transfer

You learn a lot more about motion vectors in Chapter 9.

Translating speed and direction into dx and dy values is the purpose of the calcVector() method. After you've got a handle on what the function should do, its actual implementation is pretty simple:

```
def calcVector(self):
    if self.dir == 0:
        self.dx = 1
        self.dy = 0
    elif self.dir == 45:
        self.dx = .7
        self.dy = -.7
    elif self.dir == 90:
        self.dx = 0
        self.dy = -1
    elif self.dir == 135:
        self.dx = -.7
        self.dy = -.7
    elif self.dir == 180:
        self.dx = -1
        self.dy = 0
    elif self.dir == 225:
        self.dx = -.7
        self.dy = .7
    elif self.dir == 270:
        self.dx = 0
        self.dy = 1
```

```
    elif self.dir == 315:
        self.dx = .7
        self.dy = .7
    else:
        print "something went wrong here"

    self.dx *= self.speed
    self.dy *= self.speed
```

In this particular program, the `calcVector()` method is easy to understand, if a bit repetitive. Here's what it does:

1. Examines the sprite's current direction.

Use an `if` structure to examine the possible direction values:

```
if self.dir == 0:
    . . .
elif self.dir == 45:
    . . .
```

Use an `if-elif` structure to test for all the possible direction values.

2. Sets dx and dy to appropriate values.

Use the values in Table 8-2 to set the values of `self.dx` and `self.dy` according to the current direction. For example, direction 0 (East) looks like this:

```
self.dx = 1
self.dy = 0
```

3. Prints an error message if necessary.

Be sure to check for any surprise angles. The `else` clause will trigger if none of the previous conditions were `True`.

```
else:
    print "something went wrong here"
```

4. Multiplies the dx and dy values by the sprite's speed attribute.

The dx and dy values in Table 8-2 are designed to move the sprite exactly 1 pixel per frame in the designated direction. Of course, the `move8dir.py` program allows the user to set the speed to anything from –3 to +10 pixels per frame. If you know how to move the sprite 1 pixel in any direction, just multiply the dx and dy attributes by the desired speed.

```
self.dx *= self.speed
self.dy *= self.speed
```

Accepting user input

The user will interact with this program using the arrow keys. The main loop is modified to accept the input and send appropriate instructions to the sprite:

```
while keepGoing:
    clock.tick(30)
    for event in pygame.event.get():
        if event.type == pygame.QUIT:
            keepGoing = False
        elif event.type == pygame.KEYDOWN:
            if event.key == pygame.K_LEFT:
                ship.turnLeft()
            elif event.key == pygame.K_RIGHT:
                ship.turnRight()
            elif event.key == pygame.K_UP:
                ship.speedUp()
            elif event.key == pygame.K_DOWN:
                ship.slowDown()
```

The only issue here is to check for all four arrow keys. Here's the drill:

1. **Check for a keyboard event.**

Check to see if the user has pressed a key on the keyboard during the current frame.

2. **Check for the left arrow key.**

Use the `pygame.K_LEFT` constant to see if the current key is the left arrow.

3. **Call the sprite's `turnLeft()` method.**

The main loop is a good place to check for keyboard input, but it shouldn't really worry about the details of what's going on in the sprite. It simply invokes one of the sprite's methods.

4. **Repeat for the other arrows.**

This particular sprite can speed up, slow down, turn left, and turn right. The main loop simply reads the keyboard and calls the appropriate sprite method.

 Step Into the Real World

The arrow keys are a natural way to control the object, but the actual keys pressed aren't important to the sprite. It's good to separate the actual keyboard input from the sprite's actions. This will allow you to assign alternate keystrokes or incorporate more advanced control techniques (like the joystick) as you learn how to do these things. This approach (calling sprite methods) also takes advantage of encapsulation. In the main loop code, you really need to focus on what the sprite is doing (turning left or slowing down, for example) rather than the details of the process (changing `speed`, `dx`, and `dy` attributes).

Implementing the sprite's control methods

The sprite has a number of methods that are called from the main loop. These methods take the user's intentions and translate them to changes in the sprite's `speed` and `dir` attributes. These variables will later be used to modify `dx` and `dy`, which will eventually change the position of the sprite on the screen. Here's what you do:

1. **Manage left and right turns.**

The `turnLeft()` and `turnRight()` methods are replicated exactly from the `rotate.py` program.

```
def turnLeft(self):
    self.dir += 45
    if self.dir == 360:
        self.dir = 0

def turnRight(self):
    self.dir -= 45
    if self.dir < 0:
        self.dir = 315
```

Don't forget to check for boundary values.

2. **Speed up the sprite.**

The `speedUp()` method doesn't speed up the sprite directly. Instead, it increments the `speed` attribute.

```
def speedUp(self):
    self.speed += 1
```

3. **Check for a maximum speed.**

Give your sprites a speed limit, or they'll get going too fast to see on the screen. I imposed a maximum speed of 8 pixels per frame on my sprite.

```
if self.speed > 8:
```

4. **Don't let the speed surpass the maximum.**

If the speed is larger than the maximum value, reset it to the maximum value.

```
self.speed = 8
```

5. **Build another method for slowing down.**

If the user presses the down arrow, he wants to slow the sprite down. The `slowDown()` method is very much like `speedUp()`.

```
def slowDown(self):
    self.speed -= 1
    if self.speed < -3:
        self.speed = -3
```

6. **Decrement the speed by 1.**

Subtracting 1 from the speed will cause the sprite to move 1 less pixel per frame.

7. **Check for a minimum speed.**

If you don't want the sprite to go backwards, test for a speed less than 0. If you allow negative speeds, the sprite will go backwards.

Finishing up the program

Be sure to look over the `move8dir.py` program in its entirety; I haven't shown you all the code in this section. That's because the elements I haven't covered here have been described completely in other parts of the book. They include these two:

- **The overall IDEA/ALTER structure.** As the code gets longer, I assume you understand the overall structure of the program.

- **The `checkBounds()` method.** I used a standard wrapping technique for this program.

Combining Motion with Animation

The `cowEast.py` program illustrated in Figure 8-17 shows a cow walking toward the east. The figure can't do this program justice, as the real program shows a realistic walking motion, with the head and tail swaying as the cow walks.

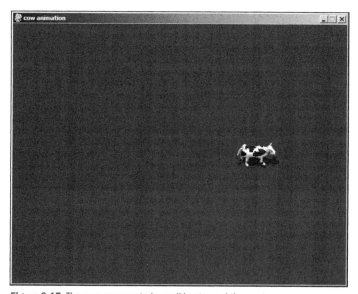

Figure 8-17: The cow appears to be walking toward the east.

Making an animated sprite move combines several ideas from earlier in this chapter. To keep things simple, this program will only move the cow in one direction.

Transfer

In the next section of this chapter, I'll explain how to animate the sprite in other directions.

Initializing the cow sprite

The cowEast.py program is the first step in making a multi-frame, multi-direction animation. Begin by making a cow sprite that walks in only one direction. All the interesting stuff happens in the cow sprite itself.

```
class Cow(pygame.sprite.Sprite):

    def __init__(self, screen):
        self.screen = screen
        pygame.sprite.Sprite.__init__(self)
        self.image = pygame.image.load              ↩
("cowImages/stopped0002.bmp")
        self.image = self.image.convert()
        tranColor = self.image.get_at((1, 1))
        self.image.set_colorkey(tranColor)
        self.rect = self.image.get_rect()
        self.rect.center = (320, 240)

        self.img = []
        self.loadPics()

        self.frame = 0
        self.delay = 3
        self.pause = self.delay
        self.dx = 4
```

You put the cow sprite into motion — like most moving sprites — via these steps:

1. **Use a screen parameter.**

   Like most moving sprites, the Cow instance will need access to the screen for its boundary-detection routine:

```
        def __init__(self, screen):
            self.screen = screen
```

2. **Initialize the image.**

   Load up a default image for test purposes: Make sure you've got the cow sprite visible with one image before you go through the complexity of adding a bunch of other images.

```
            self.image = pygame.image.load          ↩
("cowImages/stopped0002.bmp")
            self.image = self.image.convert()
            tranColor = self.image.get_at((1, 1))
```

```
            self.image.set_colorkey(tranColor)
            self.rect = self.image.get_rect()
            self.rect.center = (320, 240)
```

3. **Build a list of images for the animation.**

The cow images from Reiner's Tilesets include eight images walking toward the east. Create a list to hold the images and use the `loadPics()` method to store the images in the list.

```
        self.img = []
        self.loadPics()
```

4. **Initialize other sprite attributes.**

The sprite will need attributes to handle the animation. Initialize these attributes to appropriate starting values.

```
        self.frame = 0
        self.delay = 3
        self.pause = self.delay
        self.dx = 4
```

Loading the images

The `loadPics()` method loads up all the images necessary to animate the cow walking. If you examine the cow images supplied in Reiner's Tilesets, you can see that there are eight images of the cow walking toward the east. They are named `walking e0000.bmp` through `walking_e0007.bmp`. The `loadPics()` method here is similar to the `cowMoo.py` example from earlier in this chapter.

```
def loadPics(self):
    for i in range(8):
        imgName = "cowImages/walking e000%d.bmp" % i
        tmpImg = pygame.image.load(imgName)
        tmpImg.convert()
        tranColor = tmpImg.get_at((0, 0))
        tmpImg.set_colorkey(tranColor)
        self.img.append(tmpImg)
```

Here's how you load the images:

1. **Repeat eight times.**

The cow images are numbered from 0 to 7, so the `for i in range(8)` statement will produce exactly the numbers you need to re-create the filenames:

```
        for i in range(8):
```

2. **Build the current filename.**

Use string interpolation to create each filename in turn:

```
            imgName = "cowImages/walking e000%d.bmp" % i
```

3. Load the image into a variable called `tmpImg`.

```
            tmpImg = pygame.image.load(imgName)
```

4. Prepare `tmpImage` by converting it and setting its `colorkey`.

```
            tmpImg.convert()
            tranColor = tmpImg.get_at((0, 0))
            tmpImg.set_colorkey(tranColor)
```

5. Add `tmpImg` to the `img` list.

This is the list of images to be used in the animation.

```
            self.img.append(tmpImg)
```

Updating the animated cow

The `update()` method combines motion with animation as you can see in the following code and steps:

```
def update(self):

    self.pause -= 1
    if self.pause <= 0:
        self.pause = self.delay

        self.frame += 1
        if self.frame > 7:
            self.frame = 0

        self.image = self.img[self.frame]

        self.rect.centerx += self.dx
        if self.rect.centerx > self.screen.get_width():
            self.rect.centerx = 0
```

Step Into the Real World

You might wonder why my image-movement and boundary-checking routines are so simple here when they were more complex in previous examples. For example, I added dx directly to the `self.rect.centerx` attribute. I did this deliberately. When building something complex, it's always smart to start simply and then add complexity. Right now I'm going to make the cow move only to the east with an animation. After that's working properly, I'll fit the program with the other details necessary for walking in multiple directions (the keyboard-input commands, direction and speed-management methods, and more sophisticated movement and boundary-checking routines). You'll see all these things added in the next section.

1. **Incorporate a delay mechanism in the animation.**

Use the `pause` and `delay` variables to delay the animation to 10 frames per second, like this:

```
self.pause -= 1
if self.pause <= 0:
    self.pause = self.delay

    self.frame += 1
    if self.frame > 7:
        self.frame = 0
```

Transfer

Check the discussion of animation delays earlier in this chapter if you need a refresher on how these variables are used to slow the animation.

2. **Extract the current image from the `img` list:**

```
self.image = self.img[self.frame]
```

3. **Move the image:**

```
self.rect.centerx += self.dx
```

4. **Check for boundaries:**

```
if self.rect.centerx > self.screen.get_width():
    self.rect.centerx = 0
```

Building an Eight-Direction Animation

Finally you have all the tools you need to build an animation that walks smoothly in eight directions. This animation seems very simple to the user, but now you know that it's really pretty complicated. The cow can move in eight directions, and walking in each direction requires eight frames of animation. The simple cow is really 64 separate images. Your program has to organize these images in a structure which makes them easy to manage, and make sure the game retrieves the right image for each situation based on the cow's direction of travel and current frame.

Figure 8-18 shows the `cow.py` program. As in all the programs for this chapter, you can't really appreciate the animation from the book. You'll need to run it yourself to see how it works. The user controls the cow with the arrow keys.

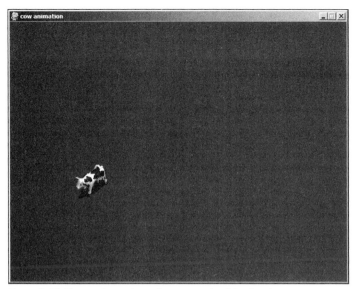

Figure 8-18: The cow has animated movement in eight directions.

Managing complexity with data structures

The key problem in the `cow.py` program is handling all those images in a sensible way. Making the cow walk in a single direction requires eight frames of animation, but you need it to walk in *eight* directions. Every image needed to animate the walking cow can be specified by a direction and frame. It makes sense to put these images into a list. With eight directions of travel and eight images for each direction, so the program really requires a list of lists! Fortunately, Python lists can contain anything, even other lists. To access any image in the `imgList` attribute in the final version of Cow, I actually use two parameters, like this:

```
self.imgList[self.dir][self.frame]
```

where `self.dir` is the direction the cow is currently pointing, and `self.frame` is the animation frame for walking in that direction.

Setting up direction constants

The first trick is to control the directions in a meaningful way. Previously I managed directions with the degree measurements. This is okay for basic programs, but it becomes problematic when you want to do more than simply rotate an image. The actual degree measurement isn't important here, because I won't rotate the images — instead, I'll load in a different image set for each direction of travel. In this example, it's easier if the directions are represented by integers between 0 and 7. I think of each direction as a state, and create constants to help remember the direction values.

```
#direction constants
EAST = 0
NORTHEAST = 1
NORTH = 2
NORTHWEST = 3
WEST = 4
SOUTHWEST = 5
SOUTH = 6
SOUTHEAST = 7
```

Notice that I arranged the direction constants in order as they appear in the mathematical approach to angle measurement.

Initializing the sprite

The Cow sprite's __init__() method incorporates most of the ideas discussed in this chapter:

```
    def __init__(self, screen):
        self.screen = screen
        pygame.sprite.Sprite.__init__(self)
        self.image = pygame.image.load                    ↩
("cowImages/stopped0002.bmp")
        self.image = self.image.convert()
        tranColor = self.image.get_at((1, 1))
        self.image.set_colorkey(tranColor)
        self.rect = self.image.get_rect()
        self.rect.center = (320, 240)

        self.imgList = []
        self.loadPics()

        self.dir = EAST
        self.frame = 0
        self.delay = 3
        self.pause = self.delay
        self.speed = 4

        self.dxVals = (1,   .7,   0,  -.7,  -1,  -.7,  0,  .7)
        self.dyVals = (0,  -.7,  -1,  -.7,   0,   .7,  1,  .7)
```

The __init__() method seems long, but only a couple of unfamiliar things crop up in it.

⊛ **Creates an image list.** The imageList attribute begins life as an empty list. The loadPics() method creates a large data structure that loads up all the necessary images and makes each image accessible by direction and animation frame.

Creates tuples to manage dx and dy values. I added two tuples, dxVals and dyVals. These two tuples are arranged to hold the dx and dy values for each direction. The tuples are another form of Table 8-2. You can use these tuples to extract dx and dy values for any direction value. For example, remember that EAST is 0, so to make a cow going east, get the dx value from self.dxVals[0], and dy from self.dyVals[0]. This technique makes the calcVector method a lot simpler, because it will no longer need the long if-elsif structure to calculate dx and dy.

Information Kiosk

The calcVector() method is the only method that needs access to dxVals and dyVals. I didn't define the attributes there, because the __init__ () method happens only one time (when the sprite is first built). The calcVector() method is called each frame, and redefining the attributes 30 times per second is unnecessary processing.

Loading up the pictures

The loadPics() method is modified to build the data structure necessary for holding all those images. Considering that the program requires 64 images to be loaded, the loadPics() method is not all that complex. See for yourself:

```
def loadPics(self):
    fileBase = [
        "cowImages/walking e000",
        "cowImages/walking ne000",
        "cowImages/walking n000",
        "cowImages/walking nw000",
        "cowImages/walking w000",
        "cowImages/walking sw000",
        "cowImages/walking s000",
        "cowImages/walking se000"
    ]

    for dir in range(8):
        tempList = []
        tempFile = fileBase[dir]
        for frame in range(8):
            imgName = "%s%d.bmp" % (tempFile, frame)
            tmpImg = pygame.image.load(imgName)
            tmpImg.convert()
            tranColor = tmpImg.get_at((0, 0))
            tmpImg.set_colorkey(tranColor)
            tempList.append(tmpImg)
        self.imgList.append(tempList)
```

The `loadPics()` method uses a pair of `for` loops to create the necessary data structure as shown in the following steps:

1. Create a list of filenames.

The filenames include some information about the direction being traveled, followed by a frame name and the .bmp extension. The easiest way to manage filenames is to store them in a list organized by direction:

```
fileBase = [
    "cowImages/walking e000",
    "cowImages/walking ne000",
    "cowImages/walking n000",
    "cowImages/walking nw000",
    "cowImages/walking w000",
    "cowImages/walking sw000",
    "cowImages/walking s000",
    "cowImages/walking se000"
    ]
```

This list will be used in Step 6 to create the image filenames necessary to load up all the files efficiently.

2. Create a `dir` variable that will contain all the directions.

Use a `for` loop to handle all eight directions:

```
for dir in range(8):
```

3. Build a temporary list.

Each direction will need a list of images. These lists of images will go into another list.

```
tempList = []
```

4. Build a temporary file name. Get the beginning of the filename from the `fileBase` list. Use the `dir` variable to extract the file name based on the current direction.

```
tempFile = fileBase[dir]
```

5. Create a frame counter that will repeat eight times.

Each direction has eight frames of animation, so make a variable that will range from 0 to 7.

```
for frame in range(8):
```

6. Build a filename combining the direction and frame number.

```
imgName = "%s%d.bmp" % (tempFile, frame)
```

Use string interpolation to build an image filename based on the current temp file and frame number.

7. Load the image into a temporary variable.

Load the image into a variable and do all the normal initializations:

```
tmpImg = pygame.image.load(imgName)
tmpImg.convert()
tranColor = tmpImg.get_at((0, 0))
tmpImg.set_colorkey(tranColor)
```

8. Append the image onto the temporary list.

Repeat the loop until you've loaded all the images for this direction onto the temporary list:

```
tempList.append(tmpImg)
```

9. Append the temporary list onto the `imageList`.

Repeat this process for each direction:

```
self.imgList.append(tempList)
```

At the end of this process, `self.imgList` is a *two-dimensional data structure,* which is a list that can be accessed through two indices.

Creating the update() method

The `update()` method for this sprite isn't modified too much — it simply takes into account the direction and frame.

```
def update(self):

    self.pause -= 1
    if self.pause <= 0:
        self.pause = self.delay

        self.frame += 1
        if self.frame > 7:
            self.frame = 0

        self.calcVector()
        self.image = self.imgList[self.dir][self.frame]

        self.rect.centerx += self.dx
        self.rect.centery += self.dy

        self.checkBounds()
```

Everything in this method is familiar, and here's what it looks like step by step:

1. Set up a delay mechanism.

The animation will play more slowly than the game's frame rate, so set up a delay mechanism, as you have throughout this chapter:

```
self.pause -= 1
if self.pause <= 0:
    self.pause = self.delay

    self.frame += 1
    if self.frame > 7:
        self.frame = 0
```

2. Calculate the new values for dx and dy.

The `calcVector()` method will do all the work for you:

```
self.calcVector()
```

3. Select the image.

This line is the only one that's new in this code. The image is now extracted from a two-dimensional data structure (the nested lists), so it needs two indices. The first index indicates the direction, and the second is the frame. The direction is modified by the `moveLeft()` and `moveRight()` functions, and the frame was modified in the delay section at the beginning of this method:

```
self.image = self.imgList[self.dir][self.frame]
```

4. Move the image.

Use dx and dy to move the image to its new position on the screen:

```
self.rect.centerx += self.dx
self.rect.centery += self.dy
```

5. Check for boundaries.

The boundary checking is entirely routine, and is handled in the standard method:

```
self.checkBounds()
```

Calculating the vector

If you look back at the `move8dir.py` program earlier in this chapter, you'll see that I calculated the `dx` and `dy` values with a series of `if-elif` statements. This approach is easy to understand, but it's a little awkward to write. I added two special list attributes to the cow back in the `__init__()` method:

```
self.dxVals = (1,   .7,   0, -.7, -1, -.7, 0, .7)
self.dyVals = (0, -.7, -1, -.7,   0,   .7, 1, .7)
```

These two attributes are used to hold the values of `dx` and `dy` for each of the directions. After they're in place, the `calcVector()` method is a lot easier to write than it was in `move8dir.py`:

```
def calcVector(self):
    self.dx = self.dxVals[self.dir]
    self.dy = self.dyVals[self.dir]

    self.dx *= self.speed
    self.dy *= self.speed
```

As long as the `dxVals` and `dyVals` lists are created properly, it becomes easy to extract the appropriate `dx` and `dy` because the sprite's `dir` attribute can be used as an index. The `dx` and `dy` values can then be multiplied by the `speed` attribute to compensate for the sprite's speed.

Watch Your Step

When animating things that are walking (like the cow), you have to calibrate the animation delay with the object's motion. If the object is moving too fast or too slowly for the animation, it will look like the sprite is "skating" along the surface. Experiment to get the right combination.

Finishing up the program

The `turnLeft()`, `turnRight()`, and `checkBounds()` methods are pretty standard. I include them here for the sake of completeness. Here's how the whole thing looks:

```
def turnLeft(self):
    self.dir += 1
    if self.dir > SOUTHEAST:
        self.dir = EAST

def turnRight(self):
    self.dir -= 1
```

```
                if self.dir < EAST:
                    self.dir = SOUTHEAST

    def main():
        screen = pygame.display.set_mode((640, 480))
        pygame.display.set_caption("cow animation")

        background = pygame.Surface(screen.get_size())
        background.fill((0, 0x66, 0))
        screen.blit(background, (0, 0))

        cow = Cow(screen)
        allSprites = pygame.sprite.Group(cow)

        clock = pygame.time.Clock()
        keepGoing = True
        while keepGoing:
            clock.tick(30)
            for event in pygame.event.get():
                if event.type == pygame.QUIT:
                    keepGoing = False
                elif event.type == pygame.KEYDOWN:
                    if event.key == pygame.K_LEFT:
                        cow.turnLeft()
                    elif event.key == pygame.K_RIGHT:
                        cow.turnRight()


            allSprites.clear(screen, background)
            allSprites.update()
            allSprites.draw(screen)

            pygame.display.flip()

    if __name__ == "__main__":
        main()
```

There are only a few things to watch in these parts of the program:

- **Direction now is stored in constant values.** The directions are no longer measured in degrees in the `turnLeft()` and `turnRight()` methods. This program uses constants to determine direction, so turning the sprite really amounts to modifying the constant by positive or negative 1.

- **Add event handling to receive keyboard input.** The user can control the cow's direction through the left and right arrow keys, so I added the appropriate event-handling routines in the main loop.

Making Better Motion

You've learned the basics of sprite motion and animation in this chapter. Turn to the next chapter to build more realistic motion and realistically moving vehicles.

animation delay: A technique to control animation speed using delay and pause attributes.

bouncing: When a sprite hits a screen boundary, its dx or dy attribute is inverted to give the appearance of bouncing off the wall.

motion vector: The current direction and speed of the sprite. Can be stored in speed and dir attributes, but must be translated to dx and dy attributes to actually move the object.

multi-dimension data structure: A list or tuple containing more lists or tuples.

position: The location of a sprite on the game surface. Sometimes stored in float x and y attributes to account for pygame's tendency to do all position math in integers.

scrolling: When a sprite encounters a screen boundary, it stays in place, but the background image moves to give the illusion of motion.

sprite animation: Swapping through several images in succession to give the impression that a sprite is moving.

state constant: A sprite with multiple states often has constants defined to describe each state.

stopping: When a sprite hits a screen boundary, its dx and dy attributes are set to 0 so the sprite stops moving.

tile set: A series of images (whether in separate files or combined into one large image file) representing several states of animation and/or direction for a sprite.

wrapping: When a sprite hits a screen boundary, it re-enters on the opposite side with the same speed and direction of travel.

Command	Arguments	Description
A.blit(B, pos, (offset, size))	A: surface to be drawn on B: surface to extract image from pos: surface position at which the image will be drawn offset: upper-left position of sub-image size: size of extracted image	Extracts a sub-image from one image and draws it to another. Useful when several images are stored on the same image file.
pygame.transform.rotate (Surface, angle)	surface: Surface object (image) to be rotated angle: amount of rotation in degrees (increasing counterclockwise)	Rotates an image the specified angle and returns a new image.
pygame.transform.scale (surface, size)	surface: Surface object (image) to be resized) size: new size of objects in pixels (width, height)	Changes an image's size. Can result in a loss of detail.

Practice Exam

1. Write a version of `moo.py` that uses the eating animation in Reiner's tile set.

2. Find another animated sprite set (or create your own) and build an animation.

3. Write a slide show that displays a series of images 2 seconds apart. (Hint: load the filenames into a list or tuple or give them consistent names on the hard drive.)

4. Change `cow.py` so it can moo in any direction. (This is harder than it sounds!)

5. When might you incorporate a bouncing boundary-checking algorithm?

_____

_____

_____

6. Which is *not* a standard boundary-checking algorithm?

A) Wrapping

B) Bouncing

C) Drifting

D) Stopping

7. In the *mathematical* approach to angle measurement, where is 0 degrees?

A) North

B) East

C) South

D) West

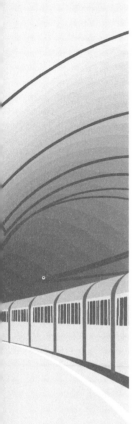

8. How are angles increased in the mathematical scheme?

   A) Clockwise

   B) Counterclockwise

   C) Up and down

   D) Mathematicians don't increase angles.

9. Why is .7 used for diagonal values in `dx` and `dy`?

   A) It results in a unit vector of length 1, which makes speed calculation easier.

   B) Because .7 is the square root of 2.

   C) Darned if I know.

   D) It makes game programmers seem smart.

10. Why do we sometimes add a delay factor to sprite animations?

   A) You never want to slow things down! Make your animations as fast as possible!

   B) So the processor will have time to catch up with the animation

   C) To enable more accurate event handling

   D) To make the animation easier to see

9

Realistic Movement

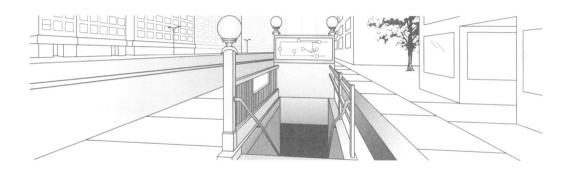

Enter the Station

Questions

1. What are the basic terms and ideas that describe how objects move?

2. How are position, velocity, and acceleration related to each other?

3. How can a sprite get access to the keyboard without using the `event` object?

4. How can you build a smoothly rotating sprite?

5. How do you get a sprite to launch a missile or bullet?

6. How do you incorporate variable drag, turning, and power into a motion model?

7. How can you make a sprite point toward the mouse or another sprite?

8. How do you manage gravity calculations?

9. How can you mimic the flight of a spacecraft?

10. How do you make one sprite orbit another?

A Lesson in Phuzzy Physics

Game programming is ultimately about creating things that move around. Often, the basis for the movement will be some real-world object (a chicken or a car) or an imaginary object (an enraged antigravity-enhanced zombie robot opossum, for example) that follows some variation of real-world principles. In either case, you need to have a basic understanding of how things move. The science of physics studies various things, including the nature of motion. An understanding of some very basic physics concepts can be extremely handy to a game developer. In this chapter you will begin by understanding these basic principles. You will then apply the principles in some very useful ways to make all kinds of interesting motion. By the end of the chapter, your sprites will be able to zoom, turn, twist, fall, shoot, and orbit!

 ### Watch Your Step

While I am using real-world physics as a foundation, the realities of arcade-game programming often require simplifications and modifications to physics principles. While this chapter can be an adequate introduction to essential ideas of Newtonian motion, it is by no means complete. If you want to be a really *good* game programmer, you owe it to yourself to read some physics books or take some classes so you can model reality more accurately. Most professional game programmers prepare themselves with several years of physics and mathematical studies.

Newton's Laws of Motion

About 300 years ago, Sir Isaac Newton developed several rules to describe how objects move. His observations provide plenty of insight into game development, but Newton's three Laws of Motion are especially useful. Through the years, I've devised my own translations of Newton's Three Laws of Motion. (I give you a more formal definition, too.)

I. If It's Moving, It's Moving. If It Ain't, It Ain't.

Newton's First Law is more officially stated like this:

An object at rest tends to stay at rest. An object in motion tends to stay in motion unless acted on by some external force.

This law has practical aspects for game developers. A vehicle or object stays motionless until something acts on it (you change its dx or dy). It remains in motion until something acts on it again (you change dx or dy again). Of course, cannonballs don't fly forever, and cars eventually stop when you don't apply the gas, so there needs to be some way to model these external forces, including drag and gravity. I show you some simple ways to approximate these forces throughout this chapter.

II. If You Want It to Go Faster, Kick It Harder

While my summary has a certain cachet, Newton's Second Law is more formally stated like this:

The rate of change of the momentum of a body is directly proportional to the net force acting on it, and the direction of the change in momentum takes place in the direction of the net force.

Newton's Second Law is normally summarized by this formula:

F = ma, or Force = mass * acceleration

Newton's Second Law is extremely important in real life, because it explains mathematically the relationship between force, mass, and acceleration. It allows us to calculate exactly how much force is needed to get a particular acceleration for a particular mass in a particular direction.

In arcade games, we normally approximate Newton's second law by taking into account an object's mass and the power of its propulsion system. It's important to understand that heavier objects need more force to get the same acceleration.

III. When You Throw a Rock, the Rock Throws You

Newton's Third Law of Motion is equally important:

To every action (force applied) there is an equal but opposite reaction (equal force applied in the opposite direction).

This law is important because it makes space travel possible (rockets depend on it). You can move an object simply by applying force in the opposite direction. Game programmers don't use this law as frequently as the other two, because we don't need a real propulsion system except to add realism. If you tell an object to move, it moves. It's still good to know about it, so you can accurately model vehicle behavior.

Step Into the Real World

You might have heard that Newton's Laws have been made obsolete by Einstein's work on special relativity and by recent discoveries in quantum mechanics. Newton's Laws are still completely applicable to most observable forms of motion. Special relativity explains how things change at extremely high speeds (near the speed of light,) and quantum mechanics explains how things change at an extremely small (submicroscopic) scale. Most arcade game topics stay well within the range of Newtonian physics. Of course, you could write a very interesting game modeling these more esoteric phenomena. (A relativity roller coaster that goes so fast that you age slowly? A quantum Pac-Man that can be in two places at once?)

Terms of motion

A few terms are frequently used in the discussion of motion. It's extremely important to understand how these terms relate to game programming so you can use them properly.

- **Vector.** A vector is an object characterized by *direction* and *magnitude*. In game programming, it's often easiest to think of an object's motion as a vector, because the object's `dir` attribute indicates the direction, and the `speed` attribute indicates the magnitude of the vector.

- **Vector components.** A vector is useful because it relates to real life. If you want a ball to move in a certain direction at a certain speed, you kick it with a particular force in the desired direction. The kicking action is the *force vector*. If you want to actually move the object in a Cartesian coordinate system (the kind that computers use is characterized by x- and y-coordinate pairs) you have to translate the vector's angle and magnitude into x and y components, normally called `dx` and `dy`. Once you've *projected* (converted) the vector into components, it's trivial to add these components to the object's current `x` and `y` attributes to move it.

    ## Transfer

    You used a basic form of vector projection in Chapter 8 when you built an eight-direction animation. In this chapter, you apply mathematical principles to build a much more robust form of vector projection that allows motion at any angle and any speed.

- **Position.** This is the current position of the object. It's normally described as an (x, y) coordinate pair.

- **Velocity.** Velocity is simply a change in position during a unit of time. If a vehicle sprite in a computer program is at (0, 0) and it moves to (10, 0) within a single frame, it has a velocity of 10 pixels per frame in x, or 10 pixels per frame at an angle of 0 degrees. Velocity is normally considered a vector, with an angle and a magnitude. In programming, it's commonly useful to convert the vector to its components, which are `dx` (difference in x) and `dy` (difference in y). Vector projection converts a vector into its components.

- **Acceleration is a change in *velocity*.** Any force which causes a change in an object's velocity is technically acceleration, even if it slows down the vehicle's forward motion. Acceleration is normally considered a vector, although it is commonly broken into `ddx` and `ddy` components. Sometimes acceleration is also called a *force vector* to indicate that it is force applied to the current velocity in a current direction.

Information Kiosk

Technically, acceleration would be considered ddx and ddy (the difference in delta-x and delta-y), but this doesn't really add much clarity, so game programmers often call acceleration vectors dx and dy too. It doesn't matter too much, because you use exactly the same technique to convert any vector to its x and y components, regardless of what the original vector measures.

Adding force vectors

The Newtonian idea of motion is relatively straightforward. A non-moving object basically stays put (Newton's first law). The object has a force vector of magnitude 0 and an undetermined direction. At some point, a force is applied to the object (it fires a rocket, is pushed, whatever). The force is a force vector, which influences the object's motion vector, making the object speed up in a particular direction. If you want to turn an object, you apply another force in another direction. Slowing the object down requires yet another force vector. Environmental conditions (for example, wind resistance, rolling resistance, and other kinds of drag) can impose their own force vectors on an object, influencing its actual direction and speed. The velocity of an object is ultimately the result of the many force vectors acting at the same time.

That might sound daunting, but it's actually easy to calculate a bunch of force vectors. Imagine an empty balloon. It might be pulled downward by gravity with a force of 1 pixel per frame. If you inflate that balloon with helium, the helium may exert a lift force of 3 pixels per frame upward, giving the balloon a net climb rate of 2 pixels per frame.

You can decompose force vectors to dx and dy components, and then simply add up the dx and dy values to get an overall motion vector for the object. For example, imagine the same balloon with the following forces acting on it.

Force	x component	y component
Gravity	0	1
Buoyancy	0	-3
Wind	4	0
Total	4	-2

If you break each force into its dx and dy components, you can easily combine all the dx values to get a total dx, and all the dy components to get a total dy. You'll write programs throughout this chapter that move an object by manipulating its dx and dy values. Each time you add something to an object's dx and dy, you are applying a force vector to the object.

Getting Continuous Keyboard Input

In the last chapter, you built sprites that can turn and move in eight directions. However, there's no reason a sprite has to point in only the eight major directions. The `turret.py` program shown in Figure 9-1 illustrates a gun turret that rotates smoothly under keyboard control.

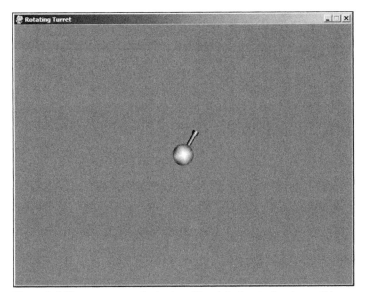

Figure 9-1: The user can use the keyboard to rotate the gun turret smoothly.

The turret uses only one sprite image, rotated with functions in the `pygame.transform` module. The more interesting part of the program is actually the keyboard input, which has some new characteristics:

- **The sprite handles the keystroke on its own.** There's no event-handling in the main program except the normal test for quitting. The turret sprite handles its own events.

- **Keyboard input is continuous.** The keyboard technique you've used throughout the book so far returns one event per key press. In the rotation programs in Chapter 8, you had to press an arrow key several times to get a rotation.

- **Rotation appears to be much smoother.** The new rotation seems smoother because it is. Rather than jumping in 45-degree increments as your earlier rotations have done, the turret turns in 10-degree increments. In fact, you can make the rotation as smooth as you want by turning in 5- or 1-degree increments if that gives you the best effect. Of course, the smaller the increments, the more slowly the turret will rotate.

Building the Turret class

The Turret class is a relatively standard sprite object, with a few new features. The initialization is pretty routine:

```
class Turret(pygame.sprite.Sprite):
    def __init__(self):
        pygame.sprite.Sprite.__init__(self)
        self.imageMaster = pygame.image.load("turret.gif")
        self.imageMaster = self.imageMaster.convert()
        self.rect = self.imageMaster.get_rect()
        self.rect.center = (320, 240)
        self.turnRate = 10
        self.dir = 0
```

The __init__() method has a few interesting elements which allow you to do the following:

- **Prepare the turret image.** I just built a simple turret using GIMP. I love gradient fills, because they are such a great way to build pseudo-3D objects. The turret is saved as a GIF file with transparency so I didn't need to store a colorkey value. I also made the default master image pointing to the east to simplify rotation.

- **Load the turret image into the imageMaster attribute.** Since the turret can rotate to any arbitrary angle, it's not reasonable to load a different image for each direction because there's just too many possible images needed. The pygame. transform.rotate() function will create an appropriate image dynamically. When using the rotation technique, keep a master image unchanged to minimize the effects of multiple transformations:

  ```
          self.imageMaster = pygame.image.load("turret.gif")
          self.imageMaster = self.imageMaster.convert()
  ```

- **Set the center to the middle of the screen.** In this program, I'm not going to have the turret travel elsewhere on the screen, so I'll put it in the middle of the screen so it's easy to see:

```
    self.rect = self.imageMaster.get_rect()
    self.rect.center = (320, 240)
```

Set up a `turnRate` constant. This value will be used to determine how many degrees per frame the object can turn. A large value leads to quick-but-jerky turns. Smaller values lead to smoother and slower turns. Be sure to play around with the value of `self.turnRate` in the finished program to see how it works.

```
    self.turnRate = 10
```

Set the initial direction. Although the turret won't move around on the screen, it still needs a direction attribute, to determine which way the barrel is pointing (which for now is east).

```
    self.dir = 0
```

Updating the turret

As your sprites become more complex, the `update()` method starts to get cluttered. It's often smart to encapsulate the `update()` method, sending controls to other more specific methods.

```
def update(self):
    self.checkKeys()
    self.rotate()
```

Looking at this code, it's clear that two main things happen during the sprite's update of each frame: The keys are checked and the image is rotated.

Checking the keyboard

This program uses a different form of keyboard checking than you've used so far. In the technique you already know, the event loop (in the main loop) produces an `event` object. You then examine this object to see whether it's a key press. If so, you look further to see which key was pressed — then (usually) you invoke an object's method to make the object respond to the keyboard input. The technique here is a little different. Pygame has a special module called `key`, which has several functions for working with the keyboard. The `pygame.key.get_pressed()` function is especially interesting, because it returns a tuple of Boolean values: one for each key on the keyboard. You can use this function to find out whether any key on the keyboard is currently being pressed:

Store `pygame.key.get_pressed()` in a variable. The variable will be a large tuple. For this example, I stored the function results in a variable called `keys`.

`keys` is a tuple of all keys on the keyboard with 0 (`False`) and 1 (`True`) values indicating whether the particular key is currently pressed or not.

Use a keyboard constant to refer to a particular key. If you're want to know the status of the spacebar, for example, use the pygame constant `pygame.K_SPACE`.

Check the tuple to see whether the key is currently pressed. It's a lot easier than it sounds.

```
if keys[pygame.K_SPACE]:
```

This checks the `keys` tuple to see whether the value corresponding to the spacebar is 1 (`True`, meaning the key is currently pressed) or 0 (`False`).

The `checkKeys()` function uses this technique to look for arrow keys:

```
def checkKeys(self):
    keys = pygame.key.get_pressed()
    if keys[pygame.K_LEFT]:
        self.dir += self.turnRate
        if self.dir > 360:
            self.dir = self.turnRate
    if keys[pygame.K_RIGHT]:
        self.dir -= self.turnRate
        if self.dir < 0:
            self.dir = 360 - self.turnRate
```

The process is straightforward. Here's what you do:

1. Store `key.get_pressed()` in the local variable `keys`.

```
keys = pygame.key.get_pressed()
```

2. Check to see whether the left arrow is currently pressed.

Use the left arrow constant as the index to the `keys` tuple to determine whether the left arrow is currently being pressed:

```
if keys[pygame.K_LEFT]:
```

3. Add `self.turnRate` to `self.dir`.

This will cause the direction to rotate counterclockwise. Use `turnRate` rather than a specific literal value so you can easily change the turning rate later:

```
self.dir += self.turnRate
```

4. Check for a maximum angle.

If the `dir` value has become larger than 360, it should reset to the value of `turnRate`. (If you reset to 0, the sprite will appear to stop momentarily because 0 and 360 degrees are the same value.)

```
if self.dir > 360:
    self.dir = self.turnRate
```

5. **Repeat for right turns.**

The process is nearly the same for right turns, except of course you subtract `turnRate` from `dir` and check for a minimum value.

```
if keys[pygame.K_RIGHT]:
    self.dir -= self.turnRate
    if self.dir < 0:
        self.dir = 360 - self.TURNRATE
```

Rotating the turret

Changing the sprite's `dir` attribute is important, but it doesn't automatically cause the turret to turn in the right direction. Use the `rotate()` method for that task:

```
def rotate(self):
    oldCenter = self.rect.center
    self.image = pygame.transform.rotate(self.imageMaster, self.dir)
    self.rect = self.image.get_rect()
    self.rect.center = oldCenter
```

Rotating a sprite is done just in the same way as it was in Chapter 8. Here's a quick review:

1. **Store the current center position because the center may change during the rotation.**

2. **Transform the master image to create a new value for `self.image`.**

3. **Retrieve the `rect` from the new image.**

The `rect` may have changed because the image size changed.

4. **Restore the previous center.**

Since all this work is done before the screen is updated, the user will see a smooth animation with none of the jitter described in chapter 7 as the image resizes and moves around.

Step Into the Real World

This form of keyboard checking (called *hardware polling*, if you care) is very handy for use inside sprite objects, because the sprite can determine which key was pressed, even without having access to the main program's `event` object. Of course, you can send an `event` object to a sprite's `__init__()` method and have the sprite do the traditional keyboard input too, if you want.

Building the main loop

The most interesting thing about the main loop of the turret.py program is what's *not* there: It has no arrow event-handling code! The main loop still checks for quit events, but all other keyboard checking is relegated to the turret object.

```python
def main():
    screen = pygame.display.set_mode((640, 480))
    pygame.display.set_caption ("Rotating Turret")

    background = pygame.Surface(screen.get_size())
    background.fill((0x00, 0xCC, 0x00))
    screen.blit(background, (0, 0))

    turret = Turret()
    allSprites = pygame.sprite.Group(turret)

    clock = pygame.time.Clock()
    keepGoing = True
    while keepGoing:
        clock.tick(30)
        for event in pygame.event.get():
            if event.type == pygame.QUIT:
                keepGoing = False

        allSprites.clear(screen, background)
        allSprites.update()
        allSprites.draw(screen)
        pygame.display.flip()

if __name__ == "__main__":
    main()
```

Watch Your Step

The event.get() loop is still important. Pygame uses the event mechanism to tell the checkKeys() method which key is being pressed, so you still need the event loop mechanism that you've used throughout the IDEA/ALTER framework. If you want to use key.get_pressed() for all of your keyboard events (including testing for a quit event) make sure to include pygame.event.pump() somewhere inside your main loop. This tells pygame to empty the event list and tell all the other objects (such as the checkKeys() method) what events have happened in the current frame.

Vector Projection

You can rotate a sprite to any angle, but moving the sprite in an arbitrary direction seems problematic. You learned some techniques for converting a direction and speed into dx and dy variables. Those techniques work fine, but only for a limited number of directions. What if you want to be able to move an object at any speed, in any direction? The turretFire.py program shown in Figure 9-2 demonstrates one way this technique might be used:

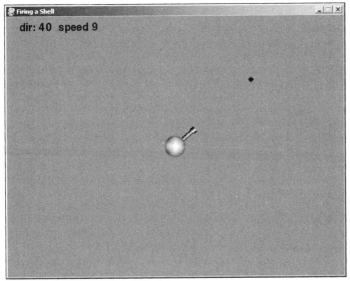

Figure 9-2: When you press the spacebar, the turret fires a shell in the current direction.

The user can rotate the turret as before, but now s/he can also press the spacebar. A shell will fire from the gun in whatever direction the turret is pointing. The user can configure the turret's direction and the charge that will be applied to the shell, which will effect the direction and speed the shell can travel. If the turret can turn only in increments of 10 degrees, and the charge can be any integer between 0 and 20 pixels per frame, that means there are 720 possible values for dx and dy! It would be very awkward to use if statements or even a set of nested lists to track all these values.

It would be great if there was a way to figure out the appropriate dx and dy values for any speed and direction. Fortunately, the ancient Greeks came up with a system for solving exactly this kind of problem. Once you understand this technique, called *vector projection*, you'll be able to calculate the dx and dy values for any angle, any speed.

Examining the problem

It's easiest to think about a sprite's motion in terms of its speed and direction. These two characteristics taken together are called the sprite's *motion vector*. A vector is simply a mathematical construct that has a direction and a magnitude (or length). If you want to move a sprite at a certain speed in a certain direction, you need a way to translate the motion vector into dx and dy values, so you know exactly how much to add to x and y during the current frame. (dx and dy are sometimes known as the *vector components,* or the *component form* of the vector.) Take a look at Figure 9-3 to see some notation commonly used in this kind of problem:

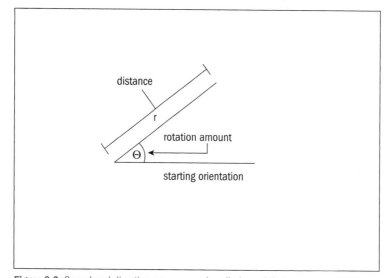

Figure 9-3: Speed and direction are commonly called r and theta.

For the sake of argument, presume that you want to make a sprite travel at a speed called r, in a direction called theta. The symbol Θ as it appears on the diagram is pronounced "thay-tah." It is a letter in the Greek alphabet.

Step Into the Real World

It might bother you to use the Greek symbol theta when there are plenty of perfectly good letters in the Roman alphabet we normally use. You can use any symbol you want to refer to the angle, but mathematicians typically use Greek symbols to denote angles so they are easily distinguished from other kinds of values. You'll undoubtedly see the theta symbol used in math texts, so you might as well get used to it. Besides, since the ancient Greeks discovered so much about angles, it's only fair to use some of their characters!

It is important to notice that the rotation amount is measured from the x axis. In fact, the whole vector projection business you're learning here is one reason that mathematicians use this particular kind of angle measurement.

Building a triangle

Given any r and theta values, you can easily make a right triangle by drawing horizontal and vertical lines as in the dashed lines in Figure 9-4.

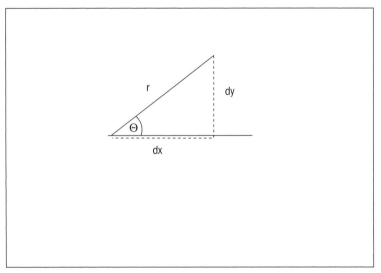

Figure 9-4: Draw horizontal and vertical lines to make a right triangle.

Once you've created the triangle, it's easy to see how dx and dy are related to r and theta. The length of the horizontal line shows exactly how far you have to move in the x axis to get from the beginning to the end of the line. The length of this horizontal line will be the value for dx. The vertical line indicates how far you have to travel in the y axis to get from the beginning to the end of the line, so the length of the vertical line is dy.

Enter Chief SOHCAHTOA

Now comes the clever part: The Greeks noticed that every right triangle preserves certain ratios. For example, if theta is 30 degrees, the ratio between the lengths of dx and r will remain the same, no matter how long they are. If you have access to these ratios, and you know one angle and one side length of a right triangle, you can figure out all the other angles and side lengths.

Figure 9-5 shows the notation used to think about right triangles in this way:

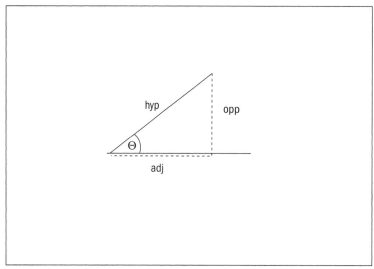

Figure 9-5: The sides of right triangles have different names in trigonometry.

It's easier to think about the triangle if you give the sides some new names:

- **The hypotenuse (hyp):** The longest side, opposite the right angle in a right triangle. This side is also the length the sprite will move.

- **The adjacent side (adj):** The side touching the angle in question. For this problem, the adjacent side is also dx.

- **The opposite side (opp):** The side opposite theta. For vector-projection problems, the opposite side is dy.

Math teachers sometimes refer to the mythical Indian chief SOHCAHTOA as a mnemonic device for remembering how the various rations work. Here's what it means:

- **SOH:** The length of the opposite side divided by the length of the hypotenuse is called the *sine* of theta. This is abbreviated sin(theta) = opp/hyp or SOH.

- **CAH:** The length of the adjacent side divided by the length of the hypotenuse is called the *cosine* of theta. This is abbreviated cos(theta) = adj/hyp or CAH.

- **TOA:** The opposite side length divided by the adjacent side length is called the *tangent* of theta. The tangent relationship is sometimes stated tan(theta) = opp/adj or TOA.

Solving for dx and dy

Once you have all this notation in place, it's actually not that difficult to solve for dx. Figure 9-6 shows the formula:

$$\sin \Theta = \frac{opp}{hyp} = \frac{dy}{r}$$

$$dy = r* \,(\sin \Theta)$$

$$\cos \Theta = \frac{opp}{adj} = \frac{dx}{r}$$

$$dx = r* \,(\cos \Theta)$$

Figure 9-6: Here's how to solve for dx.

It's not nearly as frightening as it looks. Here's how you do it:

1. Determine the trigonometry function you need.

The cosine of theta is "adjacent over hypotenuse." This will be handy for figuring out the value of dx.

2. Translate to vector terms.

Translate the formula into the terms of the original problem (dx and r): cos(theta) = dx / r.

3. Solve for dx.

With a little algebra, you can transpose the problem so it solves for dx. The formula is dx = r * cos(theta). Given any length (r) and angle (theta), you can use this formula to determine dx.

4. Repeat for dy.

The process is almost the same for dy, except the sin() function turns out to be more useful.

Dealing with radians

Python has a `math` module with the trig functions you need. There's one problem, though. So far, you've done your angle measurements in degrees. The trigonometry functions require all angle measurements to be in a different notation called *radians*. It seems like a lot of unnecessary trouble at first, but radians actually make more sense than degrees, because radians are intimately tied to the nature of the circle, while degrees are an arbitrary measurement.

For any circle, the entire circumference of the circle is exactly two times pi radians. Figure 9-7 shows several common angle measurements described in radians.

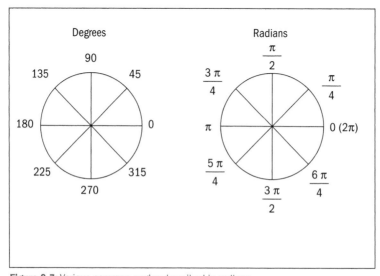

Figure 9-7: Various common angles described in radians.

Step Into the Real World

I like to use a true story to describe radians. When my wife and I were dating, she had a pleasant but not-very-smart dog. They had no fence, so the dog had a leash attached to a spike in the back yard. It's not surprising that the dog eventually wore a circular path in the back yard. One day, the leash came untied from the spike. The dog was still walking around in a circle, dragging the leash behind. The leash is the radius (distance from the center to the outside) of the circle. When you drag that leash along the circle (as the dog was doing) the angle described by the length of the leash along the circle is one radian. I was so excited by this unintentional math moment that I jumped around cheering about the dog doing geometry. The dog looked at me with a puzzled expression and kept on walking. (Despite this early indication of my geeky nature, the dog's owner and I are still happily married.)

It's actually pretty easy to convert from degrees to radians, or vice versa. If you have degrees and you want radians, multiply the degree measurement by pi and divide by 180. (If you have radians and need degrees, multiply the radian measurement by 180 and divide by pi.)

Writing a vector-projection program

All this math might be making you a little bit dizzy. It pays off, though, when you see vecProj.py, featured in Figure 9-8.

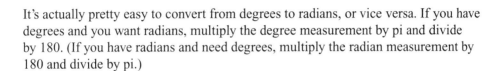

Figure 9-8: This text-based program takes any speed and direction and converts it into dx and dy values.

I made vecProj.py as a pure text-based program to keep it simple. In the next section I explain how to incorporate vector projection into sprites.

```
""" vecProj
    given any angle and distance,
    converts to dx and dy
    No GUI.
"""

import math

def main():
    keepGoing = True
    while keepGoing:
        print
        print "Give me an angle and distance,"
        print "and I'll convert to dx and dy values"
        print
        r = float(raw_input("distance: "))
        degrees = float(raw_input("angle (degrees): "))

        theta = degrees * math.pi / 180
        dx = r * math.cos(theta)
```

```
    dy = r * math.sin(theta)

    # compensate for inverted y axis
    dy *= -1

    print "dx: %f, dy: %f" % (dx, dy)
    response = raw_input("Again? (Y/N)")
    if response.upper() != "Y":
        keepGoing = False

if __name__ == "__main__":
    main()
```

The vecProj.py program can return dx and dy values for any angle and distance. Here's how you put it to use:

1. **Import the math module.**

   You'll need access to some trigonometry functions and the constant pi. Fortunately, these things are built into Python's math module. Be sure to import it to have access to these important features.

   ```
   import math
   ```

2. **Begin a loop.**

   For convenience, the main() function features a loop. This way you can try several vectors at a time to see how it works.

   ```
   def main():
       keepGoing = True
       while keepGoing:
   ```

3. **Input values for angle and distance.**

   Use the raw_input() function to retrieve these values. Don't forget to convert the input into real numbers so you can do math on them.

   ```
   print
   print "Give me an angle and distance,"
   print "and I'll convert to dx and dy values"
   print
   r = float(raw_input("distance: "))
   degrees = float(raw_input("angle (degrees): "))
   ```

4. **Convert the angle to radians.**

   Use the formula specified earlier in this chapter.

   ```
   theta = degrees * math.pi / 180
   ```

5. **Calculate dx and dy.**

   Use the standard formulas developed earlier in this chapter.

   ```
   dx = r * math.cos(theta)
   dy = r * math.sin(theta)
   ```

6. **Invert the dy value.**

In mathematics, the dy axis increases upwards. In the computing world, the Y axis increases downwards. Compensate for this by multiplying dy by −1:

```
# compensate for inverted y axis
dy *= -1
```

7. **Output the values.**

Print out values for dx and dy. Use string interpolation to simplify the output:

```
print "dx: %f, dy: %f" % (dx, dy)
```

8. **Ask if user wants to repeat.**

Use another `raw_input()` command to determine whether the user wants to try another vector:

```
if response.upper() != "Y":
    keepGoing = False
```

Converting components back to vectors

It's also possible to go in the other direction. For example, you might know two points and want to know the angle and direction between them. To calculate the angle, return to SOHCAHTOA. If you divide the opposite side (dy) by the adjacent side (dx), you'll get the tangent of theta. Using the arctangent function (usually abbreviated `atan`) you can get the angle between dx and dy in radians. This can then be converted to degrees. Likewise, you can use the famous Pythagorean Theorem to determine the distance between any two points. Figure 9-9 illustrates the formulas used to determine the angle and distance between any two points.

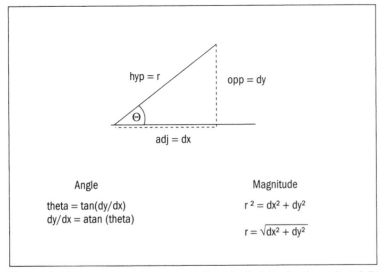

Figure 9-9: Given any two points, you can mathematically determine the angle and distance between them.

This technique is useful when you want to move one object towards another. A guided missile can follow an enemy, or you can turn a turret to follow the mouse pointer, as I'll do later in this chapter.

Transfer

Look at the "Following the Mouse" section later in this chapter to see these formulas in action.

Making the Turret Fire

With the addition of vector projection principles, the turret program can now fire shells in whatever direction it's facing.

Adding a Label class

The `turretFire.py` program has a label printing out the turret's current direction and charge. Use the `Label` class defined in Chapter 6.

```
class Label(pygame.sprite.Sprite):
    """ Label Class
        Attributes:
            font: any pygame font object
            text: text to display
            center: desired position of label center (x, y)
    """
    def __init__(self):
        pygame.sprite.Sprite.__init__(self)
        self.font = pygame.font.SysFont("None", 30)
        self.text = ""
        self.center = (320, 240)

    def update(self):
        self.image = self.font.render(self.text, 1,     ↩
(0, 0, 0))
        self.rect = self.image.get_rect()
        self.rect.center = self.center
```

Updating the Turret class

The `Turret` class requires you to make a few modifications:

1. The `turret` instance needs to know about the `shell` instance.

The turret will be controlling the shell, so it needs a reference to the `shell` object. The `__init__()` method is slightly modified to accommodate the shell:

```
def __init__(self, shell):
    self.shell = shell
```

2. **The `Turret` class now has a charge as well as a direction.**

The `charge` attribute indicates the speed of the shell when it is shot out of the gun. The up and down arrows are used to modify the charge, which can range from 0 to 20. The `charge` attribute is defined in the `__init__()` method:

```
self.charge = 5
```

3. **The turret can fire.**

When the user presses and releases the spacebar, the turret will fire the shell in the appropriate direction.

The `checkKeys()` method still checks all the possible keyboard events:

```
def checkKeys(self):
    keys = pygame.key.get_pressed()
    if keys[pygame.K_LEFT]:
        self.dir += self.turnRate
        if self.dir > 360:
            self.dir = self.turnRate
    if keys[pygame.K_RIGHT]:
        self.dir -= self.turnRate
        if self.dir < 0:
            self.dir = 360 - self.turnRate

    if keys[pygame.K_UP]:
        self.charge += 1
        if self.charge > 20:
            self.charge = 20
    if keys[pygame.K_DOWN]:
        self.charge -= 1
        if self.charge < 0:
            self.charge = 0

    if keys[pygame.K_SPACE]:
        self.shell.x = self.rect.centerx
        self.shell.y = self.rect.centery
        self.shell.speed = self.charge
        self.shell.dir = self.dir
```

Step Into the Real World

I called this attribute `charge` rather than `speed` because the turret doesn't move around. Instead, it has a value it passes to the shell's speed. The term `charge` more accurately describes what this variable does. Of course, I might want to make a version of the turret that can move, so it would need a `speed` attribute to handle this behavior.

In addition to checking for left and right arrow keys (which the `checkKeys()` method of the original `Turret` class already did), the improved turret program also checks for the up and down arrow keys, as the next steps illustrate:

4. **If the player presses the up arrow, the `charge` attribute increments by 1.**

```
if keys[pygame.K_UP]:
    self.charge += 1
```

5. **You need to set a maximum charge of 20.**

The charge will correspond to the shell's speed (in pixels per frame). A speed higher than 20 ppf (pixels per frame) will be hard for the user to see, so I set this as the maximum charge:

```
if self.charge > 20:
    self.charge = 20
```

6. **You'll have to allow the user to lower the charge with the down arrow.**

The down-arrow code is similar, but it decreases the `charge` attribute, with a minimum charge of 0.

```
if keys[pygame.K_DOWN]:
    self.charge -= 1
    if self.charge < 0:
        self.charge = 0
```

Finally, the `checkKeys()` method looks for the spacebar — and if it has been pressed, the shell is set into motion. (You'll see the `Shell` class described in detail in the next section.)

When the user fires the turret, these are the things you need to do:

1. **Move the shell to the turret's current position.**

It should appear that the shell flies out of the turret's barrel. You move the shell so it has the same center as the turret. If the shell is placed underneath the turret, the shell will not appear until it flies out of the barrel, and will look like it's coming from the barrel.

```
if keys[pygame.K_SPACE]:
    self.shell.x = self.rect.centerx
    self.shell.y = self.rect.centery
```

2. **Set the shell's speed according to the turret's charge.**

The shell's `speed` attribute is set equal to the turret's `charge` attribute.

```
self.shell.speed = self.charge
```

3. **Set the shell's direction equal to the turret's direction.**

The shell will fly in whatever direction the turret is currently pointed.

```
self.shell.dir = self.dir
```

Creating the Shell class

The artillery shell is a typical sprite, except for a few idiosyncrasies:

- ○ **The shell appears to be created by the turret.** As you'll see, this is actually an illusion.

- ○ **The shell is given a direction and speed by the turret.** The shell doesn't respond to keyboard input at all. Instead, its speed and direction are determined by the turret.

- ○ **It "dies" when it hits the edge of the screen.** As soon as the shell leaves the screen, it seems to vanish forever.

> ## Information Kiosk
>
> It's certainly possible to create a new shell every time the player fires the turret, and kill the shell when it reaches the edge of the screen, but I chose an easier expedient. There's only one `shell` instance in the whole game, and it's reused each time the player fires the gun. If the shell isn't currently flying on the screen, I hide it offstage until it's needed. This is a pretty common technique in game development, because it's easier on both the programmer and the system's resources.

Building the `Shell` class is relatively simple:

Initializing the shell

Using the `Shell` class's `__init__()` method you build the shell in a mostly standard way as shown in the following steps:

1. **Include the `screen` object as a parameter.**

The shell will need to check for screen boundaries, so it needs access to the `screen` object from the main program. Copy the `screen` parameter to a local variable so you have access to it throughout your code.

```
class Shell(pygame.sprite.Sprite):
    def __init__(self, screen):
        pygame.sprite.Sprite.__init__(self)
        self.screen = screen
```

Step Into the Real World

I wasn't exactly sure what size the bullet should be, so I created something close (a circle with a radius of 5 on a 10×10 surface) and then scaled it to exactly the right size. This is a pretty good practice; it allows you to tweak your visuals until they look right.

2. **Create the image.**

Since the bullet is just a circle, I decided to draw it rather than import an image. I made a 10 × 10 surface, gave it a transparent background, drew a circle on it, and then scaled it to the appropriate size.

```
self.image = pygame.Surface((10, 10))
self.image.fill((0xff, 0xff, 0xff))
self.image.set_colorkey((0xff, 0xff, 0xff))
pygame.draw.circle(self.image, (0, 0, 0), (5, 5), 5)
self.image = pygame.transform.scale(self.image, (5, 5))
```

3. **Move the shell off stage.**

The shell will always be available in this program, but when it isn't needed, it will be hidden motionless off stage. Get the image's `rect`, and set the center to someplace where the sprite won't be seen.

```
self.rect = self.image.get_rect()
self.rect.center = (-100, -100)
```

Information Kiosk

When you transform an image, remember that some transformations change the image size. Extract the rectangle after all the transformations are done, so the `rect` reflects the size of the image after the transformations are complete.

4. **Set up sprite properties.**

The shell sprite has all the properties you've come to expect of a moving sprite. It's particularly important that you set the speed to 0 at this point, so the sprite doesn't wander onto the stage until you want it there.

```
self.speed = 0
self.dir =0
self.reset()
```

Updating the shell

The `Shell` class' `update()` method is a triumph of encapsulation. Most of the code calls other methods to perform specific tasks. The final step takes the calculated position (the x and y attributes) and transfers them to the sprite's `rect`, moving the sprite where it's supposed to go.

```
def update(self):
    self.calcVector()
    self.calcPos()
    self.checkBounds()
    self.rect.center = (self.x, self.y)
```

Calculating the vector

Calculate the shell's dx and dy attributes using the vector-projection principle. Once you understand how it works, the code is surprisingly simple.

```python
def calcVector(self):
    radians = self.dir * math.pi / 180

    self.dx = self.speed * math.cos(radians)
    self.dy = self.speed * math.sin(radians)
    self.dy *= -1
```

Calculating the shell's position

The shell's next position is easy to obtain. Remember to add `self.dx` and `self.dy` to `self.x` and `self.y` (rather than `self.rect.centerx` and `self.rect.centery`) because the floating-point x and y attributes are more accurate than the integer `rect` values.

```python
def calcPos(self):
    self.x += self.dx
    self.y += self.dy
```

Checking for boundaries

The boundary-checking method is simple. When the shell hits any screen boundary, it should reset itself so it is no longer visible. Since the reset functionality is needed several times, I made it a method of the object.

```python
def checkBounds(self):
    screen = self.screen
    if self.x > screen.get_width():
        self.reset()
    if self.x < 0:
        self.reset()
    if self.y > screen.get_height():
        self.reset()
    if self.y < 0:
        self.reset()
```

Resetting the shell

The shell's `reset()` method is called whenever the shell leaves a screen boundary. If there were any targets on the screen, I'd also reset the shell when it hits a target, so it appears to go away. Resetting the shell does not delete the sprite. It simply moves it out of the way and sets the speed to 0 — that way it stays hidden until needed again.

```python
def reset(self):
    """ move off stage and stop"""
    self.x = -100
    self.y = -100
    self.speed = 0
```

Modifying the main program

The main program doesn't need many modifications, but it does need to know about the shell, and it needs to connect the shell to the turret. Also, the label is there to help you see the value of direction and charge, so the code for manipulating the label is part of the main logic. Here's what you do:

1. **Create instances of all three sprites.**

Be sure you keep track of what parameters each sprite needs. The `Turret` class is now expecting a `shell` instance, and the `Shell` class needs the screen. The label expects no parameters, but you can change its center to position it.

```
shell = Shell(screen)
turret = Turret(shell)
lblOutput = Label()
lblOutput.center = (100, 20)
```

Watch Your Step

The order in which these sprites are created matters. Because the turret needs a shell as part of its initialization, you have to create the shell first.

2. **Add the sprites to a sprite group.**

As usual, most sprite manipulation is handled by a sprite group. Add all three sprites to the same group. Be sure to add the shell before the turret, so the shell will appear underneath the turret in the game:

```
allSprites = pygame.sprite.Group(shell, turret, lblOutput)
```

3. **Update the label.**

I found it easiest to update the label within the main loop, so I added some code to update the label's text with the turret's direction and charge:

```
#update label
lblOutput.text = "dir: %d  speed %d" % (turret.dir, turret.charge)
```

Step Into the Real World

I could have put the label-updating code inside the label, but I decided not to do that. Doing so would have required passing the `turret` instance to the label as an argument. I prefer to keep the `Label` class simpler and more generic, so I simply added the code in the main loop.

Following the Mouse

You can use vector projection to convert any angle and distance to dx and dy components, but sometimes you want to calculate in the other direction. If you know the location of two points on the screen, you can easily calculate the angle and distance between them. To illustrate, take a look at the followMouse.py program shown in Figure 9-10.

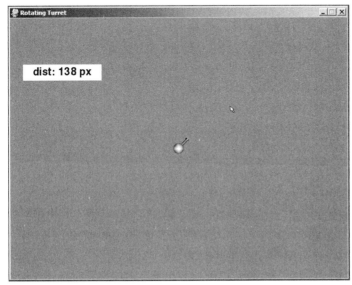

Figure 9-10: The turret always points directly at the mouse cursor.

The program is modified from turret.py, but rather than using keyboard input, the turret compares its own position with that of the mouse cursor to determine the turret's current direction.

Updating the turret

The Turret class has a slightly different update() method that calls a followMouse() method rather than the more standard checkKeys() method.

```
def update(self):
    self.followMouse()
    self.rotate()
```

The rotate() method is still needed to rotate the turret image, but there is no need for a calcVector() method, because the followMouse() method will calculate the vector from the mouse position.

Calculating the direction to the mouse

The `followMouse()` method compares the turret's position to that of the mouse, and uses an arctangent function (`atan2()`) to return the direction between the two objects.

```
def followMouse(self):
    (mouseX, mouseY) = pygame.mouse.get_pos()
    dx = self.rect.centerx - mouseX
    dy = self.rect.centery - mouseY
    dy *= -1

    radians = math.atan2(dy, dx)
    self.dir = radians * 180 / math.pi
    self.dir += 180

    #calculate distance
    self.distance = math.sqrt((dx * dx) + (dy * dy))
```

It isn't difficult to calculate the direction to another object. Here's how you go about it:

1. Get the current mouse position.

It's easiest to have two separate variables for the mouse's X and Y positions. Use tuple-unpacking syntax to get the two variables:

```
(mouseX, mouseY) = pygame.mouse.get_pos()
```

2. Calculate dx and dy.

These values can be determined by subtracting the relevant coordinate points. Subtract the mouse's x from the turret's x to get dx, and subtract the mouse's y from the turret's y to get dy.

```
dx = self.rect.centerx - mouseX
dy = self.rect.centery - mouseY
```

 Watch Your Step

It matters whether you subtract mouse positions from turret positions or the other way around. If you don't get exactly the angle you're expecting, try subtracting the other way around.

3. Compensate for the inverted y axis.

The y axis increases downward in programming and upward in math. Multiply dy by −1 to incorporate this effect:

```
dy *= -1
```

4. Calculate the angle between the turret and the mouse.

Python's `math` module actually includes two different arctangent functions. The "official" `atan()` function does the job, but it's a little tricky to work with. Arctangent has an undefined value when `dy` is `0`, because division by zero is undefined in mathematics. (Remember, the tangent is defined as dx/dy.) The `atan2()` function handles this situation properly. Remember that the result of this function will be an angle measured in radians.

```
radians = math.atan2(dy, dx)
```

5. Convert the radian measure into degrees.

The `rotate()` method expects `self.dir` to be expressed in degrees, so do the appropriate conversion.

```
self.dir = radians * 180 / math.pi
```

6. Offset the result by 180 degrees.

The result of the `atan2()` call will be in the range between -180 and 180 degrees. The `rotate()` method is expecting a value between 0 and 360, so add 180 degrees to the `dir` attribute.

```
self.dir += 180
```

7. Calculate the distance between the turret and the mouse.

Although it isn't necessary for this particular exercise, it can be very handy to know the distance between two points. Use a variation of the Pythagorean Theorem to extract this value:

```
#calculate distance
self.distance = math.sqrt((dx * dx) +     ↵
(dy * dy))
```

Step Into the Real World

If you look at the source code for the `followMouse.py` program, you'll notice that I display the distance in a special object called `LblDist`, which is derived from the label in `turretFire.py`. I needed a label much like one I had already made, so I simply imported it from a previous file and added my own new features to it. This is the real joy of object-oriented programming; once you make something useful you can re-use it in a lot of other ways. Experienced programmers often build libraries of really handy objects (like the label used here) that they can use over and over. You'll build a toolkit of objects specialized for making games in the next chapter.

Simulating Basic Gravity

The turret game is happening now, and if you're looking at the turret from a top-down perspective, it's pretty cool. However, a lot of artillery games are based on a side view of the gun, which looks something like `turretGrav.py` in Figure 9-11.

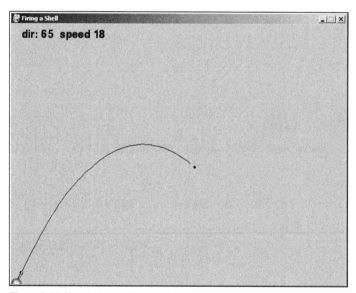

Figure 9-11: The shells now fly in a realistic arc.

There is an important difference, though, in viewing the turret from this perspective. If you view a gun firing from the ground, gravity plays an important role in the shell's trajectory.

An object under the influence of a strong gravitational force (like the Earth) has certain characteristics:

- **Its path describes a parabola.** The path of such an object isn't a straight line. It forms a unique mathematical curve called a *parabola*. I put a path-drawing feature into the program (see Figure 9-11) so you can see that the shell does follow a parabolic path. Every combination of angle and charge gives a slightly different parabola.

- **The horizontal speed is relatively constant.** In reality, wind resistance causes objects to slow down their horizontal motion slightly (provided there's an atmosphere present). However, this slowing effect is so minor over the length of a shell's flight it is usually ignored in arcade games. The dx component assigned to a shell when it leaves the turret remains constant during the entire flight.

The vertical speed is constantly changing. The gravitational attraction between the shell and the earth is constantly affecting the shell's vertical speed (dy). As soon as the shell leaves the turret, its vertical speed is being slowed. Eventually, gravity overcomes the shell's initial vertical speed, and the shell appears to float momentarily at the top of the arc. The shell then picks up speed again, hitting the ground at the same speed it left the turret. The turretGrav.py program accurately reflects this dynamic as well.

All these rules about how an object behaves under the influence of gravity might be scaring you a little bit. If you've taken a physics class, you've doubtless encountered formulas about all this. The code to make an object respond to a large gravitational influence (as we're doing in this example) is ridiculously easy. I made a few very simple changes to turret.py to incorporate gravity. Most of the changes really have more to do with drawing the trajectory than the actual physics!

Transfer

I show you another approach to gravity later in this chapter, where you create spacecraft that can orbit planets. Both effects are really the same phenomenon, but this easier variant is used in most Earthbound games that use gravity.

1. **Include the background as a parameter to the `shell` object.**

The shell will draw its path on the background, so I add the background object to the shell.

```
def __init__(self, screen, background):
    pygame.sprite.Sprite.__init__(self)
    self.screen = screen
    self.background = background
```

Step Into the Real World

If you've taken a physics class, you know that the standard gravitational constant on Earth is about 9.86 meters/second². You might wonder then why I'm using .5 as my gravitational constant. It's all about units of measurement. In arcade games, I don't usually use real-world measurement units. Rather than measuring velocity in meters per second, I'm using pixels per frame. Experiment to find the gravity that looks right for the scale and style of your game. Of course, you can modify gravity any way you want, so if you have a gravitational constant that works fine on Earth, divide that value by 6 to simulate the moon's gravity (one-sixth of Earth's), or multiply it by 2.5 to simulate the gravity of Jupiter (two-and-a-half times Earth's).

2. Add a gravitational constant to the shell.

This figure determines the effect of gravity on the shell. It should be a relatively small value, as it will be added to dy during each animation frame. This should be done as part of the shell's __init__() method:

```
self.gravity = .5
```

3. Calculate the shell's vector only once, when the shell is first initialized.

The shell gets its starting direction only once — when it is first created. The dy values will be modified throughout the life of the shell. Call the shell's calcVector() method once, when the shell is created (in the turret's checkKeys() method):

```
if keys[pygame.K_SPACE]:
    self.shell.x = self.rect.centerx
    self.shell.y = self.rect.centery
    self.shell.speed = self.charge
    self.shell.dir = self.dir
    self.shell.calcVector()
```

4. Remove `calcVector()` from the shell's `update()` method.

The calcVector() method is used to calculate dx and dy from an initial speed and dir. The dy attribute will change from these initial settings, so it's not necessary to call calcVector() each frame. The vector will actually be modified during the calcPos() method.

```
def update(self):
    self.calcPos()
    self.checkBounds()
    self.rect.center = (self.x, self.y)
```

5. Clear the background in `calcVector()`.

In this particular game, I want to draw a new arc each time the user fires the cannon. The most convenient way to do this was to refill the background graphic each time calcVector() is called (which happens immediately after firing the cannon).

```
#clear the background
self.background.fill((0x00, 0xCC, 0x00))
```

6. Compensate for gravity in `calcPos()`.

The calcPos() method is the natural place to add the gravity modification. Add the gravity factor to the shell's dy attribute during each frame to simulate the cumulative effect of gravity.

```
def calcPos(self):
    #compensate for gravity
    self.dy += self.gravity
```

7. **Draw the shell's path on the background.**

To make the image in Figure 9-11 easier to understand, I traced the shell's path. During each `calcPos()` call, draw a small line from the shell's previous point to the new (`self.x, self.y`) point.

```
#get old position for drawing
oldx = self.x
oldy = self.y

self.x += self.dx
self.y += self.dy

pygame.draw.line(self.background, (0,0,0),  ↵
(oldx, oldy), (self.x, self.y))
```

8. **Blit the background image rather than relying on `allSprites.clear()`.**

The sprite group `clear()` method you normally use for erasing a sprite's previous position relies on a nonchanging background image. Because I'm drawing on the background during each frame, it's better to comment out this line and replace it with a standard `blit()` method in the main loop.

```
#blit the background for drawings
screen.blit(background, (0, 0))

#allSprites.clear(screen, background)
allSprites.update()
allSprites.draw(screen)
pygame.display.flip()
```

Building a Vector-Based Vehicle

Of course, the concepts used to build the turret can also be applied to a steerable moving sprite. The `carVec.py` program shown in Figure 9-12 uses the vector technique to create a smoothly turning car. (I made it a car, but of course the image can be whatever you want)

The `car` sprite combines the simple motion model used in Chapter 8 with the vector-projection principles described earlier in this chapter.

Initializing the car

The `car` sprite's initialization is familiar, but it incorporates several variables to help make the car turn smoothly rather than the sharp 45-degree angles of the cow model:

```
import pygame, math
pygame.init()

class Car(pygame.sprite.Sprite):
```

```
def __init__(self, screen):
    pygame.sprite.Sprite.__init__(self)
    self.screen = screen
    self.imageMaster = pygame.image.load("car.gif")
    self.imageMaster = self.imageMaster.convert()
    self.imageMaster = pygame.transform.scale(self.imageMaster, (50, 35))
    self.rect = self.imageMaster.get_rect()
    self.dir = 0
    self.turnRate = 3
    self.accel = .1
    self.x = 320.0
    self.y = 240.0
    self.speed = 0
    self.rect.center = (self.x, self.y)
```

Figure 9-12: The car turns smoothly as it races around the screen.

Creating the `Car` class is pretty standard stuff by now, but here are the steps anyway:

1. **Import the math module.**

   Vector projection requires the trig functions built into the `math` module, so be sure to import it.

   ```
   import pygame, math
   ```

2. **Include the screen as a parameter for boundary-checking.**

   The sprite will wrap around boundaries, so it needs to know the size of the screen. Accept this value as a parameter, and store it in attribute (cleverly) called `screen`.

```
class Car(pygame.sprite.Sprite):
    def __init__(self, screen):
        pygame.sprite.Sprite.__init__(self)
        self.screen = screen
```

3. **Attach a car image to the sprite.**

I drew a race car image (pointing east) and loaded it into the sprite as
`imageMaster`. I converted and scaled the image so it would be the proper
size. If you'll be rotating an image, be sure to save an unaltered version so you
don't lose detail during the rotations.

```
self.imageMaster = pygame.image.load("car.gif")
self.imageMaster = self.imageMaster.convert()
self.imageMaster = pygame.transform.scale(self.imageMaster, (50, 35))
self.rect = self.imageMaster.get_rect()
```

4. **Set attributes for the car's motion values.**

The car needs `dir` and `speed` attributes to indicate which direction and speed the
user intends the car to move. The `turnRate` attribute determines how much the
car will turn on each frame (in degrees) when the user turns the car. The `accel`
attribute indicates how much the car will accelerate during each frame if the
user steps on the gas. Finally, the `x` and `y` attributes will hold floating-point values for the car's position — they offer more accurate placement of the car than
the integer `rect.centerx` and `rect.centery` attributes can provide.

```
self.dir = 0
self.turnRate = 3
self.accel = .1
self.x = 320.0
self.y = 240.0
self.speed = 0
self.rect.center = (self.x, self.y)
```

Updating the car

The `Car` class's `update()` method relegates most of the work to specialized methods:

```
def update(self):
    self.checkKeys()
    self.rotate()
    self.calcVector()
    self.checkBounds()
    self.rect.center = (self.x, self.y)
```

The purpose of each of these methods should be obvious from their titles, but they are
described in the following sections. After all the various operations have been done,
the `self.x` and `self.y` attributes are copied over to the sprite's `rect.center`
attribute, preparing the sprite to actually move during the next render.

Checking the keyboard

The car's keyboard-checking method is very similar to the one for the turret. It looks for the four arrow keys and changes attributes of the car accordingly:

```
def checkKeys(self):
    keys = pygame.key.get_pressed()
    if keys[pygame.K_RIGHT]:
        self.dir -= self.turnRate
        if self.dir < 0:
            self.dir = 360 - self.turnRate
    if keys[pygame.K_LEFT]:
        self.dir += self.turnRate
        if self.dir > 360:
            self.dir = self.turnRate
    if keys[pygame.K_UP]:
        self.speed += self.accel
        if self.speed > 10:
            self.speed = 10
    if keys[pygame.K_DOWN]:
        self.speed -= self.accel
        if self.speed < -3:
            self.speed = -3
```

Here's how you use the keyboard-checking routine:

1. **Store the keyboard information in a tuple called keys.**

Use the pygame.key.get_pressed() function to query the current status of the keyboard.

2. **Turn the car left or right.**

If the left or right arrow keys are pressed, change the dir attribute accordingly. Use turnRate to determine how much to turn the car. Be sure to check for angles greater than 360 and smaller than 0, so dir is always a legal value.

3. **Adjust the speed.**

The up and down arrow keys modify the speed. Because the hardware-polling technique reads the keyboard continuously, the accel variable doesn't need to be very big. Accelerating the vehicle by 0.1 pixels per frame (as I'm doing here) actually amounts to a 3-pixel-per-second acceleration, because the game runs at 30 frames per second. As usual, check for maximum and minimum values to keep the vehicle within reasonable bounds.

Rotating the car

You rotate the car's image just as you did the turret in the earlier example:

```
def rotate(self):
    oldCenter = self.rect.center
    self.image = pygame.transform.rotate(self.imageMaster, self.dir)
    self.rect = self.image.get_rect()
    self.rect.center = oldCenter
```

Copy the image's old center, use the `pygame.transform.rotate()` function to rotate the image master, re-calculate the `rect`, and re-center the image. Check back with the turret examples earlier in this chapter if you are unclear how the image rotation is done.

Calculating the vector

Rotating the image does not cause the car to travel in the right direction. The car needs `dx` and `dy` values for that. The `calcVector()` method uses standard vector-projection principles to get these values:

```
def calcVector(self):
    radians = self.dir * math.pi / 180
    self.dx = math.cos(radians)
    self.dy = math.sin(radians)

    self.dx *= self.speed
    self.dy *= self.speed
    self.dy *= -1

    self.x += self.dx
    self.y += self.dy
```

Here's what you need to do:

1. **Convert the sprite's `dir` value to radians.**

Use the standard formula for this task:

```
radians = self.dir * math.pi / 180
```

2. **Calculate `dx` and `dy` using trig functions.**

```
self.dx = math.cos(radians)
self.dy = math.sin(radians)
```

3. **Multiply `dx` and `dy` by the sprite's speed.**

The calculated `dx` and `dy` variables move the sprite 1 pixel in the indicated direction. Multiply each of these values by `self.speed` to incorporate speed.

```
self.dx *= self.speed
self.dy *= self.speed
```

4. **Multiply `dy` by -1.**

The standard formulas assume that y increases upward (as it does in mathematics). Multiply dy by -1 to account for the inverted y axis in computer graphics.

```
self.dy *= -1
```

5. **Update x and y.**

```
self.x += self.dx
self.y += self.dy
```

Use the newly calculated values of dx and dy to update x and y.

Checking the boundaries

The boundary-checking method is the same wrapping technique you've seen many times by now:

```
def checkBounds(self):
    if self.x > self.screen.get_width():
        self.x = 0
    if self.x < 0:
        self.x = self.screen.get_width()
    if self.y > self.screen.get_height():
        self.y = 0
    if self.y < 0:
        self.y = self.screen.get_height()
```

Building the main loop

The main() function has no surprises either. You should be well acquainted with this loop by now — except (of course) for one change: the sprite group includes the car sprite.

```
def main():
    screen = pygame.display.set_mode((640, 480))
    pygame.display.set_caption("vector projection")

    background = pygame.Surface(screen.get_size())
    background.fill((0xcc, 0xcc, 0xcc))
    screen.blit(background, (0, 0))

    car = Car(screen)
    allSprites = pygame.sprite.Group(car)

    keepGoing = True
    clock = pygame.time.Clock()

    while keepGoing:
        clock.tick(30)
        for event in pygame.event.get():
```

```
            if event.type == pygame.QUIT:
                keepGoing = False

        allSprites.clear(screen, background)
        allSprites.update()
        allSprites.draw(screen)

        pygame.display.flip()

if __name__ == "__main__":
    main()
```

Making a More Versatile Vehicle Model

The vehicle motion technique used in `carVec.py` provides basic motion, but the technique can be improved. Look at the `carParam.py` program in Figure 9-13.

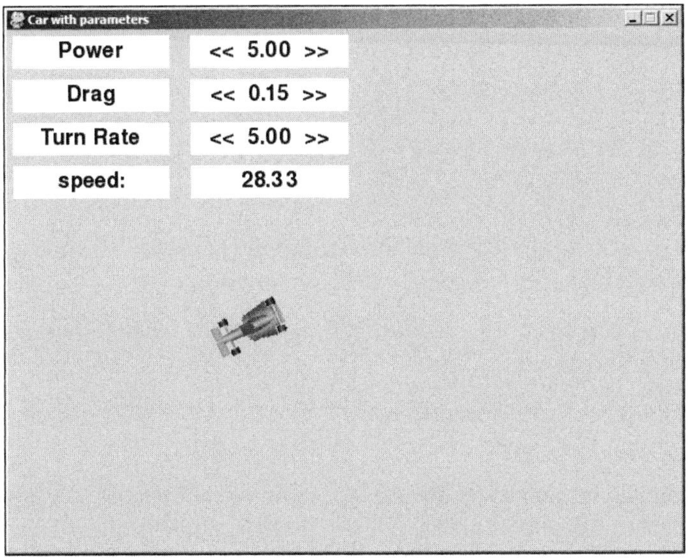

Figure 9-13: This car has several parameters that can be modified by the user.

The user can modify several parameters of this car to give it different handling characteristics:

- **Power:** Indicates the strength of the vehicle's engine in comparison to its weight. The power is measured in pixels of acceleration per frame. More power generally means faster acceleration and top speed.

Drag: All the various factors that will cause a vehicle to slow down. Wind resistance and other forms of friction are the main things that cause drag in a vehicle. A vehicle with a very low drag coefficient will accelerate quickly, and will retain its speed longer when no longer under acceleration. A vehicle with a high drag coefficient will slow down quickly as soon as acceleration is no longer applied. Drag is described as a ratio between 0 (no drag whatsoever) to 1 (infinitely high drag — which means the vehicle will never move).

Turn Rate: The turning rate describes how quickly the vehicle turns. It is measured in degrees turned per frame. A higher turning rate means quicker turns.

Speed: The user doesn't directly indicate the top speed. Instead, the speed is determined by the interplay of power and drag. Speed is measured in pixels per frame.

Adding the Interface objects

I made some custom interface objects for this program, stored in `miniGUI.py`. The program uses two custom classes: `Labels` and `Scrollers`. The `Label` class was described in Chapter 6. The `Scroller` class is an advanced label used to manage a numeric value easily. (It will be described more fully in Chapter 10, but I'm using it here, for illustration purposes.)The `Scroller` class has the following characteristics:

- The `center` attribute determines where on the screen the scroller should be placed.

- The `fgColor` and `bgColor` attributes determine the scroller's color.

- The `value` attribute is used to set and retrieve the numeric value associated with the scroller.

- The `minValue` and `maxValue` attributes describe the range of possible values the scroller will return.

- The `increment` attribute describes how much the value will be changed each time the scroller is clicked.

- The scroller can be clicked. If the user clicks on the left half of the scroller, the value decreases. If the user clicks on the right half of the scroller, the value increases.

Information Kiosk

The `Scroller` class is interesting, but it's not central to this discussion. If you're curious about how it is made, read ahead in Chapter 10, where I describe it and several other custom classes thoroughly. All of the useful tools in the `miniGUI` module are described in full in the next chapter, where they're incorporated into a full-blown game development module.

To add the various `Label`, `Button`, and `Scroller` classes to your own programs, import the `miniGUI.py` module included with this chapter's notes. Here's how I did it in `carParam.py`:

1. **Import `miniGUI.py` at the beginning of the program, just as you import the `pygame` and `math` modules.**

```
import pygame, math
import miniGUI
```

2. **Create a label for power.**

In the `main()` function for the program, make an instance of the `miniGUI.Label` class for a quick and functional label. Set the `center` and `text` attributes so the label appears as you wish.

```
#Make some labels and scrollers
lblPower = miniGUI.Label()
lblPower.center = (80, 20)
lblPower.text = "Power"
```

3. **Create a scroller to go with the Power label.**

The scroller lets the user actually change the power setting. I want the power to go from 0 to 10 by .5 increments, so I set the values accordingly

```
scrPower = miniGUI.Scroller()
scrPower.center = (250, 20)
scrPower.bgColor = (0xFF, 0xFF, 0xFF)
scrPower.value = 5
scrPower.maxValue = 10
scrPower.increment = .5
```

4. **Repeat for drag and turning rate.**

Create labels and scrollers to manage the other two parameters. Set the scroller attributes to be appropriate to the particular data type. (For example, the drag should range from 0 to 1 by .01 increments.)

```
lblDrag = miniGUI.Label()
lblDrag.center = (80, 60)
lblDrag.text = "Drag"

scrDrag = miniGUI.Scroller()
scrDrag.center = (250, 60)
scrDrag.bgColor = (0xFF, 0xFF, 0xFF)
scrDrag.value = .15
scrDrag.maxValue = 1
scrDrag.increment = .01

lblTurn = miniGUI.Label()
lblTurn.center = (80, 100)
```

```
                          lblTurn.text = "Turn Rate"

                          scrTurn = miniGUI.Scroller()
                          scrTurn.center = (250, 100)
                          scrTurn.bgColor = (0xFF, 0xFF, 0xFF)
```

5. **Create two labels for speed.**

Even though the user can't edit the speed, it's nice to show the user the current speed. I used two labels for this, because the user can't edit the speed directly. The second label starts empty, but will be modified throughout the main loop with the car's current speed.

```
                          lblSpeed0 = miniGUI.Label()
                          lblSpeed0.text = "speed:"
                          lblSpeed0.center = (80, 140)

                          lblSpeed1 = miniGUI.Label()
                          lblSpeed1.text = ""
                          lblSpeed1.center = (250, 140)
```

Managing the sprites in the main loop

All the labels and scrollers are sprites, so their management is pretty straightforward:

```
        allSprites = pygame.sprite.OrderedUpdates(lblPower,   ↵
scrPower,
                                        lblDrag, scrDrag,
                                        lblTurn, scrTurn,
                                        lblSpeed0, lblSpeed1,
                                        car)

    keepGoing = True
    clock = pygame.time.Clock()

    while keepGoing:
        clock.tick(30)
        for event in pygame.event.get():
            if event.type == pygame.QUIT:
                keepGoing = False

        # read scrollers
        car.power = scrPower.value
        car.turnRate = scrTurn.value
        car.drag = scrDrag.value
        lblSpeed1.text = "%.2f" % car.speed

        allSprites.clear(screen, background)
        allSprites.update()
```

```
allSprites.draw(screen)

pygame.display.flip()
```

The scrollers need a small amount of attention within the main loop. Here's how you go about it:

1. **Add all the labels and scrollers to the `allSprites` group.**

   Put all the sprites in the group so they will be updated and displayed in every frame. I found it disconcerting that the car sometimes drives under the labels and scrollers, so note that I made the sprite group a `sprite.OrderedUpdates` group to ensure the sprites would all be displayed in the order they were placed in the group.

2. **Read values from each of the scrollers.**

   The purpose of the `scroller` objects is to let the user change various parameters on the fly. Transfer the `value` attribute from the scroller to the appropriate attribute in the `Car` class.

   ```
   car.power = scrPower.value
   car.turnRate = scrTurn.value
   car.drag = scrDrag.value
   ```

3. **Update the `speed` label with the car's current speed.**

   The `speed` label should be updated with the car's current speed value. Using the string-interpolation technique makes it easy to format the car's speed to two decimal points.

Customizing the car sprite

The `Car` class just requires minor modifications to accept the various parameters, yet those parameters provide nearly endless variety in the vehicle's handling characteristics.

Define the car attributes

Some attributes (`power`, `turnRate`, and `drag`) are directly edited by the user. Other attributes are defined by the interplay between the primary attributes and other user input. Define all the attributes you will need in the `Car` class's `__init__()` method.

```
class Car(pygame.sprite.Sprite):

    def __init__(self, screen):
        pygame.sprite.Sprite.__init__(self)

        self.screen = screen

        self.imageMaster = pygame.image.load("car.gif")
```

```
self.imageMaster = self.imageMaster.convert()
self.rect = self.imageMaster.get_rect()

#define attributes
self.x = 320
self.y = 230
self.dx = 0
self.dy = 0
self.speed = 0
self.dir = 0
self.turnRate = 2
self.power = 1
self.drag = .3
```

Information Kiosk

Some of the initial attribute values don't really matter, because they will be pulled from the on-screen controls. Still, I put values here for the first version of the program (that didn't allow user-editable values) and to show the typical range of the value.

Manage the car's behavior

The update() method contains a list of methods to perform during each frame:

```
def update(self):
    self.checkKeys()
    self.rotate()
    self.calcVector()
    self.calcPos()
    self.checkBounds()
    self.rect.center = (self.x, self.y)
```

Most of these methods act exactly as they did in earlier versions of the program, but there are a few new twists.

Adjust the keyboard input

The checkKeys() method has a few relatively minor changes:

```
def checkKeys(self):
    keys = pygame.key.get_pressed()
    if keys[pygame.K_RIGHT]:
        self.dir -= self.turnRate
        if self.dir < 0:
            self.dir = 360 - self.turnRate
    if keys[pygame.K_LEFT]:
        self.dir += self.turnRate
        if self.dir > 360:
```

```
        self.dir = self.turnRate
if keys[pygame.K_UP]:
    self.speed += self.power
    #no need to check for a max speed anymore
if keys[pygame.K_DOWN]:
    self.speed -= self.power
    if self.speed < -3:
        self.speed = -3
```

- **The up and down keys now affect `self.power` rather than `self.accel`.** The term `power` seemed more appropriate to the new version of the car, because the acceleration is now a function of the interaction between power and drag.

- **There's no need to check for a maximum speed.** The maximum speed will be determined by the interplay between the power and drag ratio rather than by an arbitrary top speed. This leads to smoother and more realistic acceleration characteristics.

- **Use power to handle braking as well.** If you want, you can add a braking factor as well. Truthfully, you won't need brakes much with this technique, because the car's drag will slow the car down and eventually stop it. (Besides, what self-respecting arcade car has brakes?)

Compensate for drag

The most important new effect is the drag coefficient. Most arcade games use an expedient for drag that isn't perfect physics, but simulates drag in a fairly effective way. Essentially, subtract the drag coefficient from 1, and multiply the speed by this new rate. If the drag coefficient is 0.05, for example, the speed will be multiplied by .95 each frame, gradually slowing the car. If the car is accelerating, the car will speed up. If the accelerator is not currently pressed, the car will eventually slow down. The drag calculations can be done as part of the `calcVector()` method:

```
def calcVector(self):
    radians = self.dir * math.pi / 180
    self.dx = math.cos(radians)
    self.dy = math.sin(radians)

    #compensate for drag
    self.speed *= (1 - self.drag)
    if self.speed < .5:
        if self.speed > -.5:
            self.speed = 0

    self.dx *= self.speed
    self.dy *= self.speed
    self.dy *= -1
```

Most of the method is the same as it's always been, but the speed is modified by the drag ratio before it is applied to dx and dy. Follow these steps:

1. Subtract drag from 1.

The drag factor is actually 1 minus the drag ratio. That way, small values of the coefficient represent more efficient vehicles, as is true in the real world. The resulting value is a percentage of the car's velocity that is kept as it moves to the next frame — though it slows down frame by frame.

2. Multiply the speed by the resulting percentage.

If there is no (or little) acceleration, the net effect will slow the car down. If there is sufficient acceleration, the car will speed up. As the speed increases, the amount taken away by drag also increases. At some point, the loss will equal the acceleration, and the car will reach its natural maximum velocity.

3. Manage drag at very slow speeds.

This quick approach to drag works pretty well except at very slow speeds. The car will get slower and slower with this technique, but it will never come to a complete stop. If the car speed drops within a certain range (I chose –0.5 to 0.5 pixels per frame), simply set the speed to 0.

```
if self.speed < .5:
    if self.speed > -.5:
        self.speed = 0
```

Step Into the Real World

Although the basic idea of this drag coefficient is correct, don't take the actual value too seriously. It's rare for a car to have a drag coefficient better than .30 in the real world, yet the car in this example has a starting drag of .15. This is because I'm not using real-world measurement values in the game, but the somewhat arbitrary units of pixel distance and frame-based time. The feel is more important than the reality. If you want to have a speedometer that simulates real world speed, use this technique:

- **Create a power/drag ratio** that feels right through experimentation.
- **Find the top speed of your model** in pixels-per-frame (about 28 ppf with the default settings in carParam).
- **Determine the approximate top speed** of the actual vehicle (let's say 230 m.p.h. for an Indy car).
- **Divide** the actual top speed (230) by the ppf top speed (28) to get a real-world ratio (roughly 8.21).
- **Report speed using the ratio.** During the game, multiply ppf speed by the ratio to get the "virtual" m.p.h. reading. For example, if the car is going 10 ppf, multiply 10 by 8.21 and tell the player the car is traveling at 82.1 miles per hour.

Handle the other car characteristics

All the other `car` methods are exactly as described earlier in this chapter. Please see the complete `carParam.py` code on the companion Web site for all the details.

Building a Spacecraft Model

No discussion of arcade game vehicles would be complete without spacecraft. Spaceships were featured in the first computer game, and they're still a standard.

> ### Information Kiosk
>
> That's right. *Pong* wasn't the first computer game. That honor belongs to *SpaceWar*, a two-player game featuring realistic physics and player-controlled spacecraft that debuted on a PDP-1 at MIT in 1962. Several arcade versions of the game were released, but they were commercial failures, because the game was too complicated, and just too far from anybody's experience. *Pong* became a hit partially because it was both new and familiar, and easy to understand.

Figure 9-14 shows `space.py`, which features a simple spacecraft flying around in space.

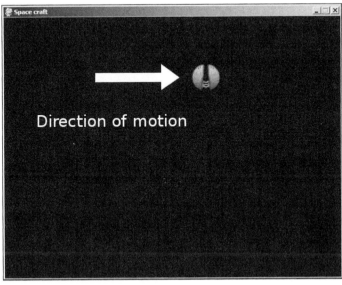

Figure 9-14: The spaceship is moving sideways even though it's pointing up. (I added the arrow and text.)

Spacecraft (at least the arcade kind) have a fundamentally different kind of movement than earthbound vehicles. Most vehicles move in whatever direction they're pointed, and eventually slow down if they are not under power. When you fire a spaceship's engine, you apply a force vector in the direction the ship is pointing — but there's no friction to speak of in space. So when you turn a moving spacecraft, it keeps going in the same direction until you change its course by applying thrust in a different direction.

Creating the spacecraft sprite

The __init__() method for the Ship class is pretty standard.

```
class Ship(pygame.sprite.Sprite):
    def __init__(self, screen):
        pygame.sprite.Sprite.__init__(self)
        self.screen = screen

        self.imageThrust = pygame.image.load("shipThrust.png")
        self.imageThrust = self.imageThrust.convert()
        self.imageCruise = pygame.image.load("shipCruise.png")
        self.imageCruise = self.imageCruise.convert()
        self.imageLeft = pygame.image.load("shipLeft.png")
        self.imageLeft = self.imageLeft.convert()
        self.imageRight = pygame.image.load("shipRight.png")
        self.imageRight = self.imageRight.convert()

        self.imageMaster = self.imageCruise
        self.image = self.imageMaster
        self.rect = self.image.get_rect()

        self.x = 100
        self.y = 100
        self.dx = 0
        self.dy = 0
        self.dir = 0
        self.turnRate = 5
        self.speed = 0
```

Here's what you do along the way:

1. **Include the screen as a parameter.**

   The spacecraft, like most sprites, needs to know about the screen size to handle boundary-checking information.

2. **Load four master images.**

   In this simulation, it's important that the user can see she is applying thrust to the craft. For that reason, (and just because it's cool) I made four versions of the spaceship (modified from Ari's spriteLib). One version, called imageCruise shows the ship puttering happily along with no thrust in any direction. imageThrust shows the main engine blazing away, and imageLeft and imageRight demonstrate maneuvering thrusters. All four images need to be loaded and converted.

Whenever a particular image is needed, it will be copied to imageMaster, which will then be rotated in the rotate() method and displayed as the ship's image.

```
self.imageThrust = self.imageThrust.convert()
self.imageCruise = pygame.image.load("shipCruise.png")
self.imageCruise = self.imageCruise.convert()
self.imageLeft = pygame.image.load("shipLeft.png")
self.imageLeft = self.imageLeft.convert()
self.imageRight = pygame.image.load("shipRight.png")
self.imageRight = self.imageRight.convert()

self.imageMaster = self.imageCruise
self.image = self.imageMaster
self.rect = self.image.get_rect()
```

3. Set up the normal properties.

The ship will have the same general properties as any moving sprite: x, y, dx, dy, dir, and turnRate. Note that the ship does not have a speed attribute. The user won't directly affect the ship's speed. Instead, a thrust attribute indicates how much acceleration the ship has.

```
self.x = 100
self.y = 100
self.dx = 0
self.dy = 0
self.dir = 0
self.turnRate = 5
self.thrust = 0
```

Updating the ship

The ship's update() method is also relatively routine. Spacecraft do all the same things as normal vehicles, but the internal details are a bit different (ooh, polymorphism!).

```
def update(self):
    self.checkKeys()
    self.rotate()
    self.calcVector()
    self.setPos()
    self.checkBounds()
    self.rect.center = (self.x, self.y)
```

Checking for keyboard input

The checkKeys() method checks the arrow keys as normal, but each key indicates a different image. Also, the up and down arrows affect the ship's thrust attribute instead of changing the ship's speed directly. There's no need to handle the down arrow here, because spaceships don't have brakes. Slow down by facing backwards and firing the main thrusters. (It's true, some spaceships might have retro-rockets, but humor me.)

```python
def checkKeys(self):
    keys = pygame.key.get_pressed()
    self.imageMaster = self.imageCruise
    if keys[pygame.K_RIGHT]:
        self.dir -= self.turnRate
        if self.dir < 0:
            self.dir = 360 - self.turnRate
        self.imageMaster = self.imageRight
    if keys[pygame.K_LEFT]:
        self.dir += self.turnRate
        if self.dir > 360:
            self.dir = self.turnRate
        self.imageMaster = self.imageLeft
    if keys[pygame.K_UP]:
        self.thrust = .1
        self.imageMaster = self.imageThrust
    else:
        self.thrust = 0
```

Here's what you do at each stage of the code:

1. **Set the default image to `imageCruise`.**

If none of the arrow keys are pressed, the ship should show its normal status with the `imageCruise` image. It's easiest to begin with this basic image and change it if any of the arrows is pressed.

```python
self.imageMaster = self.imageCruise
```

2. **Turn left and right in the normal way.**

Use the `turnRate` attribute to determine how quickly the ship turns. Switch the `imageMaster` value to the appropriate image. Remember, turning the ship merely changes the value of the `dir` attribute. The `rotate()` method will change the actual orientation on the screen.

```python
if keys[pygame.K_RIGHT]:
    self.dir -= self.turnRate
    if self.dir < 0:
        self.dir = 360 - self.turnRate
    self.imageMaster = self.imageRight
if keys[pygame.K_LEFT]:
    self.dir += self.turnRate
    if self.dir > 360:
        self.dir = self.turnRate
    self.imageMaster = self.imageLeft
```

3. **Set the thrust level to non-zero when the user presses the up arrow.**

When the user presses the up arrow, he intends to add a new motion vector to the spacecraft. The thrust amount indicates how much of a change should happen to the motion vector. Any positive non-zero value will cause the ship's motion vector to change.

```
if keys[pygame.K_UP]:
    self.thrust = .1
```

4. **Replace the image with the engine-firing version.**

Use the image version with flames to indicate to the user that the engine is being fired. This would also be a good place for a rocket sound effect.

```
self.imageMaster = self.imageThrust
```

5. **If the user is not firing the engine, turn it off.**

Set the thrust to 0 and the motion vector will not change during the frame. It isn't necessary to set the image if no keys are pressed, because the default setting of the image was set to the cruise image at the beginning of the method.

Calculating the new motion vector

The new motion vector is calculated a little differently for spacecraft than for cars. The spacecraft motion technique is actually truer to Newton's First Law of Motion. The motion thrust is a small vector that is added to the sprite's existing motion vector.

```
def calcVector(self):
    radians = self.dir * math.pi / 180

    thrustDx = self.thrust * math.cos(radians)
    thrustDy = self.thrust * math.sin(radians)
    thrustDy *= -1

    self.dx += thrustDx
    self.dy += thrustDy
    self.speed = math.sqrt((self.dx * self.dx) + ↵
(self.dy * self.dy))
```

Here's the actual steps you carry out along the way:

1. **Convert the ship's direction to radians.**

Use the standard conversion function for this task.

```
radians = self.dir * math.pi / 180
```

2. **Calculate a thrust vector.**

The thrust vector indicates how much *change* in velocity will happen during the frame rather than indicating the speed of the ship directly (as you did with basic car motion). The formulas are still standard vector projection fare. If the user is pressing the up arrow, `self.thrust` is non-zero, and there will be changes in `dx` and `dy`. If the user is not firing the main engines, `self.thrust` will be 0, and there will be no change to the ship's motion.

```
thrustDx = self.thrust * math.cos(radians)
thrustDy = self.thrust * math.sin(radians)
thrustDy *= -1
```

3. **Add the thrust vector to the ship's current motion vector.**

Add `thrustDx` to the ship's `dx` attribute and `thrustDy` to the ship's `dy` attribute. This will cause the current motion vector to be modified by the thrust vector.

```
self.dx += thrustDx
self.dy += thrustDy
```

Information Kiosk

The spaceship model clearly demonstrates the relationship between velocity and acceleration. `dx` and `dy` are the ship's *velocity* vector (in component form). `thrustDx` and `thrustDy` are added to the velocity, so they are the ship's *acceleration* vector (also in component form).

4. **Calculate the ship's current speed.**

The spaceship demo doesn't need to know the speed, but it can be handy in further calculation. Use the Pythagorean Theorem to determine the ship's current speed, based on the values of `dx` and `dy`.

```
self.speed = math.sqrt((self.dx * self.dx) + ↵
(self.dy * self.dy))
```

Introducing Orbiting Spacecraft

Spacecraft have very simple behavior in regular space. Things are much more interesting when there is some large body (like a star or planet) close enough to exert gravitational force. Figure 9-15 shows `orbit.py`, with a spacecraft orbiting around a planet. (I added a drawing feature to the program so you can see the orbital path.)

Orbital physics can seem pretty challenging, but you have just a few factors to keep in mind when considering orbits in 2D:

Each object exerts a gravitational force on each other object. This force is amplified when one or both of the objects are large, and when the objects are close to each other.

- **If there is no other motion vector, a small object will be pulled into a large one.** Once a motionless object is close enough to an object with a lot of mass, the gravitational effects will cause them to collide. The small object will have almost no effect on the larger object, but the larger object will appear to pull in the smaller one.

- **If a small object has enough velocity, it can skip past a larger object.** It's possible for a smaller object to not be pulled into a larger one if the smaller one is moving quickly.

- **Orbits happen when a small object is constantly "falling" toward a larger object, but is moving laterally fast enough to avoid crashing.**

- **The orbital speed means everything.** If the ship is going too slowly, it will eventually hit the planet. If it goes too quickly, it will eventually leave the influence of the larger planet.

- **Lower orbits are faster.** The closer to the planet the ship is, the faster it will move.

- **Raise an orbit by firing prograde (that is, in the direction of the orbit).** To make part of an orbit higher (farther from the planet), fire thrusters in the direction of the orbit (*prograde*) on the *opposite* point of the orbit. (Play around with `orbit.py` to see how this works.)

- **Lower an orbit by firing retrograde.** To make part of an orbit lower (closer to the planet), fire thrusters against the direction of the orbit (*retrograde*) on the opposite point of the orbit.

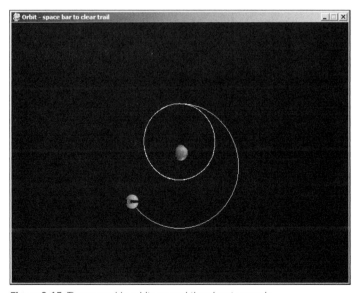

Figure 9-15: The spaceship orbits around the planet properly.

Play around with the `orbit.py` program yourself to confirm these facts. Practice making various kinds of orbits.

Taking gravity seriously

Isaac Newton thought a lot about gravity, and he created a very useful formula for determining the gravitational attraction between two objects. Figure 9-16 shows Newton's law of Universal Gravitation.

$$f = \frac{m_1 * m_2}{d^2} G$$

f = force
m_1 = mass of object 1
m_2 = mass of object 2
d = distance between objects
G = gravitational constant

Figure 9-16: Newton's law of Universal gravitation.

Essentially, this law means that any two objects will exert a pull on each other — and the force of gravity is applied to an object according to Newton's First Law. The force is determined by the product of the masses of the two objects divided by the distance between them squared. A few things about this formula are useful for us:

The masses of the two objects are important. The masses of the objects are important in determining how intensive the gravitational pull will be.

Watch Your Step

As usual, I'm making up my own units here, but I start with a mass of 1 for the ship and 500 for the planet. That means that the planet is only 500 times heavier than the ship. This is completely unrealistic, but that's fine for arcade use. I'll be able to adjust later using the gravitational constant G.

The distance between the objects is important. Gravitational forces are much stronger when objects are close together than when they are farther apart. To determine the gravitational attraction of two objects, you need to know the distance between them.

There's a universal gravitational constant. In the real world, there's a special gravitational constant called G used to make actual calculations. In this simplified form of orbital math, I'll leave G out, but you can put it back in if you find your planets are exerting too much or too little orbital force.

Both objects exert the force on each other. When an apple falls to the earth, clearly the earth is exerting a gravitational force on the apple. The apple is also exerting a force on the earth, but since the apple is so much smaller, the force is immeasurably small. Thus when I calculate the orbit of a ship around a planet, I don't usually calculate the ship's pull on the planet because it's too small to be important.

Modifying the ship

The `orbit.py` program is based on `space.py` with a few modifications.

The ship now has a `mass` attribute of 1. The mass will be used in the gravity calculation. Since the actual mass isn't as important as the relative mass (the ratio of mass between the two objects) I start the ship with a mass attribute of 1. This code is in the ship's `__init__()` method, along with the other attribute values.

```
self.mass = 1
```

The ship no longer needs the `checkBounds()` method. I commented out the `checkBounds()` method call in the `update()` method because screen wrapping caused some very strange effects when I was modeling planetary orbits. I chose to let the ship fly outside the visual part of the screen, and this seems to work well for this simulation.

The ship now draws its own path. The trace of the ship's motion is useful for seeing the orbits. (Besides, the screen shots would have been very boring without this feature.) The drawing commands require the ship to have access to the background object. The ship then draws a small line on the background surface during each frame. I wrote the drawing code in the setPos() method.

```
def setPos(self):
    oldCenter = (self.x, self.y)
    self.x += self.dx
    self.y += self.dy

    pygame.draw.line(self.background, (0xFF,        ↩
0xFF, 0xFF), (oldCenter), (self.x, self.y))
```

Information Kiosk

Don't forget that when you draw on the background, the spriteGroup.clear() method is no longer the best way to clear the frame for each screen. In the main loop, simply re-blit the background during each frame to incorporate the drawings into your final game. I commented out the allSprites.clear() line and added the following:

```
#re-blit background for drawing command
        screen.blit(background, (0, 0))
```

There is a simple planet object. The Planet class is basic, but important. The Planet class's __init__() method is standard for a nonmoving sprite:

```
class Planet(pygame.sprite.Sprite):
    def __init__(self):
        pygame.sprite.Sprite.__init__(self)
        self.image = pygame.image.load("pluto.gif")
        self.image = self.image.convert()
        self.image = pygame.transform.scale        ↩
(self.image, (30, 30))
        self.rect = self.image.get_rect()
        self.mass = 500
        self.x = 320
        self.y = 240
        self.rect.center = (self.x, self.y)
```

The only thing about the planet that is new is its mass attribute, which is used in the gravity calculations. Also notice that I gave the planet x and y attributes because I need to know the position of the planet, even though the planet will not move.

The Planet class has a gravitate() method. This method allows the planet to calculate what kind of gravitational pull it exerts on some other object. The gravitate() method takes another object as a parameter. It assumes that both objects will have a mass attribute as well as x and y attributes. The gravitate() method applies a variation of Newton's law of Universal Gravitation to the ship. I explain the gravitate() code fully in the next section.

The `planet` instance calculates its gravity effect on the ship in the main loop. The most convenient way to incorporate planetary gravity is to call the planet's `gravitate()` method from within the program's main loop: That way the planet can exert its gravitational pull on anything, including other ships and even planets.

```
planet.gravitate(ship)
```

Building the gravitate() method

The `gravitate()` method is obviously an important part of this program. While its behavior is complex, the method itself is surprisingly simple. The method calculates the force of gravity between the ship and the planet, calculates a vector of acceleration based on that force, and adds the resulting force to the ship's dx and dy attributes.

```
def gravitate(self, body):
    """ calculates gravitational pull on
        object """

    (self.x, self.y) = self.rect.center

    #get dx, dy, distance
    dx = self.x - body.x
    dy = self.y - body.y
    distance = math.sqrt((dx * dx) + (dy * dy))

    #normalize dx and dy
    dx /= distance
    dy /= distance

    force = (body.mass * self.mass)/(math.pow     ↩
(distance, 2))
    dx *= force
    dy *= force

    body.dx += dx
    body.dy += dy
```

The `gravitate()` method is an application of Newton's Law of Universal Gravitation. Here's how to implement it on-screen:

1. **Accept a body object as a parameter.**

   The other body will be a ship, satellite, or other orbiting object. The calculations assume that the body has a `mass` attribute.

   ```
   def gravitate(self, body):
   ```

2. **Calculate the current x and y values of the planet.**

Although the planet won't move (yet), it's handy to calculate the x and y values so the center of the planet can be moved after the planet has initialized. For example, you may want the planet to be able to orbit around a star or something.

```
(self.x, self.y) = self.rect.center
```

3. **Calculate the dx and dy values between the objects.**

Determine the difference in x values by subtracting the planet (self) x from the body's x, and the planet's y from the body's y value.

```
#get dx, dy, distance
dx = self.x - body.x
dy = self.y - body.y
```

Watch Your Step

You must subtract the body's position from the planet's position, because if you don't, you get a force pushing the ship *away* from the planet rather than pulling it in, as gravity should do.

Also notice that dx and dy don't have anything to do with the motion of the planet. They are just variables, used to determine the differences in x and y between the planet and the ship.

4. **Calculate the distance between the two objects.**

Use the Pythagorean Theorem to determine the distance between the objects.

```
distance = math.sqrt((dx * dx) + (dy * dy))
```

5. **Normalize the direction vector.**

The dx and dy values are a vector showing the direction and distance between the two objects. The formula will create a new vector in the same direction, but at a force calculated by Newton's Law. Normalize the initial value (that is, make its length equal to 1) by dividing both dx and dy by distance. Now dx and dy create a vector of length 1. You can multiply the components by any value (including the force that will be generated soon) to make the vector that long.

```
#normalize dx and dy
dx /= distance
dy /= distance
```

6. **Calculate the force of gravity.**

Newton's Law of Universal Gravitation finally comes into effect here. Notice I used the math.pow() function as an alternative way to square distance. Also, I ignored the gravitational constant G, because I'm pretty happy with the results. If I were working in real-world units, or felt that the gravity was too weak or too powerful for my game, I'd multiply by some constant to adjust the force of gravity. (Grandiose, isn't it?)

```
force = (body.mass * self.mass)/(math.pow(distance, 2))
```

7. **Multipy dx and dy by the gravitational force.**

Adjust dx and dy by multiplying them by the force of gravity you just calculated.

```
dx *= force
dy *= force
```

8. **Add the new gravity vector to the object's motion vector.**

Add dx and dy, (the gravity vector) to body.dx and body.dy (the body's motion vector). This causes the gravitational effect to modify whatever other forces are acting on the ship.

```
body.dx += dx
body.dy += dy
```

Building more advanced gravity situations

The beauty of the gravitate() technique is it's reusability. If you want to have a satellite, moon, or space station orbit the planet, you can do it pretty easily. Simply build the new object, and apply the planet's gravitate() method to the second object in the main loop. You can also do seemingly complex simulations, such as orbits around two bodies. twoPlanets.py, shown in Figure 9-17, shows the elegant orbital path that can occur in this situation.

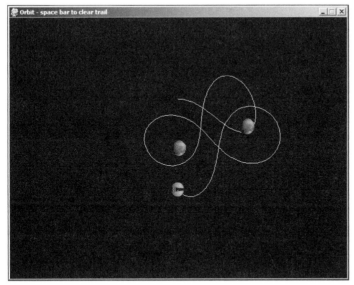

Figure 9-17: This ship is orbiting around two planets!

Creating an orbit around two planets seems difficult, but it's actually very easy, once you've written the gravitate() method. Follow these steps:

1. **Build a second instance of the `planet` object.**

   You've done all the work for creating an object in the class definition. You can make a second planet by making another instance of the `Planet` class.

   ```
   planet2 = Planet()
   ```

2. **Set the second planet's center and mass.**

   The effect of the second planet is determined by its center and mass.

   ```
   planet2.rect.center = (450, 200)
   planet2.mass = 600
   ```

3. **Add the second planet to the sprite group.**

   Of course, you want the second planet to be visible (unless it's a black hole! *That* would be fun!), so add it to the sprite group.

   ```
   allSprites = pygame.sprite.Group(ship, planet,  ↵
   planet2)
   ```

4. **Calculate the effect of each planet's gravity on the ship in the main loop.**

   Each planet has its own `gravitate()` function, which can be used to add a gravitational factor to the ship's motion.

   ```
   planet.gravitate(ship)
   planet2.gravitate(ship)
   ```

Moving Forward

You have learned a lot in this chapter. Now you can use the basic laws of physics to control how an object moves — in realistic and fun ways. Your basic knowledge of fundamental motion allows you to bend the rules to make more interesting motion and effects. In the next chapter, you'll apply all the concepts in the book to make a powerful gaming library and create several starter games.

acceleration: Change in velocity. A vector or d̈x, d̈y components.

arctangent (atan): The inverse operation of tangent, to determine the angle between two sides.

cosine (`cos`): In trigonometry, a ratio representing the adjacent side divided by the hypotenuse.

direction: The angle at which something is moving or pointed. Angles are usually calculated in radians but often specified in degrees.

force vector: Another term for acceleration.

hardware-polling: A technique for reading information from the keyboard directly. Use the `pygame.key.get_pressed()` method to determine which key is currently pressed.

hypotenuse: In trigonometry, the term for the longest side of a right triangle.

magnitude: The length of a vector and can indicate speed, distance, or force.

motion vector: Another term for velocity.

Newton's Laws of Motion: A basic set of rules that accurately describes the motion of most objects.

parabola: The shape formed by the trajectory of a projectile under the influence of gravity. Also the shape described by a quadratic equation.

position: The x and y coordinates of an object.

prograde: In the direction of orbit. Use prograde thrust to create a larger orbit.

Pythagorean Theorem: An important mathematical theorem used to calculate the distance between two points. Usually summarized $A^2 + B^2 = C^2$.

radian: The common unit of angle measurement in mathematics. One radian is the length of the radius described on the circle. A complete circle has 2 * pi radians.

retrograde: In exactly the opposite direction of orbit. Use retrograde thrust to create a smaller orbit.

sine (`sin`): In trigonometry, a ratio representing the opposite side divided by the hypotenuse.

tangent (`tan`): In trigonometry, a ratio representing the opposite side divided by the adjacent side.

Theta (Θ): The symbol commonly used for an angle in trigonometry.

trajectory: The path an object makes as it travels.

vector: Data involving direction and magnitude. A vector can indicate position, velocity, and acceleration.

vector components: A vector stated in `dx`, `dy` format. Vector components are useful because they make it easy to determine where the sprite should move.

vector projection: A technique using trigonometry for converting a vector to its components and vice versa.

velocity: Change in an object's position. A vector with direction and magnitude (or dx and dy components).

Command	Arguments	Description
pygame.key.get_pressed()	*<none>*	Returns a tuple of Boolean values, one for each key.
pygame.event.pump()	*<none>*	Used if the program has no event.get() call, so as to ensure that event-handling is processed.
math.sin(*theta*)	*theta*: an angle in radians	Performs the sine function on *theta*.
math.cos(*theta*)	*theta*: an angle in radians	Performs the cosine function on *theta*.
math.atan2(*dy*, *dx*)	*dy*: the vertical component of a vector *dx*: the horizontal component of a vector	Returns the angle of a triangle with the dx and dy component sides. Result is in radians.
math.pi	*<none>*	Returns an approximation of the constant *pi*: approximately 3.1415927.

Last Stop

Practice Exam

1. **Which is the best approximation of Newton's First Law?**

A) An object in motion tends to stay in motion; one at rest stays at rest.

B) Force = mass * acceleration.

C) A train leaves Pittsburg at 3:00 P.M. . . .

D) $A^2 + B^2 = C^2$

2. **True or false: Velocity and acceleration are the same thing.**

_____

3. **Which is _not_ an advantage of the keyboard-polling technique?**

A) It allows a sprite to read keystrokes without passing the event object.

B) It allows continuous reads of the keyboard.

C) It can also be used to read the mouse position.

D) It can be used to access any key in the pygame constants.

4. **Why is vector projection so important?**

A) It allows you to program motion in any direction at any speed.

B) It encourages accurate physics by combining force vectors.

C) It doesn't require complex `if` structures or lists to implement.

D) All of the above

5. **Describe how you might add gravity to a Lunar Lander–style game.**

_____

_____

_____

_____

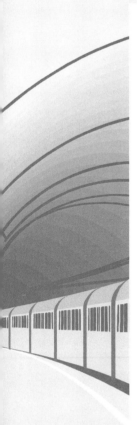

6. Add a small component to the lander's dy attribute during each frame to simulate the cumulative force of gravity.

7. Add a target to the turret game. Use a collision-detection routine to determine whether the shell hit the target.

8. Make a two-player turret game. Optionally allow motion or advanced projectiles.

9. Create a car game using the parameterized car model. Allow the user to purchase improvements in the car's speed and performance.

10. Build a satellite that orbits a planet. Create a game where the user tries to match orbits with the satellite.

11. Re-create the original *SpaceWar* game. (Look online for its features.)

Building a Game Engine

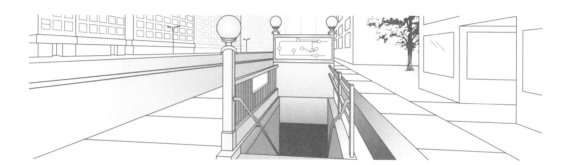

 # Enter the Station

Questions

1. Why might you use a higher-level game engine?

2. What features should go into an improved sprite class?

3. How can you make a sprite have automated boundary-checking?

4. How can you simplify the IDEA/ALTER structure through encapsulation?

5. Why is inheritance useful in the design of GUI widgets?

6. How can you create a simple device for choosing numeric values?

7. How might you build games using a high-level engine?

Introducing the Game Engine

You've learned a lot about how games work. You can create sprites, move them around, bounce them into each other, manage user input, and do all kinds of things. You've learned a lot so far. That's great, but it's also a problem. There's a lot of detail in game programming, and sometimes you just want to write games. In this chapter, you'll learn how to build and use a *game engine* that incorporates everything else you've done — but hides all the details so you can just concentrate on writing games. The game engine is a special module you can use to make your game development easier and more powerful. A tool that hides complexity is often called a *high-level* environment, and that's exactly what the game engine is.

First I show you how to use the game engine as a programmer, and then I open the hood and show you how it works. Finally — and most importantly — I use it to make a few interesting games.

Making a scene

Figure 10-1 shows a program that moves a sprite slowly across the screen.

Figure 10-1: This is not a pretty program, but it sure was easy to make.

That's no big deal; you've been doing that for half of this book. What makes this interesting is the code. Take a look, and you'll see what I mean:

```
""" simpleGe.py
    example of simplest possible
    game engine program
"""

import pygame, gameEngine

game = gameEngine.Scene()
game.start()
```

Yes, that's it. That's all there is to it. After the `import` statements, I have a working pygame animation in only two lines of code. That's pretty phenomenal! Here's what you do:

1. Import the **pygame** and **gameEngine** modules.

The gameEngine module is the powerhouse of this chapter.

```
import pygame, gameEngine
```

2. Create a **gameEngine.Scene** object.

The gameEngine module has a special class called the Scene class. This class encapsulates the entire IDEA/ALTER mechanism into a fancy object that just knows what to do. I made an instance of the Scene class called game.

```
game = gameEngine.Scene()
```

3. Start the **Scene**.

Creating the scene instance handles all the basic initialization of a typical pygame program (essentially the IDEA part). The start() method begins the main loop (the ALTER part).

```
game.start()
```

4. The rest is automatic.

The default Scene object has a sprite already built in, so you can see it's working. Amazingly, the custom sprite seems to have wrapping behavior built in. When it leaves the edge of the screen, it automatically wraps around the screen.

 Information Kiosk

The easiest way to use the gameEngine is to install it using the installation program on the Web site. Check Appendix C for more details also.

Adding a SuperSprite

The Scene class simplifies pygame development by hiding many details, but it's not the only new thing in the gameEngine module. The module features an improved sprite called the SuperSprite, which can do all kinds of interesting things. Figure 10-2 shows superSprite.py, which introduces the new type of sprite.

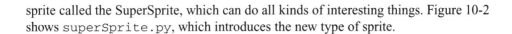

Figure 10-2: The sprite has a custom image with interesting built-in behavior.

The superSprite.py program features a sprite named ship. The sprite does some things you've seen before:

- **It can move in an arbitrary direction.** For this example, I set the direction to 135 degrees.

- **It can move at an arbitrary speed.** I set the speed at 5 pixels per frame.

- **It "knows" how to handle screen boundaries.** I told the sprite to bounce off screen boundaries rather than using the default wrapping behavior.

None of those things are earth-shattering; you've seen them all done throughout the book. What's interesting is how simple the code is:

```
""" superSprite.py
    show a very basic form of supersprite
"""

import pygame, gameEngine

def main():
    game = gameEngine.Scene()
    ship = gameEngine.SuperSprite(game)

    #customize the ship sprite
    ship.setImage("ship.gif")
```

```
ship.setAngle(135)
ship.setSpeed(5)
ship.setBoundAction(ship.BOUNCE)

#customize the scene
game.setCaption("Introducing Super Sprite!")
game.background.fill((0x33, 0x33, 0x99))
game.sprites = [ship]

#let 'er rip!
game.start()

if __name__ == "__main__":
    main()
```

The code is so short because it takes advantage of the gameEngine class to handle all the details. The main code is focused on how to make the specific behavior needed for this game. Here's what you do:

1. Import **pygame** and **gameEngine**.

Most of the real work is still being done through pygame, but just as pygame provides a layer of abstraction to the underlying SDL graphics library, gameEngine adds a layer of abstraction to pygame, making it easier to use.

```
import pygame, gameEngine
```

2. Create instances of the **Scene** and **SuperSprite** classes.

The two primary classes in the gameEngine module are Scene and SuperSprite. The Scene class handles the big-picture game-management duties, and SuperSprite is a souped-up Sprite class.

```
game = gameEngine.Scene()
ship = gameEngine.SuperSprite(game)
```

The SuperSprite class requires a scene instance as its one parameter. The sprite uses this instance to access details of the scene it belongs to, primarily the screen size for boundary checking.

3. Give the ship a custom graphic.

The SuperSprite class has some convenient methods and attributes you can access. The setImage() method allows you to easily apply any image to the sprite. The setImage() method takes care of storing the image to a master image, converting it to pygame's preferred image format, and storing it for use with rotations — all in one line:

```
ship.setImage("ship.gif")
```

4. Set the ship's angle and speed.

The setAngle() method allows you to determine the sprite's angle. This changes both the rotation of the ship's visual orientation on the screen (which is stored as `rotation`) and the `dir` attribute (which determines the direction of travel). The `setSpeed()` method is used along with `setAngle()` (in the `__calcVector()` method) to determine the sprite's `dx` and `dy` attributes automatically. You don't have to do a thing, because the conversion is done quietly under the hood.

```
ship.setAngle(135)
ship.setSpeed(5)
```

5. **Tell the ship how to handle screen boundaries.**

`SuperSprite` objects can react to screen boundaries in four different ways, all indicated by constants built into the `SuperSprite` class. The following constants describe what happens when a sprite encounters a screen boundary:

◎ WRAP

◎ BOUNCE

◎ STOP

◎ CONTINUE

All you have to do is send the appropriate parameter to the `setBoundAction()` method. The `SuperSprite` object does the rest for you.

```
ship.setBoundAction(ship.BOUNCE)
```

6. **Initialize the game object.**

The `game` instance of the `Scene` class has a few tricks up its sleeve as well. You can use the `setCaption()` method to set its caption. The scene's background object is an attribute, so you can use pygame's `fill()` method to set it to whatever color you like, or blit a background image onto it.

```
#customize the scene
game.setCaption("Introducing Super Sprite!")
game.background.fill((0x33, 0x33, 0x99))
```

7. **Assign sprites to the sprite group.**

Like most pygame loops, the `game` object relies on a group to manage the sprites. You can easily attach sprite objects (including `SuperSprites`) to the main sprite group by assigning them to the `sprites` attribute. This attribute is a list (thus the square brackets), but the list can have any number of elements in it. All sprites in `game.sprites` will be added to the main sprite group, which is automatically cleared, updated, and drawn at the appropriate points in the animation cycle.

```
game.sprites = [ship]
```

8. **Start the engine.**

The `game.start()` method begins the main loop, and the program begins chugging along. Of course, there's a `stop()` method too, so you can tell the `game` instance to stop whenever you want.

```
game.start()
```

Step Into the Real World

Since `gameEngine` is so much easier to use than straight pygame, you might wonder why the author of pygame (Pete Shinners) didn't just build in a class as simple to use as `gameEngine`. He certainly could have, but by leaving pygame at a relatively low level, he freed programmers to work directly in pygame when they want, and build their own abstraction layers — as I have done with `gameEngine`. `gameEngine` doesn't eliminate the need to use pygame directly. It just simplifies the more tedious, repetitive tasks such as building standard sprites and game loops. Besides, not everyone agrees on what a good extraction is, so it's good to be able to build your own.

Adding events to the SuperSprite

Just as with the pygame `Sprite` class, you can extend the `SuperSprite` class to make your own classes. The `carGE.py` program in Figure 10-3 creates a car that responds to keyboard commands, moving around on the screen according to input from the arrow keys.

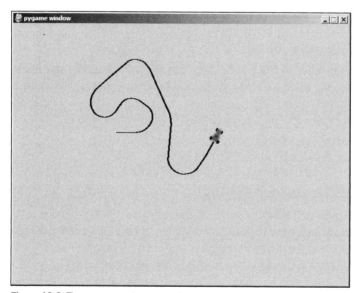

Figure 10-3: The car responds to arrow keys to turn, speed up, and slow down.

Making a car that can respond to keyboard input is nothing new, but it's much easier to make this sort of sprite if you base it on the `gameEngine.SuperSprite` class than if you base it on the regular `pygame.Sprite` class. Here's what that streamlined approach looks like:

```
""" carGE.py
    extend SuperSprite to add keyboard input
"""

import pygame, gameEngine

class Car(gameEngine.SuperSprite):
    def __init__(self, scene):
        gameEngine.SuperSprite.__init__(self, scene)
        self.setImage("car.gif")

    def checkEvents(self):
        keys = pygame.key.get_pressed()
        if keys[pygame.K_LEFT]:
            self.turnBy(5)
        if keys[pygame.K_RIGHT]:
            self.turnBy(-5)
        if keys[pygame.K_UP]:
            self.speedUp(.2)
        if keys[pygame.K_DOWN]:
            self.speedUp(-.2)

def main():
    game = gameEngine.Scene()
    game.background.fill((0xCC, 0xCC, 0xCC))

    car = Car(game)
    game.sprites = [car]

    game.start()

if __name__ == "__main__":
    main()
```

This program creates a new class based on the gameEngine.SuperSprite class. The Car class inherits all the nifty features of SuperSprite, and has an easy mechanism to add event handling. Here's what you do along the way:

1. First you create a subclass of SuperSprite.

You can extend any class, even those that are already extensions of other classes. By extending SuperSprite, your new Car class has everything that SuperSprite has. Because it's a new class, you can add a few more features that make the new class act exactly like you want.

```
class Car(gameEngine.SuperSprite):
```

2. Initialize the Car class.

The init() method begins by calling SuperSprite's __init__() method. This is important because SuperSprite takes care of several details for you, including setting up a bunch of useful attributes. After calling SuperSprite.init(), add any special initializations you need for the car. In this case, I simply change the image to be a basic car image:

```
def __init__(self, scene):
    gameEngine.SuperSprite.__init__(self, scene)
    self.setImage("car.gif")
```

3. Add an event-handling routine.

The SuperSprite class automatically calls a special method called checkEvents() at the beginning of each frame. Create a SuperSprite. checkEvents() method in the Car class, and all the code in this method will be evaluated once per frame.

```
def checkEvents(self):
```

 Information Kiosk

I intended checkEvents() to be for event-handling code (reading mouse, keyboard, or joystick input), but you can put any code you want in here. Any code in this event will run at the beginning of the update() method (before the sprite is moved).

4. Check the keyboard.

The Car class uses a basic speed and direction mechanism, so I'll check the keyboard with the pygame.key.get_pressed() technique.

```
keys = pygame.key.get_pressed()
```

5. Turn the sprite if left or right arrows are pressed.

The left and right arrows are used to turn the car. All the details of turning the sprite are hidden in SuperSprite.turnBy(), so I just give it a turn amount (in degrees) and all the calculations are done for me automatically:

```
if keys[pygame.K_LEFT]:
    self.turnBy(5)
if keys[pygame.K_RIGHT]:
    self.turnBy(-5)
```

Information Kiosk

The turnBy() method turns both the sprite's rotation (visual orientation) and direction (direction of travel if speed is not 0). The rotateBy() method allows you to rotate the sprite without effecting its direction of travel (as you do in space games).

6. Change the speed if the user presses up or down arrows.

The up and down arrows are used to speed up — or slow down — the car. SuperSprite instances have a built-in maximum speed of 10 pixels per frame (ppf) and a minimum of -3 pixels per frame, and the `car` instance inherits these attributes. You can set new speed limits By using the `SuperSprite` class's `speedUp()` method, but I'll use the default values for this simple example.

```
if keys[pygame.K_UP]:
    self.speedUp(.2)
if keys[pygame.K_DOWN]:
    self.speedUp(-.2)
```

7. Initialize the game.

The main loop begins by setting up a `scene` instance and giving it an appropriate background color.

```
def main():
    game = gameEngine.Scene()
    game.background.fill((0xCC, 0xCC, 0xCC))
```

8. Create a car sprite.

Make an instance of the `Car` class you just created, and add it to the game's sprite group.

```
car = Car(game)
game.sprites = [car]
```

9. Start the game.

The game's `start()` method puts it all in motion.

```
game.start()
```

Extending the Scene class

The other primary class in `gameEngine` is the `Scene` class. You can also extend the `Scene` class to add event-handling behavior. The `spaceGE.py` program in Figure 10-4 illustrates how to add event handling in a customized `Scene` object. It also shows how to implement space-style motion in the game engine.

If you don't need any major changes in the `SuperSprite` class, you can extend `Scene` instead and add event handling to it — like this:

```
""" spaceGE.py
    extend the Scene class for input
    and demonstrate space-style motion
"""

import pygame, gameEngine

class Game(gameEngine.Scene):
    def __init__(self):
        gameEngine.Scene.__init__(self)
        self.setCaption("Space-style Motion in GameEngine")
        self.ship = gameEngine.SuperSprite(self)
```

```
            self.ship.setImage("ship.gif")
            self.sprites = [self.ship]


    def update(self):
        #change rotation to change orientation of ship
        #but not direction of motion

        keys = pygame.key.get_pressed()

        if keys[pygame.K_RIGHT]:
            self.ship.rotateBy(-5)

        if keys[pygame.K_LEFT]:
            self.ship.rotateBy(5)

        if keys[pygame.K_UP]:
            #add a force vector to the ship in the
            #direction it's currently pointing
            self.ship.addForce(.2, self.ship.rotation)

def main():
    game = Game()
    game.start()

if __name__ == "__main__":
    main()
```

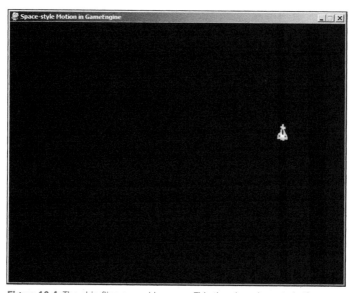

Figure 10-4: The ship flies around in space. This time I read events in the Scene class.

It's pretty easy to make a game based on an extension of the Scene class, as you can see in these steps:

1. Create a new class based on gameEngine.Scene.

Extend the Scene class to make a new class based on its characteristics:

```
class Game(gameEngine.Scene):
```

2. Run the Scene class's __init__() method.

As is usual in an extended class, begin by calling the parent class's constructor. Set the caption and background if you want. (I want a black background — which is the default — so I don't specify a background fill.)

```
def __init__(self):
    gameEngine.Scene.__init__(self)
    self.setCaption("Space-style Motion in GameEngine")
```

3. Add a ship sprite.

In this program, the ship sprite will be an instance of the standard gameEngine.SuperSprite() class. Set its image attribute, and assign it to the Scene objects's sprite list.

```
self.ship = gameEngine.SuperSprite(self)
self.ship.setImage("ship.gif")
self.sprites = [self.ship]
```

> **ℹ Information Kiosk**
>
> Notice that I made the ship as an attribute of the Scene object. Although it's not completely necessary, I find it handy because it makes it possible to refer to every sprite from every other sprite through the scene. Get in the habit now, and it will pay dividends when you create games with hundreds of sprites in them.

4. Add an update() method.

The gameEngine.Scene class has an update() method that's called during each frame. This method (just like update() in the pygame.Sprite class) is automatically called once per frame. If you're creating a subclass of gameEngine.Scene, build an update() method to handle any code you want to perform during each frame.

```
def update(self):
    #change rotation to change orientation of ship
    #but not direction of motion
```

5. Turn right or left.

The turnBy() method demonstrated in carGE.py changes both the rotation and direction of travel at the same time. If you want to rotate a sprite without changing its motion vector, use the SuperSprite class's rotateBy() method instead.

```
keys = pygame.key.get_pressed()

if keys[pygame.K_RIGHT]:
    self.ship.rotateBy(-5)

if keys[pygame.K_LEFT]:
    self.ship.rotateBy(5)
```

Like turnBy() the rotateBy() method automatically checks to ensure the rotation angle stays within legal limits (0 to 360 degrees).

6. Apply a force vector.

When the user presses the up arrow key, the spacecraft applies a motion vector in the direction of thrust. I'm assuming normal rockets (rather than retro-rockets pointing backward) so I'll add a force in the sprite's current rotation direction.

```
if keys[pygame.K_UP]:
    #add a force vector to the ship in the
    #direction it's currently pointing
    self.ship.addForce(.2, self.ship.rotation)
```

The SuperSprite class's addForce() method accepts an amount and an angle, calculates dx and dy values for the force vector, adds these to the sprite's current dx and dy values, and modifies the ship's speed and direction accordingly.

7. Create an instance of the customized Scene class.

Now that you've made a customized class based on the Scene class, make an instance and start it up to begin your game:

```
def main():
    game = Game()
    game.start()
```

Step Into the Real World

You might wonder why I have a custom method that happens in each frame built into the Scene object, when exactly the same feature is built into SuperSprite. The reason is flexibility. Sometimes I want to handle events inside the sprite, and sometimes I want to do it at the scene level. Many games will have some event handling performed at each level. For example, the Lunar Lander game presented near the end of this chapter has keyboard-checking embedded into the lander object, but the scene checks for collisions between the lander and the platform.

Exploring graphical widgets

Most high-end programming environments include some kind of support for graphical interface tools like labels, buttons, and scrollbars. These toolkits are sometimes called *graphical user interface* (GUI) tools, and the individual elements are sometimes called *widgets*. Python supports several powerful and popular GUI toolkits, including Tk and wxWidgets. Unfortunately, these tool kits don't work well with pygame. It would be nice to have some basic graphical tools that fit well within the pygame interface. I've been using a few of these objects throughout the book, so I included them in the gameEngine framework. Figure 10-5 shows the major GUI controls included in gameEngine in a program called GUIdemoGE.py.

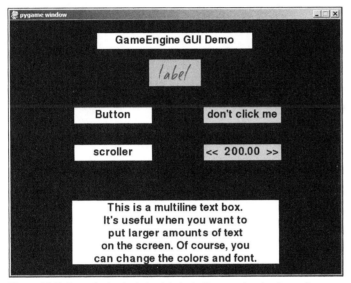

Figure 10-5: GameEngine includes labels, buttons, and a simple scroller.

Notice that the original version of this program has a yellow background. The gameEngine module has the following widgets:

- **Label class.** A label is a simple sprite designed to display text. It has a text attribute that determines what text will be displayed. The fgColor and bgColor attributes determine the label's color scheme. Its position and size are determined by appropriately named attributes. The label's font attribute can be modified to use any typeface or font size.

- **Button class.** A button is a special form of label. It is a subclass of the Label class, so it has all of Label's characteristics. In addition, it has two special Boolean attributes. active is True if the mouse pointer is currently over the button, and clicked is True when the mouse button is pressed and released with the pointer over the on-screen button.

If you click the button in GUIdemo.py, the associated label will change captions. Figure 10-6 shows what happens after the user has clicked the (irresistible) button.

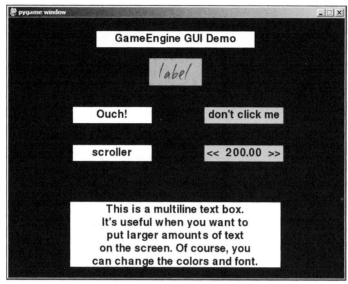

Figure 10-6: If you want to be SURE that your users click the button, tell them not to.

Notice that the background of the entire program has turned to black.

Scroller. A *scroller* is a simpler form of scroll bar. It's useful for getting numeric information from the user in a graphical form. My Scroller class is a subclass of my Button class. It has a numeric value that is always displayed. If the scroller is clicked anywhere left of its center point, the number decrements; if the right side of the scroller is clicked, the number increments. Its attributes allow you to set the minimum and maximum values, read or set the current value, and set the increment amount (how much the value will change when you click the scroller). In GUIdemoGE.py, the value displayed in the scroller also controls the position of one of the labels. Figure 10-7 shows what happens when I change the scroller value.

MultiLine Text. The basic Label class is fine, but it isn't really useful for large amounts of text, because it only allows one line at a time. If you want to allow multiple lines of text, you need to use the MultiLabel class. It has all the typical GUI attributes, but rather than a text attribute, it has textLines, which is a list of strings. The MultiLabel class does its best to put all the text inside the designated size, but you'll probably have to mess with the size and font to get exactly the look you're expecting.

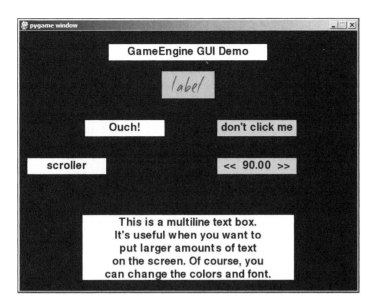

Figure 10-7: I can use scrollers to let the user change any numeric data, including the position of a label.

Using the widgets

The widgets are all extensions of the ordinary `pygame.Sprite` class, so they're easy to integrate into your games. As far as your program is concerned, widgets are simply sprites. The following sections show how to put the `GUIdemoGE.py` program together.

Building a scene

You can use widgets in any pygame program, but since they're in the `gameEngine` module, you might as well start by extending the `Scene` object for simplicity:

```
class Game(gameEngine.Scene):
    def __init__(self):
        gameEngine.Scene.__init__(self)
        #initialize background to yellow
        self.background.fill((0xff, 0xff, 0x00))

        self.addLabels()
        self.addButton()
        self.addScroller()
        self.addMultiLabel()

        self.sprites = [self.lblTitle, self.label,
                        self.lblButton, self.button,
                        self.lblScroller, self.scroller,
                        self.multi]
```

Step Into the Real World

Most mouse actions don't really happen when you click the mouse! Generally the program waits to do anything until the user releases the mouse. This is done for two main reasons. First, if the user clicks on a button but then decides not to commit, she can move off the button before releasing the mouse — in which case, the action doesn't happen. From a more practical standpoint, the mouse button could be held down for hundreds of frames at a time. Button clicks are about a specific instance of time. The mouse button is only released once per click, so it's easier to code for a mouse button being *lifted* than released.

The GUIdemoGE.py program is based on a game instance. The Game class is a subclass of gameEngine.Scene. The Game class's __init__() method provides insight into the overall structure of the program.

- **You can build the components.** While the components are not difficult to create, they do have a number of parameters and options, so I broke the various types of widgets into groups, and created each group in its own method. I explain each of these methods in detail in the following sections:

  ```
  self.addLabels()
  self.addButton()
  self.addScroller()
  self.addMultiLabel()
  ```

- **You can add widgets to the sprites list.** Since the widgets are essentially sprites, simply add them to the sprites list, and they will be correctly placed and updated on the screen. (The actual widgets are created in the various methods you've already created.)

Making labels

Labels are pretty basic, but they form the foundation for all the other GUI widgets. Build them by making instances of the gameEngine.Label class and then modifying their attributes as needed:

```
def addLabels(self):
    self.lblTitle = gameEngine.Label()
    self.lblTitle.text = "GameEngine GUI Demos"
    self.lblTitle.center = (320, 40)
    self.lblTitle.size = (300, 30)

    self.label = gameEngine.Label()
    self.label.font = pygame.font.Font
("goodfoot.ttf", 40)
```

```
self.label.text = "Label"
self.label.fgColor = (0xCC, 0x00, 0x00)
self.label.bgColor = (0xCC, 0xCC, 0x00)
self.label.center = (320, 100)
self.label.size = (100, 50)
```

Here's how you build the labels:

1. **Build the title label.**

The main label is an instance of the `gameEngine.Label` class.

```
self.lblTitle = gameEngine.Label()
```

2. **Apply text to the label.**

Use the `text` attribute to determine what the label says:

```
self.lblTitle.text = "GameEngine GUI Demo"
```

3. **Determine the label's position.**

The `center` attribute is used to determine the label's position on the screen.

```
self.lblTitle.center = (320, 40)
```

4. **Set the label's size.**

Labels have a default size of 100 pixels wide by 30 pixels tall. If that is not large enough, set the size parameter to something more appropriate.

```
self.lblTitle.size = (300, 30)
```

5. **Set the label's font.**

The second label (the one called simply "label") has a custom font. (Use the font tricks described in Chapter 4 to build a font for the label.)

```
self.label.font = pygame.font.Font("goodfoot.ttf",    ↩
40)
```

6. **Set the label's colors.**

You can use `fgColor` and `bgColor` to determine the label's color scheme. This and the `font` attribute are great ways to dress up otherwise-boring labels.

```
self.label.fgColor = (0xCC, 0x00, 0x00)
self.label.bgColor = (0xCC, 0xCC, 0x00)
```

Building the button

The button is also easy to create. I built it and an associated label in the `addButton()` method:

```
def addButton(self):
    self.lblButton = gameEngine.Label()
    self.lblButton.center = (200, 180)
```

```
        self.lblButton.text = "Button"

        self.button = gameEngine.Button()
        self.button.center = (450, 180)
        self.button.text = "don't click me"
```

Buttons have all the same attributes as text, so they can be set up in exactly the same way. You can modify the text, font, center, fgColor, and bgColor attributes. Buttons have a default background color different from that of labels, but of course you can change this. The most important aspect of buttons is the clicked attribute, which only makes sense in the context of event handling.

 Transfer

Look ahead to the section on responding to events in game to see how I use the button's clicked attribute.

Adding a scroller

The scroller is added to the program like any other widget. This code does the job:

```
def addScroller(self):
    self.lblScroller = gameEngine.Label()
    self.lblScroller.text = "scroller"
    self.lblScroller.center = (200, 250)

    self.scroller = gameEngine.Scroller()
    self.scroller.center = (450, 250)
    self.scroller.minValue = 0
    self.scroller.maxValue = 250
    self.scroller.value = 200
    self.scroller.increment = 5
```

The scroller is paired with a label. Since the scroller is based on the Label class, it has all the same basic attributes. However, scrollers are designed to work with numeric values rather than text, so the scroller's text value is calculated from a numeric attribute called value. The scroller has a few extra attributes that allow you to control its behavior better:

- **You can set minValue and maxValue.** These control the scroller's range of possible values. If you're using the scroller to create color values, for example, you'd use 0 for minValue and 255 for maxValue.

- **You can set the default value.** The value attribute determines the current value of the scroller. The scroller's text is constantly created from this attribute.

- **You can set the increment.** This attribute determines how much the value will change each time the user holds the mouse down over the scroller. If you specify a floating-point increment, the scroller will create floating-point values.

Making a MultiLabel

The `MultiLabel` class is an easy tool to use, but it usually requires some minor tweaking. It's similar to `gameEngine.Label`, so it has all the attributes you've grown to know and love. The one original attribute is `textLines`. This attribute replaces `text`, and requires a list of strings:

```
def addMultiLabel(self):
    self.multi = gameEngine.MultiLabel()
    self.multi.textLines = [
        "This is a multiline text box.",
        "It's useful when you want to",
        "put larger amounts of text",
        "on the screen. Of course, you",
        "can change the colors and font."
        ]
    self.multi.size = (400, 120)
    self.multi.center = (320, 400)
```

You'll generally have to adjust the size and font to make sure everything shows up just the way you want in your `MultiLabel` instance.

Responding to events in game

The `Game` class has an `update()` method that's called once each frame. This is an ideal place to put code that responds to GUI input:

```
def update(self):
    if self.button.clicked:
        self.lblButton.text = "Ouch!"

    self.lblScroller.center = (self.scroller.value, 250)
```

Use this code to check for changes in GUI elements, as follows:

1. Check to see whether the button has been clicked.

Buttons have two Boolean attributes. `active` is `True` when the mouse is currently being pressed over the button. (This attribute isn't used all that often on its own. It's used to help set up the `clicked` attribute, and in the `Scroller` class.) The `clicked` attribute contains the value `True` when the user has pressed the mouse and released it over the object.

```
        if self.button.clicked:
```

2. If the button was pressed, change something.

Just for the sake of example, I change the caption in `lblButton`. Often your buttons will do something a bit more momentous — such as letting the user begin the program or move to another part of the game.

```
            self.lblButton.text = "Ouch!"
            self.background.fill((0x00, 0x00, 0x00))
            self.screen.blit(self.background, (0, 0))
```

3. Respond to the scroller's value.

The scroller generates a numeric value. Simply map that value to some numeric attribute to see it in action. As a silly example, I copy the scroller's `value` attribute to the `lblScroller`'s x attribute. When the user changes the scroller's value, the `update()` method immediately modifies the position of the label.

Transfer

Take a look at the `adventure.py` program later in this chapter to see an example using most of the graphical widgets.

Examining the gameEngine Module

The `gameEngine` code might seem daunting from the outside, but it's really nothing new. Almost everything in the module is stuff you've done before in this book. The only thing that's really new is the way it's been put together in one comprehensive package. In this section, I take you through the module code and show you what's inside. Once you know how the code is written, you can use it to your advantage. Also, you can add your own improvements!

Information Kiosk

As always, be sure to look at the real file for this project. It loses something when it's broken up and transferred to the written page. Also, I took out a few non-essential elements (mainly comments that are repeated in the book's text here) to save space. I'm also focusing more on the big picture than details in this description. Almost all the code is described in much more detail earlier in the book.

Initializing the engine

The game engine is written as a module. It's intended to provide classes that can either be directly instantiated (that is, used as-is) or extended to generate custom objects:

```
""" gameEngine.py
    high-level tools to simplify pygame programming
    for Game Programming - The L-Line
    by Andy Harris, 2006
"""

import pygame, math
pygame.init()
```

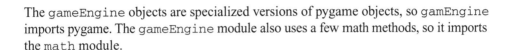

The gameEngine objects are specialized versions of pygame objects, so gamEngine imports pygame. The gameEngine module also uses a few math methods, so it imports the math module.

Building the SuperSprite

The most interesting class in gameEngine is the SuperSprite. This class is an extension of the basic pygame Sprite class. It incorporates a number of new attributes and methods that make it easier to use as a general-purpose sprite object.

```
class SuperSprite(pygame.sprite.Sprite):
    """ An enhanced Sprite class
        expects a gameEngine.Scene class as its one
        parameter
        Use attributes to change image, direction, speed
        Will automatically travel in direction and speed
        indicated
        Automatically rotates to point in indicated
        direction
        Five kinds of boundary collision
    """
```

It's always important to document your code, but it's even more important when you're building code you intend to reuse. Make sure you clearly indicate what each object does, what each method does, and what parameters and attributes can be changed. This information will be extremely useful to the programmer using the object (whether that programmer is you or somebody else).

Initializing SuperSprite

The SuperSprite __init__() method does the same job as most sprite initializing code. It accepts parameters, sets up class-level constants, and initializes the most important attributes of the class.

```
    def __init__(self, scene):
        pygame.sprite.Sprite.__init__(self)
        self.scene = scene
        self.screen = scene.screen

        #create constants
        self.WRAP = 0
        self.BOUNCE = 1
        self.STOP = 2
        self.HIDE = 3
        self.CONTINUE = 4

        #create a default text image as a placeholder
        #This will usually be changed by a setImage call
```

```
self.font = pygame.font.SysFont(None, 30)
self.imageMaster = self.font.render(">sprite>",
    True, (0, 0,0), (0xFF, 0xFF, 0xFF))
self.image = self.imageMaster
self.rect = self.image.get_rect()

#create attributes
#most will be changed through method calls
self.x = 200
self.y = 200
self.dx = 0
self.dy = 0
self.dir = 0
self.rotation = 0
self.speed = 0
self.maxSpeed = 10
self.minSpeed = -3
self.boundAction = self.WRAP
self.pressed = False
self.oldCenter = (100, 100)
```

The __init__() method helps you do a few important things such as the following:

- **Import the scene instance.** Every gameEngine.SuperSprite instance must be passed the name of a gameEngine.Scene instance to which it belongs. This allows the SuperSprite to have access to all the Scene object's attributes. This is important for boundary checking. It also allows (potentially) every sprite in the game to have access to every other sprite, if you set up all sprites as attributes of the Scene object.

- **Set up constants.** The only constants the SuperSprite needs are the various boundary behaviors.

- **Set up standard attributes.** The superSprite has a number of attributes which control its basic functioning. The dx, dy, x, y, and speed attributes are used in the same way you've used them throughout the book.

- **Separate dir and rotation attributes.** To make a sprite more flexible, I've separated the sprite's direction data into two separate variables. rotation refers to the sprite's visual orientation on the screen. The dir attribute refers to the sprite's direction of travel. Ordinarily, these two attributes have the same value, but a vehicle can travel in a direction different from the one it's pointed in.

- **Specify speed boundaries.** The SuperSprite has built-in attributes for setting the sprite's minimum (minSpeed) and maximum speed (maxSpeed).

- **Store the oldCenter attribute.** This attribute is used in the drawTrace() method to draw a line on the background indicating the position of the sprite.

- **Specify boundary behavior.** The SuperSprite has five kinds of boundary-checking built in. The boundActinon attribute indicates which of those behaviors will be used. (Of course, you can also generate your own boundary-checking scheme if you want.) The value of boundAction should normally be one of the boundary behavior constants.

- **Initialize `self.pressed` to `False`.** This attribute is used to determine whether the user is currently clicking the sprite.

Controlling overall flow with update()

The update() method controls the behavior of the sprite under normal conditions. If you set the sprite's speed and dir attributes (directly or through methods), the sprite will travel in the indicated direction automatically until it reaches a screen boundary — after which the sprite will act according to the current setting of boundAction. Here's what that looks like:

```
def update(self):
    self.oldCenter = self.rect.center
    self.checkEvents()
    self.__rotate()
    self.__calcVector()
    self.__calcPosition()
    self.__checkBounds()
    self.rect.center = (self.x, self.y)
```

You generally won't change the update() method in your sprites that are based on SuperSprite, because it does most everything that's needed. If you need to change a sprite's behavior, overwrite checkEvents() rather than update(), Also, checkEvents() will run before most of the other frame code, so it's ideal for adding event handling at the sprite level. The one other interesting thing in update() is storing the self.oldCenter attribute. This is used for the drawTrace() method, so it can draw a line from the sprite's current center to the next event.

Setting up an event handler with checkEvents()

The checkEvents() method is interesting — because it doesn't do anything! The pass command tells Python that no action should happen here. The checkEvents() method doesn't do anything in an ordinary SuperSprite instance. If you make a new class based on SuperSprite, that class will call checkEvents() automatically during every frame. If your new class overrides checkEvents(), the new code automatically runs at the start of update() without requiring any extra work from you:

```
def checkEvents(self):
    """ overwrite this method to add your own event ↩
code """
    pass
```

Step Into the Real World

Having an empty method like `checkEvents()` may seem strange to you, but you've actually been taking advantage of a similar mechanism since your first pygame programs. The built-in `pygame.sprite.Sprite` class has a method called `update()` that does nothing. When you run the sprite group's `update()` method, this calls the `update()` methods of each sprite in the group. If you added a custom `update()` method to your sprites, it automatically runs at the appropriate time without requiring any more effort from you.

The main purpose of `checkEvents()` is to provide a placeholder for you to add your own event-handling code when you subclass `SuperSprite`. Look back at the `carGE.py` code earlier in this chapter to see how to use `checkEvents()`.

Changing visual orientation with the __rotate() method

The `__rotate()` method changes the visual orientation of the sprite image, and looks like this:

```
def __rotate(self):
    """ change visual orientation based on
        rotation attribute.
        automatically called in update().
        change rotation attribute directly or with
        rotateBy(), setAngle() methods
    """
    oldCenter = self.rect.center
    self.image = pygame.transform.rotate(self.imageMaster, self.rotation)
    self.rect = self.image.get_rect()
    self.rect.center = oldCenter
```

The `__rotate()` method is not meant to be called directly. It is called automatically by `update()` when needed. The two underscores in front of the method indicate that `__rotate()` is a *private* method. Private methods can be called from inside the class definition, but not by other code. Note that you *don't* use `__rotate()` to change the sprite's angle. The `__rotate()` method is used by `update()` to rotate the visual image only. There are several other methods available to handle rotating the image.

Watch Your Step

Python doesn't actually support *truly* private methods. The technique I'm showing is a workaround, and it's well known to have some problems. Don't use private methods unless you have a good reason. Since I have some methods that I don't want anyone to use from outside the class definition, I'll make them private in this situation.

Also, even though the `__init__()` method begins with two underscores, it is not a private method. Python uses leading and trailing underscores to indicate certain other special methods and attributes, too.

Vector Projection with __calcVector()

The __calcVector() method is another private method called by the update() function. It automatically calculates the dx and dy attributes based on the speed and direction.

```
def __calcVector(self):
    """ calculates dx and dy based on speed, dir
        automatically called in update()
    """
    theta = self.dir / 180.0 * math.pi
    self.dx = math.cos(theta) * self.speed
    self.dy = math.sin(theta) * self.speed
    self.dy *= -1
```

Calculating the sprite's position with __calcPosition()

The __calcPosition() method is nothing new. It's just like the one in Chapter 9.

```
def __calcPosition(self):
    """ calculates the sprites position adding
        dx and dy to x and y.
        automatically called in update()
    """
    self.x += self.dx
    self.y += self.dy
```

Transfer

The __rotate, __calcVector(), and __calcPosition() methods are identical to similar methods described in Chapter 9. If you're not sure how they work, please refer to that chapter for a complete discussion.

Building multiple boundary-checks in checkBounds()

The checkBounds() method combines all the boundary-checking behavior shown throughout the book into one powerful method. This method is the most involved method in SuperSprite, but it isn't overly complex. Here's what you do, step by step:

1. **Document the method.**

The documentation is especially important in this method, because the behavior of the method is dependant on a particular attribute. The programmer needs to understand this relationship to use the method correctly.

```
def checkBounds(self):
    """ checks boundary and acts based on
        self.BoundAction.
        WRAP: wrap around screen (default)
        BOUNCE: bounce off screen
```

```
STOP: stop at edge of screen
CONTINUE: keep going at present course
and speed
automatically called by update() but can
be overwritten (not private)
"""
```

Information Kiosk

Notice that `checkBounds()` is not a private method (it doesn't begin with underscores). That's because it's conceivable that you would have a sprite that needs specialized boundary checking. In such a case, you can overwrite `checkBounds()`. You shouldn't overwrite a private method, so I made it public.

2. **Build variables to hold screen parameters.**

The screen width and height are a little awkward to extract, and I need them a lot, so I make variables to simplify the code:

```
scrWidth = self.screen.get_width()
scrHeight = self.screen.get_height()
```

3. **Create Booleans to clarify various off-screen situations.**

Several variables will be used to indicate the sprite's position. Begin by setting all the variables to `False`.

```
#create variables to simplify checking
offRight = offLeft = offTop = False
offBottom = offScreen = False
```

Information Kiosk

Every once in a while, you want to set several variables to the same value. The syntax I use here is perfect to use in this situation. I still broke the code into two lines to make it easier to read.

4. **Populate the situation variables by performing standard boundary checks.**

```
if self.x > scrWidth:
    offRight = True
if self.x < 0:
    offLeft = True
if self.y > scrHeight:
    offBottom = True
if self.y < 0:
    offTop = True

if offRight or offLeft or offTop or offBottom:
    offScreen = True
```

5. Handle wrapping.

If the programmer wants the sprite to wrap around the screen, s/he has indicated so by setting the boundAction attribute to self.WRAP. If this is the case, wrap the sprite as needed. Note how easy it is to understand the code with the Boolean variables in place:

```
if self.boundAction == self.WRAP:
    if offRight:
        self.x = 0
    if offLeft:
        self.x = scrWidth
    if offBottom:
        self.y = 0
    if offTop:
        self.y = scrHeight
```

6. Handle bouncing.

If boundAction is self.BOUNCE, the programmer wants the sprite to bounce off the screen. Reverse the sprite's dx when it hits a horizontal wall, and reverse dy when it hits a vertical wall.

```
elif self.boundAction == self.BOUNCE:
    if offLeft or offRight:
        self.dx *= -1
    if offTop or offBottom:
        self.dy *= -1

    self.updateVector()
    self.rotation = self.dir
```

Watch Your Step

Whenever you directly change the value of dx or dy in SuperSprite (as I did in this method,) be sure to call the updateVector() method to copy that change over to the sprite's speed and dir attributes.

7. Handle stopping.

If the boundAction attribute is set to STOP, set the sprite's speed to 0 as soon as it encounters any screen boundary.

```
elif self.boundAction == self.STOP:
    if offScreen:
        self.speed = 0
```

8. Hide the sprite when needed.

Certain sprites (especially bullets) should move offstage and stop when they reach the edge of the screen. The code that handles the HIDE attribute takes care of this behavior:

```
elif self.boundAction == self.HIDE:
    if offScreen:
        self.speed = 0
        self.setPosition((-1000, -1000))
```

9. **Allow sprite to continue on indefinitely.**

Some of your sprites should keep going off the screen. If you do this, you should either have some mechanism for eventually returning the sprite (such as orbital physics) or some mechanism for telling the user where the sprite is and where it's heading (as in an air-traffic-control simulation).

```
elif self.boundAction == self.CONTINUE:
    pass
```

10. **Treat any other value of boundAction as a CONTINUE.**

Handle any unforeseen events, just in case:

```
else:
    # assume it's CONTINUE - keep going forever
    pass
```

Setting the sprite's speed attribute in setSpeed()

The setSpeed() method provides an easy way to set the object's speed directly to whatever value you want. setSpeed() does *not* check for maximum or minimum speed.

```
def setSpeed(self, speed):
    """ immediately sets the objects speed to the
        given value.
    """
    self.speed = speed
```

Changing sprite speed with speedUp()

The speedup() method is the primary mechanism for changing, the sprite's speed. Use a positive value to speed the sprite up, and a negative value to slow it down. The speedup() method takes into account the minSpeed and maxSpeed parameters.

```
def speedUp(self, amount):
    """ changes speed by the given amount
        Use a negative value to slow down
    """
    self.speed += amount
    if self.speed < self.minSpeed:
        self.speed = self.minSpeed
    if self.speed > self.maxSpeed:
        self.speed = self.maxSpeed
```

Changing sprite direction and rotation with setAngle()

The `setAngle()` method is used to set the direction of the sprite immediately. Using this method automatically sets both the visual representation of the object and the direction of travel. The direction angle is measured in degrees, using mathematical notation (0 degrees is the X axis) that increases counterclockwise:

```
def setAngle(self, dir):
    """ sets both the direction of motion
        and visual rotation to the given angle
        If you want to set one or the other,
        set them directly. Angle measured in degrees
    """
    self.dir = dir
    self.rotation = dir
```

Changing sprite direction and rotation with turnBy()

The `turnBy()` method changes the sprite's rotation and direction by the indicated number of degrees. A positive value rotates the sprite to the left, and negative towards the right.

```
def turnBy (self, amt):
    """ turn by given number of degrees. Changes
        both motion and visual rotation. Positive is
        counterclockwise, negative is clockwise
    """
    self.dir += amt
    if self.dir > 360:
        self.dir = amt
    if self.dir < 0:
        self.dir = 360 - amt
    self.rotation = self.dir
```

Changing sprite's visual orientation with rotateBy()

In some game situations, you want to change the sprite's visual rotation without affecting the direction of travel. The `rotateBy()` method performs this task:

```
def rotateBy(self, amt):
    """ change visual orientation by given
        number of degrees. Does not change direction
        of travel.
    """
    self.rotation += amt
    if self.rotation > 360:
        self.rotation = amt
    if self.rotation < 0:
        self.rotation = 360 - amt
```

Setting up the sprite's image master with setImage()

Because the `SuperSprite()` object repeatedly rotates its primary image, the `setImage()` command accepts an image filename and loads the corresponding image into an `imageMaster` attribute, which is used for all rotations:

```
def setImage (self, image):
    """ loads the given file name as the master image
        default setting should be facing east. Image
        will be rotated automatically """
    self.imageMaster = pygame.image.load(image)
    self.imageMaster = self.imageMaster.convert()
```

Determining a sprite's boundary action in setBoundAction()

The `setBoundAction()` method is used to specify how the sprite should behave when it encounters a screen boundary:

```
def setBoundAction (self, action):
    """ sets action for boundary. Values are
        self.BOUNCE (bounce off screen changing
            direction,)
        self.STOP (stop at edge of screen,)
        self.WRAP (wrap around edge - default)
        self.HIDE (move offstage and stop)
        self.CONTINUE (move on forever)
        Any other value allows the sprite to move on
            forever
    """
    self.boundAction = action
```

Using setPosition() to directly move sprite to a position

If you want to move a sprite directly to a point on the screen, use `setPosition()`. This method can be used to make a virtual mouse cursor by hiding the mouse and setting a sprite's position to the mouse position.

```
def setPosition (self, position):
    """ place the sprite directly at the given position
        expects an (x, y) tuple
    """
    (self.x, self.y) = position
```

Moving sprite a particular amount with moveBy()

If you want to move the sprite by a certain amount, one time only, you use the `moveBy()` method to accomplish this task. It expects one (dx, dy) vector as a parameter. The method moves the sprite, but it doesn't change the sprite's speed or direction. In the next frame, the sprite will move according to its speed and direction attributes.

```
def moveBy (self, vector):
    """ move the sprite by the (dx, dy) values in vector
        automatically calls checkBounds. Doesn't change
        speed or angle settings.
    """
    (dx, dy) = vector
    self.x += dx
    self.y += dy
    self.__checkBounds()
```

Moving sprite forward in the current direction

Sometimes an object just cruises — so you may want to move the sprite forward by some amount along the direction it's currently pointed. The `forward()` method does this without changing the sprite's underlying speed and direction attributes:

```
def forward(self, amt):
    """ move amt pixels in the current direction
        of travel
    """

    #calculate dx dy based on current direction
    radians = self.dir * math.pi / 180
    dx = amt * math.cos(radians)
    dy = amt * math.sin(radians) * -1

    self.x += dx
    self.y += dy
```

Adding a force vector to a sprite with addForce()

The powerful `addForce()` method allows you to add any force vector to a sprite by specifying the angle and strength (`amt`) of that force. `addForce()` converts the force to `dx` and `dy` components, adds these values to the sprite's `dx` and `dy`, and then maps these new values back to `speed` and `dir` so the sprite's overall behavior is affected by the new force vector.

Transfer

Check Chapter 9 if you need a refresher on how to use force vectors.

```
def addForce(self, amt, angle):
    """ apply amt of thrust in angle.
        change speed and dir accordingly
        add a force straight down to simulate gravity
        in rotation direction to simulate spacecraft thrust
        in dir direction to accelerate forward
        at an angle for retro-rockets, etc.
```

```
"""

#calculate dx dy based on angle
radians = angle * math.pi / 180
dx = amt * math.cos(radians)
dy = amt * math.sin(radians) * -1

self.dx += dx
self.dy += dy
self.updateVector()
```

Changing the speed and direction to reflect dx or dy changes with updateVector()

The updateVector() method is a utility method used primarily by other methods in SuperSprite. It takes the sprite's current dx and dy values and calculates corresponding dir and speed attributes.

```
def updateVector(self):
    #calculate new speed and angle based on dx, dy
    #call this any time you change dx or dy

    self.speed = math.sqrt((self.dx * self.dx) + (self.dy * self.dy))

    dy = self.dy * -1
    dx = self.dx

    radians = math.atan2(dy, dx)
    self.dir = radians / math.pi * 180
```

Information Kiosk

You might wonder why I need to calculate speed and direction from dx and dy, when dx and dy are calculated from speed and direction in the calcVector() method. It comes down to a design decision in SuperSprite. I feel that when I'm writing a game, it's often easier to think of a sprite's motion in terms of speed and direction than dx and dy, so I wrote a method to automatically convert speed and dir to dx and dy during each frame. If I set the dx or dy values directly, these values will be reset the next time calcVector() runs. The updateVector() function sidesteps this problem by converting dx and dy to speed and dir. If all this is still fuzzy to you, just remember this: If you want to change dx or dy, either use the built-in functions or call updateVector() to make sure those changes take effect.

Setting dx and dy attributes directly

Complex objects like the SuperSprite often contain methods to handle changing all the important attributes. If possible, use these methods rather than directly changing the attributes. The setDX and setDY methods each change the corresponding parameter with the added updateVector() call. The setComponts() method lets you change both dx and dy at once:

```
def setDX(self, dx):
    """ changes dx value and updates vector """
    self.dx = dx
    self.updateVector()

def setDY(self, dy):
    """ changes dy value and updates vector """
    self.dy = dy
    self.updateVector()

def setComponents(self, components):
    """ expects (dx, dy) for components
        change speed and angle according to
        dx, dy values """

    (self.dx, self.dy) = components
    self.updateVector()
```

Adding a value to dx or dy

Sometimes you'll want to nudge an object a little bit in dx or dy. SuperSprite has methods to do that correctly, so you don't have to remember the updateVector() method:

```
def addDX(self, amt):
    """ adds amt to dx, updates vector """
    self.dx += amt
    self.updateVector()

def addDY(self, amt):
    """ adds amt to dy and updates vector """
    self.dy += amt
    self.updateVector()
```

Using setSpeedLimits() to determine the minimum and maximum speed

The setSpeedLimits() method determines the maximum and minimum speeds that the sprite can attain through the speedUp() method:

```
def setSpeedLimits(self, max, min):
    """ determines maximum and minimum
        speeds you will allow through
        speedUp() method. You can still
        directly set any speed you want
        with setSpeed() Default values:
            max: 10
            min: -3
    """
    self.maxSpeed = max
    self.minSpeed = min
```

Using dataTrace() to report the sprite's vital statistics

As you're debugging your games, you might want to know all the basic stats about a sprite. The `dataTrace()` method is a special programmer's utility that spits out the most pertinent details of a sprite to the console.

```
def dataTrace(self):
    """ utility method for debugging
        print major attributes
        extend to add your own attributes
    """
    print "x: %d, y: %d, speed: %.2f, dir: %.f, dx: %.2f, dy: %.2f" % \
        (self.x, self.y, self.speed, self.dir, self.dx, self.dy)
```

Checking for mouse clicks with mouseDown()

The `mouseDown()` method checks to see whether the mouse button is currently clicked over the sprite. It returns the value `True` if the mouse is currently clicked and over the sprite, and `False` otherwise. You can use `mouseDown()` to turn any sprite object into a basic button. The current mouse button status is stored in the `self.pressed` attribute.

```
def mouseDown(self):
    """ boolean function. Returns true if the mouse is
        clicked over the sprite, false otherwise
    """
    self.pressed = False
    if pygame.mouse.get_pressed() == (1, 0, 0):
        if self.rect.collidepoint(pygame.mouse.get_pos()):
            self.pressed = True
    return self.pressed
```

> **ℹ Information Kiosk**
>
> The `mouseDown()` method can be used to add drag-and-drop behavior to a sprite. See `dragDrop.py` later in this chapter for an example of this behavior.

Checking for mouse clicks with clicked()

The `clicked()` method is something like `mouseDown()`, but it returns `True` only when the mouse button has been clicked and released. `clicked` only returns `True` if `self.pressed` is `True` and the mouse button is subsequently released over the sprite. Check the value of `clicked()` to make any sprite act like a button.

```
def clicked(self):
    """ Boolean function. Returns True only if mouse
        is pressed and released over sprite

    """
    released = False
```

```
        if self.pressed:
            if pygame.mouse.get_pressed() == (0, 0, 0):
                if self.rect.collidepoint(pygame.mouse.get_pos()):
                    released = True
        return released
```

Checking for collisions using collidesWith()

The `collidesWith()` method provides a simple technique for determining whether
the sprite is currently colliding with some other sprite. It returns a Boolean value:
`True` if the sprites are currently colliding, `False` otherwise — like this:

```
def collidesWith(self, target):
    """ boolean function. Returns True if the sprite
        is currently colliding with the target sprite,
        False otherwise
    """
    collision = False
    if self.rect.colliderect(target.rect):
        collision = True
    return collision
```

Checking for collision with a group using collidesGroup()

The `collidesGroup()` method is used to determine whether the sprite is colliding
with any objects in a group. This is especially useful for games with a lot of enemies,
because you can use one collision check for all of them.

```
def collidesGroup(self, target):
    """ wrapper for pygame.sprite.spritecollideany() method
        simplifies checking sprite - group collisions
        returns result of collision check (sprite from group
        that was hit or None)
    """
    collision = pygame.sprite.spritecollideany(self, target)
    return collision
```

Transfer

See the `asteroids.py` game starter later in this chapter for
an example of group collision checking.

Determining distanceTo() a point or sprite

The `distanceTo()` method tells the distance between the sprite and a point. It can
be handy as an alternate form of collision detection, or if you want to calculate the
range between two objects. If you can determine the distance between two points, you
can essentially create a circular type of collision-detection, minimizing the problems
with bounding boxes.

```
def distanceTo(self, point):
    """ returns distance to any point in pixels
        can be used in circular collision detection
    """
    (pointx, pointy) = point
    dx = self.x - pointx
    dy = self.y - pointy

    dist = math.sqrt((dx * dx) + (dy * dy))
    return dist
```

Finding direction to a point or sprite with dirTo()

The dirTo() method provides the angle to a specific point. It can be used to have a sprite point towards the mouse cursor, or to create a guided missile or smart opponent. If you want an enemy to run away, calculate the direction from that opponent to the player, and add or subtract 180 degrees:

```
def dirTo(self, point):
    """ returns direction (in degrees) to
        a point """

    (pointx, pointy) = point
    dx = self.x - pointx
    dy = self.y - pointy
    dy *= -1

    radians = math.atan2(dy, dx)
    dir = radians * 180 / math.pi
    dir += 180
    return dir
```

Drawing the sprite's path on the screen with drawTrace()

Throughout the book it's been handy to draw a sprite's path on the screen. I added a feature to the SuperSprite object so it could do this.

```
def drawTrace(self, color=(0x00, 0x00, 0x00)):
    """ traces a line between previous position
        and current position of object
    """
    pygame.draw.line(self.scene.background, color,
                     self.oldCenter,
                     self.rect.center, 3)
    self.screen.blit(self.scene.background, (0, 0))
```

The drawTrace() method uses the pygame.draw.line() method to draw a line on the background indicating where the sprite has been. The line color can be accepted as a parameter or default to black. The line is drawn from `self.oldCenter` (which is updated at the beginning of every `update()` method) to the sprite's current `self.rect.center`. The drawing is made to the background, which is blitted to the primary surface.

Information Kiosk

The result of `drawTrace()` isn't a smooth line, but a series of dots, because I am modifying a background that's being updated with the dirty `rect` technique. If you blit the background, you no longer need the dirty `rect` technique, and in fact it causes you problems. I could have fixed this by having further code that only does dirty `rect` updating when I'm not drawing, but that was too much effort for a technique I'm not sure I'll ever use.

Examining the Scene class

The `SuperSprite` class is truly a powerful and impressive object, but the actual motivation for the `gameEngine` module was to build a simple object that can simplify the repetitive task of building and maintaining the IDEA/ALTER structure. The `Scene` class encapsulates that entire structure into a simple, clean object that's easy to use and modify. The `SuperSprite` class is used to represent the various characters in the game; the `Scenes` class is used to create playing fields. A game typically has one primary scene to manage game play, and other scenes for introduction, score-keeping, and so on.

Building the basic scene

The `Scene` object is unique because it isn't derived from any other class. It isn't a sprite, or anything else. To specify that the scene is a top-level object, extend the core object. As usual, comments are critical for an object in a reusable library. I indicate which attributes can be modified by the programmer. Here's the drill:

```
class Scene(object):
    """ encapsulates the IDEA / ALTER framework
        attributes:
        sprites - a list of sprite objects
            that forms the primary sprite group
        background - the background surface
        screen - the display screen

        it's generally best to add all sprites
        as attributes, so they can have access
        to each other if needed
    """
```

Initializing the scene

The Scene class's __init__() method is nothing more than the beginning part of an IDEA framework. Most of the code is completely familiar to you:

```
def __init__(self):
    """ initialize the game engine
        set up a sample sprite for testing
    """
    pygame.init()
    self.screen = pygame.display.set_mode((640, 480))
    self.background = pygame.Surface(self.screen.get_size())
    self.background.fill((0, 0, 0))

    self.sampleSprite = SuperSprite(self)
    self.sampleSprite.setSpeed(3)
    self.sampleSprite.setAngle(0)
    self.sampleSprite.boundAction = self.sampleSprite.WRAP
    self.sprites = [self.sampleSprite]
    self.groups = []
```

The __init__() method does have a couple of features that bear special mention:

- **The scene comes with a sample sprite.** I added a SuperSprite instance to even the most basic scene just so I could test both objects easily. Notice that I used text to create the sprite's image so I can ship the gameEngine library without an image.

- **The sample sprite is created as an attribute of the Scene class.** Other methods of the Scene class will need access to the sprite, so I create it as an attribute.

- **The sample sprite is the lone member of the sprites list.** The sprites list is a convenient way to add a list of sprites to the scene. Any sprites in this list will be added to the mainSprites sprite group automatically.

- **An empty list of sprite groups is created.** You can create multiple sprite groups with methods provided in the Scene class. The groups attribute is a list of all the sprite groups. This list of groups is automatically maintained by the object. The programmer never needs to worry about it directly.

Starting up the scene

The start() method makes all the final preparations and begins the main loop.

```
def start(self):
    """ sets up the sprite groups
        begins the main loop
    """
    self.mainSprites = pygame.sprite.Group(self.sprites)
    self.groups.append(self.mainSprites)

    self.screen.blit(self.background, (0, 0))
    self.clock = pygame.time.Clock()
    self.keepGoing = True
```

```
while self.keepGoing:
    self.__mainLoop()
```

 Information Kiosk

It might seem strange to separate __init__() and start(), because you'll usually start a scene shortly after you create it. There's a good reason, though. After you initialize a scene, you'll probably want to modify its background, set its caption, and add sprites to it. Once all these elements are in place, you're ready to start the scene's main loop.

Stopping the scene

If you can start a scene up, it's only logical that you can stop it as well. Note that stopping a scene doesn't automatically end the program. Your game can have many scenes (as Mail Pilot did in Chapter 7). The stop() method stops the current scene. If this is the last (or only) scene, the entire game ends, too.

```
def stop(self):
    """stops the loop"""
    self.keepGoing = False
```

Controlling the main loop

The __mainLoop() method of the Scene object encapsulates a standard IDEA/ALTER loop, but it has a few twists that make it even more powerful. Here's how you make your way through the code:

1. **You need to pause as usual.**

The __mainLoop() method isn't really a loop at all, but it's the code that happens in each frame inside the loop. Use the clock.tick() method to keep the game at 30 frames per second:

```
def __mainLoop(self):
    """ manage all the main events
        automatically called by start
    """
    self.clock.tick(30)
```

2. **Check for a quit event.**

Every game that runs in a window should check for the quit event — so put the normal code in an event handler. This event-handling code has the added benefit of checking all events so there is no need to call event.pump(). All events that have happened within a frame will be registered, so queries to the mouse, key, and joystick objects will work correctly.

```
for event in pygame.event.get():
    if event.type == pygame.QUIT:
        self.keepGoing = False
```

3. **Now you set up an extended event handler.**

A programmer will generally extend the `Scene` class to make a game. The `Scene` class therefore has an empty method called `doEvents()`. This method will be called automatically, and will have access to the `event` object. If the programmer wants to incorporate standard event handling, she can do so by extending the `doEvents()` method.

```
self.doEvents(event)
```

4. **Call the `update()` method.**

The `Scene` class also has an empty `update()` method that's called during every frame. This method is meant to be overwritten with any code that needs to run each frame. The `update()` method is especially handy for event handling using pygame's various device modules (`pygame.mouse`, `pygame.key`), and for managing collisions between various objects.

```
self.update()
```

5. **Manage all the sprite groups.**

The `Scene` class always has one sprite group stored in the `self.groups` attribute. More can be added with the `makeSpriteGroup()` and `addGroup()` methods. Each group is cleared, updated, and drawn inside a basic `for` loop.

```
for group in self.groups:
    group.clear(self.screen, self.background)
    group.update()
    group.draw(self.screen)

pygame.display.flip()
```

Building a sprite group

Simple games with only a few sprites do fine with only one sprite group. If that's all you need, simply create your sprites and add them to the `Scene.sprites` list. Sometimes it makes more sense to have multiple sprite groups. The `asteroids.py` program later in this chapter has a main group containing the ship and bullet, and another group containing the asteroids. This simplifies collision detection, because you can check for a collision with all the asteroids with only one line of code if they are all in the same group. The `makeSpriteGroup()` method simplifies creation of a sprite group because it expects a list of sprites as its single parameter and it returns a `pygame.sprite.Group` instance.

```
def makeSpriteGroup(self, sprites):
    """ create a group called groupName
        containing all the sprites in the sprites
        list. This group will be added after the
        sprites group, and will automatically
        clear, update, and draw
    """
```

```
tempGroup = pygame.sprite.Group(sprites)
return tempGroup
```

Adding a sprite group

Once you've created a sprite group, you need a mechanism for adding it to Scene's group list. The addGroup() method performs this task easily.

```
def addGroup(self, group):
    """ adds a sprite group to the groups list for
        automatic processing
    """
    self.groups.append(group)
```

Creating the event handlers

The doEvents() and update() methods are both empty methods intended to be overwritten. They give the programmer a convenient place to write event code in classes that extend the Scene class. The only difference between the two event routines is that doEvents() takes as a parameter the event object from the loop's main event handler. If you need to do traditional event handling (by examining the event object), put your code in this method. Otherwise, use the update() method:

```
def doEvents(self, event):
    """ overwrite this method to add your own events.
        Works like normal event handling, passes event
        object
    """
    pass

def update(self):
    """ happens once per frame, after event parsing.
        Overwrite to add your own code, esp event
        handling
        that doesn't require event obj.
        (pygame.key.get_pressed,
        pygame.mouse.get_pos, etc)
        Also a great place for collision detection
    """
    pass
```

Setting the caption

The final method of the Scene class is a simple utility that allows the programmer to change the scene's caption:

```
def setCaption(self, title):
    """ set's the scene's title text """
    pygame.display.set_caption(title)
```

Step Into the Real World

You might wonder why I didn't just combine the `makeSpriteGroup()` and `addGroup()` methods into one method that does both tasks. I actually started that way, but I wanted a mechanism for naming the sprite group so later code can refer to it. It is possible to create code that builds variables based on string values, but the technique is awkward. I found it much simpler to simply create two separate methods. Look at the `asteroids.py` program to see how this is done. Sometimes the simplest way is the best.

Building the Label class

The remaining classes in the `gameEngine` module provide basic user interface components. The most essential of these is the `Label` class. The `Label` is a basic (but highly flexible) sprite designed to incorporate text. To use a label, follow these steps:

1. **Create an instance of the Label class.**

2. **Set up the label instance's attributes to give it a unique look.**

You can modify the text, font, color, size, and position.

3. **You can change the label attributes at any time.**

All the label's attributes are modified during the `update()` method, if you change a label's position or text, the change will take effect on the next frame.

```python
class Label(pygame.sprite.Sprite):
    """ a basic label
        attributes:
            font: font to use
            text: text to display
            fgColor: foreground color
            bgColor: background color
            center: position of label's center
            size: (width, height) of label
    """

    def __init__(self):
        pygame.sprite.Sprite.__init__(self)
        self.font = pygame.font.SysFont(None, 30)
        self.text = ""
        self.fgColor = ((0x00, 0x00, 0x00))
        self.bgColor = ((0xFF, 0xFF, 0xFF))
        self.center = (100, 100)
        self.size = (150, 30)

    def update(self):
        self.image = pygame.Surface(self.size)
```

```
        self.image.fill(self.bgColor)
        fontSurface = self.font.render(self.text,    ↵
True, self.fgColor, self.bgColor)
        #center the text
        xPos = (self.image.get_width() -             ↵
fontSurface.get_width())/2

        self.image.blit(fontSurface, (xPos, 0))
        self.rect = self.image.get_rect()
        self.rect.center = self.center
```

The Label object creates its own surface based on the current size attribute, font setting, and text value.

Information Kiosk

The program uses an external font (freesansbold.ttf) that comes with pygame. You may need to include this font in the same directory as your game if you use the Label class. If you use the installer I provide in Appendix C, the font will be automatically provided.

Building the Button class

The Button class is based on the Label class. It has all the same basic attributes inherited from Label. In addition, the Button class's update() method returns two binary values:

- **active** is True when the mouse button is pressed over the button, and False otherwise. The active attribute provides continuous information about the current state of the button.

- **clicked** is only True when the mouse button has been pressed and released over the button. The clicked state is active for only a brief moment. Generally you'll test for the clicked state rather than active.

Initializing the Button

The button is initialized in the normal way.

```
class Button(Label):
    """ a button based on the label
        same attributes as label +
        active: True if user is clicking on sprite
                False if user is not currently clicking
        clicked: True when user releases mouse over a
                currently active button
    """
```

Here's a breakdown of what you're doing in the code along the way:

1. Inherit from the `Label` class.

Note that since the button is based on the `Label` class, it calls `Label`'s `__init__()` method (which in turn calls `Sprite`'s). The `Button` class has access to all the `Label` class's attributes and methods, and the new code can be devoted to making this new class act more like a button.

```
def __init__(self):
    Label.__init__(self)
```

2. Create attributes for `active` and `clicked`.

Initialize both to `False`.

```
self.active = False
self.clicked = False
```

3. Set a different default background color.

Buttons should look different than labels, so the user knows he can click them. There are lots of ways to do that, but for now just change the default background color to gray.

```
self.bgColor = (0xCC, 0xCC, 0xCC)
```

Updating the Button

The `Button` class's `update()` method is where the `active` and `clicked` attributes are changed.

```
def update(self):
```

Inside the `update()` method is where all the checking to determine the button's status occurs, as you can see by following these steps:

1. Call the `Label`'s `update()` method.

The button is still primarily a label — so if you want all the label features (like the ability to update itself with new text and position), you need to call the `Label` class's `update()` method. Any further code is an extension that handles updates to the button's behavior.

```
Label.update(self)
```

2. Initialize `self.clicked` to `False`.

Each time through the loop, assume that `self.clicked` is `False`. Do not initialize `self.active`, because its value should last over more than one frame.

```
self.clicked = False
```

3. Check to see whether the mouse is currently pressed over the button.

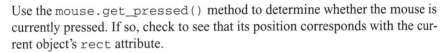

Use the `mouse.get_pressed()` method to determine whether the mouse is currently pressed. If so, check to see that its position corresponds with the current object's `rect` attribute.

```
#check for mouse input
if pygame.mouse.get_pressed() == (1, 0, 0):
    if self.rect.collidepoint(pygame.mouse.get_pos()):
        self.active = True
```

4. Check for mouse button release.

If the object is active (the mouse was pressed over it) and the mouse button then gets released over the object, the button has been clicked, so set the `self.clicked` attribute accordingly.

```
#check for mouse release
if self.active == True:
    if pygame.mouse.get_pressed() == (0, 0, 0):
        self.active = False
        if self.rect.collidepoint(pygame.mouse.get_pos()):
            self.clicked = True
```

Information Kiosk

The `Button` class uses Boolean attributes to record whether the button is currently clicked or not, and the `SuperSprite` object uses methods. Using attributes leads to slightly cleaner code, but it requires that the mouse be checked on every single frame. Buttons are meant to be clicked, so checking on every frame is reasonable overhead for a button. Most sprite objects are not clicked as frequently, so the `mouseDown()` and `clicked()` methods of `SuperSprite` are called only when needed.

Creating a scroller

The `Scroller` class is a very simple version of the common scroll bar. Use this class when you want to let the user provide some sort of numeric input. The `Scroller` class has a `value` attribute that indicates its current value, and attributes to determine its minimum and maximum values, as well as how much it increments.

```
class Scroller(Button):
    """ like a button, but has a numeric value that
        can be decremented by clicking on left half
        and incremented by clicking on right half.
        new attributes:
            value: the scroller's numeric value
            minValue: minimum value
            maxValue: maximum value
            increment: How much is added or subtracted
    """
```

Initializing the scroller

The `Scroller` class has a long heritage. It is inherited from the `Button` class, which is inherited from the `Label`, which is inherited from pygame's `Sprite` class. It enjoys features of all of them. The `__init__()` method is dedicated to providing the new attributes that make the `Scroller` class stand apart from its predecessors.

```
def __init__(self):
    Button.__init__(self)
    self.minValue = 0
    self.maxValue = 10
    self.increment = 1
    self.value = 5
    self.format = "<<  %.2f  >>"
```

The first line of `__init__()` calls the initialization of the `Button` class, which cascades the initialization all the way up the line to the `pygame.Sprite` class. This ensures that all the features of the various parent classes will be available.

The `self.format` variable is a string interpolation template. The default value is set up for a floating-point value with two decimal points. Change this template if you want the value to be displayed in a different format.

Updating the scroller

The `Scroller` class's `update()` method performs the main task of the class. It checks to see whether the user is clicking the scroller, then either adds or subtracts from the `value` attribute. Here's how you go about it:

1. **Update the parent classes.**

The `Scroller` class depends on the `value` attribute of the `Button` class and the `text` attribute of the `Label` class. Calling the `Button.update()` method makes sure these two other `update()` methods are called. The rest of the `Scroller` class's `update()` method contains code unique to the scroller:

```
def update(self):
    Button.update(self)
```

2. **Check to see whether the user is clicking the scroller.**

The scroller does all its work when the user clicks it. Fortunately, the `Button` class already provides the very useful `active` attribute, which clearly indicates whether this is happening.

```
if self.active:
```

3. **Retrieve the mouse's position.**

It's actually easier to get the mouse position as a tuple than as individual values, but you can easily use this syntax to extract the values directly to `mousex` and `mousey` variables. Note that I don't really need `mousey`, but it doesn't hurt anything to create it in this local context.

```
                    (mousex, mousey) = pygame.mouse.get_pos()
```
4. If the mouse is to the left of the label's center, decrement the `value` attribute.

```
            if mousex < self.rect.centerx:
                self.value -= self.increment
                if self.value < self.minValue:
                    self.value = self.minValue
```

5. Otherwise, increment the `value`.

In either case, check for the appropriate boundary:

```
            else:
                self.value += self.increment
                if self.value > self.maxValue:
                    self.value = self.maxValue
```

6. Display the value.

Use `self.format` to define how the value will be printed. Apply the resulting string to the `text` attribute (inherited from `Label`) and the value will automatically be displayed.

```
            self.text = self.format % self.value
```

Building the MultiLabel class

The `MultiLabel` class is designed to handle one deficiency in the `gameEngine`. `Label` class. The standard label only allows one line of text. In many cases, you'll want to print several lines of text onto the screen. The `MultiLabel` class provides this capability.

```
class MultiLabel(pygame.sprite.Sprite):
    """ accepts a list of strings, creates a multi-line
        label to display text
        same attributes as label except textLines
        is a list of strings. There is no text
        attribute.
        Set the size manually. Vertical size should be at
        least 30 pixels per line (with the default font)
    """
```

Initializing the MultiLabel class

I was tempted to have the `MultiLabel` class inherit the `Label`, but decided against it, because the two classes are more different than they might appear. Rather than a single `text` attribute, the `MultiLabel` class requires a list of text values, one per line. The technique for placing these text values is a bit different, so it was easier to just start over than to try to make the `MultiLabel` class fit the `Label` mold. Still, you'll see that `MultiLabel` has a lot of the same attributes as `Label`.

```
def __init__(self):
    pygame.sprite.Sprite.__init__(self)
    self.textLines = ["This", "is", "sample", "text"]
    self.font = pygame.font.SysFont(None, 30)
    self.fgColor = ((0x00, 0x00, 0x00))
    self.bgColor = ((0xFF, 0xFF, 0xFF))
    self.center = (100, 100)
    self.size = (150, 100)
```

Updating MultiLabel

The `MultiLabel` class works by creating one large surface for itself (the `image` attribute) and a smaller surface for each line of text. Each of the smaller images is blitted onto the `image` surface to make the larger image. Here's the steps:

1. **Create the background image.**

You will probably need to mess around with the `size` attribute to make sure the overall size is appropriate. Changing the text or the font will have an effect on how much space it requires.

```
self.image = pygame.Surface(self.size)
self.image.fill(self.bgColor)
```

2. **Determine the number of lines.**

It's important to know how many lines of text the programmer intends to print. This can be extracted through the `len()` function.

```
numLines = len(self.textLines)
```

3. **Determine the vertical space allocated for each line.**

Divide the `image` height by the number of lines to determine the vertical space allocated for each line on the final surface. If the image isn't tall enough, the text lines will overlap each other.

```
vSize = self.image.get_height() / numLines
```

4. **Render each line into its own surface.**

Use the `font.render` method to create a small surface for each line in `textLines`.

```
for lineNum in range(numLines):
    currentLine = self.textLines[lineNum]
    fontSurface = self.font.render(currentLine,
        True, self.fgColor, self.bgColor)
```

5. **Determine the position of the each text surface.**

The x position will be the center of the main image. The y position is the line's index times the designated `vSize`.

For example, if you have five lines and `size` is `(100, 100)`, the `vSize` will be `20` (`100 / 5 = 20`). Line zero's y coordinate will be `0 *20 = 0`. The first line will be `1 * 20 = 20`. At the end, the surfaces will all be centered, and will evenly be spaced along the y axis.

```
#center the text
xPos = (self.image.get_width() - fontSurface.get_width())/2
yPos = lineNum * vSize
```

6. Blit the text surface onto the main image.

The faithful `blit()` method is used to paste the text surface onto the main `image` surface.

```
self.image.blit(fontSurface, (xPos, yPos))
```

7. Reset the sprite's `rect` attribute.

Any time you have an operation that potentially changes the size and location of a sprite, you should reset the `rect` attribute.

```
self.rect = self.image.get_rect()
self.rect.center = self.center
```

Testing the game engine

The `gameEngine` module is not really meant to be run on its own. It provides a series of classes that are intended to be imported and extended into other programs. You may be surprised to discover that the `gameEngine` module has a `main()` method, but it does — and for a very good reason: testing. Every time you make changes to the engine, you need to test it. To make that simple, I create a basic scene that runs only when I'm directly running the `gameEngine.py` script. It won't happen when `gameEngine` is imported as a module.

```
if __name__ == "__main__":
    ge = Scene()
    button = Button()
    button.text = "button"
    ge.sprites = [button]

    ge.start()
```

Step Into the Real World

Would it be better if the `MultiLabel` class automatically determined what size it needed to be? Maybe. You can examine the rendered surfaces to see how large each is — and automatically adjust the size of the primary surface so it's large enough. In real page layout, adaptable components can cause a lot of problems because they may block out other components. I've found it's often better to determine the size first and *then* adjust the other attributes (`font` and `text`) to make the `MultiLabel` instance fit in the designated screen real estate.

The code here won't normally be run. I used it so I could test various features of the game engine without having to write another program. You can run the gameEngine code directly, and it will always do *something*. If you make your own changes to the gameEngine class, you can also put your own test code in the main area to see whether it's working.

Remember, the __name__ == "__main__" test checks to see if gameEngine is being run as a standalone Python program, or as a module. The code in this section will only be run if gameEngine is the main code being run. If gameEngine is being run as a module (as it usually will be) this main code will be ignored.

And Now for Some Sample Games

The whole purpose of the gameEngine class is to hide all the details so you can write games faster. The last part of this chapter gives you basic starting code for a number of games and shows how quickly you can build them with the gameEngine module.

The Adventure game

The Adventure game makes use of the GUI tools primarily. Figure 10-8 shows the Adventure game running.

The actual programming of the Adventure game was pretty easy. Designing the game, however, is a bit more difficult. Figure 10-9 shows the diagram I used to think through the game's various nodes.

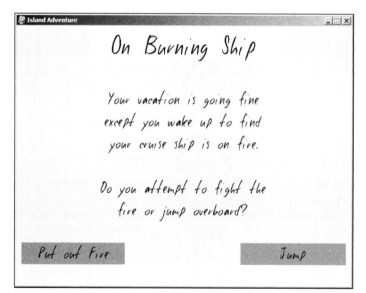

Figure 10-8: Click a button to choose your destiny . . . .

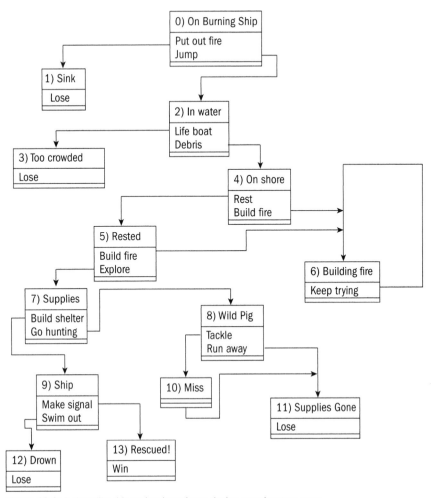

Figure 10-9: A chart like this makes it easier to design an adventure game.

Creating a Node

The heart of the Adventure game is a custom class I call a `Node`. This object has no methods except for `__init__()`. It's just a convenient way to hold all the data needed for each decision point in the game.

```
class Node(object):
    def __init__(self, title, desc, aText, aIndex, bText, bIndex):
        self.title = title
        self.description = desc
        self.aText = aText
        self.aIndex = aIndex
        self.bText = bText
        self.bIndex = bIndex
```

Building the game screen

The Adventure game consists of one customized Scene object. I built the screen with reusable components. Each time the player makes a choice, the screen elements are updated to make it look like a new scene:

```
class GameScreen(gameEngine.Scene):
    def __init__(self):
        gameEngine.Scene.__init__(self)

        self.lblTitle = gameEngine.Label()
        self.lblTitle.font = pygame.font.Font("goodfoot.ttf", 50)
        self.lblTitle.center = (320, 35)
        self.lblTitle.size = (350, 60)

        self.lblDescription = gameEngine.MultiLabel()
        self.lblDescription.font = pygame.font.Font("goodfoot.ttf", 30)
        self.lblDescription.bgColor = (0xff, 0xff, 0x99)
        self.lblDescription.center = (320,240)
        self.lblDescription.size = (400, 250)

        self.btnA = gameEngine.Button()
        self.btnA.bgColor = (0x99, 0x99, 0x66)
        self.btnA.font = pygame.font.Font("goodfoot.ttf", 30)
        self.btnA.center = (110, 420)
        self.btnA.size = (200, 40)

        self.btnB = gameEngine.Button()
        self.btnB.bgColor = (0x99, 0x99, 0x66)
        self.btnB.font = pygame.font.Font("goodfoot.ttf", 30)
        self.btnB.center = (530, 420)
        self.btnB.size = (200, 40)

        self.sprites = [self.lblTitle, self.lblDescription,
                        self.btnA, self.btnB]

        self.background.fill((0xff, 0xff, 0x99))
```

Loading up the Node

The key to the game is the `loadNode()` method of the `gameScreen` class, which takes a `node` instance and loads it into the game screen:

```
def loadNode(self, node):
    self.lblTitle.text = node.title
    self.lblDescription.textLines = node.description
    self.btnA.text = node.aText
    self.btnB.text = node.bText
    self.aIndex = node.aIndex
    self.bIndex = node.bIndex
```

Populating the Node List

The game architecture is completely divorced from the game content. The actual game data is stored in a list of nodes:

```
def main():

    nodeList = []

    #0
    nodeList.append( Node(
        "On Burning Ship",
        [   "Your vacation is going fine",
            "except you wake up to find",
            "your cruise ship is on fire.",
            "",
            "Do you attempt to fight the",
            "fire or jump overboard?"
        ],
        "Put out Fire", 1,
        "Jump", 2
        ))
```

I was careful to make sure each node is set up in the correct format (a string for the title, a list of strings for the description, the caption and destination of each button), then simply made more nodes and loaded them onto the list.

Transfer

I only print one node here to save space. Take a look at the Adventure game on the Web site to see all the actual code.

Extending the Adventure game

The great advantage of this design is its extensibility. You can easily create any Adventure game you want by simply changing the node data. Here are some other ways you can customize the game:

- **Save and load adventures.** Investigate Python's file-management features (especially the `pickle()` module) for ways to save and load complex data structures.

- **Build an adventure editor that allows the user to enter data.** You might need to do this on the command line; pygame doesn't have any easy text-input features.

- **Add an image and sound effect to each node.** The easiest way to do this is to add filenames for these resources, and have the program load up the file when needed. Be sure to allow for nodes without an image or sound effect.

- **Add interactive sprites.** Have things moving around on the screen the user has to interact with.

The Lunar Lander game

The Lunar Lander game is a classic (I played a text-only version on a teletype-computer terminal in 1975). The version featured in Figure 10-10 is a bit more modern.

The Lunar Lander game uses custom classes based on `SuperSprite` and `Scene`.

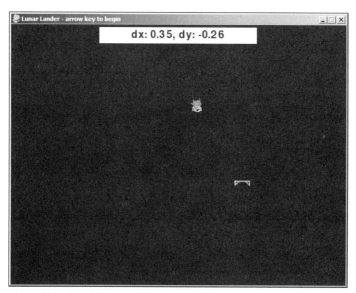

Figure 10-10: Land the spaceship on the platform.

Building the Lander class

The `Lander` class is based on `SuperSprite`. It responds automatically to arrow-key input. Here's what it looks like:

```
class Lander(gameEngine.SuperSprite):
    def __init__(self, scene):
        gameEngine.SuperSprite.__init__(self, scene)
        self.thrust = .1
        self.sideThrust = .05
        self.setImage("lander.gif")
        self.setAngle(90)
        self.inFlight = True

    def checkEvents(self):
        self.checkKeys()

    def checkKeys(self):
        keys = pygame.key.get_pressed()

        if keys[pygame.K_UP]:
            self.dy -= self.thrust
            self.inFlight = True

        if keys[pygame.K_LEFT]:
            self.dx += self.sideThrust
            self.inFlight = True

        if keys[pygame.K_RIGHT]:
            self.dx -= self.sideThrust
            self.inFlight = True

        self.updateVector()
```

Building the Platform class

The `Platform` class is a simpler `SuperSprite` with the ability to reset its position:

```
class Platform(gameEngine.SuperSprite):
    def __init__(self, scene):
        gameEngine.SuperSprite.__init__(self, scene)
        self.setImage("platform.gif")
        self.reset()

    def reset(self):
        #pick random position on screen
        self.x = random.randint(0, self.screen.get_width())

        #make sure it's in bottom half of screen
        screenHeight = self.screen.get_height()
        self.y = random.randint(screenHeight/2,
        screenHeight)
```

Note that the platform only positions itself in the bottom half of the screen. It's a lot harder to land on if it's near the top of the screen.

Building the game

As usual with gameEngine games, once you've built the sprites, just put them together with a scene instance and add any unique features. In this game, the most important part is the collision detection between the lander and the platform. This happens in the Game class, which is based on the gameEngine.Scene class.

```python
class Game(gameEngine.Scene):
    def __init__(self):
        gameEngine.Scene.__init__(self)
        self.setCaption("Lunar Lander - arrow key to begin")
        self.lander = Lander(self)

        self.platform = Platform(self)

        self.lblInfo = gameEngine.Label()
        self.lblInfo.center = (320, 20)
        self.lblInfo.size = (300, 30)

        self.sprites = [self.lander, self.platform, self.lblInfo]
        self.gravity = .02

    def update(self):
        #add force of gravity
        if self.lander.inFlight == True:
            self.lander.addDY(self.gravity)
        self.checkLanding()

        self.updateInfo()

    def checkLanding(self):
        #check collisions
        if self.lander.collidesWith(self.platform):
            #check for good landing
            if self.lander.dx < .5:
                if self.lander.dx > -.5:
                    if self.lander.dy >= 0:
                        if self.lander.dy < 1:
                            print "nice landing"
                        else:
                            print "too much vertical velocity"
                    else:
                        badDY = self.lander.dy
                        print "must approach from top %.2f" % badDY
                else:
                    print "going too fast to left"
            else:
                print "going too fast to right"

            self.lander.dx = 0
            self.lander.dy = 0
```

```
            self.lander.updateVector()
            self.lander.inFlight = False

    def updateInfo(self):
        info = "dx: %.2f, dy: %.2f" % (self.lander.dx, self.lander.dy)
        self.lblInfo.text = info

def main():
    game = Game()
    game.start()

if __name__ == "__main__":
    main()
```

The `checkLanding()` method in the `Game` class makes sure that the lander is within certain performance parameters. The `inFlight` attribute ensures the lander stops falling when it is currently in contact with a surface.

Making a better Lunar Lander game

In the current state, the game is only a demo. To turn it into a full-fledged game, it needs a few more features:

- **On-screen information.** Right now all the user feedback happens in the command console. That's okay for testing purposes, but it will never fly for a real game. Add some labels explaining what's going on.

- **Limited fuel supply.** You can't just keep blasting away forever. Each time the user expends some thrust, take a small amount of fuel away. When there's no more fuel, don't respond to input any more.

- **New situation.** Once the player has crashed or landed, reset the situation (maybe with a mouse press or spacebar).

- **New obstacles.** Put stuff in the way. Space monsters, asteroids, gravity fields, and UFOs might make the game more interesting.

- **Powerups.** You can almost always make a game more interesting by adding toys. Let the user rescue an astronaut for extra points, pick up extra fuel, or earn a "hyperspace" bonus (that moves the spacecraft to a random spot on the screen).

The Asteroids game

Asteroids was one of the biggest video games ever. Figure 10-11 shows a basic version of this game, done in just a few lines.

It's actually quite easy to make Asteroids using `gameEngine`:

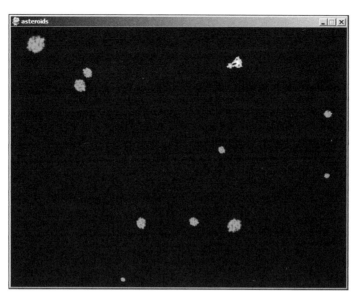

Figure 10-11: Shoot the rocks and don't crash into them.

Building the ship

The ship works just like the version in `space.py`:

```
class Ship(gameEngine.SuperSprite):
    def __init__(self, scene):
        gameEngine.SuperSprite.__init__(self, scene)
        self.setImage("ship.gif")
        self.setSpeed(0)
        self.setAngle(0)

    def checkEvents(self):
        keys = pygame.key.get_pressed()
        if keys[pygame.K_LEFT]:
            self.rotateBy(5)
        if keys[pygame.K_RIGHT]:
            self.rotateBy(-5)
        if keys[pygame.K_UP]:
            self.addForce(.2, self.rotation)
        if keys[pygame.K_SPACE]:
            self.scene.bullet.fire()
```

The `rotateBy()` and `addForce()` methods make this sprite simple to build. If the user presses the spacebar, invoke the `Bullet` class's `fire()` method.

Making a Bullet class

The `Bullet` class is also extremely simple. It takes advantage of several other features of `SuperSprite`:

```
class Bullet(gameEngine.SuperSprite):
    def __init__(self, scene):
        gameEngine.SuperSprite.__init__(self, scene)
        self.setImage("bullet.gif")
        self.imageMaster = pygame.transform.scale(self.imageMaster, (5, 5))
        self.setBoundAction(self.HIDE)
        self.reset()

    def fire(self):
        self.setPosition((self.scene.ship.x, self.scene.ship.y))
        self.setSpeed(12)
        self.setAngle(self.scene.ship.rotation)

    def reset(self):
        self.setPosition ((-100, -100))
        self.setSpeed(0)
```

The bullet fires by positioning itself under the ship, setting its direction equal to the ship's rotation value, and setting its speed to 12.

The reset() method simply moves the bullet off-screen and stops its motion (just like the HIDE constant of the SuperSprite class).

Creating a Rock class

The Rock class is another simple extension of SuperSprite:

```
class Rock(gameEngine.SuperSprite):
    def __init__(self, scene):
        gameEngine.SuperSprite.__init__(self, scene)
        self.setImage("rock.gif")
        self.reset()

    def checkEvents(self):
        self.rotateBy(self.rotSpeed)

    def reset(self):
        """ change attributes randomly """

        #set random position
        x = random.randint(0, self.screen.get_width())
        y = random.randint(0, self.screen.get_height())
        self.setPosition((x, y))

        #set random size
        scale = random.randint(10, 40)
        self.setImage("rock.gif")
        self.imageMaster = \
            pygame.transform.scale(self.imageMaster, (scale, scale))

        self.setSpeed(random.randint(0, 6))
        self.setAngle(random.randint(0, 360))
        self.rotSpeed = random.randint(-5, 5)
```

An instance of the Rock class starts with a random size, rotation, direction, and speed.

Building the Game

The Game class is an extension of Scene. It creates a list of rocks, and incorporates collision checking between the ship and the rocks, as well as between the bullet and rocks.

```python
class Game(gameEngine.Scene):
    def __init__(self):
        gameEngine.Scene.__init__(self)
        self.ship = Ship(self)
        self.bullet = Bullet(self)

        self.rocks = []
        for i in range(10):
            self.rocks.append(Rock(self))

        self.rockGroup = self.makeSpriteGroup(self.rocks)
        self.addGroup(self.rockGroup)
        self.sprites = [self.bullet, self.ship]
        self.setCaption("asteroids")

    def update(self):
        rockHitShip = self.ship.collidesGroup(self.rocks)
        if rockHitShip:
            rockHitShip.reset()

        rockHitBullet = self.bullet.collidesGroup(self.rocks)
        if rockHitBullet:
            rockHitBullet.reset()
            self.bullet.reset()

def main():
    game = Game()
    game.start()

if __name__ == "__main__":
    main()
```

Extending the Asteroids game

Of course, there's a lot you could do to turn this into a functional game. Here are a few starting points:

- **Add some kind of scorekeeping.** There's no benefit to shooting rocks, and no disadvantage to being pummeled by an asteroid. That's got to change.

- **Make big rocks turn into little rocks.** The original *Asteroids* game began with a few big rocks. Shooting big rocks made medium rocks, which made small rocks. This provided an important strategic element to the game. It will take a few small modifications to the code to make this feature work right.

- **Add obstacles.** Gravity would be fun, especially if it affects rocks and the ship. You can also add bad guys shooting at you, and other nasty surprises.

- **Add powerups.** Hyperspace, shields, and extra lives come to mind.

Transfer

I make a slightly more sophisticated version of this program in Appendix B. That extended version features an intro screen, scorekeeping, and an end-of-game scenario.

Taking It from Here

In this chapter, you put together much of what you've learned throughout the book — so you not only can make games, you can make toolkits for creating better games. The gameEngine module is a good place to start, but it's only the beginning. Where you go from here is up to you. You now have the skills to build any 2D arcade game you can think of. I can't wait to see what you build. Keep in touch!

Andy
aharris@cs.iupui.edu

abstraction: Hiding the details of some process inside a seemingly simple object or procedure. The Scene object is a good example of abstraction, because the programmer doesn't have to think of all the details of the IDEA/ALTER framework, simply what a scene is, which sprites are attached to it, and what event handling should happen.

component: Another generic term for a GUI widget.

Graphic User Interface (GUI): Generally a set of tools and screen objects that allow the user to interact with a program in a predictable way.

high-level code: Code that attempts to move away from the details of the programming language and deal more closely with the problem at hand. The gameEngine module is an attempt at a higher-level wrapper to the pygame modules.

method overriding: If you create a method in a subclass that already exists in the parent class, you are overriding the parent's method. The subclass version takes precedence. If you want, you can still call the parent class from within the subclass. Method overriding is used in the gameEngine module to simplify event handling.

private method: A method intended to be used only inside its own class definition. It cannot be called or overridden from the outside.

widget: The specific tools in a GUI (label, button, scroller, and so on) are often called widgets.

Command	Arguments	Description
Pass	*<none>*	Does nothing. Typically used to indicate that a method is meant to be overwritten.
def __*method*	*<none>*	A method name beginning with two underscores defines the method as private. Two underscores can also be used to define a private attribute.

Last
Stop

Practice Exam

1. **What is a private method? Why would you use one?**

_____

_____

_____

_____

2. **What's the best definition of method overriding?**

A) Two different objects with the same method

B) A subclass with a method name that also exists in the parent class

C) A method with two different parameters

D) A class with two methods with the same name

3. **Why might you use abstraction?**

A) It clarifies your code.

B) It separates implementation details from game logic.

C) It makes writing programs faster and easier.

D) All of the above

4. **Why might you build a custom class to keep track of game information (as in the adventure game)?**

_____

_____

_____

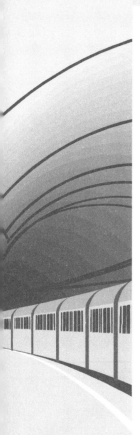

5. Why is the `Button` class extended from the `Label` class?

   A) It's impossible to make a button without a label.

   B) If it didn't extend `Label`, it wouldn't handle text.

   C) There's no need to duplicate the work for making a label; simply add those things that make it a button.

   D) The `Button` class is not extended from `Label`.

6. Rebuild an earlier game (such as Mail Pilot) using `gameEngine`.

7. Create your own adventure game based on `adventure.py`.

8. Add any of the enhancements to the games in this chapter.

9. Create a new game entirely of your own design.

A

The Practice Exam Answers

his appendix lists the answers to all of the Practice Exams found at the end of each chapter.

Chapter 1

1. Describe three ways game programming is useful for beginning programmers.

> **Answer:** It's highly visual, motivating, fun. Teaches transferable skills. Provides the same challenges as other programming. It's not boring.

2. Describe three reasons to use Python as a first game programming language.

> **Answer:** It's easy, fun, straightforward syntax, platform-independent, and free.

3. Which is the best description of a variable in Python?

- A) A place to hold numbers but not text data.
- B) A named place in memory to hold information.
- C) A command without an argument.
- D) Python doesn't have variables. It uses constants instead.

> **Answer:** B) A variable is a place in memory that can hold information. It has a name and a value.

4. Which of the following is the best name for a variable to hold a person's shoe size?

- A) `ss`
- B) `thePersonsShoeSize`
- C) `7 1/2 wide`
- D) `shoeSize`

> **Answer:** D) `shoeSize`

5. What's the best way to read the code `result = 5 + 7`?

> **Answer:** Result gets 5 + 7

6. Why might you use IDLE for writing your Python programs?

> **Answer:** It stores files in plain text. It has a built-in console, it automatically colors your text, it has a built-in text editor.

7. Why should your programs begin with a docstring?

Answer: It provides useful information about your program to other programmers and yourself.

8. Why are comments used in Python?

Answer: To help explain the code

9. How does the `print` statement work?

Answer: It prints out some value to the screen.

10. True or false (and explain why): The `print` statement prints quoted text differently than arguments without quotes.

Answer: True. Quoted values are repeated exactly to the screen. If a value is not in quotes, it is interpreted as a variable name.

11. If the `raw_input()` function is used for input, why does it output something to the screen?

Answer: The user will not know what to enter unless he is prompted.

12. Write a program that asks the user's name and then responds with a customized greeting. For example, if the user's name is "Elizabeth," the program says `"Hi, Elizabeth!"`

13. What is an object method?

A) Something that happens to an object

B) A characteristic of an object

C) An attribute

D) Something an object can do

Answer: D) Something an object can do

14. Name some methods of the string object.

Answer: `upper()`, `lower()`, `title()`, `replace()`, and so on.

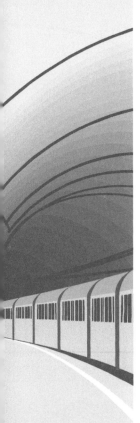

15. Describe the result of the following code:

```
var = "programming"
print var[3:7]
```

A) 'gram'

B) 'prog'

C) 'programming'

D) 'GRAM'

Answer: A) 'gram'

16. What is the primary purpose of string slicing?

Answer: To get a subset of a string value.

Chapter 2

1. What kind of data goes in a string variable?

Answer: Text

2. Why should you convert numeric values you received from `raw_input()`?

Answer: `raw_input` only returns text values. If you want to do calculations, you'll need to convert to a numeric type.

3. When does the plus sign concatenate rather than add?

Answer: When both operands are strings.

4. Why should you be careful about dividing integer values?

Answer: Because Python will incorrectly return an integer result

5. **How do you create a list variable?**

Answer: Simply create a variable with many values inside square braces, separated by commas.

6. **How similar are string and list slicing?**

Answer: They are nearly identical, except string slicing extracts characters and list slicing extracts elements.

7. **What's the easiest way to work with each element of a list?**

A) You can't work with elements individually

B) Use a `for` loop

C) Copy each individual variable to a list

D) Use a lambda function

Answer: B

8. **What two parameters does a `for` loop require in Python?**

Answer: A variable which will contain all values and a list

9. **Why must the line after a `for` loop be indented?**

Answer: Python uses indentation to indicate program structure.

10. **Why is it good to know how to use the debugger?**

Answer: It helps you gain insight into what your code is doing, especially when things are going badly.

11. **What are the three possible parameters of the `range()` function?**

Answer: starting value, maximum value, and increment value

12. **Why should you organize your thoughts before you begin programming?**

Answer: As soon as you start dealing with code details, you're bound to lose sight of the big picture. A careful process avoids mistakes.

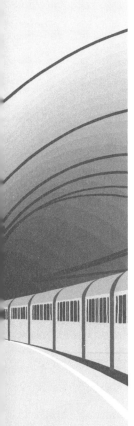

Chapter 3

1. **Name one way computers are different than most machines.**

> **Answer:** They appear capable of making decisions.

2. **Why should you indent your Python code?**

> A) You don't have to, but it makes the code easier to read.
>
> B) Python uses indentation to figure out how code is organized.
>
> C) You must use tabs rather than spaces to indent code in Python.
>
> D) If you use curly braces (`{ }`) you don't have to indent.
>
> **Answer:** B

3. **What's the best definition of a condition?**

> An _____ that can be _____ to _____ or _____
>
> **Answer:** expression, evaluated, `True`, `False`

4. **Which is NOT a legal comparison operator in Python?**

> A) `==`
>
> B) `!=`
>
> C) `<`
>
> D) `=`
>
> **Answer:** D

5. **Describe one way to make multiple comparisons in Python?**

> **Answer:** Use an `if` statement followed by a series of `elif` clauses and an `else` clause to catch any unanticipated results.

6. **Why must you understand Python's shortcut evaluations?**

> **Answer:** Because of how shortcut evaluation works, the order in which you place `elif` clauses is important.

7. **When would you choose a `while` loop rather than a `for` loop?**

> **Answer:** When you don't know exactly how many times something will happen.

8. **Name three recommendations for avoiding endless loops:**

> **Answer:**
> 1) Initialize the sentry variable.
> 2) Be sure the condition can be triggered.
> 3) Change the code inside the loop to make the condition `False`.

9. **Which is the best explanation of *encapsulation*?**

> A) The process of loading an astronaut into a spacecraft.
>
> B) Using loops and variables in your programs.
>
> C) Using functions to hide complexity and variables from the main program.
>
> D) Heavy use of global variables.
>
> **Answer:** C

10. **Which would be the output of the following code:**

```
print "%s said that a circle's circumference is %d times
%.3f radians" % ("Bob", 2, 3.1415927)
```

> A) "%s said that a circle's circumference is %d times %.3f radians" % ("Bob", 2, 3.1415927)
>
> B) "2 said that a circle's circumference is Bob times 3.1415927 radians"
>
> C) "Bob said that a circle's circumference is 2 times 3.14 radians"
>
> D) "Bob said that a circle's circumference is 2 times 3.142 radians"
>
> **Answer:** D

11. **True or false: A variable created inside a function is available to code outside that function.**

> **Answer:** False.

12. **What's the best definition of a parameter?**

> **Answer:** A temporary variable that is created when the function is called. If you define a function using parameters, you must call it with values for the parameters.

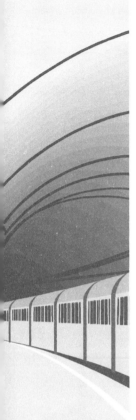

13. **How do you return some value from a function?**

Answer: Use the `return` statement.

14. **How do you build a loop with more than one exit point?**

Answer: The best solution is to use a Boolean sentry variable. All situations that should cause the loop to end should simply change the value of that sentry.

Chapter 4

1. **Why do most games use a graphics API?**

Answer: Graphics work requires speed and special functionality provided by the API.

2. **Which is NOT a graphics API?**

A) OpenGL

B) Python

C) DirectX

D) SDL

Answer: B

3. **The speed of a game is called its _____ _____**

Answer: Frame rate

4. **What's the name of one dot on the screen?**

A) A pixel

B) A dot

C) A frame

D) An origin

Answer: A

5. **Which action is NOT normally part of a gaming loop?**

A) Checking for user events

B) Initializing pygame

C) Updating object variables

D) Refreshing the screen

   Answer: B

6. **How is pygame related to SDL?**

A) They are the same thing.

B) SDL is a special version of pygame.

C) pygame is a wrapper that gives Python programmers access to SDL.

D) pygame actually uses DirectX because SDL only works on Windows machines.

   Answer: C

7. **Please summarize the steps in IDEA:**

I _____

D _____

E _____

A _____

   Answer:
   I - Import/Initialize
   D - Display setup
   E - Entity creation
   A - Action/ALTER

8. **Please summarize the steps in ALTER:**

A _____

L _____

T _____

E _____

R _____

Answer:
A - Assign variables
L – Loop
T – Timing
E - Event handling
R - Refresh screen

9. **Briefly describe double buffering.**

Answer: Graphics are prepared in an off-screen memory buffer, and then quickly transferred to the display hardware using the `flip()` function.

Chapter 5

1. **Which is NOT a common feature of an advanced programming editor?**

A) Syntax completion

B) Integrated debugging

C) Code translation

D) Syntax highlighting

Answer: C

2. **Why is it best to put most of your code in functions?**

Answer: You are less likely to have variable scope errors; code is easier to manage.

3. **True or false: The `__name__ == "__main__"`: business prevents your code from running accidentally.**

Answer: True. Without this check, importing or documenting your code can cause it to run.

4. **What's the general strategy for drawing basic shapes in pygame?**

A) You can't. You have to import them as graphics.

B) Use the `pygame.draw` module.

C) Use the various drawing methods of the `Surface` object, like `surface.drawCircle()`.

D) There are special pygame objects called `Line`, `Circle`, `Ellipse`, and so on.

Answer: B

5. **How do you load an image into pygame?**

Answer: Assign the result of `pygame.image.load("filename")` to a `Surface` object.

6. **What does `event.key` return?**

A) A numeric code corresponding to a key that was pressed.

B) The name of the key that was pressed.

C) A list of keys that have been pressed since the last call to `event.key`.

D) The coordinates on the keyboard of the key.

Answer: A

7. **What's the downside of using a system font?**

A) There's no downside. They're great!

B) What's installed on your system may not be on your users'.

C) There's never very many system fonts installed.

D) You can only use the default font.

Answer: B

8. **If your game uses a standard `pygame.font.Font` command, you'll also need to supply _____ .**

Answer: The font file itself.

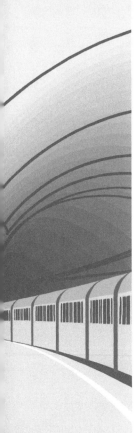

Chapter 6

1. **Which is the best audio format for pygame programming?**

A) MP3

B) aup

C) Ogg Vorbis

D) wav

Answer: C

2. **Why do we use `Sprite` objects?**

A) They attach all the sprite's characteristics to the sprite.

B) They use encapsulation.

C) They are easy to re-use.

D) All of the above

Answer: D

3. **Name three components of objects:**

Answer:
Properties (attributes)
Events
Methods (constructor)

4. **True or false: Inheritance refers to hiding code details.**

Answer: False

5. **Why would you inherit a class rather than build a new class?**

Answer: To use the features of the existing class.

6. How do you create a class initializer in Python?

A) def __init__(self):

B) def init(self)

C) def __constructor__(self)

D) pygame.sprite.Sprite.__init__(self)

Answer: A

7. What is a class most like?

A) A cake

B) A recipe

C) A fish

D) A banana

Answer: B) A class is a recipe, an instance is the cake.

8. What is an instance most like?

A) A cake

B) A recipe

C) A fish

D) A banana

Answer: A

9. Why might you create a class library?

Answer: To store a series of classes for easy re-use.

10. What is a color key used for?

A) To unlock a color

B) To choose a primary key

C) To determine a transparent color

D) Color keys are not used in pygame.

Answer: C

Chapter 7

1. **Name at least two techniques to make a game more appealing:**

Answer:
Display the previous high score
Have a changeable level of difficulty
Make it easy to restart the game

2. **What information should go into the game sketch?**

A) The player's view of the game

B) All the sprites

C) Behaviors and collisions

D) All of the above

Answer: D

3. **Why should you break a game plan into smaller goals?**

A) So you have a series of achievable goals.

B) To conform with rules of the game programmers' union.

C) Python won't let you write long code in one session.

D) It's really not a good idea to have smaller goals.

Answer: A

4. **True or false: Collision detection and sound effects are often implemented together:**

Answer: True

5. **How do you design a graphic for use as a scrolling background?**

A) Larger than the screen

B) With no visible seams

C) Duplication at the top and bottom of the image

D) All of the above

Answer: D

6. Why did I make a sprite for the scoreboard?

A) I just love sprites.

B) It allows me to combine the scores with the mechanism to display them.

C) I didn't. The scoreboard isn't a sprite!

D) What's a scoreboard?

Answer: B

7. Why is the notion of state important to game programmers?

A) You pay different tax rates depending on the state you live in.

B) All games have exactly three states.

C) The idea of state helps you design the overall flow of your game.

D) Every function in a game is represented by a state.

Answer: C

8. What characteristics should be included in a state transition diagram?

Answer:
Entry and exit points
States (labeled)
Transitions between states (with labels and directions)

Chapter 8

5. When might you incorporate a bouncing boundary-checking algorithm?

Answer: When you want to simulate a small space with objects bouncing off solid walls

6. Which is *not* a standard boundary-checking algorithm?

A) Wrapping

B) Bouncing

C) Drifting

D) Stopping

Answer: C

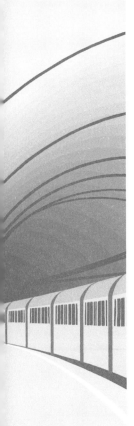

7. In the *mathematical* approach to angle measurement, where is 0 degrees?

A) North

B) East

C) South

D) West

Answer: B

8. How are angles increased in the mathematical scheme?

A) Clockwise

B) Counterclockwise

C) Up and down

D) Mathematicians don't increase angles.

Answer: B

9. Why is .7 used for diagonal values in dx and dy?

A) It results in a unit vector of length 1, which makes speed calculation easier.

B) Because .7 is the square root of 2.

C) Darned if I know.

D) It makes game programmers seem smart.

Answer: A

10. Why do we sometimes add a delay factor to sprite animations?

A) You never want to slow things down! Make your animations as fast as possible!

B) So the processor will have time to catch up with the animation

C) To enable more accurate event handling

D) To make the animation easier to see

Answer: D

Chapter 9

1. **Which is the best approximation of Newton's First Law?**

A) An object in motion tends to stay in motion; one at rest stays at rest.

B) Force = mass * acceleration.

C) A train leaves Pittsburgh at 3:00 P.M. . . .

D) $A^2 + B^2 = C^2$

Answer: A

2. **True or false: Velocity and acceleration are the same thing.**

Answer: False. Acceleration is the change in Velocity

3. **Which is *not* an advantage of the keyboard-polling technique?**

A) It allows a sprite to read keystrokes without passing the event object.

B) It allows continuous reads of the keyboard.

C) It can also be used to read the mouse position.

D) It can be used to access any key in the pygame constants.

Answer: C

4. **Why is vector projection so important?**

A) It allows you to program motion in any direction at any speed.

B) It encourages accurate physics by combining force vectors.

C) It doesn't require complex `if` structures or lists to implement.

D) All of the above

Answer: D

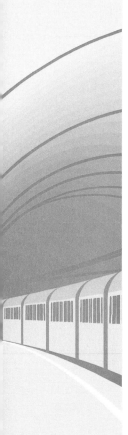

Chapter 10

1. **What is a private method? Why would you use one?**

Answer: A method that's meant to be called only inside the current class. It provides a utility or process not needed from the outside.

2. **What's the best definition of method overriding?**

A) Two different objects with the same method

B) A subclass with a method name that also exists in the parent class

C) A method with two different parameters

D) A class with two methods with the same name

Answer: B

3. **Why might you use abstraction?**

A) It clarifies your code.

B) It separates implementation details from game logic.

C) It makes writing programs faster and easier.

D) All of the above

Answer: D

4. **Why might you build a custom class to keep track of game information (as in the adventure game)?**

Answer: A class can hold a great deal of information in named attributes, can also have methods to work with the data, and can be stored in a list for easy manipulation.

5. **Why is the `Button` class extended from the `Label` class?**

A) It's impossible to make a button without a label.

B) If it didn't extend `Label`, it wouldn't handle text.

C) There's no need to duplicate the work for making a label; simply add those things that make it a button.

D) The `Button` class is not extended from `Label`.

Answer: C

Index

built-in sprite attributes, 231–233
built-in sprite methods, 233
buoyancy, 400
`Button` class, 475, B–5
buttons, 121
By Color Select tool, GIMP, D–2

C

`calcPosition( )` method, 487
Calculator program, 45–46
`calcVector( )` method, 374–375, 385, 423, 433, 441, 487, 494
`carGE.py` program, 468–470
`carParam.py` program, 435–438
Cartesian coordinate system, 146, 399
`carVec.py` program, 429–433
case-sensitivity, 19
center-and-radius technique, 174
`center` attribute
  `Button` class, B–5
  `Label` class, B–4
  `Scroller` class, 436, B–5 to B–6
  sprite, 250
  sprite rect, 232, 251
`centerx` attribute, sprite rect, 232
`centery` attribute, sprite rect, 232
`checkBorders( )` method, 234
`checkBounds( )` method, 338–343, 372, 378, 389–390, 451, 487–490, B–11
`checkCollisions( )` methods, Python, 233
`checkEvents( )` method, 470, 485, B–11
`checkKeys( )` function, 200–206, 404, 406
`checkKeys( )` method, 440–441, 445
`checkLanding( )` method, `Game` class, 519
chopper image, size and position of, 359
`chopper.py` program, 358
`Chopper` sprite, 360
`chorus( )` function, 104
`Circle` class, 245, 268

circle position, 244
circles, drawing, 171–172, 244. *See also* arcs
`circles.bmp` file, 184
`circle` sprite, 242–243, 244
Civilization II game, 334
`class className(parentClass)` command, 272
classes
  defined, 271
  re-using, 259–262
`class` keyword, Python, 234
`class` module, 271
`clear( )` method, 240, 309, 452
`clicked` attribute, 480, B–5
`clicked( )` method, 496–497, 507, B–10
`clock.tick( )` method, 136, 154, 353
`clock` variable, 135
Clone Brush, GIMP, D–8
Clone Tool, GIMP, D–2
`Cloud` class, `mpIsland.py` program, 298
clouds, Mail Pilot game, 297–301
  creating cloud sprite, 298–300
  incorporating cloud into game, 300–301
  using multiple clouds, 310–312
code, storing in files, 12–14
`collidepoint(point)` attribute, sprite rect, 232
`colliderect( )` method, `Rect` object, 262
`colliderect(rect2)` attribute, sprite rect, 232
`collidesGroup( )` method, 497, B–10
`collidesWith( )` method, 497, B–10
`collisionObjects.py` program, 257–258, 261
collisions
  bounding rectangles, 269–270
  checking for, 497
  checking for sprite-on-sprite collisions, 262–264
  checking for collisions with a group, 497
  colliding with multiple objects, 264–267
  improving on a class, 268–269

event list, 137
events, 129, 137–138
events, defined, 152, 271
events element, 229
`event.type` command, 154, 193–194
`event.type` if statement, 194
`event` variable, `paint.py` program, 200
experiments, visualizing, 163
extensibility of Python, 5
extra lives, 326

J

K

L

P